SQL For Dummies
4th Edition

Cheat Sheet

Criteria for Normal Forms

First Normal Form (1NF)

Table must be two-dimensional, with rows and columns.

Each row contains data that pertains to one thing or one portion of a thing.

Each column contains data for a single attribute of the thing being described.

Each cell (intersection of row and column) of the table must be single-valued.

All entries in a column must be of the same kind.

Each column must have a unique name.

No two rows may be identical.

The order of the columns and of the rows does not matter.

Second Normal Form (2NF)

Table must be in first normal form (1NF).

All nonkey attributes (columns) must be dependent on all of the key.

Third Normal Form (3NF)

Table must be in second normal form (2NF).

Table has no transitive dependencies.

Domain Key Normal Form (DKNF)

Every constraint on the table is a logical consequence of the definition of keys and domains.

SQL Data Types

Exact Numerics
INTEGER
SMALLINT
NUMERIC

Approximate Numerics
REAL
DOUBLE PRECISION
FLOAT

Character Strings
CHARACTER
CHARACTER VARYING (VARCHAR)
NATIONAL CHARACTER
NATIONAL CHARACTER VARYING

Bit Strings
BIT
BIT VARYING

Datetimes
DATE
TIME
TIMESTAMP
TIME WITH TIMEZONE
TIMESTAMP WITH TIMEZONE

Intervals
INTERVAL DAY
INTERVAL YEAR

New Types in SQL:1999
BOOLEAN
BLOB
CLOB
ROW
ARRAY
Abstract Data Types
Distinct Types

SQL For Dummies®
4th Edition

WHERE Clause Predicates

Comparison Predicates

=	Equal
<>	Not equal
<	Less than
<=	Less than or equal
>	Greater than
>=	Greater than or equal

Other Predicates

BETWEEN
IN
NOT IN
LIKE
NOT LIKE
NULL
ALL
SOME, ANY
EXISTS
UNIQUE
OVERLAPS
MATCH
SIMILAR
DISTINCT

Set Functions

COUNT	Returns the number of rows in the specified table
MAX	Returns the maximum value that occurs in the specified table
MIN	Returns the minimum value that occurs in the specified table
SUM	Adds up the values in a specified column
AVG	Returns the average of all the values in the specified column

Value Functions

String Value Functions

SUBSTRING	Extracts a substring from a source string
UPPER	Converts a character string to all uppercase
LOWER	Converts a character string to all lowercase
TRIM	Trims off leading or trailing blanks
TRANSLATE	Transforms a source string from one character set to another
CONVERT	Transforms a source string from one character set to another

Numeric Value Functions

POSITION	Returns the starting position of a target string within a source string
CHARACTER_LENGTH	Returns the number of characters in a string
OCTET_LENGTH	Returns the number of octets (bytes) in a character string
BIT_LENGTH	Returns the length of a bit string
EXTRACT	Extracts a single field from a datetime or interval

Datetime Value Functions

CURRENT_DATE	Returns the current date
CURRENT_TIME(p)	Returns the current time; (p) is precision of seconds
CURRENT_TIMESTAMP(p)	Returns the current date and the current time; (p) is precision of seconds

Hungry Minds™

For Dummies: Bestselling Book Series for Beginners

by Allen G. Taylor

Hungry Minds™

Best-Selling Books • Digital Downloads • e-Books • Answer Networks • e-Newsletters • Branded Web Sites • e-Learning

New York, NY ◆ Cleveland, OH ◆ Indianapolis, IN

SQL For Dummies, 4th Edition

Published by
Hungry Minds, Inc.
909 Third Avenue
New York, NY 10022
www.hungryminds.com
www.dummies.com

Library of Congress Control Number: 00-109290

ISBN: 0-7645-0737-0

Printed in the United States of America

10 9 8 7 6 5 4 3 2

4O/RS/RQ/QR/IN

Distributed in the United States by Hungry Minds, Inc.

Distributed by CDG Books Canada Inc. for Canada; by Transworld Publishers Limited in the United Kingdom; by IDG Norge Books for Norway; by IDG Sweden Books for Sweden; by IDG Books Australia Publishing Corporation Pty. Ltd. for Australia and New Zealand; by TransQuest Publishers Pte Ltd. for Singapore, Malaysia, Thailand, Indonesia, and Hong Kong; by Gotop Information Inc. for Taiwan; by ICG Muse, Inc. for Japan; by Intersoft for South Africa; by Eyrolles for France; by International Thomson Publishing for Germany, Austria and Switzerland; by Distribuidora Cuspide for Argentina; by LR International for Brazil; by Galileo Libros for Chile; by Ediciones ZETA S.C.R. Ltda. for Peru; by WS Computer Publishing Corporation, Inc., for the Philippines; by Contemporanea de Ediciones for Venezuela; by Express Computer Distributors for the Caribbean and West Indies; by Micronesia Media Distributor, Inc. for Micronesia; by Chips Computadoras S.A. de C.V. for Mexico; by Editorial Norma de Panama S.A. for Panama; by American Bookshops for Finland.

For general information on Hungry Minds' products and services please contact our Customer Care Department within the U.S. at 800-762-2974, outside the U.S. at 317-572-3993 or fax 317-572-4002.

For sales inquiries and reseller information, including discounts, premium and bulk quantity sales, and foreign-language translations, please contact our Customer Care Department at 800-434-3422, fax 317-572-4002, or write to Hungry Minds, Inc., Attn: Customer Care Department, 10475 Crosspoint Boulevard, Indianapolis, IN 46256.

For information on licensing foreign or domestic rights, please contact our Sub-Rights Customer Care Department at 212-884-5000.

For information on using Hungry Minds' products and services in the classroom or for ordering examination copies, please contact our Educational Sales Department at 800-434-2086 or fax 317-572-4005.

For press review copies, author interviews, or other publicity information, please contact our Public Relations Department at 317-572-3168 or fax 317-572-4168.

For authorization to photocopy items for corporate, personal, or educational use, please contact Copyright Clearance Center, 222 Rosewood Drive, Danvers, MA 01923, or fax 978-750-4470.

Hungry Minds™ is a trademark of Hungry Minds, Inc.

About the Author

Allen G. Taylor is a 30-year veteran of the computer industry and the author of 18 computer-related books, including *Database Development For Dummies, dBASE for Windows Solutions, File Formats, Voodoo OS/2,* and *Unix Guide for DOS Users.* He is Director of Technical Services for E-Business at HMH, an integrated communications company in Portland, Oregon. Allen lives with his family on a small farm outside of Oregon City, Oregon. You can contact Allen at allen.taylor@ieee.org.

Dedication

This book is dedicated to my partner and teacher, Joyce C. Taylor.

Author's Acknowledgments

Many people have contributed to improving the quality and content of this book. I would especially like to thank David Kalman and Chris Date for their helpful advice. I am deeply indebted to Phil Shaw for his careful scrutiny of the manuscript and many valuable suggestions. I have enjoyed working with my editor, Mica Johnson. My thanks go to all those at IDG Books who have helped make this edition possible, including copy editors Amy Pettinella, Rebekah Mancilla, and Barry Childs-Helton, and project coordinator Maridee Ennis.

I very much appreciate the help I have received from my technical editor, Eric Rudie. Thanks to my agent, Matt Wagner, for his ongoing assistance in furthering my career, and to my brother David Taylor, who, as far as I know, is still the only person in the world who has bought a copy of every one of my books, including foreign translations. Here's yet another, Dave.

My biggest thanks go to my wife Joyce, for being who she is.

Publisher's Acknowledgments

We're proud of this book; please send us your comments through our Online Registration Form located at www.dummies.com.

Some of the people who helped bring this book to market include the following:

Acquisitions, Editorial, and Media Development

Project Editor: Mica Johnson

Acquisitions Editor: Debra Williams Cauley

Copy Editors: Barry Childs-Helton, Rebecca Mancilla, Amy Pettinella

Proof Editor: Mary SeRine

Technical Editor: Eric Rudie

Editorial Manager: Jeanne Criswell

Media Development Manager: Laura Carpenter

Media Development Supervisor: Richard Graves

Editorial Assistant: Candace Nicholson

Production

Project Coordinator: Maridee Ennis

Layout and Graphics: Heather Pope, Jacque Schneider, Kendra Span, Julie Trippetti, Jeremey Unger, Erin Zeltner

Proofreaders: David Faust, Susan Moritz, Angel Perez, York Production Services, Inc.

Indexer: York Production Services, Inc.

Special Help

Sheri Replin

Hungry Minds Technology Publishing Group: Richard Swadley, Senior Vice President and Publisher; Mary Bednarek, Vice President and Publisher, Networking; Joseph Wikert, Vice President and Publisher, Web Development Group; Mary C. Corder, Editorial Director, Dummies Technology; Andy Cummings, Publishing Director, Dummies Technology; Barry Pruett, Publishing Director, Visual/Graphic Design

Hungry Minds Manufacturing: Ivor Parker, Vice President, Manufacturing

Hungry Minds Marketing: John Helmus, Assistant Vice President, Director of Marketing

Hungry Minds Production for Branded Press: Debbie Stailey, Production Director

Hungry Minds Sales: Michael Violano, Vice President, International Sales and Sub Rights

Contents at a Glance

Cartoons at a Glance

By Rich Tennant

page 119

page 291

page 5

page 261

page 403

page 393

page 327

page 71

Cartoon Information:
Fax: 978-546-7747
E-Mail: richtennant@the5thwave.com
World Wide Web: www.the5thwave.com

Table of Contents

Introduction

●●

*W*elcome to database development using the industry standard *query language* (SQL). Many database management system (DBMS) tools run on a variety of hardware platforms. The differences among the tools can be great, but all serious products have one thing in common: They support SQL data access and manipulation. If you know SQL, you can build relational databases and get useful information out of them.

About This Book

Relational database management systems are vital to many organizations. People often think that creating and maintaining these systems are extremely complex activities — the domain of database gurus who possess enlightenment beyond that of ordinary mortals. This book sweeps away the database mystique. In this book, you:

- Get to the roots of databases.
- Find out how a DBMS is structured.
- Discover the major functional components of SQL.
- Build a database.
- Protect a database from harm.
- Operate on database data.
- Determine how to get the information you want out of a database.

The purpose of this book is to help you build relational databases and get valuable information out of them by using SQL. SQL is the international standard language used around the world to create and maintain relational databases. This edition covers the latest version of the standard, SQL:1999.

This book doesn't tell you how to design a database (I do that in *Database Development For Dummies, also published by IDG Books Worldwide, Inc.*). Here I assume that you or somebody else has already created a valid design. I then illustrate how you implement that design using SQL. If you suspect that you don't have a good database design, by all means, fix your design before you try to build the database. The earlier you detect and correct problems in a development project, the cheaper are the corrections you must make.

Who Should Read This Book?

If you need to store or retrieve data from a DBMS, you can do a much better job with a working knowledge of SQL. You don't need to be a programmer to use SQL, and you don't need to know programming languages, such as COBOL, C, or Basic. SQL's syntax is like English.

If you are a programmer, you can incorporate SQL into your programs. SQL adds powerful data manipulation and retrieval capability to conventional languages. This book tells you what you need to know to enable you to use SQL's rich assortment of tools and features inside your programs.

How This Book Is Organized

This book contains eight major parts. Each part contains several chapters. You may want to read this book from cover to cover once, although you don't have to. After that, this book becomes a handy reference guide. You can turn to whatever section is appropriate to answer your questions.

Part I: Basic Concepts

Part I introduces the concept of a database and distinguishes relational databases from other types. It describes the most popular database architectures, as well as the major components of SQL.

Part II: Using SQL to Build Databases

You don't need SQL to build a database. This part shows how to build a database by using an interactive Rapid Application Development (RAD) tool, and then you get to build the same database by using SQL. In addition to defining database tables, this part covers other important database features: domains, character sets, collations, translations, keys, and indexes.

Throughout this part, I emphasize protecting your database from corruption, which is a bad thing that can happen many ways. SQL gives you the tools, but you must use them to prevent problems caused by bad database design, harmful interactions, operator error, and equipment failure.

Part III: Storing and Retrieving Data

After you have some data in your database, you want to do things with it: add to the data, change it, or delete it. Ultimately, you want to retrieve useful information from the database. SQL tools enable you to do all this. These tools give you low-level, detailed control over your data.

Part IV: Controlling Operations

A big part of database management is protecting the data from harm, which comes in a variety of shapes and forms. People may accidentally or intentionally put bad data into database tables, for example. You can protect yourself by controlling who can access your database and what they can do. Another threat to data comes from unintended interaction of concurrent users' operations. SQL provides powerful tools to prevent this too. SQL provides much of the protection automatically, but you need to understand how the protection mechanisms work so you get all the protection you need.

Part V: SQL in the Real World

SQL is different from most other computer languages in that it operates on a whole set of data items at once, rather than dealing with them one at a time. This difference in operational modes makes combining SQL with other languages a challenge, but you can face it by using the information in this book. I describe in depth how to use SQL to transfer data across the Internet or an intranet.

Part VI: Advanced Topics

In this part, you include set-oriented SQL statements in your programs and figure out how to get SQL to deal with data one item at a time.

Part VI also covers error handling. SQL provides you with a lot of information whenever something goes wrong in the execution of an SQL statement, and you find out how to retrieve and interpret that information.

Part VII: The Part of Tens

This section provides some important tips on what to do, and what not to do, in designing, building, and using a database.

Part VIII: Appendixes

Appendix A lists every one of SQL:1999's reserved words. These are words that have a very specific meaning in SQL and cannot be used for table names, column names, or anything other than their intended meaning. Appendix B gives you a basic glossary on some frequently used terms.

Icons Used in This Book

Tips save you a lot of time and keep you out of trouble.

Pay attention to the information marked by this icon — you may need it later.

Heeding the advice that this icon points to can save you from major grief. Ignore it at your peril.

This icon alerts you to the presence of technical details that are interesting but not absolutely essential to understanding the topic being discussed.

This icon indicates a new feature that first appeared in the SQL:1999 specification.

Getting Started

Now for the fun part! Databases are the best tools ever invented for keeping track of the things you care about. After you understand databases and can use SQL to make them do your bidding, you wield tremendous power. Co-workers come to you when they need critical information. Managers seek your advice. Youngsters ask for your autograph. But most important, you know, at a very deep level, how your organization really works.

Part I
Basic Concepts

The 5th Wave   By Rich Tennant

"DO YOU WANT ME TO CALL THE COMPANY AND HAVE THEM SEND ANOTHER REVIEW COPY OF THEIR DATABASE SOFTWARE SYSTEM, OR DO YOU KNOW WHAT YOU'RE GOING TO WRITE?"

In this part . . .

In Part I, I present the big picture. Before talking about SQL itself, I explain what databases really are and how they're different from data that early humans used to store in crude, Stone Age-style, unstructured files. I go over the most popular database models and discuss the physical systems on which these databases run. Then I move on to SQL itself. I give you a brief look at what SQL is, how the language came about, and what it is today, based on the latest international standard, SQL:1999.

Chapter 1

Relational Database Fundamentals

SQL (short for *structured query language*) is an industry-standard language specifically designed to enable people to create databases, add new data to databases, maintain the data, and retrieve selected parts of the data. Various kinds of databases exist, each adhering to a different conceptual model. SQL was originally developed to operate on data in databases that follow the *relational model*. In this chapter, I discuss data storage, devote a section to how the relational model compares with other major models, and provide a look at the important features of relational databases.

Before I talk about SQL, however, first things first: I need to nail down what I mean by the term *database*. Its meaning has changed as computers have changed the way people record and maintain information.

Keeping Track of Things

Today, people use computers to perform many tasks formerly done with other tools. Computers have replaced typewriters for creating and modifying documents. They've surpassed electromechanical calculators as the best way to do math. They've also replaced millions of pieces of paper, file folders, and file cabinets as the principal storage medium for important information. Compared to those old tools, of course, computers do much more, much faster — and with greater accuracy. These increased benefits do come at a cost, however. Computer users no longer have direct physical access to their data.

Small is beautiful

Computers really shine in the area of data storage, packing away all kinds of information — text, numbers, sounds, graphic images, TV programs, or animations — as binary data. A computer can store data at very high densities, enabling you to keep large quantities of information in a very small space. As technology continues to advance, more and more data can occupy smaller and smaller spaces. These days computers continue to pop up everywhere — gas pumps, your new car, and a bewildering array of toys. Before long, we could see computerized shoes that alter the resilience of their soles depending on whether you're walking, running, or taking a jump shot. If you're a basketball star, maybe you can get shoes that store records of all your endorsement accounts in a tiny database. . . .

When computers occasionally fail, office workers may wonder whether computerization really improved anything at all. In the old days, a manila file folder only "crashed" if you dropped it — then you merely knelt down, picked up the papers, and put them back in the folder. Barring earthquakes or other major disasters, file cabinets never "went down," and they never gave you an error message. A hard drive crash is another matter entirely: You can't "pick up" lost bits and bytes. Mechanical, electrical, and human failures can make your data go away into the Great Beyond, never to return.

Taking the necessary precautions to protect yourself from accidental data loss allows you to start cashing in on the greater speed and accuracy that computers provide.

If you're storing important data, you have four main concerns:

- ✔ Storing data needs to be quick and easy, because you're likely to do it often.
- ✔ The storage medium must be reliable. You don't want to come back later and find some (or all) of your data missing.
- ✔ Data retrieval needs to be quick and easy, regardless of the number of items you store.
- ✔ You need an easy way to sift the exact information that you want from the tons of data that you don't want.

State-of-the-art computer databases satisfy these four criteria. If you store more than a dozen or so data items, you probably want to store those items in a database.

What Is a Database?

The term *database* has fallen into loose use lately, losing much of its original meaning. To some people, a database is any collection of data items (phone books, laundry lists, parchment scrolls . . . whatever). Other people define the term more strictly.

In this book, I define a *database* as a self-describing collection of integrated records. And yes, that does imply computer technology, complete with languages such as SQL.

A *record* is a representation of some physical or conceptual object. Say, for example, that you want to keep track of a business's customers. You assign a record for each customer. Each record has multiple *attributes*, such as name, address, and telephone number. Individual names, addresses, and so on are the *data*.

A database, however, consists of both data and *metadata*. Metadata is the data that describes the structure of the data within a database. If you know how your data is arranged, then you can retrieve it. Because the database contains a description of its own structure, it's *self-describing*. The database is *integrated* because it includes not only data items but also the relationships among data items.

The database stores metadata in an area called the *data dictionary,* which describes the tables, columns, indexes, constraints, and other items that make up the database.

Because a flat file system (described later in this chapter) has no metadata, applications written to work with flat files must contain the equivalent of the metadata as part of the application program.

Database Size and Complexity

Databases come in all sizes, from simple collections of a few records to mammoth systems holding millions of records.

A *personal database* is designed for use by a single person on a single computer. Such a database usually has a rather simple structure and a relatively small size. A *departmental* or *workgroup database* is used by the members of a single department or workgroup within an organization. This type of database is generally larger than a personal database and is necessarily more complex; such a database must handle multiple users trying to access the same data at the same time. An *organizational database* can be huge. Organizational databases may model the critical information flow of entire large organizations.

What Is a Database Management System?

Glad you asked. A *database management system (DBMS)* is a set of programs used to define, administer, and process databases and their associated applications. The database being "managed" is, in essence, a structure that you build to hold valuable data. A DBMS is the tool you use to build that structure and operate on the data contained within the database.

Many DBMS programs are on the market today. Some run only on mainframe computers, some only on minicomputers, and some only on personal computers. A strong trend, however, is for such products to work on multiple platforms or on networks that contain all three classes of machines.

A DBMS that runs on platforms of multiple classes, large and small, is called *scalable.*

Whatever the size of the computer that hosts the database — and regardless of whether the machine is connected to a network — the flow of information between database and user is the same. Figure 1-1 shows that the user communicates with the database through the DBMS. The DBMS masks the physical details of the database storage so that the application need only concern itself with the logical characteristics of the data, not how the data is stored.

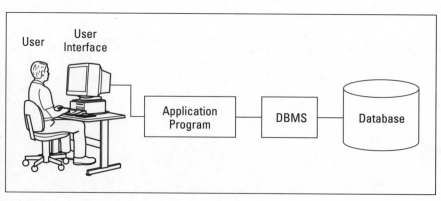

Figure 1-1: Block diagram of a DBMS-based information system.

The value is not in the data, but in the structure

Years ago, some overly clever person calculated that if you reduce human beings to their components of carbon, hydrogen, oxygen, and nitrogen atoms (plus traces of others), they would be worth only 97 cents. However droll this assessment, it's misleading. People aren't composed of mere isolated collections of atoms. Our atoms combine into enzymes, proteins, hormones, and many other substances that would cost millions of dollars per ounce on the pharmaceutical market. The precise structure of these combinations of atoms is what gives them that value. By analogy, database structure makes possible the interpretation of seemingly meaningless data. The structure brings to the surface patterns, trends, and tendencies in the data. Unstructured data — like uncombined atoms — has little or no value.

Flat Files

Where structured data is concerned, the flat file is as simple as it gets. No, a flat file isn't a folder that's been squashed under a stack of books. *Flat files* are so called because they have minimal structure. If they were buildings, they'd barely stick up from the ground. A flat file is simply a collection of one data record after another in a specified format — the data, the whole data, and nothing but the data — in effect, a list. In computer terms, a flat file is simple. Because the file doesn't store structural information (metadata), its overhead (stuff in the file that is not data) is minimal.

Say that you want to keep track of the names and addresses of your company's customers in a flat file system. The system may have a structure something like this:

```
Harold Percival26262 S. Howards Mill Rd Westminster CA92683
Jerry Appel     32323 S. River Lane Rd   Santa Ana   CA92705
Adrian Hansen   232   Glenwood Court      Anaheim     CA92640
John Baker      2222  Lafayette St        Garden GroveCA92643
Michael Pens    77730 S. New Era Rd       Irvine      CA92715
Bob Michimoto   25252 S. Kelmsley Dr      Stanton     CA92610
Linda Smith     444   S.E. Seventh St     Costa Mesa  CA92635
Robert Funnell  2424  Sheri Court         Anaheim     CA92640
Bill Checkal    9595  Curry Dr            Stanton     CA92610
Jed Style       3535  Randall St          Santa Ana   CA92705
```

As you can see, the file contains nothing but data. Each field has a fixed length (the Name field, for example, is always exactly 15 characters long), and no structure separates one field from another. The person who created the database assigned field positions and lengths. Any program using this file must "know" how each field was assigned, since that information is not contained in the database itself.

Such low overhead means that operating on flat files can be very fast. On the minus side, however, application programs must include logic that manipulates the data in the file at a very low level of complexity. The application must know exactly where and how the file stores its data. Thus, for small systems, flat files work fine. The larger a system is, however, the more cumbersome a flat file system becomes. Using a database instead of a flat file system eliminates duplication of effort. Although database files themselves may have more overhead, the applications can be more portable across various hardware platforms and operating systems. A database also makes writing application programs easierbecause the programmer doesn't need to know the physical details of where and how the files store their data.

Databases eliminate duplication of effort, because the DBMS handles the details of data manipulation. Applications written to operate on flat files must include those details in the application code. If multiple applications all access the same flat file data, these applications must all (redundantly) include that data manipulation code. By using a DBMS, you don't need to include such code in the applications at all.

Clearly, if a flat file-based application includes data-manipulation code that only runs on a particular hardware platform, then migrating the application to a new platform is a headache waiting to happen. You have to change all the hardware-specific code — and that's just for openers. Migrating a similar DBMS-based application to another platform is much simpler — fewer complicated steps, fewer aspirin consumed.

Database Models

Different as databases may be in size, they are generally always structured according to one of three database models:

- ✔ **Relational.** Nowadays, new installations of database-management systems are almost exclusively of the relational type. Organizations that already have a major investment in hierarchical or network technology may add to the existing model, but groups that have no need to maintain compatibility with "legacy systems" nearly always choose the relational model for their databases.

- ✔ **Hierarchical.** Hierarchical databases are aptly named because they have a simple hierarchical structure that allows fast data access. They suffer from redundancy problems and a structural inflexibility that makes database modification difficult.

- ✔ **Network.** Network databases have minimal redundancy but pay for that advantage with structural complexity.

The first databases to see wide use were large organizational databases, built according to either the hierarchical or the network model. Systems built according to the relational model followed several years later. SQL is a strictly modern language; it applies only to the relational model and its descendant, the object-relational model. So here's where this book says, "so long, it's been good to know ya" to the hierarchical and network models.

New database-management systems that are not based on the relational model probably conform to the newer object model or the hybrid object-relational model.

Relational model

Dr. E. F. Codd of IBM first formulated the relational database model in 1970, and this model started appearing in products about a decade later. Ironically, IBM did not deliver the first relational DBMS. That distinction went to a small start-up company, which named its product Oracle.

Relational databases have replaced databases built according to earlier models because the relational type has valuable attributes that distinguish relational databases from those other database types. Probably the most important of these attributes is that, in a relational database, you can change the database structure without requiring changes to applications that were based on the old structures. Suppose, for example, that you add one or more new columns to a database table. You don't need to change any previously written applications that will continue to process that table, unless you alter one or more of the columns with which those applications deal.

Of course, if you remove a column that an existing application references, you experience problems no matter what database model you follow. One of the best ways to make a database application crash is to ask it to retrieve a kind of data that your database doesn't contain.

Why relational is better

In applications written with DBMSs that follow the hierarchical or the network model, database structure is *hard-coded* into the application — that is, the application is dependent on the specific physical implementation of the database. If you add a new attribute to the database, you must change your application to accommodate the change, whether or not the application uses the new attribute.

Relational databases offer structural flexibility; applications written for those databases are easier to maintain than similar applications written for hierarchical or network databases. That same structural flexibility enables you to retrieve combinations of data that you may not have anticipated needing at the time of the database's design.

Components of a relational database

Relational databases gain their flexibility because their data resides in tables that are largely independent of each other. You can add, delete, or change data in a table without affecting the data in the other tables, provided that the affected table is not a *parent* of any of the other tables. (Parent-child table relationships are explained in Chapter 5, and no, it doesn't mean discussing allowances over dinner.) In this section, I show what these tables consist of and how they relate to the other parts of a relational database.

Guess who's coming to dinner?

At holiday time, many of my relatives come to my house and sit down at my table. Databases have relations, too, but each of their relations has its own table. A relational database is made up of one or more relations.

A *relation* is a two-dimensional array of rows and columns, containing single-valued entries and no duplicate rows. Each cell in the array can have only one value, and no two rows may be identical.

Most people are familiar with two-dimensional arrays of rows and columns, in the form of electronic spreadsheets such as Microsoft Excel or Lotus 1-2-3. The offensive statistics listed on the back of a major-league baseball player's baseball card are another example of such an array. On the baseball card are columns for year, team, games played, at-bats, hits, runs scored, runs batted in, doubles, triples, home runs, bases on balls, steals, and batting average. A row covers each year that the player has played in the major leagues. You can also store this data in a relation (a table), which has the same basic structure. Figure 1-2 shows a relational database table holding the offensive statistics for a single major-league player. In practice, such a table would hold the statistics for an entire team, or perhaps the whole league.

Columns in the array are *self-consistent,* in that a column has the same meaning in every row. If a column contains a player's last name in one row, the column must contain a player's last name in all rows. The order in which the rows and columns appear in the array has no significance. As far as the DBMS is concerned, it doesn't matter which column is first, which is next, and which is last. The DBMS processes the table the same way regardless of the order of the columns. The same is true of rows. The order of the rows simply doesn't matter to the DBMS.

Figure 1-2: A
table
showing a
baseball
player's
offensive
statistics.

Player	Year	Team	Game	At Bat	Hits	Runs	RBI	2B	3B	HR	Walk	Steals	Bat. Avg.
Roberts	1988	Padres	5	9	3	1	0	0	0	0	1	0	.333
Roberts	1989	Padres	117	329	99	81	25	15	8	3	49	21	.301
Roberts	1990	Padres	149	556	172	104	44	36	3	9	55	46	.309

Every column in a database table embodies a single attribute of the table.
The meaning of a column is the same for every row of the table. A table may,
for example, contain the names, addresses, and telephone numbers of all an
organization's customers. Each row in the table (also called a *record,* or a
tuple) holds the data for a single customer. Each column holds a single
attribute, such as customer number, customer name, customer street, cus-
tomer city, customer state, customer postal code, or customer telephone
number. Figure 1-3 shows some of the rows and columns of such a table.

The development community commonly calls relations *tables.* Academics and
theoreticians, on the other hand, prefer the term *relation,* but both terms
mean the same thing. In this book, I call them tables.

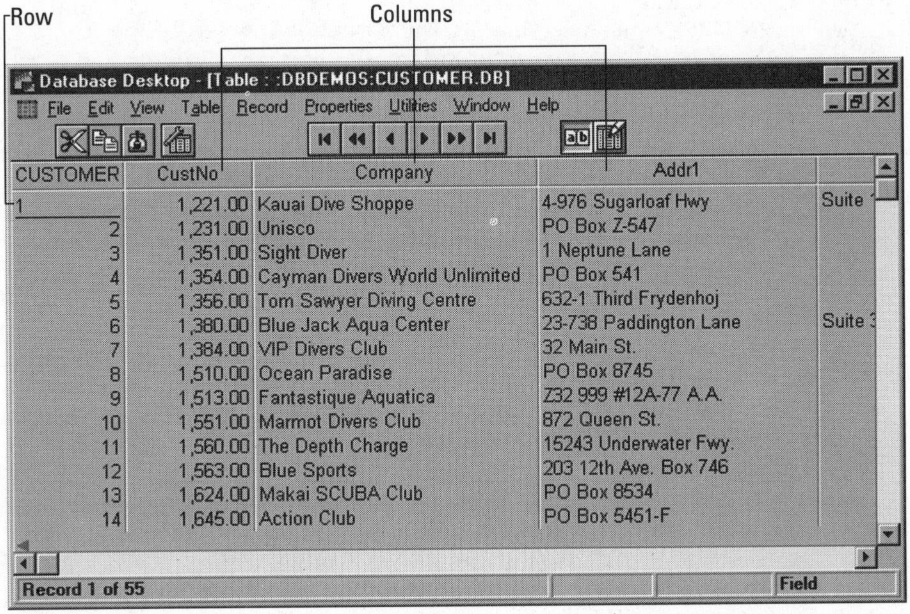

Figure 1-3:
Each
database
row
contains a
record;
each
database
column
holds a
single
attribute.

```
┌Row                              Columns
Database Desktop - [Table : :DBDEMOS:CUSTOMER.DB]
 File  Edit  View  Table  Record  Properties  Utilities  Window  Help
     ✂ 📋 📇  🗄          ◄◄ ◄◄ ◄ │ ▶ ▶▶ ▶│        ab 📋

 CUSTOMER   CustNo            Company                      Addr1
 1                1,221.00  Kauai Dive Shoppe         4-976 Sugarloaf Hwy      Suite
        2        1,231.00  Unisco                    PO Box Z-547
        3        1,351.00  Sight Diver               1 Neptune Lane
        4        1,354.00  Cayman Divers World Unlimited  PO Box 541
        5        1,356.00  Tom Sawyer Diving Centre  632-1 Third Frydenhoj
        6        1,380.00  Blue Jack Aqua Center     23-738 Paddington Lane   Suite 3
        7        1,384.00  VIP Divers Club           32 Main St.
        8        1,510.00  Ocean Paradise            PO Box 8745
        9        1,513.00  Fantastique Aquatica      Z32 999 #12A-77 A.A.
       10        1,551.00  Marmot Divers Club        872 Queen St.
       11        1,560.00  The Depth Charge          15243 Underwater Fwy.
       12        1,563.00  Blue Sports               203 12th Ave. Box 746
       13        1,624.00  Makai SCUBA Club          PO Box 8534
       14        1,645.00  Action Club               PO Box 5451-F

 Record 1 of 55                                               Field
```

Enjoy the view

One of my favorite views is the Yosemite Valley seen from the mouth of the Wawona Tunnel, late on a spring afternoon. Golden light bathes the sheer face of El Capitan, Half Dome glistens in the distance, and Bridal Veil Falls forms a silver cascade of sparkling water, while a trace of wispy clouds weaves a tapestry across the sky. Databases have views as well — even if they're not quite that picturesque. The beauty of database views is their sheer usefulness when you're working with your data.

Tables can contain many columns and rows. Sometimes all that data interests you, and sometimes it doesn't. Only some of the columns of a table may interest you or only rows that satisfy a certain condition. Some columns of one table and some other columns of a related table may interest you. To eliminate data that is not relevant to your current needs, you can create a view. A *view* is a subset of a database that an application can process. It may contain parts of one or more tables.

Views are sometimes called *virtual tables*. To the application or the user, views behave exactly the same as tables. Views, however, have no independent existence. Views allow you to look at data, but views are not part of the data.

Say, for example, that you're working with a database that has a CUSTOMER table and an INVOICE table. The CUSTOMER table has columns CUSTOMER_ID, FIRST_NAME, LAST_NAME, STREET, CITY, STATE, ZIPCODE, and PHONE. The INVOICE table has columns INVOICE_NUMBER, CUSTOMER_ID, DATE, TOTAL_SALE, TOTAL_REMITTED, and FORM_OF_PAYMENT.

A national sales manager wants to look at a screen that contains only the customer's first name, last name, and telephone number. Creating from the CUSTOMER table a view that contains only those three columns enables the manager to view only the needed information without having to see all of the unwanted data in the other columns. Figure 1-4 shows the derivation of the national sales manager's view.

A branch manager may want to look at the names and phone numbers of all customers whose zip code falls between 90000 and 93999 (Southern and Central California). A view that places a restriction on the rows it retrieves as well as the columns it displays does the job. Figure 1-5 shows the sources for the branch manager's view's columns.

The accounts payable manager may want to look at customer names from the CUSTOMER table and DATE, TOTAL_SALE, TOTAL_REMITTED, and FORM_OF_PAYMENT from the INVOICE table, where TOTAL_REMITTED is less than TOTAL_SALE. The latter would be the case if full payment hasn't yet been made. This need requires a view that draws from both tables. Figure 1-6 shows data flowing into the accounts payable manager's view from both the CUSTOMER and INVOICE tables.

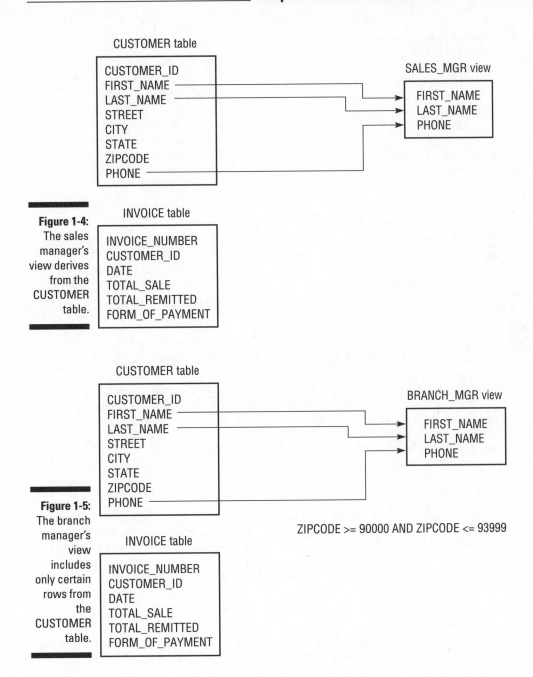

Figure 1-4:
The sales manager's view derives from the CUSTOMER table.

Figure 1-5:
The branch manager's view includes only certain rows from the CUSTOMER table.

Views are useful because they enable you to extract and format database data without physically altering the stored data. Chapter 6 illustrates how to create a view using SQL.

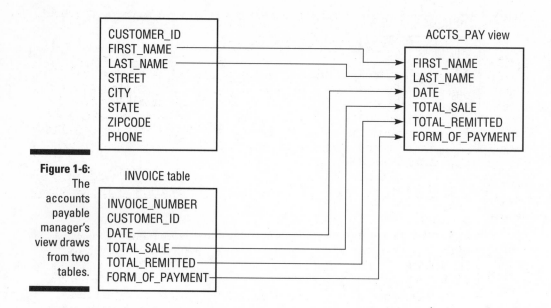

CUSTOMER_ID
FIRST_NAME
LAST_NAME
STREET
CITY
STATE
ZIPCODE
PHONE

ACCTS_PAY view

FIRST_NAME
LAST_NAME
DATE
TOTAL_SALE
TOTAL_REMITTED
FORM_OF_PAYMENT

Figure 1-6:
The
accounts
payable
manager's
view draws
from two
tables.

INVOICE table

INVOICE_NUMBER
CUSTOMER_ID
DATE
TOTAL_SALE
TOTAL_REMITTED
FORM_OF_PAYMENT

Schemas, domains, and constraints

A database is more than a collection of tables. Additional structures, on several levels, help to maintain the integrity of the data. A database's *schema* provides an overall organization to the tables. The *domain* of a table column tells you what values you may store in the column. You can apply *constraints* to a database table to prevent anyone (including yourself) from storing invalid data in the table.

Schemas

The structure of an entire database is its *schema,* or *conceptual view.* This structure is sometimes also called the *complete logical view* of the database. The schema is metadata — as such, it's part of the database. The metadata itself, which describes the structure of the database, is stored in tables that are just like the tables that store the regular data. Even metadata is data; that's the beauty of it.

Domains

An attribute of a relation (that is, a column of a table) can assume some finite number of values. The set of all such values is the *domain* of the attribute.

Historical perspectives

In the early 1980s, personal databases appeared for the first time on personal computers. The earliest products were based on flat file systems, but some early products attempted to follow the relational model. As they evolved, the most popular PC DBMSs came ever closer to being truly relational, as defined by Dr. Codd. Since the late 1980s, more and more PCs in organizations are hooked together into workgroups or departmental networks. To fill this new market niche, relational DBMSs that originated on large mainframe computers have migrated down to — and relational PC DBMSs have migrated up from — stand-alone personal computers.

Say, for example, that you're an automobile dealer who handles the newly introduced Curarri GT 4000 sports coupe. You keep track of the cars you have in stock in a database table that you name INVENTORY. You name one of the columns of that table COLOR, which holds the exterior color of each car. The GT 4000 comes in only four colors: blazing crimson, midnight black, snowflake white, and metallic gray. Those four colors are the domain of the COLOR attribute.

Constraints

Constraints are an important, although often overlooked, component of a database. Constraints are rules that determine what values the attributes of a table can assume.

By applying tight constraints to a column, you can prevent people from entering invalid data into that column. Of course, every value that is legitimately in the domain of the column must satisfy all the column's constraints. As I mentioned in the preceding section, the domain of a column is the set of all values that the column can contain. A constraint is a restriction on what a column may contain. The characteristics of a table column, plus the constraints that apply to that column, determine the column's domain. By applying constraints, you can prevent the entry into a column of data that falls outside the column's domain.

In the auto dealership example, you can constrain the database to accept only those four values in the COLOR column. If a data entry operator then tries to enter in the COLOR column a value of, for example, forest green, the system refuses to accept the entry. Data entry can't proceed until the operator enters a valid value into the COLOR field.

The object model challenges the relational model

The relational model has been fantastically successful in a wide variety of application areas. However, it is not problem free. The problems have been made more visible by the rise in popularity of object-oriented programming languages such as C++ and Smalltalk. Such languages are capable of handling more complex problems than traditional languages due to such features as user-extensible type systems, encapsulation, inheritance, dynamic binding of methods, complex and composite objects, and object identity. I am not going to explain what all those things mean in this book (although we will touch on some of them later). Suffice it to say that the classic relational model does not mesh well with many of these features. As a result, database management systems based on the object model have been developed and are available on the market. As yet their market share is relatively small.

Object-relational model

Database designers, like everyone else, are constantly searching for the best of all possible worlds. They mused, "Wouldn't it be great if we could have the advantages of an object-oriented database system, and still retain compatibility with the relational system that we have come to know and love?" This kind of thinking led to the hybrid object-relational model. Object-relational DBMSs extend the relational model to include support for object-oriented data modeling. Object-oriented features have been added to the international SQL standard, allowing relational DBMS vendors to transform their products into object-relational DBMSs, while retaining compatibility with the standard. Thus, whereas the SQL-92 standard describes a purely relational database model, SQL:1999 (formerly known as SQL3) describes an object-relational database model.

In this book I describe ISO/IEC international standard SQL. This is primarily a relational database model. I also include the object-oriented extensions to the standard that were introduced in SQL:1999. The object-oriented features of the new standard allow developers to apply SQL databases to problems that are too complex to address with the older, purely relational, paradigm. (Ah, paradigms. Ya gotta love 'em.)

Database Design Considerations

A database is a representation of a physical or conceptual structure, such as an organization, an automobile assembly, or the performance statistics of all the major-league baseball clubs. The accuracy of the representation depends on the level of detail of the database design. The amount of effort that you put into database design should depend on the type of information you want to get out of the database. Too much detail is a waste of effort, time, and hard drive space. Too little detail may render the database worthless. Decide how much detail you need now and how much you may need in the future — and then provide exactly that level of detail in your design (no more and no less) — but don't be surprised if you have to adjust it to meet real-world needs.

Today's database management systems, complete with attractive graphical user interfaces and intuitive design tools, can give the would-be database designer a false sense of security. These systems make designing a database seem comparable to building a spreadsheet or engaging in some other relatively straightforward task. No such luck. Database design is difficult. If you do it incorrectly, you get a database that becomes gradually more corrupt as time goes on. Often the problem doesn't turn up until after you devote a great deal of effort to data entry. By the time you know that you have a problem, it's already serious. In many cases, the only solution is to completely redesign the database and reenter all the data. The up side is that you get better at it.

Chapter 2

SQL Fundamentals

SQL is a flexible language that you can use in a variety of ways. It's the most widely used tool for communicating with a relational database. In this chapter, I explain what SQL is and what SQL isn't — specifically, what distinguishes SQL from other types of computer languages. Then I introduce the commands and data types that standard SQL supports and explain key concepts: *null values* and *constraints*. Finally, I give an overview of how SQL fits into the client/server environment, as well as the Internet and organizational intranets.

What SQL Is and Isn't

The first thing to understand about SQL is that SQL isn't a *procedural language,* as are FORTRAN, Basic, C, COBOL, Pascal, and Ada. To solve a problem in one of those procedural languages, you write a procedure that performs one specific operation after another until the task is complete. The procedure may be a linear sequence or may loop back on itself, but in either case, the programmer specifies the order of execution.

SQL, on the other hand, is *nonprocedural.* To solve a problem using SQL, simply tell SQL *what* you want (as if you were talking to Aladdin's genie) instead of telling the system *how to get* you what you want. The database management system (DBMS) decides the best way to get you what you request.

All right. I just told you that SQL is not a procedural language. This is essentially true. However, millions of programmers out there (and you are probably one of them) are accustomed to solving problems in a procedural manner — so, in recent years, there has been a lot of pressure to add some procedural functionality to SQL. Thus the new version of the SQL specification, SQL:1999, incorporates procedural language facilities, such as BEGIN blocks, IF statements, functions, and procedures. These facilities have been added so you can store programs at the server, where multiple clients can use these programs repeatedly.

To illustrate what I mean by "tell the system what you want," suppose that you have an EMPLOYEE table and you want to retrieve from that table the rows that correspond to all your "senior" people. You want to define a senior person as anyone older than age 40 or anyone earning more than $60,000 per year. You can make the desired retrieval by using the following query:

```
SELECT * FROM EMPLOYEE WHERE AGE>40 OR SALARY>60000 ;
```

This statement retrieves all rows from the EMPLOYEE table where either the value in the AGE column is greater than 40 or the value in the SALARY column is greater than 60,000. In SQL, you don't need to specify how the information is retrieved. The database engine examines the database and decides for itself how to fulfill your request. You need only to specify what data you want to retrieve.

A *query* is a question you ask the database. If any of the data in the database satisfies the conditions of your query, SQL retrieves that data.

Current implementations of SQL lack many of the basic programming constructs fundamental to most other languages. Real-world applications usually require at least some of these programming constructs, which is why SQL is actually a data *sublanguage*. Even with the extensions that were added to SQL in SQL:1999, you will still need to use SQL in combination with one of the procedural languages, such as C, to create a complete application.

You can extract information from a database in one of two ways:

✔ **Make an *ad hoc query* from a computer console** by just typing an SQL statement and reading the results from the screen. *Console* is the traditional term for the computer hardware that does the job of the keyboard and screen used in current PC-based systems. Queries from the console are appropriate when you want a quick answer to a specific question. To meet an immediate need, you may require information that you never needed before from a database. You're likely never to need that information again either, but you need it now. Enter the appropriate SQL query statement from the keyboard, and in due time the result appears on your screen.

✔ **Execute a program that collects information from the database and then reports on the information, either on-screen or in a printed report.** You can use SQL either way. Incorporating an SQL query directly into a program is a good way to run a complex query that you're likely to run again in the future. That way, you need to formulate the query only once. Chapter 18 explains how to incorporate SQL code into programs written in another language.

A (Very) Little History

SQL originated in one of IBM's research laboratories, as did relational database theory. In the early 1970s, as IBM researchers performed early development on relational DBMS (or RDBMS) systems, they created a data sublanguage to operate on these systems. They named the prerelease version of this sublanguage *SEQUEL* (*S*tructured *E*nglish *QUE*ry *L*anguage). However, when it came time to formally release their query language as a product, they wanted to make sure that people understood that the released product was different from and superior to the prerelease DBMS. Therefore, they decided to give the released product a name that was different from SEQUEL but still recognizable as a member of the same family. So they named it SQL.

IBM's work with relational databases and SQL were well known in the industry even before IBM introduced its SQL/DS RDBMS in 1981. By that time, Relational Software, Inc. (now Oracle Corporation) had already released its first RDBMS. These early products immediately set the standard for a new class of database management systems. They incorporated SQL, which became the de facto standard for data sublanguages. Vendors of other relational database management systems came out with their own versions of SQL. These other implementations typically contained all the core functionality of the IBM products but were extended in ways that took advantage of the particular strengths of the underlying RDBMS. As a result, although nearly all vendors used some form of SQL, compatibility across platforms was poor.

An *implementation* is a particular RDBMS running on a specific hardware platform.

Soon a movement began to create a universally recognized SQL standard to which everyone could adhere. In 1986, ANSI released a formal standard it named *SQL-86*. ANSI updated that standard in 1989 to *SQL-89*, and again in 1992 to *SQL-92*. As DBMS vendors proceed through new releases of their products, they try to bring their implementations ever closer to this standard. This effort has brought true SQL portability much closer to reality.

The most recent version of the SQL standard is *SQL:1999* (ISO/IEC 9075X: 1999). SQL:1999 is a major revision of SQL-92. In this book, I describe SQL, as SQL:1999 defines the language. Any specific implementation of SQL, of course, differs from the standard to a certain extent. Because the full SQL:1999 standard is very comprehensive, currently available implementations are unlikely to support it fully. However, DBMS vendors are working to support a core subset of the standard SQL language. The full ISO/IEC standards are available for purchase at `webstore.ansi.org`.

SQL Commands

The SQL command language consists of a limited number of commands that specifically relate to data handling. Some of these commands perform data-definition functions; some perform data-manipulation functions; and others perform data-control functions. I cover the data-definition commands and data-manipulation commands in Chapter 3, and the data-control commands in Chapters 16 and 17.

To comply with SQL:1999, an implementation must include all the core features. In addition, it may also include extensions to the core set (which the SQL:1999 specification also describes). But back to basics. I've provided a table of the core SQL:1999 commands.

Table 2-1	Core SQL:1999 commands	
ALTER DOMAIN	ALTER TABLE	CALL
CLOSE	COMMIT	CONNECT
CREATE ASSERTION	CREATE CHARACTER SET	CREATE COLLATION
CREATE DOMAIN	CREATE FUNCTION	CREATE METHOD
CREATE ORDERING	CREATE PROCEDURE	CREATE ROLE
CREATE SCHEMA	CREATE TABLE	CREATE TRANSFORM
CREATE TRANSLATION	CREATE TRIGGER	CREATE TYPE
CREATE VIEW	DECLARE CURSOR	DECLARE TABLE

DELETE	DISCONNECT	DROP ASSERTION
DROP CHARACTER SET	DROP COLLATION	DROP DOMAIN
DROP ORDERING	DROP ROLE	DROP SCHEMA
DROP SPECIFIC FUNCTION	DROP SPECIFIC PROCEDURE	DROP SPECIFIC ROUTINE
DROP TABLE	DROP TRANSFORM	DROP TRANSLATION
DROP TRIGGER	DROP TYPE	DROP VIEW
FETCH	FREE LOCATOR	GET DIAGNOSTICS
GRANT	HOLD LOCATOR	INSERT
OPEN	RELEASE SAVEPOINT	RETURN
REVOKE	ROLLBACK	SAVEPOINT
SELECT	SET CONNECTION	SET CONSTRAINTS
SET ROLE	SET SESSION AUTHORIZATION	SET SESSION CHARACTERISTICS
SET TIME ZONE	SET TRANSACTION	START TRANSACTION
UPDATE		

If you're among those programmers who love to try out new capabilities, rejoice.

Reserved Words

In addition to the commands, a number of other words have a special significance within SQL. These words, along with the commands, are reserved for specific uses, so you can't use them as variable names or in any other way that differs from their intended use. You can easily see why tables, columns, and variables should not be given names that appear on the reserved word list. Imagine the confusion that a statement such as the following would cause:

```
SELECT SELECT FROM SELECT WHERE SELECT = WHERE ;
```

A complete list of SQL:1999 reserved words appears in Appendix A.

Data Types

Depending on their histories, different SQL implementations support a variety of data types. The SQL:1999 specification recognizes only five predefined general types:

- ✔ numerics
- ✔ strings
- ✔ Booleans
- ✔ datetimes
- ✔ intervals

Within each of these general types may be several subtypes (exact numerics, approximate numerics, character strings, bit strings, large object strings). In addition to the built-in, predefined types, SQL:1999 also supports constructed and user-defined types.

If you use an SQL implementation that supports one or more data types that the SQL:1999 specification doesn't describe, you can keep your database more portable by avoiding these undescribed data types. Before you decide to create and use a user-defined data type, make sure that any DBMS you may want to port to in the future also supports user-defined types.

Exact numerics

As you can probably guess from the name, the *exact numeric* data types enable you to express the value of a number exactly. Four data types fall into this category:

- ✔ INTEGER
- ✔ SMALLINT
- ✔ NUMERIC
- ✔ DECIMAL

INTEGER data type

Data of the INTEGER type has no fractional part, and its precision depends on the specific SQL implementation. The database developer can't specify the precision.

The *precision* of a number is the maximum number of digits the number can have.

SMALLINT data type

The SMALLINT type is also for integers, but the precision of a SMALLINT in a specific implementation can't be any larger than the precision of an INTEGER on the same implementation. Implementations on IBM System/370 computers commonly represent SMALLINT and INTEGER with 16-bit and 32-bit binary numbers respectively. In many implementations, SMALLINT and INTEGER are the same.

If you're defining a database table column to hold integer data and you know that the range of values in the column is never going to exceed the precision of SMALLINT data on your implementation, assign the column the SMALLINT type rather than the INTEGER type. This assignment may enable your DBMS to conserve storage space.

NUMERIC data type

NUMERIC data can have a fractional component in addition to its integer component. You can specify both the precision and the scale of NUMERIC data. (Precision, remember, is the maximum number of digits possible.)

The *scale* of a number is the number of digits in its fractional part. The scale of a number can't be negative or larger than that number's precision.

If you specify the NUMERIC data type, your SQL implementation gives you exactly the precision and scale that you request. You may specify NUMERIC and get a default precision and scale, or NUMERIC (p) and get your specified precision and the default scale, or NUMERIC (p,s) and get both your specified precision and your specified scale. The parameters *p* and *s* are placeholders that would be replaced by actual values in a data declaration.

Say, for example, that the NUMERIC data type's default precision for your implementation of SQL is 12 and the default scale is 6. If you specify a database column as having a data type of NUMERIC, the column can hold numbers up to 999,999.999999. If, on the other hand, you specify a data type of NUMERIC (10) for a column, that column can hold only numbers with a maximum value of 9,999.999999. The parameter (10) specifies the maximum number of digits possible in the number. If you specify a data type of NUMERIC (10,2) for a column, that column can hold numbers with a maximum value of 99,999,999.99. In this case, you may still have ten total digits, but only two of the digits can fall to the right of the decimal point.

NUMERIC data is for values such as 595.72. That value has a precision of 5 (the total number of digits) and a scale of 2 (the number of digits to the right of the decimal point). A data type of NUMERIC (5,2) is appropriate for such numbers.

DECIMAL data type

DECIMAL data type is similar to NUMERIC. This data type can have a fractional component, and you can specify its precision and scale. The difference is that the precision your implementation supplies may be greater than what you specify, and if so, the implementation uses the greater precision. If you do not specify precision or scale, the implementation uses default values, as it does with the NUMERIC type.

An item that you specify as NUMERIC (5,2) can never contain a number with an absolute value greater than 999.99. An item that you specify as DECIMAL (5,2) can always hold values up to 999.99, but if the implementation permits larger values, the DBMS doesn't reject values larger than 999.99.

Use the NUMERIC or DECIMAL type if your data has fractional positions, and use the INTEGER or SMALLINT type if your data always consists of whole numbers. Use the NUMERIC type if you want to maximize portability, because a value that you define as NUMERIC (5,2), for example, holds exactly the same range of values on all systems.

Approximate numerics

Some quantities have a range of possible values so large (many orders of magnitude) that a computer with a given register size can't represent all the values exactly. (Examples of *register sizes* are 32 bits, 64 bits, and 128 bits.) Usually in such cases, exactness isn't necessary, and a close approximation is acceptable. SQL:1999 defines three approximate numeric data types to handle this kind of data.

REAL data type

The REAL data type gives you a single-precision floating-point number, the precision of which depends on the implementation. In general, the hardware you're using determines precision. A 64-bit machine, for example, gives you more precision than does a 32-bit machine.

A *floating-point number* is a number that contains a decimal point. The decimal point "floats" or appears in different locations in the number, depending on the number's value. 3.1, 3.14, and 3.14159 are examples of floating-point numbers.

DOUBLE PRECISION data type

The DOUBLE PRECISION data type gives you a double-precision floating-point number, the precision of which again depends on the implementation. Surprisingly, the meaning of the word DOUBLE also depends on the implementation. Double-precision arithmetic is primarily employed by scientific users.

Different scientific disciplines have different needs in the area of precision. Some implementations of SQL cater to one category of users, and other implementations cater to other categories of users.

In some systems, the DOUBLE PRECISION type has exactly twice the capacity of the REAL data type for both mantissa and exponent. (In case you've forgotten what you learned in high school, you can represent any number as a *mantissa* multiplied by ten raised to the power given by an exponent. You can write 6,626, for example, as 6.626E3. The number 6.626 is the mantissa, which you multiply by ten raised to the third power; in that case, *3* is the exponent.) You gain no benefit by representing numbers that are fairly close to one (such as 6,626 or even 6,626,000) with an approximate numeric data type. Exact numeric types work just as well and take up less space in memory. For numbers that are either very near zero or much larger than one, however, such as 6.626E-34 (a very small number), you must use an approximate numeric type. The exact numeric types can't hold such numbers. On other systems, the DOUBLE PRECISION type gives you somewhat more than twice the mantissa capacity and somewhat less than twice the exponent capacity as the REAL type. On yet another type of system, the DOUBLE PRECISION type gives double the mantissa capacity but the same exponent capacity as the REAL type. In this case, accuracy doubles, but range does not.

The SQL:1999 specification does not try to arbitrate or establish by fiat what DOUBLE PRECISION means. The specification requires only that the precision of a DOUBLE PRECISION number be greater than the precision of a REAL number. This constraint though rather weak, is perhaps the best possible in light of the great differences you encounter in hardware.

FLOAT data type

The FLOAT data type is most useful if you think that your database may someday migrate to a hardware platform with different register sizes than the one on which you originally design it. By using the FLOAT data type, you can specify a precision — for example, FLOAT (5). If your hardware supports the specified precision with its single-precision circuitry, single-precision arithmetic is what your system uses. If the specified precision requires double-precision arithmetic, the system uses double-precision arithmetic.

 Using FLOAT rather than REAL or DOUBLE PRECISION makes porting your databases to other hardware easier, because the FLOAT data type enables you to specify precision. The precision of REAL and DOUBLE PRECISION numbers is hardware-dependent.

If you aren't sure whether to use the exact numeric data types (NUMERIC/ DECIMAL) or the approximate numeric data types (FLOAT/REAL), use the exact numeric types. The exact data types are less demanding of system resources and, of course, give exact rather than approximate results. If the range of possible values of your data is large enough to require the use of the approximate data types, you can probably determine this fact in advance.

Character strings

These days, databases store many different types of data, including graphic images, sounds, and animations. I expect odors to come next. Can you imagine a three-dimensional 1600 x 1200 24-bit color image of a large slice of pepperoni pizza on your screen, while an odor sample taken at DiFilippi's Pizza Grotto replays through your super-multimedia card? Such a setup may get frustrating — at least until you can afford to add taste-type data to your system as well. Alas, you can expect to wait a long time indeed before odor and taste become standard SQL data types. These days, the data types that you use most commonly — after the numeric types, of course — are the character-string types.

You have three main types of character data: fixed character data (CHARACTER or CHAR), varying character data (CHARACTER VARYING or VARCHAR), and character large object data (CHARACTER LARGE OBJECT or CLOB). You also have three variants of these types of character data: NATIONAL CHARACTER, NATIONAL CHARACTER VARYING and NATIONAL CHARACTER LARGE OBJECT.

CHARACTER data type

If you define the data type of a column as CHARACTER or CHAR, you can specify the number of characters the column holds by using the syntax CHARACTER (x), where x is the number of characters. If you specify a column's data type as CHARACTER (16), for example, the maximum length of any data you can enter in the column is 16 characters. If you don't specify an argument (that is, you don't provide a value in place of the x), SQL assumes a field length of one character. If you enter data into a CHARACTER field of a specified length and you enter fewer characters than the specified number, SQL fills the remaining character spaces with blanks.

CHARACTER VARYING data type

The CHARACTER VARYING data type is useful if entries in a column can vary in length, but you don't want SQL to pad the field with blanks. This data type enables you to store exactly the number of characters that the user enters. No default value exists for this data type. To specify this data type, use the form CHARACTER VARYING (x) or VARCHAR (x), where x is the maximum number of characters permitted.

CHARACTER LARGE OBJECT data type

The CHARACTER LARGE OBJECT (CLOB) data type is new with SQL:1999. As its name implies, it is used with huge character strings that are too large for the CHARACTER type. CLOBs behave much like ordinary character strings, but there are a number of restrictions on what you can do with them. A CLOB may not be used in a PRIMARY KEY, FOREIGN KEY, or a UNIQUE predicate. Furthermore it may not be used in a comparison other than one for either equality or inequality. Because of their large size, applications generally do not transfer CLOBs to or from a database. Instead, a special client-side type called a *LOB locator* is used to manipulate the CLOB data. It is a parameter whose value identifies a character large object.

NATIONAL CHARACTER, NATIONAL CHARACTER VARYING and NATIONAL CHARACTER LARGE OBJECT data types

Different languages have some characters that differ from any characters in another language. For example, German has some special characters not present in the English language character set. Some languages, such as Russian, have a very different character set from the English one. If you specify, for example, the English character set as the default for your system, you can use alternate character sets because the NATIONAL CHARACTER, NATIONAL CHARACTER VARYING, and NATIONAL CHARACTER LARGE OBJECT data types function the same as the CHARACTER, CHARACTER VARYING, and CHARACTER LARGE OBJECT data types, except that the character set you're specifying is different from the default character set. You can specify the character set as you define a table column. If you want, each column can use a different character set. The following example of a table-creation statement uses multiple character sets:

```
CREATE TABLE XLATE (
    LANGUAGE_1 CHARACTER (40),
    LANGUAGE_2 CHARACTER VARYING (40) CHARACTER SET GREEK,
    LANGUAGE_3 NATIONAL CHARACTER (40),
    LANGUAGE_4 CHARACTER (40)    CHARACTER SET KANJI
    ) ;
```

The LANGUAGE_1 column contains characters in the implementation's default character set. The LANGUAGE_3 column contains characters in the implementation's national character set. The LANGUAGE_2 column contains Greek characters. And the LANGUAGE_4 column contains Kanji characters.

Bit strings

SQL:1999 also has a data type for strings of bits that don't represent alphanumeric characters or numbers. The BIT, BIT VARYING, and BINARY LARGE OBJECT data types accept any arbitrary bit string. You specify fixed-length binary data by using the BIT (x) format, where x is the number of bits. BIT without an argument defaults to one bit. If you want to accommodate data that sometimes is one length and sometimes another, use BIT VARYING (x), where x denotes the maximum number of bits that the data field accepts. You may also use the BIT and BIT VARYING data types to hold binary or hexadecimal data or to hold flags that indicate whether individual logical switches are on or off. The BINARY LARGE OBJECT (BLOB) data type is similar to the CHARACTER LARGE OBJECT data type, with the same restrictions on how it is used. The difference is that a BLOB need not contain a character string. BLOBs are often used to store image or sound information.

Booleans

The BOOLEAN data type comprises the distinct truth values *true* and *false*, as well as *unknown*. If either a Boolean *true* or *false* value is compared to a NULL or *unknown* truth value, the result will have the *unknown* value.

Datetimes

The SQL:1999 standard defines five different data types that deal with dates and times. These data types are called *datetime data types,* or simply *datetimes.* Considerable overlap exists among these data types, so some implementations you encounter may not support all five.

Implementations that do not fully support all five data types for dates and times may experience problems with databases that you try to migrate from another implementation. If you have trouble with a migration, check how both the source and the destination implementations represent dates and times.

DATE data type

The DATE type stores year, month, and day values of a date, in that order. The year value is four digits long, and the month and day values are both two digits long. A DATE value can represent any date from the year 0001 to the year 9999. The length of a DATE is ten positions, as in 1957-08-14.

Because SQL explicitly represents all four digits of a year in the DATE type, SQL data was never subject to the much-hyped *Year 2000* (Y2K) problem.

TIME WITHOUT TIME ZONE data type

The TIME WITHOUT TIME ZONE data type stores hour, minute, and second values of time. The hours and minutes occupy exactly two digits. The seconds value may be only two digits but may also expand to include an optional fractional part. This data type, therefore, represents a time of 32 minutes and 58.436 seconds past 9 a.m., for example, as 09:32:58.436.

The precision of the fractional part is implementation-dependent but is at least six digits long. A TIME WITHOUT TIME ZONE value takes up eight positions (including colons) when the value has no fractional part, or nine positions (including the decimal point) plus the number of fractional digits when the value does include a fractional part. You specify TIME WITHOUT TIME ZONE type data either as TIME, which gives you the default of no fractional digits, or as TIME WITHOUT TIME ZONE (p), where *p* is the number of digit positions to the right of the decimal. The example in the preceding paragraph represents a data type of TIME WITHOUT TIME ZONE (3).

TIMESTAMP WITHOUT TIME ZONE data type

TIMESTAMP WITHOUT TIME ZONE data includes both date and time information. The lengths and the restrictions on the values of the components of TIMESTAMP WITHOUT TIME ZONE data are the same as they are for DATE and TIME WITHOUT TIME ZONE data, except for one difference: The default length of the fractional part of the time component of a TIMESTAMP WITHOUT TIME ZONE is six digits rather than zero. If the value has no fractional digits, the length of a TIMESTAMP WITHOUT TIME ZONE is 19 positions — ten date positions, one space as a separator, and eight time positions, in that order. If fractional digits are present (six digits is the default), the length is 20 positions plus the number of fractional digits. The twentieth position is for the decimal point. You specify a field as TIMESTAMP WITHOUT TIME ZONE type by using either TIMESTAMP WITHOUT TIME ZONE or TIMESTAMP WITHOUT TIME ZONE (p), where *p* is the number of fractional digit positions. The value of *p* can't be negative, and the implementation determines its maximum value.

TIME WITH TIME ZONE data type

The TIME WITH TIME ZONE data type is exactly the same as the TIME WITHOUT TIME ZONE data type except this type adds information about the offset from *Universal Time* (UTC, formerly known as Greenwich Mean Time or GMT). The value of the offset may range anywhere from –12:59 to +13:00. This additional information takes up six more digit positions following the time — a hyphen as a separator, a plus or minus sign, and then the offset in hours (two digits) and minutes (two digits) with a colon in between the hours and minutes. A TIME WITH TIME ZONE value with no fractional part (the default) is 14 positions long. If you specify a fractional part, the field length is 15 positions plus the number of fractional digits.

TIMESTAMP WITH TIME ZONE data type

The TIMESTAMP WITH TIME ZONE data type functions exactly the same as the TIMESTAMP WITHOUT TIME ZONE data type except that this data type also adds information about the offset from Universal Time. The additional information takes up six more digit positions following the timestamp (see the preceding section for the form of the time zone information). Including time zone data sets up 25 positions for a field with no fractional part and 26 positions plus the number of fractional digits for fields that do include a fractional part (six digits is the default number of fractional digits).

Intervals

The *interval* data types relate closely to the datetime data types. An interval is the difference between two datetime values. In many applications that deal with dates, times, or both, you sometimes need to determine the interval between two dates or two times. SQL:1999 recognizes two distinct types of intervals: the *year-month* interval and the *day-time* interval. A year-month interval is the number of years and months between two dates. A day-time interval is the number of days, hours, minutes, and seconds between two instants within a month. You can't mix calculations involving a year-month interval with calculations involving a day-time interval, because months come in varying lengths (28, 29, 30, or 31 days long).

ROW types

The ROW data type is a new type introduced with SQL:1999. It's not that easy to understand, and as a beginning to intermediate SQL programmer, you may never use it. After all, people got by without it just fine between 1986 and 1999.

One of the notable things about the ROW data type is that it violates the rules of normalization that E.F. Codd declared in the early days of relational database theory. I will talk more about those rules in Chapter 5. One of the defining characteristics of First Normal Form is that a field in a table row may not be multi-valued. A field may contain one and only one value. However, the ROW data type allows you to declare an entire row of data to be contained within a single field in a single row of a table — in other words, a row nested within a row.

Consider the following SQL statement, which defines a ROW type for a person's address information:

```
CREATE ROW TYPE addr_typ (
    Street          CHARACTER VARYING (25)
    City            CHARACTER VARYING(20)
    State           CHARACTER (2)
    PostalCode      CHARACTER VARYING (9)
    ) ;
```

Once defined, the new ROW type can be used in a table definition:

```
CREATE TABLE CUSTOMER (
    CustID          INTEGER        PRIMARY KEY,
    LastName        CHARACTER VARYING (25),
    FirstName       CHARACTER VARYING (20),
    Address         addr_typ
    Phone           CHARACTER VARYING (15)
    ) ;
```

The advantage here is that if you are maintaining address information for multiple entities — such as customers, vendors, employees, and stockholders — you only have to define the details of the address specification once — in the ROW type definition.

ARRAY types

The ARRAY data type is another one that was introduced in SQL:1999. It also violates First Normal Form (1NF), but in a different way than the way the ROW type violates 1NF. The ARRAY type is not actually a distinct type in the same sense that CHARACTER or NUMERIC are distinct data types. An ARRAY type merely allows one of the other types to have multiple values within a single field of a table. For example, say it is important to your organization to be able to contact your customers whether they are at work, at home, or on the road. You would like to maintain multiple telephone numbers for them. You can do this by declaring the Phone attribute as an array, as shown in the following code:

```
CREATE TABLE CUSTOMER (
    CustID      INTEGER       PRIMARY KEY,
    LastName    CHARACTER VARYING (25),
    FirstName   CHARACTER VARYING (20),
    Address     addr_typ
    Phone       CHARACTER VARYING (15) ARRAY [3]
    ) ;
```

The ARRAY [3] notation allows you to store up to three telephone numbers in the CUSTOMER table. The three telephone numbers represent an example of a repeating group. Repeating groups are a no-no according to classical relational database theory, but this is one of several examples of cases where SQL:1999 breaks the rules. When Dr. Codd first enunciated the rules of normalization, he traded off functional flexibility for data integrity. SQL:1999 takes back some of that functional flexibility, at the cost of some added structural complexity. The increased structural complexity could translate into compromised data integrity if you are not fully aware of all the effects of actions you perform on your database.

REF types

The reference data types, like the ROW and ARRAY types are new with SQL:1999. REF types are not part of core SQL. This means that a DBMS may claim compliance with SQL:1999 without implementing REF types at all. The REF type is not a distinct data type in the sense that CHARACTER and NUMERIC are. Instead, it is a pointer to a data item, row type, or abstract data type that resides in a row of a table (a site). Dereferencing the pointer can retrieve the value stored at the target site. If you're confused, don't worry, because you're not alone. Using the REF types requires a working knowledge of object-oriented programming (OOP) principles. This book refrains from wading too deeply into the murky waters of OOP. In fact — since the REF types are not a part of core SQL — you may be better off if you don't use them anyway. If you want maximum portability across DBMS platforms, stick to core SQL.

User-Defined types

User-defined types (UDTs) represent yet another example of new features in SQL:1999 that come from the object-oriented programming world. As an SQL programmer, you are no longer restricted to the data types defined in the SQL:1999 specification. You can define your own data types, using the principles of Abstract Data Types (ADTs) found in such object-oriented programming languages as C++.

One of the most important benefits of UDTs is the fact that they can be used to eliminate the "impedance mismatch" between SQL and the host language that is "wrapped around" the SQL. A long-standing problem with SQL has been the fact the SQL's predefined data types do not match the data types of the host languages within which SQL statements are embedded. Now, with UDTs, a database programmer can create data types within SQL that match the data types of the host language. A UDT has attributes and methods, which are encapsulated within the UDT. The outside world can see the attribute definitions and the results of the methods, but the specific implementations of the methods are hidden from view. Access to the attributes and methods of a UDT can be further restricted by specifying that they are public, private, or protected. Public attributes or methods are available to all users of a UDT. Private attributes or methods are available only to the UDT itself. Protected attributes or methods are available only to the UDT itself or its subtypes. We see from this that a UDT in SQL behaves much like a class in an object-oriented programming language. More on these topics in Chapters 6 and 7.

Distinct types

Distinct types are the simplest forms of user-defined types. Multiple distinct types that are all based on a single base type are distinct from each other and are thus not directly comparable. For example, you can use distinct types to distinguish between different currencies. Consider the following type definition:

```
CREATE DISTINCT TYPE USdollar AS DECIMAL (9,2) ;
```

This creates a new data type for U.S. dollars, based on the predefined DECI-MAL data type. You can create another distinct type in a similar manner:

```
CREATE DISTINCT TYPE Euro AS DECIMAL (9,2) ;
```

You can now create tables that use these new types:

```
CREATE TABLE USInvoice (
    InvID      INTEGER        PRIMARY KEY,
    CustID     INTEGER,
    EmpID      INTEGER,
```

```
    TotalSale    USdollar,
    Tax          USdollar,
    Shipping     USdollar,
    GrandTotal   USdollar
    ) ;
```

```
CREATE TABLE EuroInvoice (
    InvID        INTEGER      PRIMARY KEY,
    CustID       INTEGER,
    EmpID        INTEGER,
    TotalSale    Euro,
    Tax          Euro,
    Shipping     Euro,
    GrandTotal   Euro
    ) ;
```

The USdollar type and the Euro type are both based on the DECIMAL type, but instances of one cannot be directly compared with instances of the other or with instances of the DECIMAL type. Now in SQL as in the "real" world, it is possible to convert U.S. dollars into Euros, but this requires a special operation (CAST). Once the conversion has been made, comparisons become possible.

Data type summary

Table 2-2 lists various data types and displays literals that conform to each type.

Table 2-2	Data Types
Data Type	*Example Value*
CHARACTER (20)	'Amateur Radio '
VARCHAR (20)	'Amateur Radio'
CLOB (1000000)	'This character string is a million characters long...'
SMALLINT **or** INTEGER	7500
NUMERIC **or** DECIMAL	3425.432
REAL, FLOAT, **or** DOUBLE PRECISION	6.626E-34
BIT (5)	B'11011'
BIT (16)	X'3FD0'

(continued)

Table 2-2 *(continued)*

Data Type	Example Value
BLOB (1000000)	'10010011101010110101010101...'
BOOLEAN	'true'
DATE	DATE '1957-08-14'
TIME (2) WITHOUT TIME ZONE[1]	TIME '12:46:02.43' WITHOUT TIME ZONE
TIME (3) WITH TIME ZONE	TIME '12:46:02.432-08:00' WITH TIME ZONE
TIMESTAMP WITHOUT TIME ZONE (0)	TIMESTAMP '1957-08-14 12:46:02' WITHOUT TIME ZONE
TIMESTAMP WITH TIME ZONE (0)	TIMESTAMP '1957-08-14 12:46:02-08:00' WITH TIME ZONE
INTERVAL DAY	INTERVAL '4' DAY
ROW	ROW (Street VARCHAR (25), City VARCHAR (20), State CHAR (2), PostalCode VARCHAR (9))
ARRAY	INTEGER ARRAY [15]
REF	Not a type, but a pointer
USER DEFINED TYPE	Currency type based on DECIMAL
DISTINCT TYPE	Euro type, USdollar type

[1] *Argument specifies number of fractional digits.*

Your specific implementation of SQL may not support all the data types that I describe in this section. Furthermore, your implementation may support non-standard data types that I don't describe here. (Your mileage may vary, and so on. You know the drill.)

Null Values

If a database field contains a data item, that field has a specific value. A field that does not contain a data item is said to have a *null value*. In a numeric field, a null value is not the same as a value of zero. In a character field, a null value is not the same as a blank. Both a numeric zero and a blank character are definite values. A null value indicates that a field's value is undefined — its value is not known.

A number of situations exist in which a field may have a null value. The following list describes a few of these situations and gives an example of each:

- *The value exists, but you don't know what the value is yet:* You set MASS to null in the Top row of the QUARK table before the mass of the top quark was accurately determined.

- *The value doesn't exist yet:* You set TOTAL_SOLD to null in the SQL For Dummies, 4th Edition row of the BOOKS table because the first set of quarterly sales figures is not yet reported.

- *The field isn't applicable for this particular row:* You set SEX to null in the C-3PO row of the EMPLOYEE table because C-3PO is a droid who has no gender.

- *The value is out of range:* You set SALARY to null in the Oprah Winfrey row of the EMPLOYEE table because you designed the SALARY column as type NUMERIC (8,2) and Oprah's contract calls for pay in excess of $999,999.99.

A field can have a null value for many different reasons. Don't jump to any hasty conclusions about what any particular null value means.

Constraints

Constraints are restrictions that you apply to the data that someone can enter into a database table. You may know, for example, that entries in a particular numeric column must fall within a certain range. If anyone makes an entry that falls outside that range, then that entry must be an error. Applying a range constraint to the column prevents this type of error from happening.

Traditionally, the application program that uses the database applies any constraints to a database. The most recent DBMS products, however, enable you to apply constraints directly to the database. This approach has several advantages. If multiple applications all use the same database, you need to apply the constraints only once rather than multiple times. Additionally, adding constraints at the database level is usually simpler than adding them to an application. In many cases, you need only to tack a clause onto your CREATE statement.

I discuss constraints and *assertions,* which are constraints that apply to more than one table, in detail in Chapter 5.

Using SQL in a Client/Server System

SQL is a data sublanguage that works on a stand-alone system or on a multi-user system. SQL works particularly well in a client/server system. On such a system, users on multiple client machines that connect to a server machine can access — via a local area network (LAN) or other communications channel — a database that resides on the server to which they're connected. The application program on a client machine contains SQL data-manipulation commands. The portion of the DBMS residing on the client sends these commands to the server across the communications channel that connects the server to the client. At the server, the server portion of the DBMS interprets and executes the SQL command and then sends the results back to the client across the communication channel. You can encode very complex operations into SQL at the client and then decode and perform those operations at the server. This type of setup results in the most effective use of the bandwidth of that communication channel.

If you retrieve data by using SQL on a client/server system, only the data you want travels across the communication channel from the server to the client. In contrast, a simple resource-sharing system, with minimal intelligence at the server, must send huge blocks of data across the channel to give you the small piece of data that you want. Needless to say, this sort of massive transmission can slow operations considerably. The client/server architecture complements the characteristics of SQL to provide good performance at a moderate cost on small, medium, and large networks.

The server

Unless it receives a request from a client, the server does nothing. It just stands around and waits. If multiple clients require service at the same time, however, servers need to respond quickly. Servers generally differ from client machines in that they have large amounts of very fast disk storage. Servers are optimized for fast data access and retrieval. And because they must handle traffic coming in simultaneously from multiple client machines, servers need a fast processor.

What the server is

The *server* (short for *database server*) is the part of a client/server system that holds the database. The server also holds the server portion of a database management system. This part of the DBMS interprets commands coming in from the clients and translates these commands into operations in the database. The server software also formats the results of retrieval requests and sends the results back to the requesting client.

What the server does

The job of the server is relatively simple and straightforward. All a server needs to do is read, interpret, and execute commands that come to it across the network from clients. Those commands are in one of several data sublanguages. A sublanguage doesn't qualify as a complete language — it implements only part of a language. A data sublanguage deals only with data handling. The sublanguage has operations for inserting, updating, deleting, and selecting data but doesn't have flow control structures such as DO loops, local variables, functions, procedures, or I/O to printers. SQL is the most common data sublanguage in use today and has become an industry standard. Proprietary data sublanguages have been supplanted by SQL on machines in all performance classes. With SQL:1999, SQL has acquired many of the features missing from traditional sublanguages. However, it is still not a complete general-purpose programming language and so must be combined with a host language to create a database application.

The client

The *client* part of a client/server system consists of a hardware component and a software component. The hardware component is the client computer and its interface to the local area network. This client hardware may be very similar or even identical to the server hardware. The software is the distinguishing component of the client.

What the client is

The primary job of the client is to provide a user interface. As far as the user is concerned, the client machine *is* the computer and the user interface *is* the application. The user may not even realize that the process involves a server. The server is usually out of sight — sometimes even in another room. Aside from the user interface, the client also contains the application program and the client part of the DBMS. The application program performs the specific task you require, such as accounts receivable or order entry. The client part of the DBMS executes the application program commands and exchanges data and SQL data-manipulation commands with the server part of the DBMS.

What the client does

The client part of a DBMS displays information on the screen and responds to user input transmitted via the keyboard, mouse, or other input device. The client may also process data coming in from a telecommunications link or from other stations on the network. The client part of the DBMS does all the application-specific "thinking." To a developer, the client part of a DBMS is the interesting part. The server part just handles the requests of the client part in a repetitive, mechanical fashion.

Using SQL on the Internet/Intranet

Database operation on the Internet and on intranets differs fundamentally from operation in a traditional client/server system. The difference is primarily on the client end. In a traditional client/server system, much of the functionality of the DBMS resides on the client machine. On an Internet-based database system, most or all of the DBMS resides on the server. The client may host nothing more than a Web browser. At most, the client holds a browser and a browser extension, such as a Netscape plug-in or an ActiveX control. Thus the conceptual "center of mass" of the system shifts toward the server. This shift has several advantages, as noted in the following list:

- The client portion of the system (browser) is low cost.
- You have a standardized user interface.
- The client is easy to maintain.
- You have a standardized client/server relationship.
- You have a common means of displaying multimedia data.

The main disadvantages of performing database manipulations on the Internet involve security and data integrity, as the following list describes:

- To protect information from unwanted access or tampering, both the Web server and the client browser must support strong encryption.
- Browsers don't perform adequate data-entry validation checks.
- Database tables residing on different servers may become desynchronized.

Client and server extensions designed to address these concerns make the Internet a feasible location for production database applications. The architecture of intranets is similar to that of the Internet, but security is less of a concern. Because the organization maintaining the intranet has physical control over all the client machines as well as the servers and the network that connects these components together, an intranet suffers much less exposure to the efforts of malicious hackers. Data-entry errors and database desynchronization, however, do remain concerns. Chapter 17 covers database on the Internet in detail, and Chapter 18 discusses the organizational intranet.

Chapter 3

The Components of SQL

SQL is a special-purpose language designed for the creation and maintenance of data in relational databases. Although the vendors of relational-database management systems have their own implementations of SQL, an ISO/ANSI standard (most recently revised in 1999) defines and controls what SQL is. All implementations differ from the standard to a greater or lesser degree. Close adherence to the standard is the key to running a database (and its associated applications) on more than one platform.

Although SQL isn't really a general-purpose programming language, it does contain some impressive tools. Three languages-within-a-language offer everything you need to create, modify, maintain, and provide security for a relational database:

✔ **The Data Definition Language (DDL):** The part of SQL that you use to create (completely define) a database, modify its structure, and destroy it after you no longer need it.

✔ **The Data Manipulation Language (DML):** Performs database maintenance. Using this powerful tool, you can specify exactly what you want to do with the data in your database — enter it, change it, or extract it.

✔ **The Data Control Language (DCL):** Armor against the many ways your database can become corrupted. Used correctly, the DCL provides security for your database; the amount of protection depends on the implementation. If your implementation doesn't provide sufficient protection, you must add that protection to your application program.

This chapter introduces the DDL, DML, and DCL.

Data Definition Language

The Data Definition Language (DDL) is the part of SQL you use to create, change, or destroy the basic elements of a relational database. Basic elements include tables, views, schemas, catalogs, clusters, and possibly other things as well. In this section, I discuss the containment hierarchy that relates these elements to each other and look at the commands that operate on these elements.

In Chapter 1, I mention tables and schemas, noting that a *schema* is an overall structure that includes tables within it. Tables and schemas, therefore, are two elements of a relational database's *containment hierarchy.* You can break down the containment hierarchy as follows: Tables contain columns and rows. Schemas contain tables and views. Catalogs contain schemas. The database itself contains catalogs. In some places, you'll find the database referred to as a *cluster.*

Creating tables

A database table is a two-dimensional array made up of rows and columns. You can create a table by using SQL's CREATE TABLE command. Within the command, you specify the name and data type of each column.

After you create a table, you can start loading the table with data. (Loading data is a DML, not a DDL, function.) If requirements change, you can change a table's structure after you create the table by using the ALTER TABLE command. Eventually, a table may outlive its usefulness or in some other way become obsolete. If that day arrives, you can eliminate the table by using the DROP command. The various forms of the CREATE and ALTER commands, together with the DROP command, make up SQL's DDL.

Say that you're a database designer and you don't want your database tables to gradually turn to guacamole as you make updates over time. You decide to structure your database tables according to the best-normalized form to ensure maintenance of data integrity. *Normalization,* which is an extensive field of study in its own right, is a way of structuring database tables so that updates do not introduce anomalies. Each table you create contains columns that correspond to attributes that are tightly linked to each other.

You may, for example, create a CUSTOMER table with the attributes CUSTOMER. CUSTOMER_ID, CUSTOMER.FIRST_NAME, CUSTOMER.LAST_NAME, CUSTOMER. STREET, CUSTOMER.CITY, CUSTOMER.STATE, CUSTOMER.ZIPCODE, and CUSTOMER.PHONE. All of these attributes are more closely related to the customer entity than to any other entity in a database that may contain many tables. These attributes contain all the relatively permanent information that your organization keeps on its customers.

Most database-management systems provide a graphical tool for creating database tables. You can, however, also create such tables by using an SQL command. The following example demonstrates a command that creates your CUSTOMER table:

```
CREATE TABLE CUSTOMER (
    CUSTOMER_ID INTEGER            NOT NULL,
    FIRST_NAME  CHARACTER (15),
    LAST_NAME   CHARACTER (20)     NOT NULL,
    STREET   CHARACTER (25),
    CITY   CHARACTER (20),
    STATE   CHARACTER (2),
    ZIPCODE INTEGER,
    PHONE   CHARACTER (13) ) ;
```

For each column, you specify its name (for example, CUSTOMER_ID), its data type (for example, INTEGER), and possibly one or more constraints (for example, NOT NULL).

Figure 3-1 shows a portion of the CUSTOMER table with some sample data in the table.

Figure 3-1:
The CUSTOMER table that you can create by using the CREATE TABLE command.

CUSTOMER_ID	FIRST_NAME	LAST_NAME	STREET	CITY	STAT	ZIPCODE
1	Harold	Percival	26262 S. Howards Mill Rd.	Westminster	CA	92683
2	Jerry	Appel	32323 S. River Lane Rd.	Santa Ana	CA	92705
3	Adrian	Hansen	232 Glenwood Ct.	Hollis	NH	3049
4	John	Baker	2222 Lafayette St.	Garden Grove	CA	92643
5	Michael	Pens	730 S. New Era Rd.	Irvine	CA	92715
6	Bob	Michimoto	25252 S. Kelmsley Dr.	Stanton	CA	92610
7	Linda	Smith	444 S.E. Seventh St.	Hudson	NH	3051
8	Robert	Funnell	2424 Sheri Ct.	Anaheim	CA	92640
9	Bill	Checkal	9595 Curry Dr.	Stanton	CA	92610
10	Jed	Style	3535 Randall St.	Santa Ana	CA	92705

If the SQL implementation you use doesn't fully implement SQL:1999, the syntax you need to use may differ from the syntax that I give in this book.

Imagine that you have the task of creating a database for your organization. Excited by the prospect of building a useful, valuable, and totally righteous structure of great importance to the future of your company, you sit right down at your computer and start entering SQL CREATE commands. Right?

Well, no. Not quite. In fact, that's a prescription for disaster. Many database development projects go awry at the very start as excitement and enthusiasm overtake careful planning. Even if you're sure you have a clear idea in your mind of how to structure your database, write everything out on paper before touching your keyboard. The following list identifies some procedures that you need to keep in mind as you plan your database:

- ✔ Identify all tables.
- ✔ Define the columns that each table must contain.
- ✔ Give each table a *primary key* that you can guarantee is unique. (I discuss primary keys in Chapters 4 and 5. You weren't going to build a database until you had read those chapters anyway, were you?)
- ✔ Make sure that every table in the database has at least one column in common with one other table in the database. These shared columns serve as logical links that enable you to relate information in one table to the corresponding information in another table.
- ✔ Put each table in third normal form (3NF) or better to ensure the prevention of insertion, deletion, and update anomalies. (I discuss database normalization in Chapter 5.)

After you complete the design on paper and verify that it is sound, you're ready to transfer the design to the computer by using SQL CREATE commands.

A room with a view

At times, you want to retrieve some specific information from the CUSTOMER table. You don't want to look at everything — only some specific columns and rows. What you need is a view.

A *view* is a virtual table. In most implementations, a view has no independent physical existence. The view's definition exists only in the database's metadata, but the actual data comes from the table or tables from which you derive the view. The view's data is not physically duplicated somewhere else in online disk storage. Some views consist of specific columns and rows of a single table. Others, known as *multitable views,* draw from two or more tables.

Single-table view

Sometimes when you have a question, the data that gives you the answer resides in a single table in your database. If all the information you want to see exists in a single table, you can create a single-table view of the data. For example, say that you want to look at the names and telephone numbers of all customers who live in the state of New Hampshire. You can create a view from the CUSTOMER table that contains only the data you want. The following SQL command creates this view:

```
CREATE VIEW NH_CUST AS
   SELECT CUSTOMER.FIRST_NAME,
          CUSTOMER.LAST_NAME,
          CUSTOMER.PHONE
      FROM CUSTOMER
      WHERE CUSTOMER.STATE = 'NH' ;
```

Figure 3-2 diagrams how you derive the view from the CUSTOMER table.

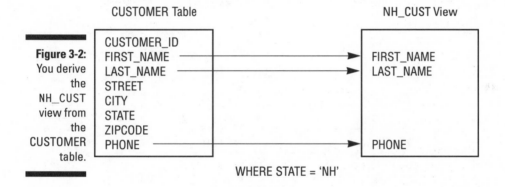

Figure 3-2: You derive the NH_CUST view from the CUSTOMER table.

This code is rigorously correct, but a little on the wordy side. You can accomplish the same thing with less typing if the SQL implementation you're using assumes that all table references are the same as the ones in the FROM clause. If your system makes that reasonable default assumption, you can reduce the command to the following lines:

```
CREATE VIEW NH_CUST AS
   SELECT FIRST_NAME, LAST_NAME, PHONE
      FROM CUSTOMER
      WHERE STATE = 'NH';
```

Although the second version is easier to write and read, it's more vulnerable to disruption from later ALTER TABLE commands. Such disruption isn't a problem for this simple case, which has no JOIN, but views with JOINs are much more robust when they use fully qualified names. I cover JOINs in Chapter 12.

Creating a multitable view

More often than not, you need to pull data from two or more tables to answer your question. For example, say that you work for a sporting goods store, and you want a list of all the customers who bought ski equipment in the last year so that you can send them a promotional mailing. You probably need information from the CUSTOMER table, the PRODUCT table, the INVOICE table, and the INVOICE_LINE table. You can create a multitable view that shows the data you need to answer your question. After you create the view, you can use that same view again and again. Each time you use the view, it reflects the changes that occurred in the underlying tables since the last time you used the view.

The sporting goods store database contains four tables: CUSTOMER, PRODUCT, INVOICE, and INVOICE_LINE. The tables are structured as shown in Table 3-1.

Table 3-1	Sporting Goods Store Database Tables		
Table	**Column**	**Data Type**	**Constraint**
CUSTOMER			
	CUSTOMER_ID	INTEGER	NOT NULL
	FIRST_NAME	CHARACTER (15)	
	LAST_NAME	CHARACTER (20)	NOT NULL
	STREET	CHARACTER (25)	
	CITY	CHARACTER (20)	
	STATE	CHARACTER (2)	
	ZIPCODE	INTEGER	
	PHONE	CHARACTER (13)	
PRODUCT			
	PRODUCT_ID	INTEGER	NOT NULL
	NAME	CHARACTER (25)	
	DESCRIPTION	CHARACTER (30)	
	CATEGORY	CHARACTER (15)	
	VENDOR_ID	INTEGER	
	VENDOR_NAME	CHARACTER (30)	
INVOICE			
	INVOICE_NUMBER	INTEGER	NOT NULL
	CUSTOMER_ID	INTEGER	
	INVOICE_DATE	DATE	
	TOTAL_SALE	NUMERIC (9,2)	
	TOTAL_REMITTED	NUMERIC (9,2)	
	FORM_OF_PAYMENT	CHARACTER (10)	

Table	Column	Data Type	Constraint
INVOICE_LINE			
	LINE_NUMBER	INTEGER	NOT NULL
	INVOICE_NUMBER	INTEGER	
	PRODUCT_ID	INTEGER	
	QUANTITY	INTEGER	
	SALE_PRICE	NUMERIC (9,2)	

Notice that some of the columns in Table 3-1 contain the constraint NOT NULL. These columns are either the primary keys of their respective tables or are columns that you, for some other reason, decide must contain a value. A table's primary key must uniquely identify each row. The primary key must contain a non-null value in every row. (I discuss keys in detail in Chapter 5.)

The tables relate to each other through the columns that they have in common. Figure 3-3 shows these relationships.

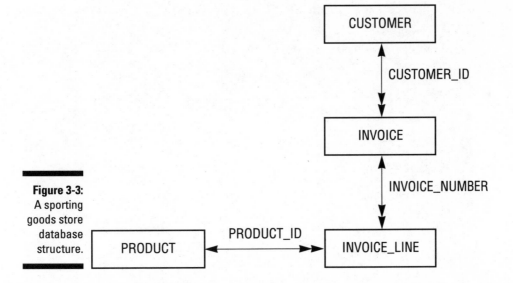

Figure 3-3:
A sporting goods store database structure.

The CUSTOMER table bears a one-to-many relationship to the INVOICE table. One customer can make multiple purchases, generating multiple invoices. Each invoice, however, deals with one and only one customer. The INVOICE table bears a one-to-many relationship to the INVOICE_LINE table. An invoice may have multiple lines, but each line appears on one and only one invoice. The PRODUCT table also bears a one-to-many relationship to the INVOICE_LINE table. A product may appear on more than one line on one or more invoices. Each line, however, deals with one, and only one, product.

The CUSTOMER table links to the INVOICE table by the common `CUSTOMER_ID` column. The INVOICE table links to the INVOICE_LINE table by the common `INVOICE_NUMBER` column. The PRODUCT table links to the INVOICE_LINE table by the common `PRODUCT_ID` column. These links are the essence of what makes this database a relational database.

To give you the information you want about customers who bought ski equipment, you need `FIRST_NAME`, `LAST_NAME`, `STREET`, `CITY`, `STATE`, and `ZIPCODE` from the CUSTOMER table; `CATEGORY` from the PRODUCT table; `INVOICE_NUMBER` from the INVOICE table; and `LINE_NUMBER` from the INVOICE_LINE table. You can create the view you want in stages by using the following commands:

```
CREATE VIEW SKI_CUST1 AS
    SELECT FIRST_NAME,
        LAST_NAME,
        STREET,
        CITY,
        STATE,
        ZIPCODE,
        INVOICE_NUMBER
    FROM CUSTOMER JOIN INVOICE
    USING (CUSTOMER_ID) ;
CREATE VIEW SKI_CUST2 AS
    SELECT FIRST_NAME,
        LAST_NAME,
        STREET,
        CITY,
        STATE,
        ZIPCODE,
        PRODUCT_ID
    FROM SKI_CUST1 JOIN INVOICE_LINE
    USING (INVOICE_NUMBER) ;
CREATE VIEW SKI_CUST3 AS
    SELECT FIRST_NAME,
        LAST_NAME,
        STREET,
        CITY,
        STATE,
        ZIPCODE,
        CATEGORY
    FROM SKI_CUST2 JOIN PRODUCT
    USING (PRODUCT_ID) ;
```

```
CREATE VIEW SKI_CUST AS
    SELECT DISTINCT FIRST_NAME,
        LAST_NAME,
        STREET,
        CITY,
        STATE,
        ZIPCODE
    FROM SKI_CUST3
    WHERE CATEGORY = 'Ski' ;
```

These CREATE VIEW statements combine data from multiple tables by using the JOIN operator. Figure 3-4 diagrams the process.

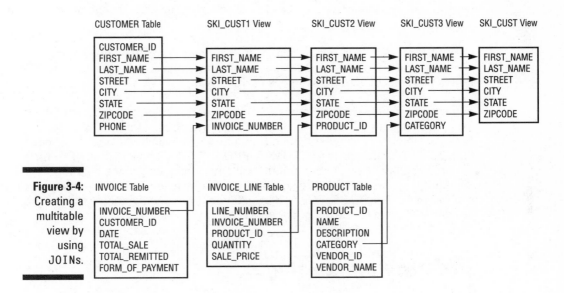

Figure 3-4: Creating a multitable view by using JOINs.

The first CREATE VIEW statement combines columns from the CUSTOMER table with a column of the INVOICE table to create the SKI_CUST1 view. The second CREATE VIEW statement combines SKI_CUST1 with a column from the INVOICE_LINE table to create the SKI_CUST2 view. The third CREATE VIEW statement combines SKI_CUST2 with a column from the PRODUCT table to create the SKI_CUST3 view. The fourth CREATE VIEW statement filters out all rows that don't have a category of 'Ski.' The end result is a view (SKI_CUST) that contains the names and addresses of all customers who bought at least one product in the 'Ski' category. The DISTINCT keyword in the fourth CREATE VIEW's SELECT clause ensures that you have only one entry for each customer, even if some customers made multiple purchases of ski items. (I cover JOINs in detail in Chapter 10.)

Collecting tables into schemas

A table consists of rows and columns and normally deals with a specific type of entity, such as customers, products, or invoices. Useful work generally requires information about several (or many) related entities. Organizationally, you collect the tables that you associate with these entities together according to a logical schema. (A *logical schema* is the organizational structure of a collection of related tables.)

In addition to a logical schema, a database also has a *physical schema*. The physical schema is the way the data and its associated items, such as indexes, are physically arranged on the system's storage devices. When I mention the schema of a database, I'm referring to the logical schema, not the physical schema.

On a system where several unrelated projects may co-reside, you can assign all tables that are related to one another to one schema. Other groups of tables you can collect into schemas of their own.

You want to name schemas to ensure that no one accidentally mixes in tables from one project with tables of another. Each project has its own associated schema, which you can distinguish from other schemas by name. Seeing certain table names (such as CUSTOMER, PRODUCT, and so on) appear in multiple projects, however, isn't uncommon. If any chance exists of a naming ambiguity, you want to qualify your table name by using its schema name as well (as in SCHEMA_NAME.TABLE_NAME). If you don't qualify a table name, SQL assigns that table to the default schema.

Ordering by catalog

For really large database systems, even multiple schemas may not prove sufficient. In a large distributed database environment with many users, you may even find duplication of a schema name. To prevent this situation from occurring, SQL:1999 adds another level to the containment hierarchy: the catalog. A *catalog* is a named collection of schemas.

You can qualify a table name by using a catalog name and a schema name. This ensures that no one confuses that table with a table of the same name in a schema with the same schema name. The catalog-qualified name appears in the following format:

```
CATALOG_NAME.SCHEMA_NAME.TABLE_NAME
```

A database's containment hierarchy has clusters at the highest level, but it's a rare system that requires use of the full scope of the containment hierarchy. Going to catalogs is enough in most cases. A catalog contains schemas; a schema contains tables and views; tables and views contain columns and rows.

The catalog also contains the *information schema.* The information schema contains the system tables. The system tables hold the metadata associated with the other schemas. In Chapter 1, I define a database as a self-describing collection of integrated records. The metadata contained in the system tables is what makes the database self-describing.

Because you distinguish catalogs by their names, you can have multiple catalogs in a database. Each catalog can have multiple schemas, and each schema can have multiple tables. Of course, each table can have multiple columns and rows. The hierarchical relationships are shown in Figure 3-5.

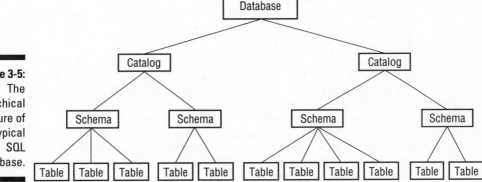

Figure 3-5:
The hierarchical structure of a typical SQL database.

Getting familiar with DDL commands

SQL's Data Definition Language consists of the CREATE, ALTER, and DROP commands. The DDL deals with the structure of a database, while the Data Manipulation Language deals with the data contained within that structure. You use the various forms of the CREATE command to build the essential structures of the database. You use the ALTER command to change structures that you create. If you apply the DROP command to a table, that command destroys not only the table's data, but its structure as well. In the following sections, I give you brief descriptions of the DDL commands. In Chapters 4 and 5, I use these commands in examples.

CREATE

You can apply the SQL CREATE command to several SQL objects, including schemas, domains, tables, and views. By using the CREATE SCHEMA statement, you can create a schema, identify its owner, and specify a default character set. An example of such a statement appears as follows:

```
CREATE SCHEMA SALES
    AUTHORIZATION SALES_MGR
    DEFAULT CHARACTER SET ASCII_FULL ;
```

Use the CREATE DOMAIN statement to apply constraints to column values or to specify a collation order. The constraints you apply to a domain determine what objects the domain can contain and what objects it can't contain. You can create domains after you establish a schema. The following example shows how you can use this command:

```
CREATE DOMAIN AGE AS INTEGER
    CHECK (AGE > 20) ;
```

You create tables by using the CREATE TABLE statement, and you create views by using the CREATE VIEW statement. Earlier in this chapter, I show you examples of the CREATE TABLE and the CREATE VIEW statements. When you use CREATE TABLE to create a new table, you can specify constraints on its columns at the same time. Sometimes, however, you may want to specify constraints that don't specifically attach to a table but that apply to an entire schema. You can use the CREATE ASSERTION statement to specify such constraints. You also have CREATE CHARACTER SETCREATE COLLATION, and CREATE TRANSLATION statements, which give you the flexibility of creating new character sets, collation sequences, or translation tables. (*Collation sequences* define the order in which you carry out comparisons or sorts. *Translation tables* control the conversion of character strings from one character set to another.)

ALTER

After you create a table, you're not necessarily stuck with that exact table forever. As you start to use the table, you may discover that it's not everything you need it to be. You can use the ALTER TABLE command to change the table by adding, changing, or deleting a column in the table. In addition to tables, you can also ALTER columns and domains.

DROP

Removing a table from a database schema is easy. Just use a DROP TABLE <tablename> command. You erase all the table's data, as well as the metadata that defines the table in the data dictionary — almost as if the table never existed.

Data Manipulation Language

As I state earlier in this chapter, the DDL is the part of SQL that creates, modifies, or destroys database structures. The DDL doesn't deal with data itself. The *Data Manipulation Language (DML)* is the part of SQL that operates on the data. Some DML statements read like ordinary English-language sentences and are easy to understand. Because SQL gives you very fine control of data, however, other DML statements can be fiendishly complex. If a DML statement includes multiple expressions, clauses, predicates, or subqueries, then understanding just what that statement is trying to do can be a real challenge. After you deal with some of these statements, you may even consider switching to an easier line of work, such as brain surgery or quantum electrodynamics. Such drastic action is probably not necessary, however, because you can come to understand such SQL statements by mentally breaking them down into their basic components and analyzing them one chunk at a time.

The DML statements you can use are INSERT, UPDATE, DELETE, and SELECT. These statements can consist of a variety of parts, including multiple clauses. Each clause may incorporate value expressions, logical connectives, predicates, aggregate functions, and subqueries. You can make fine discriminations among database records and extract more information from your data by including these clauses in your statements. In Chapter 6, I discuss the operation of the DML commands, and in Chapters 7 through 12, I delve into the details of these commands.

Value expressions

You can use *value expressions* to combine two or more values. Nine different kinds of value expressions exist, corresponding to the different data types: *numeric, string, datetime, interval, Boolean, user-defined, row,* and *collection.* The *Boolean, user-defined, row,* and *collection* types are new with SQL:1999. Some implementations may not support them right away. If you want to use any of these data types, make sure your implementation includes it.

Numeric value expressions

To combine numeric values, use the addition (+), subtraction (-), multiplication (*), and division (/) operators. The following lines show a few examples of numeric value expressions:

```
12 - 7
15/3 - 4
6 * (8 + 2)
```

The values in these examples are *numeric literals*. These values may also be column names, parameters, host variables, or subqueries — provided that those column names, parameters, host variables, or subqueries evaluate to a numeric value. The following are some examples:

```
SUBTOTAL + TAX + SHIPPING
6 * MILES/HOURS
:months/12
```

The colon in the last example signals that the following term (`months`) is either a parameter or a host variable.

String value expressions

String value expressions may include the *concatenation operator* (||). Use concatenation to join two text strings together, as shown in Table 3-2.

Table 3-2	Examples of String Concatenation
Expression	*Result*
`'military' || 'intelligence'`	`'military intelligence'`
`'oxy' || 'moron'`	`'oxymoron'`
`CITY|| ' ' ||STATE|| ' '||ZIP`	A single string with city, state, and zip code, each separated by a single space.

Some implementations of SQL use + as the concatenation operator rather than ||.

Some implementations may include string operators other than concatenation, but SQL:1999 doesn't support such operators.

Datetime and interval value expressions

Datetime value expressions deal with (surprise!) dates and times. Data of `DATE`, `TIME`, `TIMESTAMP`, and `INTERVAL` types may appear in datetime value expressions. The result of a datetime value expression is always another datetime. You can add or subtract an interval from a datetime and also specify time zone information.

One example of a datetime value expression appears as follows:

```
DUE_DATE + INTERVAL '7' DAY
```

A library may use such an expression to determine when to send a late notice. Another example, specifying a time rather than a date, appears as follows:

```
TIME '18:55:48' AT LOCAL
```

The AT LOCAL keywords indicate that the time refers to the local time zone.

Interval value expressions deal with the difference (how much time passes) between one datetime and another. You have two kinds of intervals: *year-month* and *day-time*. You can't mix the two in an expression.

As an example of an interval, say that someone returns a library book after the due date. By using an interval value expression such as that of the following example, you can calculate how many days late the book is and assess a fine accordingly:

```
(DATE_RETURNED-DATE_DUE) DAY
```

Because an interval may be of either the year-month or the day-time variety, you need to specify which kind to use. In the preceding example, I specify DAY.

Boolean value expressions

A Boolean value expression tests the truth value of a predicate. An example of a Boolean value expression would be:

```
(CLASS = SENIOR) IS TRUE
```

If this were a condition on the retrieval of rows from a student table, only rows containing the records of seniors would be retrieved. To retrieve the records of all non-seniors, you could use the following:

```
NOT (CLASS = SENIOR) IS TRUE
```

Alternatively, you could use:

```
(CLASS = SENIOR) IS  FALSE
```

To retrieve all rows that have a null value in the CLASS column, use:

```
(CLASS = SENIOR) IS UNKNOWN
```

User-defined type value expressions

User-defined types are described in Chapter 24. With this facility of SQL:1999, users can define their own data types rather than having to settle for those provided by "stock" SQL. Expressions that incorporate data elements of such a user-defined type must evaluate to an element of the same type.

Row value expressions

A row value expression, not surprisingly, specifies a row value. The row value may consist of one value expression, or two or more comma-delimited value expressions. For example:

```
('Joseph Tykociner', 'Professor Emeritus', 1918)
```

This is a row in a faculty table, showing the name, rank, and year of hire of a faculty member.

Collection value expressions

A collection value expression evaluates to an array.

Reference value expressions

A reference value expression evaluates to a value that references some other database component, such as a table column.

Predicates

Predicates are SQL equivalents of logical propositions. The following statement is an example of a proposition:

"The student is a senior."

In a table containing information about students, the domain of the CLASS column may be SENIOR, JUNIOR, SOPHOMORE, FRESHMAN, or NULL. You can use the predicate CLASS = SENIOR to filter out rows for which the predicate is false, retaining only those for which the predicate is true. Sometimes, the value of a predicate in a row is unknown (NULL). In those cases, you may choose either to discard the row or to retain it. (After all, the student *could* be a senior.) The correct course depends on the specific situation.

CLASS = SENIOR is an example of a *comparison predicate*. SQL has six comparison operators. A simple comparison predicate uses one of these operators. Table 3-3 shows the comparison predicates and examples of their use.

Table 3-3   Comparison Operators and Comparison Predicates

Operator	Comparison	Expression
=	Equal to	CLASS = SENIOR
<>	Not equal to	CLASS <> SENIOR
<	Less than	CLASS < SENIOR
>	Greater than	CLASS > SENIOR
<=	Less than or equal to	CLASS <= SENIOR
>=	Greater than or equal to	CLASS >= SENIOR

In the preceding example, only the first two entries (CLASS=SENIOR and CLASS< >SENIOR) make sense, because SOPHOMORE is considered greater than SENIOR, as SO comes after SE in the default collation sequence, which sorts in ascending alphabetical order. This interpretation, however, is probably not the one you want.

Logical connectives

Logical connectives enable you to build complex predicates out of simple ones. Say, for example, that you want to identify child prodigies in a database of high school students. Two propositions that could identify these students may read as follows:

"The student is a senior."

"The student's age is less than 14 years."

You can use the logical connective AND to create a compound predicate that isolates the student records that you want, as in the following example:

```
CLASS = SENIOR AND AGE < 14
```

If you use the AND connective, both of the component predicates must be true for the compound predicate to be true. Use the OR connective when you want the compound predicate to evaluate to true if either of the component predicates is true. NOT is the third logical connective. Strictly speaking, NOT doesn't connect two predicates, but instead reverses the truth value of the single predicate to which you apply it. Take, for example, the following expression:

```
NOT (CLASS = SENIOR)
```

This expression is true only if CLASS is, in fact, not equal to SENIOR.

Set functions

Sometimes, the information that you want to extract from a table doesn't relate to what the individual rows contain but concerns the data in the entire table taken as a set. SQL:1999 provides five *set* (or *aggregate*) *functions* to deal with such situations. These functions are COUNT, MAX, MIN, SUM, and AVG. Each function performs an action that draws data from a set of rows rather than from only a single row.

COUNT

The COUNT function returns the number of rows in the specified table. To count the number of precocious seniors in my example high school database, use the following statement:

```
SELECT COUNT (*)
      FROM STUDENT
      WHERE GRADE = 12 AND AGE < 14 ;
```

MAX

Use the MAX function to return the maximum value that occurs in the specified column. Say that you want to find the oldest student enrolled in your school. A statement such as the following returns the appropriate row:

```
SELECT FIRST_NAME, LAST_NAME, AGE
      FROM STUDENT
      WHERE AGE = (SELECT MAX(AGE) FROM STUDENT);
```

This statement returns all students whose age is equal to the maximum age. That is, if the age of the oldest student is 23, this statement returns the first and last names and the age of all students who are 23 years old.

This query makes use of a subquery. The subquery SELECT MAX(AGE) FROM STUDENT is embedded within the main query.

MIN

The MIN function works just like MAX except that MIN looks for the minimum value in the specified column rather than the maximum. To find the youngest student enrolled, you can use the following query:

```
SELECT FIRST_NAME, LAST_NAME, AGE
      FROM STUDENT
      WHERE AGE = (SELECT MIN(AGE) FROM STUDENT);
```

This query returns all students whose age is equal to the age of the youngest student.

SUM

The SUM function adds up the values in a specified column. The column must be one of the numeric data types, and the value of the sum must be within the range of that type. Thus, if the column is of type SMALLINT, the resulting sum must be no larger than the upper limit of the SMALLINT data type. In the retail database from earlier in this chapter, the INVOICE table contains a record of all sales. To find the total dollar value of all sales recorded in the database, use the SUM function as follows:

```
SELECT SUM(TOTAL_SALE) FROM INVOICE;
```

AVG

The AVG function returns the average of all the values in the specified column. As does the SUM function, AVG applies only to columns with a numeric data type. To find the value of the average sale, considering all transactions in the database, use the AVG function in the following way:

```
SELECT AVG(TOTAL_SALE) FROM INVOICE
```

Nulls, remember, have no value, so if any of the rows in the TOTAL_SALE column contain null values, those rows are ignored in the computation of the value of the average sale.

Subqueries

Subqueries, as you can see in the "Set functions" section earlier in this chapter, are queries within a query. Any place in an SQL statement where you can use an expression, you can also use a subquery. Subqueries provide a powerful tool for relating information in one table to information in another table, because you can embed a query into one table, within a query into another table. By nesting one subquery within another, you enable the access of information from two or more tables to generate a final result. When you use subqueries correctly, you can retrieve just about any information you want from a database.

Data Control Language

The *Data Control Language (DCL)* has four commands: COMMIT, ROLLBACK, GRANT, and REVOKE. These commands all involve protecting the database from harm, either accidental or intentional.

Transactions

Your database is most vulnerable to damage while you or someone else is changing it. Even in a single-user system, making a change can prove dangerous to a database. A software or hardware failure while the change is in progress can leave a database in an indeterminate state between where it was before the change starts and where it would be after the change finishes.

SQL protects your database by restricting operations that can change the database so that these operations occur only within transactions. During a transaction, SQL records every operation on the data in a log file. If anything interrupts the transaction before the COMMIT statement ends the transaction, you can restore the system to its original state by issuing a ROLLBACK statement. The ROLLBACK processes the transaction log in reverse, undoing all the actions that took place in the transaction. After you roll back the database to its state before the transaction began, you can clear up whatever caused the problem and then attempt the transaction again.

As long as a hardware or software problem can possibly occur, your database is susceptible to damage. To minimize the chance of damage, today's DBMSs close the window of vulnerability as much as possible by performing all operations that affect the database within a transaction and then committing all these operations at one time. Modern database-management systems use logging in conjunction with transactions to guarantee that hardware, software, or operational problems will not damage data. After a transaction has been committed, it's safe from all but the most catastrophic of system failures. Prior to commitment, incomplete transactions can be rolled back to their starting point and applied again, after the problem is corrected.

In a multiuser system, database corruption or incorrect results are possible even if no hardware or software failures occur. Interactions between two or more users who access the same table at the same time can cause serious problems. By restricting changes so that they occur only within transactions, SQL addresses these problems as well.

By putting all operations that affect the database into transactions, you can isolate the actions of one user from those of another user. Such isolation is critical if you want to make sure that the results you obtain from the database are accurate.

You may wonder how the interaction of two users can produce inaccurate results. For example, say that Donna reads a record in a database table. An instant later (more or less) David changes the value of a numeric field in that record. Now Donna writes a value back into that field, based on the value that she read initially. Because Donna is unaware of David's change, the value after Donna's write operation is incorrect.

Another problem can result if Donna writes to a record and then David reads that record. If Donna rolls back her transaction, David is unaware of the rollback and bases his actions on the value that he read, which doesn't reflect the value that's actually in the database after the rollback. It makes for good comedy, but lousy data management.

Users and privileges

Aside from data corruption resulting from hardware and software problems or the unintentional interaction of two users, another major threat to data integrity is the users themselves. Some people should have no access to the data at all. Others should have only restricted access to some of the data but no access to the rest. Some should have unlimited access to everything. You need, therefore, a system for classifying users and for assigning access privileges to the users in different categories.

The creator of a schema specifies who is considered its owner. As the owner of a schema, you can grant access privileges to the users you specify. Any privileges that you don't explicitly grant are withheld. You can also revoke privileges that you've already granted. A user must pass an authentication procedure to prove his identity before he can access the files you authorize him to use. That procedure is implementation-dependent.

SQL gives you the capability to protect the following database objects:

- ✔ Tables
- ✔ Columns
- ✔ Views
- ✔ Domains
- ✔ Character sets
- ✔ Collations
- ✔ Translations

I discuss character sets, collations, and translations in Chapter 5.

SQL:1999 supports several different kinds of protection: *seeing, adding, modifying, deleting, referencing,* and *using* databases, as well as protections associated with the execution of external routines.

You permit access by using the GRANT statement and remove access by using the REVOKE statement. By controlling the use of the SELECT command, the DCL controls who can see a database object such as a table, column, or view. Controlling the INSERT command determines who can add new rows in a table. Restricting the use of the UPDATE command to authorized users controls who can modify table rows, and restricting the DELETE command controls who can delete table rows.

If one table in a database contains as a foreign key a column that is a primary key in another table in the database, you can add a constraint to the first table so that it references the second table. When one table references another, the owner of the first table may be able to deduce information about the contents of the second. As the owner of the second table, you may want to prevent such snooping. SQL:1999's GRANT REFERENCES statement gives you that power. The following section discusses the problem of a renegade reference and how the GRANT REFERENCES statement prevents it. By using the GRANT USAGE statement, you can control who can use or even see the contents of a domain, character set, collation, or translation. (I cover this issue in Chapter 13.)

Table 3-4 summarizes the SQL statements that you use to grant and revoke privileges.

Table 3-4	Types of Protection
Protection Operation	*Statement*
Enable to see a table	GRANT SELECT
Prevent from seeing a table	REVOKE SELECT
Enable to add rows to a table	GRANT INSERT
Prevent from adding rows to a table	REVOKE INSERT
Enable to change data in table rows	GRANT UPDATE
Prevent from changing data in table rows	REVOKE UPDATE
Enable to delete table rows	GRANT DELETE
Prevent from deleting table rows	REVOKE DELETE
Enable to reference a table	GRANT REFERENCES
Prevent from referencing a table	REVOKE REFERENCES
Enable to use a domain, character translation, or set collation	GRANT USAGE ON DOMAIN, GRANT USAGE ON CHARACTER SET, GRANT USAGE ON COLLATION, GRANT USAGE ON TRANSLATION
Prevent the use of a domain, character set, collation, or translation	REVOKE USAGE ON DOMAIN, REVOKE USAGE ON CHARACTER SET, REVOKE USAGE ON COLLATION, REVOKE USAGE ON TRANSLATION

You can give different levels of access to different people, depending on their needs. The following commands offer a few examples of this capability:

```
GRANT SELECT
      ON CUSTOMER
      TO SALES_MANAGER;
```

The preceding example enables one person, the sales manager, to see the CUSTOMER table.

The following example enables anyone with access to the system to see the retail price list:

```
GRANT SELECT
      ON RETAIL_PRICE_LIST
      TO PUBLIC;
```

The following example enables the sales manager to modify the retail price list. She can change the contents of existing rows, but she can't add or delete rows:

```
GRANT UPDATE
      ON RETAIL_PRICE_LIST
      TO SALES_MANAGER;
```

This following example enables the sales manager to add new rows to the retail price list:

```
GRANT INSERT
      ON RETAIL_PRICE_LIST
      TO SALES_MANAGER;
```

Now, thanks to this last example, the sales manager can delete unwanted rows from the table, too:

```
GRANT DELETE
      ON RETAIL_PRICE_LIST
      TO SALES_MANAGER;
```

Referential integrity constraints can jeopardize your data

You may think that if you can control the seeing, creating, modifying, and deleting functions on a table, you're well protected. Against most threats, you are. A knowledgeable hacker, however, can still ransack the house by using an indirect method.

A correctly designed relational database has *referential integrity,* which means that the data in one table in the database is consistent with the data in all the other tables. To ensure referential integrity, database designers apply constraints to tables that restrict what someone can enter into the tables. If you have a database with referential integrity constraints, a user can possibly create a new table that uses a column in a confidential table as a foreign key. That column then serves as a link through which someone can possibly steal confidential information.

Say, for example, that you're a famous Wall Street stock analyst. Many people believe in the accuracy of your stock picks, so whenever you recommend a stock to your subscribers, many people buy that stock and its value increases. You keep your analysis in a database, which contains a table named FOUR_STAR. Your top recommendations for your next newsletter are in that table. Naturally, you restrict access to FOUR_STAR so that word doesn't leak out to the investing public before your paying subscribers receive the newsletter.

You're still vulnerable, however, if anyone other than yourself can create a new table that uses the stock name field of FOUR_STAR as a foreign key, as shown in the following command example:

```
CREATE TABLE HOT_STOCKS (
    STOCK CHARACTER (30) REFERENCES FOUR_STAR
    );
```

The hacker can now try to insert the name of every stock on the New York Stock Exchange into the table. Those inserts that succeed tell the hacker which stocks match the stocks that you name in your confidential table. At computer speeds, the hacker doesn't need long to extract your entire list of stocks.

You can protect yourself from hacks such as the one in the preceding example by being very careful about entering statements similar to the following:

```
GRANT REFERENCES (STOCK)
    ON FOUR_STAR
    TO IMASECRET_HACKER;
```

Avoid granting privileges to people who may abuse them. True, people don't come with guarantees printed on their foreheads. But if you wouldn't lend your new car to a person for a long trip, you probably shouldn't grant him the REFERENCES privilege on an important table either.

This example offers one good reason for maintaining careful control of the REFERENCES privilege.

The following list describes two other reasons for careful control of REFERENCES:

✔ If the other person specifies the constraint in HOT STOCKS by using a RESTRICT option and you try to delete a row from your table, the DBMS tells you that you can't, because doing so would violate a referential constraint.

✔ If you decide that you want to use the DROP command to destroy your table, you find that you must get the other person to first drop his constraint (or his table).

The bottom line is that enabling another person to specify integrity constraints on your table not only introduces a potential security breach, but also means that the other user sometimes gets in your way.

Delegating responsibility for security

If you want to keep your system secure, you must severely restrict the access privileges you grant and the people to whom you grant these privileges. People who can't do their work because of lack of access, however, are likely to hassle you constantly. To preserve your sanity, you're probably going to need to delegate some of the responsibility for maintaining the security of your database. SQL provides for such delegation through the WITH GRANT OPTION clause. Consider the following example:

```
GRANT UPDATE
    ON RETAIL_PRICE_LIST
    TO SALES_MANAGER WITH GRANT OPTION
```

This statement is similar to the previous GRANT UPDATE example in that the statement enables the sales manager to update the retail price list. The statement also, however, gives her the right to grant the update privilege to anyone she wants. If you use this form of the GRANT statement, you must not only trust the grantee to use the privilege wisely, but you must also trust her to choose wisely in granting the privilege to others.

The ultimate in trust, and therefore the ultimate in vulnerability, is to execute a statement such as the following:

```
GRANT ALL PRIVILEGES
    ON FOUR_STAR
    TO BENEDICT_ARNOLD WITH GRANT OPTION;
```

Be *extremely* careful about using statements such as this one.

Part II

Using SQL to Build Databases

The 5th Wave   By Rich Tennant

"I STARTED DESIGNING DATABASE SOFTWARE SYSTEMS AFTER SEEING HOW EASY IT WAS TO DESIGN OFFICE FURNITURE."

In this part . . .

The life cycle of the wild database encompasses the following four important stages:

- ✔ Creating the database
- ✔ Filling the database with data
- ✔ Manipulating and retrieving selected data
- ✔ Deleting the data

I cover all these stages in this book, but in Part II, I focus on database creation. SQL includes all the facilities you need to create relational databases of any size or complexity. I explain what these facilities are and how to use them. I also describe some common problems that relational databases suffer from and tell you about provisions in SQL that can help you prevent such problems — or at least minimize their effects.

Chapter 4

Building and Maintaining a Simple Database Structure

Computer history changes so fast that sometimes the rapid turnover of technological "generations" can be confusing. High-level (so-called third-generation) languages such as FORTRAN, COBOL, Basic, Pascal, and C were the first to be used with large databases. Later, languages specifically designed for use with databases, such as dBASE, Paradox, and R:BASE (third-and-a-half-generation languages?) came into use. The latest step in this progression is the emergence of development environments such as Access, Delphi, IntraBuilder, and C++Builder (fourth-generation languages, or 4GLs), which build applications with little or no procedural programming. You can use these graphical object-oriented tools (also known as *rapid application development,* or *RAD,* tools) to assemble application components into production applications.

If you've had a recent look at Chapters 1 through 3, you know that SQL is not a complete language. Thus it doesn't fit tidily into one of the generational categories I just mentioned. It makes use of commands in the manner of a third-generation language but is essentially nonprocedural, like a fourth-generation language. The bottom line is that how you classify SQL doesn't really matter. You can use it in conjunction with all the major third- and fourth-generation development tools. You can write the SQL code yourself, or you can move objects around on-screen and have the development environment generate equivalent code for you. The commands that go out to the remote database are pure SQL in either case.

In this chapter, I take you through the process of building, altering, and dropping a simple table by using a RAD tool, and then you find out how to build, alter, and drop the same table using SQL.

Building a Simple Database Using a RAD Tool

People use databases because they want to keep track of important information. Sometimes, the information that they want to track is simple, but sometimes it's not. A good database management system provides what you need in either case. Some DBMSs give you SQL. Others, like RADtools, give you an object-oriented graphical environment. Some DBMSs support both approaches. In the following sections, I build a simple single-table database by using a graphical database design tool so that you can see what the process involves. I use Microsoft Access, but the procedure is similar for other Windows-based development environments.

A likely scenario

The first step you make toward creating a database is to decide what facts you want to track. Consider a likely example: Imagine that you just won $101 million in the Powerball lottery. (In real life, it's about as likely as finding your car squashed by a meteorite.) People you haven't heard from in years and friends you'd forgotten you had are coming out of the woodwork. Some have sure-fire, can't-miss business opportunities in which they want you to invest. Others represent worthy causes that could benefit from your support. As a good steward of your new wealth, you realize that some business opportunities probably aren't as good as others. Some of the causes aren't as worthy as others. You decide to put all the options into a database so you don't lose any of them and so you can make fair and equitable judgments.

You decide to track the following items:

- First name
- Last name
- Address
- City
- State or province
- Postal code
- Phone
- How Known (your relationship to the person)
- Proposal
- Business or charity

Because you don't want to get too elaborate, you decide to put all the listed items into a single database table. You fire up your Access development environment and stare at the screen shown in Figure 4-1.

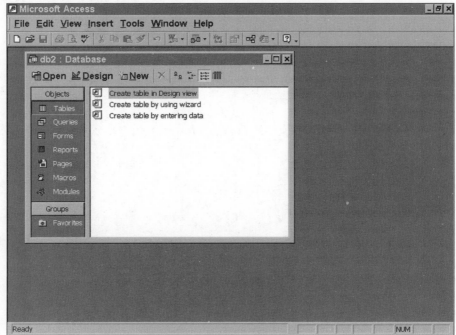

Figure 4-1:
Microsoft
Access
opening
screen.

Design view gives you full control

The screen shown in Figure 4-1 contains much more information than what previous-generation DBMS products displayed. In the old days (the 1980s), the typical DBMS presented you with a blank screen punctuated by a single-character prompt. Database management has come a long way since then, and determining what you should do first is much easier now. The workspace holds a dialog box giving three choices of how to create a database table. You should select Create Table in Design View. You could've chosen Create Table Using Wizard, but that would've been a poor choice in this case because wizards are not very flexible. The table-creating wizard builds tables from a list of predefined columns. The application is a bit unusual, so you may want to define your own columns. To define your own columns use the following steps:

1. **After opening Access, double-click the Create Table in Design View option.**

   The Table Creation dialog box appears, as shown in Figure 4-2.

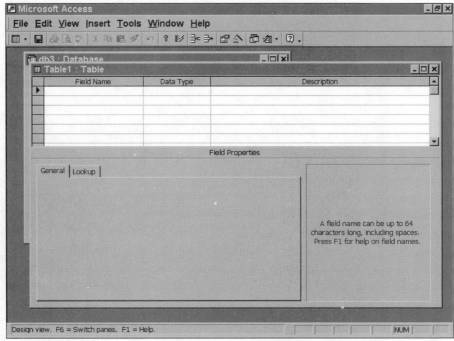

Figure 4-2:
The Table
Creation
dialog box.

2. **Fill in the Field Name, Data Type, and Description information for each attribute for your table.**

   After you make an entry in the Field Name column, a drop-down menu appears in the Data Type column

3. **Select the appropriate data types you wish to use.**

   Figure 4-3 shows that default values have been filled in for some of the Field Properties. You may want to make entries for all the fields you can identify. The fact that Access uses the *field* nomenclature rather than *column* stems from history. The original file-processing systems weren't relational and used the file, field, and record terminology common for flat-file systems.

   You may wish to retain these values, or change them as appropriate. For example, the default value for the First Name field is 50 characters, which is probably more characters than needed. You can save storage space by changing the value to something more reasonable, such as 20 characters. Figure 4-4 shows the Table Creation dialog box after all field entries are made.

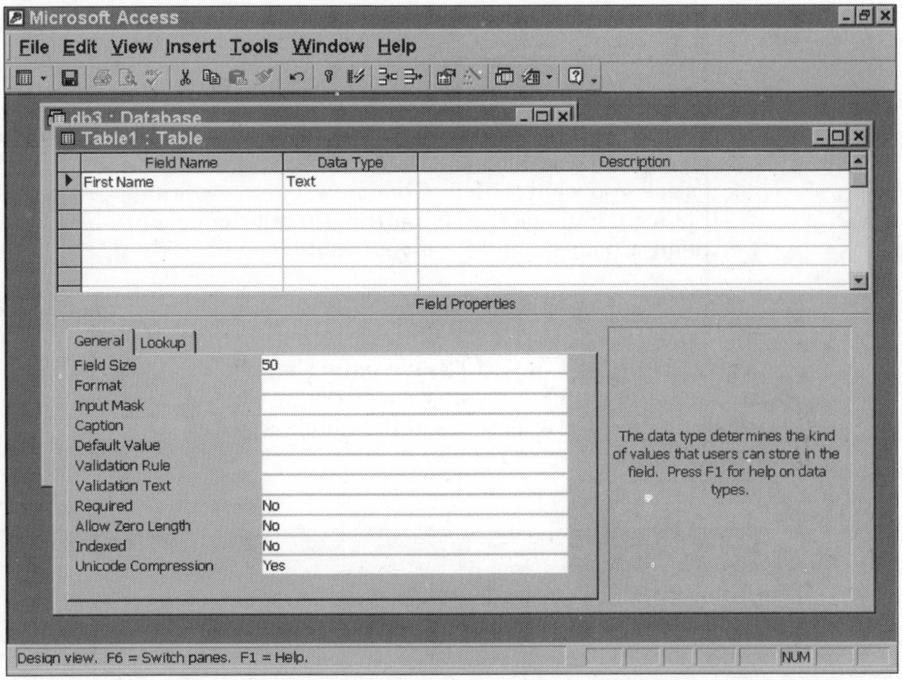

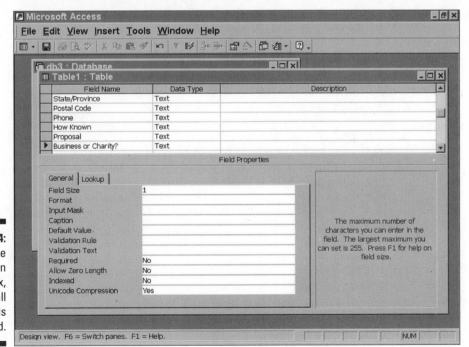

Figure 4-3:
The Table
Creation
dialog box
shows
default
entries for
First
Name Field
Properties.

Figure 4-4:
The Table
Creation
dialog box,
with all
fields
defined.

4. Now that your table is defined, save it by selecting File➪Save.

Figure 4-5 shows the dialog box that appears, asking for the name of the table you want to save. I named my table POWER.

When you try to save your new table, another dialog box appears (see Figure 4-6) that tells you that you haven't defined a primary key, and it asks if you want to define one now. I discuss primary keys a little later, but for now, click the No button. Do not define a primary key at this point. Go ahead and save your table.

After you save your table, you may decide that you may need to tweak your original design. After all, so many people have offered you enticing business deals that a few of these folks have the same first and last names as other people in the group. To keep them straight, you decide to add a unique proposal number to each record in the database table. This way, you can tell one David Lee from another.

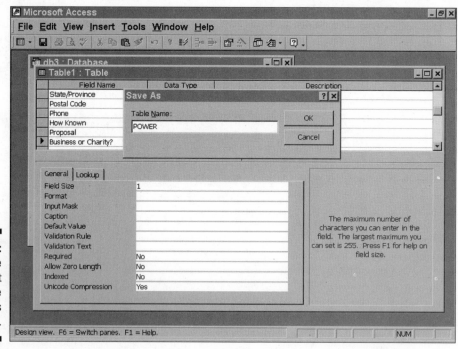

Figure 4-5:
The Table
Name: text
box in the
Save As
dialog box.

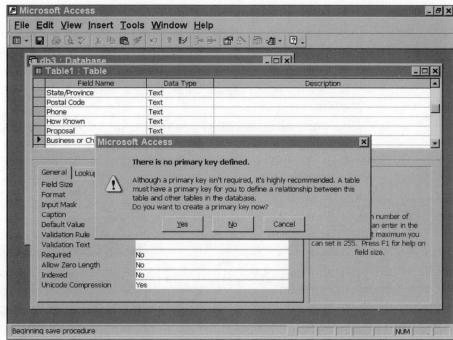

Figure 4-6:
The Primary
Key dialog
box.

Altering the structure of your table

More often than not, the database tables you create aren't right the first time you build them. If you're working for someone else, you can be virtually certain that your client is going to come to you after you create your database and tell you that management wants to keep track of another data item — perhaps even several more. If you're building a database for your own use, deficiencies in your structure, which were totally invisible before you actually built the database, inevitably become apparent *after* you create the structure. For example, perhaps you start getting proposals from outside the U.S. and need to add a Country column. Or you decide that including an e-mail address may prove helpful. In any case, you must go back in and restructure what you created. All RAD tools have a restructure capability. To demonstrate a typical one, I use Access to modify the table I'm building.

You may need to add a unique proposal number to distinguish between proposals from different people who have the same name. While you're at it, you may as well add a second Address field for people with complex addresses, and a Country field for proposals from other countries.

To insert a new row and accommodate the new changes your boss is wanting, do the following:

1. **In the Table Definition dialog box, put the cursor in the top row and select Insert⇨Rows, as shown in Figure 4-7.**

   A blank row appears at the cursor position and pushes down all the existing rows.

2. **Enter the column headings you wish to use in your table.**

   I used `Proposal Number` as the Field Name, `Number` as Data Type, and a Unique identifier for each row of the POWER table as the `Description`. In a similar way, I added an `Address 2` field below the `Address` field and a `Country` field below the `Postal Code` field. Figure 4-8 shows the result.

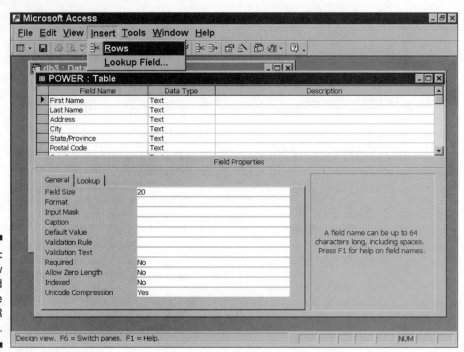

Figure 4-7: A new row is inserted in the POWER table.

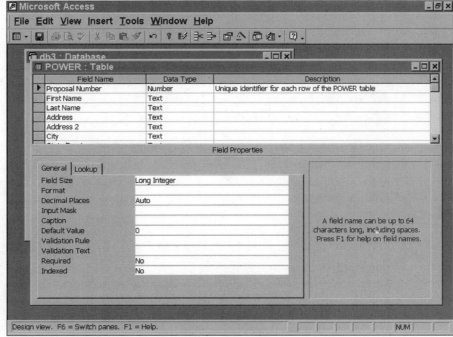

Figure 4-8:
Your revised table definition should look similar to this.

Identifying a primary key

You've already seen that the Proposal Number field uniquely identifies each row in the POWER table. A table's primary key is a field that uniquely identifies each row, so Proposal Number is a good candidate for POWER's primary key. As it happens, Proposal Number is the only field that you can be sure isn't duplicated somewhere in the table, so you should designate it as the table's primary key. You can do that by putting the cursor in the Proposal Number row of the Table Definition dialog box, and then clicking the Primary Key icon in the center of the Table Design toolbar. This puts the key icon in the left-most column of the Table Definition dialog box, which indicates that Proposal Number is the primary key of the POWER table. Figure 4-9 shows the table definition after the primary key has been declared.

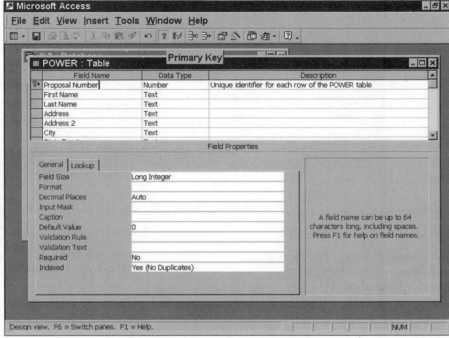

Figure 4-9:
Proposal
Number is
declared as
the primary
key.

Creating an index

Because the number of investment and charitable proposals you receive could easily grow into the thousands, you need a quick way to pull out records of interest. You may want to accomplish this task in a variety of different ways. Say, for example, that you want to look at all the proposals made by your brothers. You can isolate these offers effectively by basing your retrieval on the contents of the Last Name field, as shown in the following example:

```
SELECT * FROM POWER
    WHERE LastName = 'Marx' ;
```

That strategy, however, doesn't work for the proposals made by your brothers-in-law, but you can get those proposals by looking at another field, as shown in the following example:

```
SELECT * FROM POWER
    WHERE HowKnown = 'brother-in-law' ;
```

These queries work, but if POWER is large (tens of thousands of records), they may not work very quickly. SQL scans the entire table a row at a time, looking for entries that satisfy the WHERE clause. You can speed things up tremendously by applying *indexes* to the POWER table. (An *index* is a table of pointers. Each row in the index points to a corresponding row in the data table.)

You can define an index for each different way that you may want to access your data. If you add, change, or delete rows in the data table, you don't need to re-sort the table — you need only to update the indexes. You can update an index much faster than you can sort an entire table. After you establish an index with the desired ordering, you can use that index to access rows in the data table almost instantaneously.

Because Proposal Number is unique as well as short, using that field is always the quickest way to reach an individual record. For that reason, the primary key of any table should always be indexed. Access does this automatically. To use this field, however, you must know the Proposal Number of the record you want. You may want to create additional indexes, based on other fields, such as Last Name, Postal Code, or How Known. For a table that you index on Last Name, after a search finds the first row containing a Last Name of Marx, the search has found them all. The index keys for all the Marx rows are stored one right after another. Chico, Groucho, Harpo, Zeppo, and Karl can all be retrieved almost as fast as Chico alone.

After you create an index, that creation adds additional overhead to your system, which tends to slow down operations a bit. You must balance this slowdown against the speed you gain by accessing records through an index. Indexing fields that you use frequently to access records in a large table generally pays off in the long run. Creating indexes for fields that you never use as retrieval keys, however, costs you far more time than you gain. Creating indexes for fields that don't differentiate one record from another also makes no sense. The Business or Charity? field, for example, merely divides the table records into two categories — it doesn't make a good index.

The effectiveness of a specific index varies from one implementation to another. If you migrate a database from one platform to another, the indexes that gave the best performance on the first system may not perform the best on the new platform. In fact, they may cause worse performance than if you hadn't indexed the database at all. You must optimize your indexes for each specific DBMS and hardware configuration. Try various indexing schemes to see which one gives you the best overall performance, and consider both retrieval speed and update speed.

To create indexes for the POWER table, click the Indexes icon located to the right of the Primary Key icon in the Table Design toolbar. The Indexes dialog box appears and already has entries for Postal Code and Proposal Number. Figure 4-10 shows the Indexes dialog box.

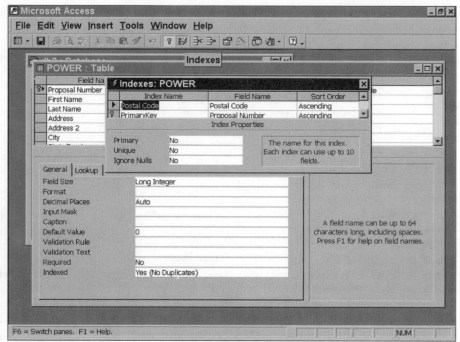

Figure 4-10:
The Indexes dialog box.

Access automatically creates an index for `Postal Code` because that field is often used for retrievals. It has automatically indexed the primary key as well.

You can see that `Postal Code` isn't a primary key and isn't necessarily unique. The opposite is true for `Proposal Number`. Create additional indexes for Last Name and How Known, because they're likely to be used for retrievals. Figure 4-11 shows how these new indexes are specified.

After you create all your indexes, you can save the new table structure by selecting File⇨Save or by clicking the diskette icon on the Table Definition toolbar.

Of course, if you use a RAD tool other than Microsoft Access, the specifics that I describe in this section don't apply to you. You would execute a roughly equivalent procedure, however, to create a database table and its indexes with a different RAD tool.

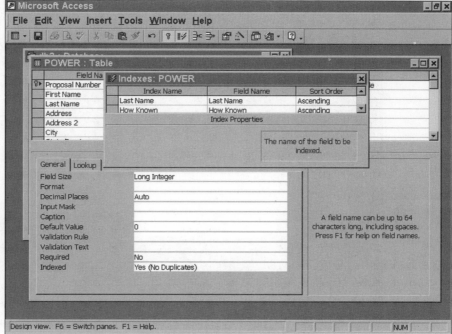

Figure 4-11:
Defining
indexes for
the Last
Name and
How Known
fields.

Deleting a table

In the course of creating a POWER table with exactly the structure you want, you may create a few intermediate forms that aren't quite right. The presence of these variant tables on your system may confuse people later, so your best course is to delete these tables while you still remember which is which. To do so, select the table that you want to delete and click the *X* icon in the menu bar of the database window, as shown in Figure 4-12.

Access asks you whether you really want to delete the selected table. Say you do, and it's permanently deleted.

If Access deletes a table, it deletes all related tables as well, including any indexes the table may have.

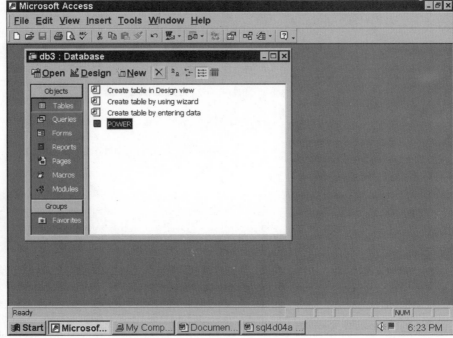

Figure 4-12:
You can
delete a
table by
selecting its
name and
clicking the
X icon.

Building POWER with SQL's DDL

All the database definition functions you can perform by using a RAD tool, such as Access, you can also accomplish by using SQL. Instead of clicking menu choices with the mouse, you enter commands from the keyboard. Some people, who prefer to manipulate visual objects, find the RAD tools easy and natural to understand and use. Other people, more oriented toward stringing words together into logical statements, find SQL commands easier and more natural. Because some things are more easily represented by using the object paradigm and others are more easily handled by using SQL, becoming proficient at using both methods is worthwhile.

In the following sections, I use SQL to perform the same table creation, alteration, and deletion operations that I used the RAD tool to perform in the preceding section.

Creating a table

To create a database table with SQL, you must enter the same information that you'd enter if you created the table with a RAD tool. The difference is that the RAD tool helps you by providing a Table Creation dialog box (or some similar data-entry skeleton) and by preventing you from entering invalid field names, types, or sizes. SQL doesn't give you as much help. You must know what you're doing before you start instead of figuring things out along the way. You must enter the entire CREATE TABLE statement before SQL even looks at it, let alone gives you any indication as to whether or not you made any errors in the statement.

The statement that creates a proposal-tracking table identical to the one created earlier uses the following syntax:

```
CREATE TABLE POWER_SQL (
    PROPOSAL_NUMBER      SMALLINT,
    FIRST_NAME           CHAR (15),
    LAST_NAME            CHAR (20),
    ADDRESS              CHAR (30),
    CITY                 CHAR (25),
    STATE_PROVINCE       CHAR (2),
    POSTAL_CODE          CHAR (10),
    COUNTRY              CHAR (30),
    PHONE                CHAR (14),
    HOW_KNOWN            CHAR (30),
    PROPOSAL             CHAR (50),
    BUSIN_OR_CHARITY     CHAR (1) );
```

As you can see, the information in the SQL statement is essentially the same as what you enter into the RAD tool (discussed earlier in this chapter). Which method you use is largely a matter of personal preference. The nice thing about SQL, however, is that the language is universal. The same standard syntax works regardless of the database-management system you use.

Any effort you put into learning SQL has long-term payoffs, because SQL's going to be around for a long time. Effort you put into becoming an expert in a particular development tool is likely to yield a lesser return on investment. No matter how wonderful the latest RAD tool may be, you can be sure that it's going to be superseded by newer technology within one to three years. If you can recover your investment in the tool in that time, great! Use it. If not, you may be wise to stick with the tried and true. Train your people in SQL, and your training investment is sure to pay dividends over a much longer period.

Creating an index

Indexes are a very important part of any relational database. Indexes serve as pointers into the tables that contain the data of interest. By using an index, you can go directly to a particular record without having to scan the table sequentially, one record at a time, to find that record. For large tables, indexes are a necessity. Without indexes, you may need to wait *years* rather than seconds for a result from a really large table. (Well, I suppose you wouldn't actually wait years. Some retrievals, however, may actually take that long if you let them keep running. Unless you have nothing better to do with your computer's time, you'd probably just abort the retrieval and do without the result. Life goes on.)

Amazingly, the SQL:1999 specification doesn't provide a means to create an index. The DBMS vendors must provide their own implementations of the function. Because these implementations aren't standardized, they may differ from one another. Most vendors provide the index creation function by adding a CREATE INDEX command to SQL. Even though two vendors may use the same words (CREATE INDEX), the way the command operates may not be the same. You're likely to find quite a few implementation-dependent clauses. You must carefully study your DBMS documentation to determine how to use that particular DBMS to create indexes.

Altering the structure of a table

To change the structure of an existing table, you can use SQL's ALTER TABLE command. Interactive SQL at your client station is not as convenient as a RAD tool. The RAD tool displays your table's structure, which you can then modify. Using SQL, you must know in advance both the table's structure and how you want to modify it. At the screen prompt, you must enter the appropriate command to perform the alteration. If, however, you want to embed the table alteration instructions in an application program, using SQL is usually the easiest way to do so.

To add a second address field to the POWER_SQL table, use the following DDL command:

```
ALTER TABLE POWER_SQL
    ADD COLUMN ADDRESS_2 CHAR (30);
```

You don't need to be an SQL guru to decipher this code. In fact, even professed computer illiterates can probably figure this one out. The command alters a table with the name POWER_SQL by adding a column to the table. The column is named ADDRESS_2, is of the CHAR data type, and is 30 characters long. This example demonstrates how easily you can change the structure of database tables by using SQL DDL commands.

SQL:1999 provides this statement for adding a column to a table and allows you to drop an existing column in a similar manner, as in the following code:

```
ALTER TABLE POWER_SQL
    DROP COLUMN ADDRESS_2;
```

Deleting a table

Deleting database tables that you no longer want cluttering up your hard disk is easy. Just use the DROP TABLE command, as follows:

```
DROP TABLE POWER_SQL ;
```

What could be simpler? If you drop a table, you erase all its data and its meta-data. No vestige of the table remains.

Deleting an index

If you delete a table by issuing a DROP TABLE command, you delete any indexes associated with that table at the same time. Sometimes, however, you may want to keep a table but remove an index from it. SQL:1999 doesn't define a DROP INDEX command, but most implementations include that command anyway. Such a command comes in handy if your system slows to a crawl and you discover that your tables aren't optimally indexed. Correcting an index problem can bring about a dramatic performance improvement that may surprise and delight users who've become accustomed to response times reminiscent of pouring molasses on a cold day in Vermont.

Portability Considerations

Any SQL implementation that you're likely to use may have extensions that give it capabilities that the SQL:1999 specification doesn't cover. Some of these features are likely to appear in the next release of the SQL specification. Others are unique to a particular implementation and probably destined to stay that way.

Often, these extensions make creating an application that meets your needs easier, and you find yourself tempted to use them. Using the extensions may be your best course, but if you do, be aware of the trade-offs. If you ever want to migrate your application to another SQL implementation, you may need to rewrite those sections in which you used extensions that your new environment doesn't support. Think about the probability of such a migration at some time in the future and also about whether the extension you're considering is unique to your implementation or fairly widespread. Forgoing use of an extension may be better in the long run, even if its use saves you some time. On the other hand, you may find no reason not to use the extension. Consider each case carefully. The more you know about existing implementations and the trends in their development, the better the decisions you can make.

Chapter 5

Building a Multitable Relational Database

*I*n this chapter, I take you through an example of how to design a multitable database. The first step to designing this type of database is to identify what to include and what not to include. The next steps are deciding how the included items relate to each other and then setting up tables accordingly. I also discuss how to use *keys,* which provide a means of accessing individual records and indexes. Keys enable you to access those records quickly.

A database must do more than merely hold your data. It must also protect the data from becoming corrupted. In the latter part of this chapter, I discuss how to protect the integrity of your data. *Normalization* is one of the key methods you can use to protect the integrity of a database, so I discuss the various "normal" forms and point out the kinds of problems that normalization solves.

Designing the Database

To design a database, follow these basic steps (I go into detail about each step in the sections that follow this list):

1. **Decide what objects you want to include in your database.**
2. **Determine which of these objects should be tables and which should be columns within those tables.**
3. **Define tables according to your determination of how you need to organize the objects.**

   Optionally, you may want to designate a table column or a combination of columns as a key. *Keys* provide a fast way of locating a particular row of interest in a table.

The following sections discuss these steps in detail, as well as some other technical issues that arise during database design.

Step 1: Defining objects

The first step in designing a database is deciding which aspects of the system are important enough to include in the model. Treat each aspect as an object and create a list containing the names of all the objects you can think of. At this stage, don't try to decide how these objects relate to each other. Just try to list them all.

You may find it helpful to have a team of several people who are familiar with the system you're modeling. These people can brainstorm and respond to each other's ideas. Working together, you'll probably develop a more complete and accurate set of objects.

When you believe that you have a reasonably complete set of objects, you can move on to the next step: deciding how these objects relate to each other. Some of the objects are major entities, crucial to giving you the results that you want. Others are subsidiary to those major entities. You ultimately may decide that some objects don't belong in the model at all.

Step 2: Identifying tables and columns

Major entities translate into database tables. Each major entity has a set of associated attributes, which translate into the columns of the table. Many business databases, for example, have a CUSTOMER table that keeps track of customers' names, addresses, and other permanent information. Each attribute of a customer, such as name, street, city, state, zip code, phone number, and Internet address, becomes a column in the CUSTOMER table.

No hard and fast rules exist about what to identify as tables and which of the attributes in the system belong to which table. You may have some reasons for assigning a particular attribute to one table and other reasons for assigning the attribute to another table. You must make a judgment based on what information you want to get from the database and how you want to use that information.

In deciding how to structure database tables, a critical consideration is to involve the future users of the database as well as the people who are going to make decisions based on database information. If the "reasonable" structure you arrive at isn't consistent with the way that people will use the information, your system turns out to be frustrating to use at best — and could even produce wrong information, which is much worse than being hard to use. Don't let this happen! Put careful effort into deciding how to structure your tables.

Take a look at an example to demonstrate the thought process that goes into creating a multitable database. Say that you just established VetLab, a clinical microbiology laboratory that tests biological specimens sent in by veterinarians. Clearly, you want to track several kinds of things, such as the items in the following list:

- Clients
- Tests that you perform
- Employees
- Orders
- Results

Each of these entities has associated attributes. Each client has a name, address, and other contact information. Each test has a name and a standard charge. Employees have contact information as well as a job classification and pay rate. For each order, you need to know who ordered it, when it was ordered, and exactly what test was ordered. For each test result, you need to know the outcome of the test, whether the results were preliminary or final, and the test order number.

Step 3: Defining tables

Now you want to define a table for each entity and a column for each
attribute. Table 5-1 shows how you may define the VetLab tables.

Table 5-1	VetLab Tables
Table	*Columns*
CLIENT	Client Name
	Address 1
	Address 2
	City
	State
	Postal Code
	Phone
	Fax
	Contact Person
TESTS	Test Name
	Standard Charge
EMPLOYEE	Employee Name
	Address 1
	Address 2
	City
	State
	Postal Code
	Home Phone
	Office Extension
	Hire Date
	Job Classification
	Hourly/Salary/Commission
ORDERS	Order Number
	Client Name
	Test Ordered
	Responsible Salesperson
	Order Date
RESULTS	Result Number
	Order Number
	Result
	Date Reported
	Preliminary/Final

You may create the tables defined in Table 5-1 by using either a rapid application development (RAD) tool or by using SQL's Data Definition Language (DDL) as shown in the following code:

```
CREATE TABLE CLIENT (
       CLIENT_NAME         CHARACTER (30)     NOT NULL,
       ADDRESS_1           CHARACTER (30),
       ADDRESS_2           CHARACTER (30),
       CITY                CHARACTER (25),
       STATE               CHARACTER (2),
       POSTAL_CODE         CHARACTER (10),
       PHONE               CHARACTER (13),
       FAX                 CHARACTER (13),
       CONTACT_PERSON      CHARACTER (30) ) ;

CREATE TABLE TESTS (
       TEST_NAME           CHARACTER (30)     NOT NULL,
       STANDARD_CHARGE     CHARACTER (30) ) ;

CREATE TABLE EMPLOYEE (
       EMPLOYEE_NAME       CHARACTER (30)     NOT NULL,
       ADDRESS_1           CHARACTER (30),
       ADDRESS_2           CHARACTER (30),
       CITY                CHARACTER (25),
       STATE               CHARACTER (2),
       POSTAL_CODE         CHARACTER (10),
       HOME_PHONE          CHARACTER (13),
       OFFICE_EXTENSION    CHARACTER (4),
       HIRE_DATE           DATE,
       JOB_CLASSIFICATION  CHARACTER (10),
       HOUR_SAL_COMM       CHARACTER (1) ) ;

CREATE TABLE ORDERS (
       ORDER_NUMBER        INTEGER            NOT NULL,
       CLIENT_NAME         CHARACTER (30),
       TEST_ORDERED        CHARACTER (30),
       SALESPERSON         CHARACTER (30),
       ORDER_DATE          DATE ) ;

CREATE TABLE RESULTS (
       RESULT_NUMBER       INTEGER            NOT NULL,
       ORDER_NUMBER        INTEGER,
       RESULT              CHARACTER(50),
       DATE_REPORTED       DATE,
       PRELIM_FINAL        CHARACTER (1) ) ;
```

These tables relate to each other by the attributes (columns) that they share, as the following list describes:

✔ The CLIENT table links to the ORDERS table by the CLIENT_NAME column.

✔ The TESTS table links to the ORDERS table by the TEST NAME (TEST ORDERED) column.

✔ The EMPLOYEE table links to the ORDERS table by the EMPLOYEE NAME (SALESPERSON) column.

✔ The RESULTS table links to the ORDERS table by the ORDER NUMBER column.

For a table to serve as an integral part of a relational database, a good practice is to link that table to at least one other table in the database by using a common column. Figure 5-1 illustrates the relationships between the tables.

The links in Figure 5-1 illustrate four different one-to-many relationships. The single arrowhead points to the "one" side of the relationship, and the double arrowhead points to the "many" side. One client can make many orders, but each order is made by one, and only one, client. Each test can appear on many orders, but each order calls for one, and only one, test. Each order is taken by one, and only one, employee (or salesperson), but each salesperson can (and, you hope, does) take multiple orders. Each order can produce several preliminary test results and a final result, but each result is associated with one, and only one, order. As you can see in the figure, the attribute that links one table to another can have a different name in each table. Both attributes must, however, have matching data types.

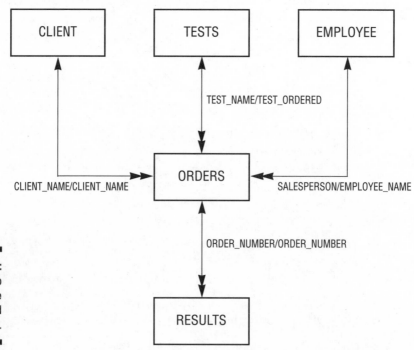

Figure 5-1:
VetLab
database
tables and
links.

Domains, character sets, collations, and translations

Although tables are the main components of a database, additional elements play a part, too. In Chapter 1, I define the *domain* of a column in a table as the set of all values that the column may assume. Establishing clear-cut domains for the columns in a table, through the use of constraints, is an important part of designing a database.

People who communicate in standard American English, however, aren't the only ones who use relational databases. Other languages — even some that use other character sets — work equally well. Even if your data isn't in a language other than English, some applications may still require a specialized character set. SQL:1999 enables you to specify the character set you want to use. In fact, you can use a different character set for each column in a table. This kind of flexibility is generally unavailable in languages other than SQL.

A *collation*, or *collating sequence*, is a set of rules that determine how strings in a character set compare with one another. Every character set has a default collation. In the default collation of the ASCII character set, *A* comes before *B* and *B* comes before *C*. A comparison, therefore, considers *A* as less than *B* and considers *C* as greater than *B*. SQL:1999, on the other hand, enables you to apply different collations to a character set. Again, this degree of flexibility isn't generally available in other languages.

Sometimes, you encode data in a database in one character set, but you want to deal with the data in another character set. Perhaps you have data in the German character set, for example, but your printer doesn't support German characters that the ASCII character set doesn't include. A *translation* is a facility of SQL:1999 that enables you to translate character strings from one character set to another. The translation may, for example, translate one character into two, such as a German *ü* to an ASCII *ue,* or the translation may translate lowercase characters to uppercase. You can even translate one alphabet into another, such as Hebrew into ASCII.

Getting into your database fast with keys

A good rule for database design is to make sure that every row in a database table is distinguishable from every other row — each row in the table should be unique. Sometimes, you may want to extract data from your database for a specific purpose, such as a statistical analysis, and in doing so, you create tables where rows aren't necessarily unique. For your limited purpose, this sort of duplication doesn't matter. Tables that you may use in more than one way, however, should not contain duplicate rows.

A *key* is an attribute or a combination of attributes that uniquely identifies a row in a table. To access a row in a database, you must have some way of distinguishing that particular row from all the other rows. Because they must be unique, keys provide such an access mechanism. Furthermore, a key must never contain a null value. If you use null keys, two rows that each contain a null key field may not be distinguishable from each other.

In my veterinary lab example, you can designate appropriate columns as keys. In the CLIENT table, CLIENT NAME makes a good key. This key can distinguish each client from all others. Entering a value in this column, therefore, becomes mandatory for every row in the table. TEST NAME and EMPLOYEE_NAME make good keys for the TESTS and EMPLOYEE tables. ORDER_NUMBER and RESULT_NUMBER make good keys for the ORDERS and RESULTS tables. In each case, make sure that you enter a unique value for every row.

You can have two kinds of keys: *primary keys* and *foreign keys.* The keys that I discuss in the preceding paragraph are actually primary keys. Primary keys guarantee uniqueness. I discuss foreign keys later in this section.

To incorporate the idea of keys into the VetLab database, you can specify the primary key of a table as you create the table. In the following example, a single column is sufficient (assuming that all VetLab's clients have unique names):

```
CREATE TABLE CLIENT (
    CLIENT_NAME         CHARACTER (30)     PRIMARY KEY,
    ADDRESS_1           CHARACTER (30),
    ADDRESS_2           CHARACTER (30),
    CITY                CHARACTER (25),
    STATE               CHARACTER (2),
    POSTAL_CODE         CHARACTER (10),
    PHONE               CHARACTER (13),
    FAX                 CHARACTER (13),
    CONTACT_PERSON      CHARACTER (30)
    ) ;
```

Here, the constraint PRIMARY KEY replaces the constraint NOT NULL, given in the earlier definition of the CLIENT table. The PRIMARY KEY constraint implies the NOT NULL constraint, because a primary key can't have a null value.

Sometimes, no single column in a table can guarantee uniqueness. In such cases, you can use a *composite key.* A composite key is a combination of columns that, together, guarantee uniqueness. Imagine that some of VetLab's clients are chains that have offices in several cities. In that case, CLIENT_NAME isn't sufficient to distinguish two different branch offices of the same client. To handle this situation, you can define a composite key as follows:

```
CREATE TABLE CLIENT (
   CLIENT_NAME            CHARACTER (30)     NOT NULL,
   ADDRESS_1              CHARACTER (30),
   ADDRESS_2              CHARACTER (30),
   CITY                   CHARACTER (25)     NOT NULL,
   STATE                  CHARACTER (2),
   POSTAL_CODE            CHARACTER (10),
   PHONE                  CHARACTER (13),
   FAX                    CHARACTER (13),
   CONTACT_PERSON         CHARACTER (30),
   CONSTRAINT BRANCH      PRIMARY KEY
      (CLIENT_NAME, CITY)
   ) ;
```

A *foreign key* is a column or group of columns in a table that corresponds to or references a primary key in another table in the database. A foreign key doesn't have to be unique itself, but it must uniquely identify the column(s) in the table that the key references. If the CLIENT_NAME column is the primary key in the CLIENT table, every row in the CLIENT table must have a unique value in the CLIENT_NAME column. CLIENT_NAME is a foreign key in the ORDERS table. This foreign key corresponds to the primary key of the CLIENT table, but the key doesn't have to be unique in the ORDERS table. In fact, you hope the foreign key *isn't* unique. If each of your clients gave you only one order and then never ordered again, you'd go out of business rather quickly. You hope, in fact, that many rows in the ORDERS table correspond with each row in the CLIENT table, indicating that nearly all your clients are repeat customers.

The following definition of the ORDERS table shows how you can add the concept of foreign keys to a CREATE statement:

```
CREATE TABLE ORDERS (
   ORDER_NUMBER           INTEGER            PRIMARY KEY,
   CLIENT_NAME            CHARACTER (30),
   TEST_ORDERED           CHARACTER (30),
   SALESPERSON            CHARACTER (30),
   ORDER_DATE             DATE,
   CONSTRAINT NAME_FK FOREIGN KEY (CLIENT_NAME)
      REFERENCES CLIENT (CLIENT_NAME),
   CONSTRAINT TEST_FK FOREIGN KEY (TEST_ORDERED)
      REFERENCES TESTS (TEST_NAME),
   CONSTRAINT SALES_FK FOREIGN KEY (SALESPERSON)
      REFERENCES EMPLOYEE (EMPLOYEE_NAME)
   ) ;
```

Foreign keys in the ORDERS table link that table to the primary keys of the CLIENT, TESTS, and EMPLOYEE tables.

Working with Indexes

The SQL:1999 specification doesn't address the topic of indexes, but that omission doesn't mean that indexes are rare or even optional parts of a database system. Every implementation of SQL supports indexes, but no universal agreement exists on how to support them. In Chapter 4, I show you how to create an index by using Microsoft Access, a rapid application development (RAD) tool. You must refer to the documentation for your particular database management system (DBMS) to see how the system implements indexes.

What's an index, anyway?

Data generally appears in a table in the order in which you originally entered the information. That order, however, may have nothing to do with the order in which you later want to process the data. Say, for example, that you want to process your CLIENT table in CLIENT_NAME order. The computer must first sort the table in CLIENT_NAME order. These sorts take time. The larger the table, the longer the sort takes. What if you have a table with 100,000 rows? What if you have a table with a million rows? In some applications, such table sizes are not rare. Even the best sort algorithms would have to make some 20 million comparisons and millions of swaps to put the table in the desired order. Even with a very fast computer, you may not want to wait that long.

Indexes can be a great time-saver. An *index* is a subsidiary or support table that goes along with a data table. For every row in the data table, you have a corresponding row in the index table. In the index table, however, the order of the rows is different.

Table 5-2 shows a small example data table.

Table 5-2		CLIENT Table		
CLIENT_NAME	*ADDRESS_1*	*ADDRESS_2*	*CITY*	*STATE*
Butternut Animal Clinic	5 Butternut Lane		Hudson	NH
Amber Veterinary, Inc.	470 Kolvir Circle		Amber	MI
Vets R Us	2300 Geoffrey Road	Suite 230	Anaheim	CA
Doggie Doctor	32 Terry Terrace		Nutley	NJ

CLIENT_NAME	ADDRESS_1	ADDRESS_2	CITY	STATE
The Equestrian Center	Veterinary Department	7890 Paddock Parkway	Gallup	NM
Dolphin Institute	1002 Marine Drive		Key West	FL
J. C. Campbell, Credit Vet	2500 Main Street		Los Angeles	CA
Wenger's Worm Farm	15 Bait Boulevard		Sedona	AZ

The rows are not in alphabetical order by CLIENT_NAME. In fact, they aren't in any useful order at all. The rows are simply in the order in which somebody entered the data.

An index for this CLIENT table may look like Table 5-3.

Table 5-3	**Client Name Index for the CLIENT Table**
CLIENT_NAME	*Pointer to Data Table*
Amber Veterinary, Inc.	2
Butternut Animal Clinic	1
Doggie Doctor	4
Dolphin Institute	6
J. C. Campbell, Credit Vet	7
The Equestrian Center	5
Vets R Us	3
Wenger's Worm Farm	8

The index contains the field that forms the basis of the index (in this case, CLIENT_NAME) and a pointer into the data table. The pointer in each index row gives the row number of the corresponding row in the data table.

Why would I want an index?

If I want to process a table in CLIENT_NAME order, and I have an index arranged in CLIENT_NAME order, I can perform my operation almost as fast as I could if the data table itself was in CLIENT_NAME order. I can work through the index sequentially, moving immediately to each index row's corresponding data record by using the pointer in the index.

If you use an index, the processing time of a table is proportional to N, where N is the number of records in the table. Without an index, the processing time for the same operation is proportional to $N \lg N$, where $\lg N$ is the logarithm of N to the base 2. For small tables, the difference is insignificant, but for large tables, the difference is great. On large tables, some operations aren't at all practical to perform without the help of indexes.

As an example, say that you have a table containing 1,000,000 records ($N = 1,000,000$) and processing each record takes one millisecond (one-thousandth of a second). If you have an index, processing the entire table takes only 1,000 seconds — less than 17 minutes. Without an index, however, you need to go through the table approximately 1,000,000 x 20 times to achieve the same result. This process would take 20,000 seconds — more than five and a half hours. I think you can agree that the difference between 17 minutes and five and a half hours is substantial. That's the difference that indexing makes on processing records.

Maintaining an index

After you create an index, something must maintain it. Fortunately, your DBMS maintains your indexes for you by updating them every time you update the corresponding data tables. This process takes a little bit of extra time, but it's worth it. After you create an index and your DBMS maintains it, the index is always available to speed your data processing, no matter how many times you need to call on it.

Clearly, the best time to create an index is at the same time you create its corresponding data table. If you create the index at the start and begin maintaining it at the same time, you don't need to undergo the pain of building the index later, with the entire operation taking place in a single, long session. Try to anticipate all the ways that you may want to access your data and then create an index for each possibility.

Some DBMS products give you the capability to turn off index maintenance. You may want to do so in some real-time applications where updating indexes takes a great deal of time and you have precious little to spare. You may even elect to update the indexes as a separate operation during off-peak hours.

Don't fall into the trap of creating an index for retrieval orders that you're unlikely ever to use. A performance penalty is associated with maintaining an index, because index maintenance is an extra operation that the computer must perform every time it modifies the index field or adds or deletes a data table row. For optimal performance, create only those indexes that you really expect to use as retrieval keys — and only for tables containing a large number of rows. Otherwise, indexes can actually degrade performance.

You may need to compile something such as a monthly or quarterly report that requires the data in an odd order that you don't ordinarily need. Create an index just before running that periodic report, run the report, and then drop the index so that the DBMS isn't burdened with maintaining the index during the long period between reports.

Maintaining Integrity

A database is valuable only if you're reasonably sure that the data it contains is correct. In medical, aircraft, and spacecraft databases, for example, incorrect data can lead to loss of life. Incorrect data in other applications may have less severe consequences but can still prove damaging. The database designer must make sure that incorrect data never enters the database.

Some problems can't be stopped at the database level. The application programmer must intercept these problems before they can damage the database. Everyone responsible for dealing with the database in any way must remain conscious of the threats to data integrity and take appropriate action to nullify those threats.

Databases can experience several distinctly different kinds of integrity — and a number of problems that can affect integrity. In the following sections, I discuss three types of integrity: *entity, domain,* and *referential.* I also look at some of the problems that can threaten database integrity.

Entity integrity

Every table in a database corresponds to an entity in the "real" world. That entity may be physical or conceptual, but in some sense, the entity's existence is independent of the database. A table has *entity integrity* if the table is entirely consistent with the entity that it models. To have entity integrity, a table must have a primary key. The primary key uniquely identifies each row in a table. Without a primary key, you can't be sure that the row retrieved is the one you want.

To maintain entity integrity, you need to specify that the column or group of columns that comprise the primary key are NOT NULL. In addition, you must constrain the primary key to be UNIQUE. Some implementations of SQL enable you to add such a constraint to the table definition. With others, you must apply the constraint later, after you specify how to add, change, or delete data from the table. Perhaps the best way to ensure that your primary key is both NOT NULL and UNIQUE is to give the key the PRIMARY KEY constraint as you create the table, as shown in the following example:

```
CREATE TABLE CLIENT (
    CLIENT_NAME      CHARACTER (30)      PRIMARY KEY,
    ADDRESS_1        CHARACTER (30),
    ADDRESS_2        CHARACTER (30),
    CITY             CHARACTER (25),
    STATE            CHARACTER (2),
    POSTAL_CODE      CHARACTER (10),
    PHONE            CHARACTER (13),
    FAX              CHARACTER (13),
    CONTACT_PERSON   CHARACTER (30)
    ) ;
```

An alternative is to use NOT NULL in combination with UNIQUE, as shown in the following example:

```
CREATE TABLE CLIENT (
    CLIENT_NAME      CHARACTER (30)      NOT NULL,
    ADDRESS_1        CHARACTER (30),
    ADDRESS_2        CHARACTER (30),
    CITY             CHARACTER (25),
    STATE            CHARACTER (2),
    POSTAL_CODE      CHARACTER (10),
    PHONE            CHARACTER (13),
    FAX              CHARACTER (13),
    CONTACT_PERSON   CHARACTER (30),
    UNIQUE (CLIENT_NAME) ) ;
```

Domain integrity

You usually can't guarantee that a particular data item in a database is correct, but you can at least determine whether a data item is valid. Many data items have a limited number of possible values. If you make an entry that is not one of the possible values, that entry must be an error. The United States, for example, has 50 states plus the District of Columbia, Puerto Rico, and a few possessions. Each of these areas has a two-character code that the U.S. Postal Service recognizes. If your database has a STATE column, you can enforce *domain integrity* by requiring that any entry into that column be one of the recognized two-character codes. If an operator enters a code that's not on the list of valid codes, that entry breaches domain integrity. If you test for domain integrity, you can refuse to accept any operation that causes such a breach.

Domain integrity concerns arise if you add new data to a table by using either the INSERT or the UPDATE statements. You can specify a domain for a column by using a CREATE DOMAIN statement before you use that column in a CREATE TABLE statement, as shown in the following example:

```
CREATE DOMAIN LEAGUE_DOM CHAR (8)
   CHECK (LEAGUE IN ('American', 'National'));
CREATE TABLE TEAM (
   TEAM_NAME        CHARACTER (20)    NOT NULL,
   LEAGUE           CHARACTER (8)     NOT NULL
   ) ;
```

The domain of the LEAGUE column includes only two valid values: American and National. Your DBMS doesn't enable you to commit an entry or update to the TEAM table unless the LEAGUE column of the row you're adding has a value of either 'American' or 'National'.

Referential integrity

Even if every table in your system has entity integrity and domain integrity, you may still have a problem because of inconsistencies in the way one table relates to another. In most well-designed databases, every table contains at least one column that refers to a column in another table in the database. These references are important for maintaining the overall integrity of the database. The same references, however, make update anomalies possible.

Update anomalies are problems that can occur after you update the data in a row of a database table.

The relationships among tables are generally not bi-directional. One table is usually dependent on the other. Say, for example, that you have a database with a CLIENT table and an ORDERS table. You may conceivably enter a client into the CLIENT table before she makes any orders. You can't, however, enter an order into the ORDERS table unless you already have an entry in the CLIENT table for the client who's making that order. The ORDERS table is dependent on the CLIENT table. This kind of arrangement is often called a *parent-child relationship,* where CLIENT is the parent table and ORDERS is the child table. The child is dependent on the parent. Generally, the primary key of the parent table is a column (or group of columns) that appears in the child table. Within the child table, that same column (or group) is a foreign key. A foreign key may contain nulls and need not be unique.

Update anomalies arise in several ways. A client moves away, for example, and you want to delete her from your database. If she's already made some orders, which you recorded in the ORDERS table, deleting her from the CLIENT table could present a problem. You'd have records in the ORDERS (child) table for which you have no corresponding records in the CLIENT (parent) table. Similar problems can arise if you add a record to a child table without making a corresponding addition to the parent table. The corresponding foreign keys in all child tables must reflect any changes to the primary key of a row in a parent table; otherwise, an update anomaly results.

You can eliminate most referential integrity problems by carefully controlling the update process. In some cases, you need to *cascade* deletes from a parent table to its children. To cascade a deletion, when you delete a row from a parent table, you also delete all the rows in its child tables that have foreign keys that match the primary key of the deleted row in the parent table. Take a look at the following example:

```
CREATE TABLE CLIENT (
    CLIENT_NAME             CHARACTER (30)      PRIMARY KEY,
    ADDRESS_1               CHARACTER (30),
    ADDRESS_2               CHARACTER (30),
    CITY                    CHARACTER (25)      NOT NULL,
    STATE                   CHARACTER (2),
    POSTAL_CODE             CHARACTER (10),
    PHONE                   CHARACTER (13),
    FAX                     CHARACTER (13),
    CONTACT_PERSON          CHARACTER (30)
    ) ;

CREATE TABLE TESTS (
    TEST_NAME               CHARACTER (30)      PRIMARY KEY,
    STANDARD_CHARGE         CHARACTER (30)
    ) ;

CREATE TABLE EMPLOYEE (
    EMPLOYEE_NAME           CHARACTER (30)      PRIMARY KEY,
    ADDRESS_1               CHARACTER (30),
    ADDRESS_2               CHARACTER (30),
    CITY                    CHARACTER (25),
    STATE                   CHARACTER (2),
    POSTAL_CODE             CHARACTER (10),
    HOME_PHONE              CHARACTER (13),
    OFFICE_EXTENSION        CHARACTER (4),
    HIRE_DATE               DATE,
    JOB_CLASSIFICATION      CHARACTER (10),
    HOUR_SAL_COMM           CHARACTER (1)
    ) ;

CREATE TABLE ORDERS (
    ORDER_NUMBER            INTEGER             PRIMARY KEY,
    CLIENT_NAME             CHARACTER (30),
```

```
    TEST_ORDERED            CHARACTER (30),
    SALESPERSON             CHARACTER (30),
    ORDER_DATE              DATE,
    CONSTRAINT NAME_FK FOREIGN KEY (CLIENT_NAME)
       REFERENCES CLIENT (CLIENT_NAME)
          ON DELETE CASCADE,
    CONSTRAINT TEST_FK FOREIGN KEY (TEST_ORDERED)
       REFERENCES TESTS (TEST_NAME)
          ON DELETE CASCADE,
    CONSTRAINT SALES_FK FOREIGN KEY (SALESPERSON)
       REFERENCES EMPLOYEE (EMPLOYEE_NAME)
          ON DELETE CASCADE
    ) ;
```

The constraint NAME_FK names CLIENT_NAME as a foreign key that references the CLIENT_NAME column in the CLIENT table. If you delete a row in the CLIENT table, you also automatically delete all rows in the ORDERS table that have the same value in the CLIENT_NAME column as those in the CLIENT_NAME column of the CLIENT table. The deletion cascades down from the CLIENT table to the ORDERS table. The same is true for the foreign keys in the ORDERS table that refer to the primary keys of the TESTS and EMPLOYEE tables.

You may not want to cascade a deletion. Instead, you may want to change the child table's foreign key to a NULL value. Consider the following variant of the previous example:

```
CREATE TABLE ORDERS (
    ORDER_NUMBER        INTEGER              PRIMARY KEY,
    CLIENT_NAME         CHARACTER (30),
    TEST_ORDERED        CHARACTER (30),
    SALESPERSON         CHARACTER (30),
    ORDER_DATE          DATE,
    CONSTRAINT NAME_FK FOREIGN KEY (CLIENT_NAME)
       REFERENCES CLIENT (CLIENT_NAME),
    CONSTRAINT TEST_FK FOREIGN KEY (TEST_ORDERED)
       REFERENCES TESTS (TEST_NAME),
    CONSTRAINT SALES_FK FOREIGN KEY (SALESPERSON)
       REFERENCES EMPLOYEE (EMPLOYEE_NAME)
          ON DELETE SET NULL
    ) ;
```

The constraint SALES_FK names the SALESPERSON column as a foreign key that references the EMPLOYEE_NAME column of the EMPLOYEE table. If a salesperson leaves the company, you delete her row in the EMPLOYEE table. New salespeople are eventually assigned to her accounts, but for now, deletion of her name from the EMPLOYEE table causes all of her orders in the order table to receive a null value in the SALESPERSON column.

Another way to keep inconsistent data out of a database is to refuse to permit an addition to a child table until a corresponding row exists in its parent table. Yet another possibility is to refuse to permit changes to a table's primary key. If you refuse to permit rows in a child table without a corresponding row in a parent table, you prevent the occurrence of "orphan" rows in the child table. This refusal helps maintain consistency across tables. If you refuse to permit changes to a table's primary key, you don't need to worry about updating foreign keys in other tables that depend on that primary key.

Potential problem areas

Data integrity is subject to assault from a variety of quarters. Some of these problems arise only in multitable databases, while others can happen even in databases that contain only a single table. You want to recognize and minimize all these potential threats.

Bad input data

The source documents or data files that you use to populate your database may contain bad data. This data may be a corrupted version of the correct data or it may not be the data you want at all. Range checks tell you whether the data has domain integrity. This type of check catches some problems but clearly not all. Field values that are within the acceptable range, but are nonetheless incorrect, aren't identified as problems.

Operator error

Your source data may be correct, but the data entry operator incorrectly transcribes the data. This type of error can lead to the same kinds of problems as bad input data. Some of the solutions are the same, too. Range checks help but they're not foolproof. Another solution is to have a second operator independently validate all the data. This approach is costly, because independent validation takes twice the number of people and twice the time. In some cases, however, the extra effort and expense may prove worthwhile if data integrity is critical.

Mechanical failure

If you experience a mechanical failure, such as a drive crash while a database table is open, the data in the table can become corrupted. Good backups are your main defense against this problem.

Malice

Consider the possibility that someone may want to intentionally corrupt your data. Your first line of defense is to deny database access to anyone who may have a malicious intent, and restrict everyone else's access to what they need. Your second defense is to maintain data backups in a safe place. Periodically reevaluate the security features of your installation. Being just a little paranoid doesn't hurt.

Data redundancy

Data redundancy is a big problem with the hierarchical database model, but the problem can plague relational databases, too. Not only does such redundancy waste storage space and slow down processing, but the problem can also lead to serious data corruption. If you store the same data item in two different tables in a database, the item in one of those tables may change, while the corresponding item in the other table remains the same. This situation generates a discrepancy, and you may have no way of telling which version is correct. A good idea is to hold data redundancy to a minimum. A certain amount of redundancy is necessary for the primary key of one table to serve as a foreign key in another. Try, however, to avoid any redundancy beyond that. The most common method for eliminating redundancy from a design is called *normalization,* splitting one database table into two simpler tables.

After you eliminate most redundancy from a database design, you may find that performance is now unacceptable. Operators very often purposefully use redundancy to speed up processing. In the previous example, the ORDERS table contains only the client's name to identify the source of each order. If you prepare an order, you must join the ORDERS table with the CLIENT table to get the client's address. If this joining of tables makes the program that prints orders run too slowly, you may decide to store the client's address redundantly in the ORDERS table. This redundancy offers the advantage of printing the orders faster but at the expense of slowing down and complicating any updating of the client's address.

A common practice is for users to initially design a database with little redundancy and with high degrees of normalization and then, after finding that important applications run slowly, to selectively add redundancy and denormalize. The key word here is *selectively.* The redundancy that you add back in has a specific purpose, and because you're acutely aware of both the redundancy and the hazard it represents, you take appropriate measures to ensure that the redundancy doesn't cause more problems than it solves.

Constraints

Earlier in this chapter, I talk about constraints as mechanisms for ensuring that the data you enter into a table column falls within the domain of that column. A *constraint* is an application rule that the DBMS enforces. After you define a database, you can include constraints (such as NOT NULL) in a table definition. The DBMS makes sure that you can never commit any transaction that violates a constraint.

You have three different kinds of constraints: column constraints, table constraints, and assertions. A *column constraint* imposes a condition on a column in a table. A *table constraint* is a constraint on an entire table. An *assertion* is a constraint that can affect more than one table.

Column constraints

An example of a column constraint is shown in the following Data Definition Language (DDL) statement:

```
CREATE TABLE CLIENT (
    CLIENT_NAME        CHARACTER (30)        NOT NULL,
    ADDRESS_1          CHARACTER (30),
    ADDRESS_2          CHARACTER (30),
    CITY               CHARACTER (25),
    STATE              CHARACTER (2),
    POSTAL_CODE        CHARACTER (10),
    PHONE              CHARACTER (13),
    FAX                CHARACTER (13),
    CONTACT_PERSON     CHARACTER (30)
    ) ;
```

The statement applies the constraint NOT NULL to the CLIENT_NAME column specifying that CLIENT_NAME may not assume a null value. UNIQUE is another constraint that you can apply to a column. This constraint specifies that every value in the column must be unique. The CHECK constraint is particularly useful in that it can take any valid expression as an argument. Consider the following example:

```
CREATE TABLE TESTS (
    TEST_NAME          CHARACTER (30)        NOT NULL,
    STANDARD_CHARGE    NUMERIC (6,2)
        CHECK (STANDARD_CHARGE >= 0.0
            AND STANDARD_CHARGE <= 200.0)
    ) ;
```

VetLab's standard charge for a test must always be greater than or equal to zero. And none of the standard tests costs more than $200. The CHECK clause refuses to accept any entries that fall outside the range 0 <= STANDARD_CHARGE <= 200. Another way of stating the same constraint is as follows:

```
CHECK (STANDARD_CHARGE BETWEEN 0.0 AND 200.0)
```

Table constraints

The PRIMARY KEY constraint specifies that the column to which it applies is a primary key. This constraint is thus a constraint on the entire table and is equivalent to a combination of the NOT NULL and the UNIQUE column constraints. You can specify this constraint in a CREATE statement, as shown in the following example:

```
CREATE TABLE CLIENT (
    CLIENT_NAME      CHARACTER (30)    PRIMARY KEY,
    ADDRESS_1        CHARACTER (30),
    ADDRESS_2        CHARACTER (30),
    CITY             CHARACTER (25),
    STATE            CHARACTER (2),
    POSTAL_CODE      CHARACTER (10),
    PHONE            CHARACTER (13),
    FAX              CHARACTER (13),
    CONTACT_PERSON   CHARACTER (30)
    ) ;
```

Assertions

An *assertion* specifies a restriction for more than one table. The following example uses a search condition drawn from two tables to create an assertion:

```
CREATE TABLE ORDERS (
    ORDER_NUMBER     INTEGER          NOT NULL,
    CLIENT_NAME      CHARACTER (30),
    TEST_ORDERED     CHARACTER (30),
    SALESPERSON      CHARACTER (30),
    ORDER_DATE       DATE
    ) ;

CREATE TABLE RESULTS (
    RESULT_NUMBER    INTEGER       NOT NULL,
    ORDER_NUMBER     INTEGER,
    RESULT           CHARACTER(50),
    DATE_REPORTED    DATE,
    PRELIM_FINAL     CHARACTER (1)
    ) ;

CREATE ASSERTION
    CHECK (NOT EXISTS (SELECT * FROM ORDERS, RESULTS
        WHERE ORDERS.ORDER_NUMBER = RESULTS.ORDER_NUMBER
        AND ORDERS.ORDER_DATE > RESULTS.DATE_REPORTED)) ;
```

This assertion ensures that you receive no reports of any result before you order its corresponding test.

Normalizing the Database

Some ways of organizing data are better than others. Some are more logical. Some are simpler. Some are better at preventing inconsistencies from arising after you start using the database.

A host of different problems (called *modification anomalies*) can plague a database if you don't structure the database correctly. To prevent these problems, you can *normalize* the database structure. Normalization generally entails splitting one database table into two simpler tables.

Modification anomalies are so named because they are generated by the addition of, change to, or deletion of data from a database table.

To illustrate how modification anomalies can occur, consider the table shown in Figure 5-2.

SALES

Customer_ID	Product	Price
1001	Laundry detergent	12
1007	Toothpaste	3
1010	Chlorine bleach	4
1024	Toothpaste	3

Figure 5-2: This SALES table leads to modification anomalies.

Your company sells household cleaning and personal-care products, and you charge all customers the same price for each product. The SALES table keeps track of everything for you. Now assume that customer 1001 moves out of the area and no longer is a customer. You don't care what he's bought in the past, because he's not going to buy again. You want to delete his row from the table. If you do so, however, you don't just lose the fact that customer 1001 has bought laundry detergent; you also lose the fact that laundry detergent costs $12. This situation is called a *deletion anomaly*. In deleting one fact (that customer 1001 bought laundry detergent), you inadvertently delete another fact (that laundry detergent costs $12).

You can use the same table to illustrate an insertion anomaly. For example, say that you want to add stick deodorant to your product line at a price of $2. You can't add this data to the SALES table until a customer wants stick deodorant.

The problem with the SALES table in the figure is that this table deals with more than one thing. The table covers which products customers buy and what the products cost. You need to split the SALES table into two tables, each one dealing with only one theme or idea, as shown in Figure 5-3.

CUST_PURCH				PROD_PRICE	
Customer_ID	Product			Product	Price
1001	Laundry detergent			Laundry detergent	12
1007	Toothpaste			Toothpaste	3
1010	Chlorine bleach			Chlorine bleach	4
1024	Toothpaste				

Figure 5-3: The SALES table is split into two tables.

Figure 5-3 shows that the SALES table is divided into two tables, CUST_PURCH and PROD_PRICE. CUST_PURCH deals with the single idea of customer purchases. PROD_PRICE deals with the single idea of product pricing. You can now delete the row for customer 1001 from CUST_PURCH without losing the fact that laundry detergent costs $12. That fact is now stored in PROD_PRICE. You can also add stick deodorant to PROD_PRICE, whether anyone has bought the product or not. Purchase information is stored elsewhere, in the CUST_PURCH table.

The process of breaking up a table into multiple tables, each of which has a single theme, is called *normalization.* A normalization operation that solves one problem may not affect others. You may need to perform several successive normalization operations to reduce each of the resulting tables to a single theme. Each database table should deal with one — and only one — main theme. Sometimes, determining that a table really deals with two or more themes is difficult.

You can classify tables according to the types of modification anomalies to which they're subject. In E. F. Codd's 1970 paper, the first to describe the relational model, Codd identified three sources of modification anomalies and defined first, second, and third *normal forms* (1NF, 2NF, 3NF) as remedies to those types of anomalies. In the ensuing years, Codd and others discovered additional types of anomalies and specified new normal forms to deal with them. The Boyce-Codd normal form (BCNF), the fourth normal form (4NF), and the fifth normal form (5NF) each afforded a higher degree of protection against modification anomalies. Not until 1981, however, did a paper, written by R. Fagin, describe domain/key normal form (DKNF). Using this last normal form enables you to guarantee that a table is free of modification anomalies.

The normal forms are *nested* in the sense that a table that's in 2NF is automatically also in 1NF. Similarly, a table in 3NF is automatically in 2NF, and so on. For most practical applications, putting a database in 3NF is sufficient to ensure a high degree of integrity. To be absolutely sure of its integrity, however, you must put the database into DKNF.

After you normalize a database as much as possible, you may want to make selected denormalizations to improve performance. If you do, be fully aware of the types of anomalies that may now become possible.

First normal form

To be in first normal form (1NF), a table must have the following qualities:

- ✔ The table is two-dimensional, with rows and columns.
- ✔ Each row contains data that pertains to some thing or portion of a thing.
- ✔ Each column contains data for a single attribute of the thing it's describing.
- ✔ Each cell (intersection of a row and a column) of the table must have only a single value.
- ✔ Entries in any column must all be of the same kind. If, for example, the entry in one row of a column contains an employee name, all the other rows must contain employee names in that column, too.
- ✔ Each column must have a unique name.
- ✔ No two rows may be identical (that is, each row must be unique).
- ✔ The order of the columns and the order of the rows is not significant.

A table (relation) in first normal form is immune to some kinds of modification anomalies but is still subject to others. The SALES table shown in Figure 5-2 is in first normal form and, as discussed previously, the table is subject to deletion and insertion anomalies. First normal form, therefore, may prove useful in some applications but unreliable in others.

Second normal form

To appreciate second normal form, you must understand the idea of functional dependency. A *functional dependency* is a relationship between or among attributes. One attribute is functionally dependent on another if the value of the second attribute determines the value of the first attribute. If you know the value of the second attribute, you can determine the value of the first attribute.

Suppose, for example, that a table has attributes (columns) STANDARD_CHARGE, NUMBER_OF_TESTS, and TOTAL_CHARGE, which relate through the following equation:

```
TOTAL_CHARGE = STANDARD_CHARGE * NUMBER_OF_TESTS
```

TOTAL_CHARGE is then functionally dependent on both STANDARD_CHARGE and on NUMBER_OF_TESTS. If you know the values of STANDARD_CHARGE and NUMBER_OF_TESTS, you can determine the value of TOTAL_CHARGE.

Every table in first normal form must have a unique primary key. That key may consist of one or more than one column. A key consisting of more than one column is called a *composite key*. To be in second normal form (2NF), all non-key attributes (columns) must depend on the entire key. Thus, every relation that is in 1NF with a single attribute key is automatically in second normal form. If a relation has a composite key, all non-key attributes must depend on all components of the key. If you have a table where some non-key attributes don't depend on all components of the key, you want to break the table up into two or more tables so that, in each of the new tables, all non-key attributes depend on all components of the primary key.

Sound pretty confusing? Look at an example to clarify matters. Consider a table like the SALES table back in Figure 5-2. Instead of recording only a single purchase for each customer, however, you add a row every time a customer buys an item for the first time. An additional difference is that "charter" customers (those with CUSTOMER_ID values of 1001 to 1009) get a discount from the normal price. Figure 5-4 shows some of this table's rows.

In Figure 5-4, CUSTOMER_ID does not uniquely identify a row. In two rows, CUSTOMER_ID is 1001. In two other rows, CUSTOMER_ID is 1010. The combination of the CUSTOMER_ID column and the PRODUCT column, however, uniquely identifies a row. These two columns together are a composite key.

If not for the fact that some customers qualify for a discount and others don't, the table wouldn't be in second normal form, because PRICE (a non-key attribute) would depend only on part of the key (PRODUCT). Because some customers do qualify for a discount, however, PRICE depends on both CUSTOMER_ID and PRODUCT, and the table is in second normal form.

SALES_TRACK

Customer_ID	Product	Price
1001	Laundry detergent	11.00
1007	Toothpaste	2.70
1010	Chlorine bleach	4.00
1024	Toothpaste	3.00
1010	Laundry detergent	12.00
1001	Toothpaste	2.70

Figure 5-4: In the SALES_ TRACK table, the CUSTOMER _ID and PRODUCT columns constitute a composite key.

Third normal form

Tables in second normal form are still subject to some types of modification anomalies. These anomalies come from transitive dependencies.

A *transitive dependency* occurs when one attribute depends on a second attribute, which depends on a third attribute. Deletions in a table with such a dependency can cause unwanted loss of information. A relation in third normal form is a relation in second normal form with no transitive dependencies.

Look again at the SALES table in Figure 5-2, which you know is in first normal form. As long as you constrain entries to permit only one row for each CUSTOMER_ID, you have a single-attribute primary key, and the table is in second normal form. The table is still, however, subject to anomalies. What if customer 1010 is unhappy with the chlorine bleach, for example, and returns the item for a refund? You want to remove the third row from the table, which records the fact that customer 1010 bought chlorine bleach. You have a problem: If you remove that row, you also lose the fact that chlorine bleach has a price of $4. This situation is an example of a transitive dependency. PRICE depends on PRODUCT, which, in turn, depends on the primary key CUSTOMER_ID.

Breaking the SALES table into two tables solves the transitive dependency problem. The two tables shown in Figure 5-3, CUST_PURCH and PROD_PRICE make up a database that's in third normal form.

Domain/key normal form (DKNF)

After a database is in third normal form, you've eliminated most, but not all, chances of modification anomalies. Normal forms beyond the third are defined to squash those few remaining bugs. Boyce-Codd normal form (BCNF), fourth normal form (4NF), and fifth normal form (5NF) are examples of such forms. Each form eliminates a possible modification anomaly but doesn't guarantee to prevent all possible modification anomalies. Domain/key normal form (DKNF), however, provides such a guarantee.

A relation is in *domain/key normal form (DKNF)* if every constraint on the relation is a logical consequence of the definition of keys and domains. A *constraint* in this definition is any rule that's precise enough that you can evaluate whether or not it's true. A *key* is a unique identifier of a row in a table. A *domain* is the set of permitted values of an attribute.

Look again at the database in Figure 5-2, which is in 1NF, to see what you must do to put that database in DKNF.

Table:	SALES (CUSTOMER_ID, PRODUCT, PRICE)
Key:	CUSTOMER_ID
Constraints:	1. CUSTOMER_ID determines PRODUCT
	2. PRODUCT determines PRICE
	3. CUSTOMER_ID must be an integer > 1,000

To enforce Constraint 3, that CUSTOMER_ID must be an integer greater than 1,000, you can simply define the domain for CUSTOMER_ID to incorporate this constraint. That makes the constraint a logical consequence of the domain of the CUSTOMER_ID column. PRODUCT depends on CUSTOMER_ID, and CUSTOMER_ID is a key, so you have no problem with Constraint 1, which is a logical consequence of the definition of the key. Constraint 2, however, *is* a problem. PRICE depends on (is a logical consequence of) PRODUCT, and PRODUCT isn't a key. The solution is to divide the SALES table into two tables. One table uses CUSTOMER_ID as a key and the other uses PRODUCT as a key. This setup is what you have in Figure 5-3. The database in Figure 5-3, besides being in 3NF, is also in DKNF.

Design your databases so they're in DKNF if possible. If you do so, enforcing key and domain restrictions causes all constraints to be met. Modification anomalies aren't possible. If a database's structure is designed so that you can't put it into domain/key normal form, you must build the constraints into the application program that uses the database. The database doesn't guarantee that the constraints will be met.

Abnormal form

Sometimes being abnormal pays off. You may get carried away with normalization and go too far. You can break up a database into so many tables that the entire thing becomes unwieldy and inefficient. Performance can plummet. Often, the optimal structure is somewhat denormalized. In fact, practical databases are almost never normalized all the way to DKNF. You want to normalize the databases you design as much as possible, however, to eliminate the possibility of data corruption that results from modification anomalies.

After you normalize the database as far as you can, make some retrievals. If performance isn't satisfactory, examine your design to see whether selective denormalization would improve performance without sacrificing integrity. By carefully adding redundancy in strategic locations and denormalizing, you can arrive at a database that's both efficient and safe from anomalies.

Part III
Storing and Retrieving Data

The 5th Wave   By Rich Tennant

"THE LCD DISPLAY WAS GOOD, PLASMA DISPLAYS WERE A LITTLE BETTER, BUT WE THINK THE LIQUID LAVA DISPLAY THAT JERRY'S DEVELOPED IS GONNA ROCK THE WEST COAST."

In this part . . .

SQL provides a rich set of tools for manipulating data in a relational database. As you may expect, SQL has mechanisms for adding new data, updating existing data, retrieving data, and deleting obsolete data. Nothing's particularly extraordinary about these capabilities (heck, human brains use 'em all the time). Where SQL shines, however, is in its capability to isolate the *exact* data you want from all the rest — and present that data to you in an understandable form. SQL's comprehensive Data Manipulation Language (DML) provides this critically important capability.

In this part, I delve deep into the riches of the DML. You discover how to use SQL tools to massage raw data into a form suitable for your present purposes — and then to retrieve the result as useful information (what a concept).

Chapter 6

Manipulating Database Data

· ·

· ·

Chapters 3 and 4 reveal that creating a sound database structure is critical to data integrity. The stuff that you're really interested in, however, is the data itself — not its structure. You want to do four things with data: Add it to tables, retrieve and display it, change it, and delete it from tables.

The SQL Data Manipulation Language (DML)

In principle, database manipulation is quite simple. Understanding how to add data to a table isn't difficult — you can add your data either one row at a time or in a batch. Changing, deleting, or retrieving table rows is also easy in practice. The main challenge to database manipulation lies in *selecting* the rows that you want to change, delete, or retrieve. Sometimes, retrieving data is like trying to put together a jigsaw puzzle with pieces that are mixed in with pieces from a hundred other puzzles. The data that you want may reside in the same database containing a much larger volume of data that you don't want. Fortunately, if you can precisely specify what you want by using an SQL SELECT statement, the computer does all the searching for you.

SQL in proprietary tools

SQL SELECT statements are not the only way to retrieve data from a database. If you're interacting with your database through a DBMS, this system probably already has proprietary tools for manipulating data. You can use these tools (many of which are quite intuitive) to add to, delete from, change, or query your database.

In a client/server system, the relational database on the server generally understands only SQL. If you develop a database application by using a DBMS or RAD tool, you can create data-entry screens that contain fields corresponding to database table fields. You can group the fields logically on-screen and explain the fields by using supplemental text. The user, sitting at a client machine, can easily examine or change the data in these fields.

Suppose that the user changes the value of some fields. The DBMS *front end* on the client takes the input that the user types into the screen form, translates that text into an SQL

UPDATE statement, and then sends the UPDATE statement to the server. The DBMS *back end* on the server executes the statement. Users who manipulate data on a relational database, therefore, are using SQL whether they realize it or not. These people may use SQL directly or indirectly through a translation process.

Many DBMS front ends give you the choice of using either their proprietary tools or SQL. In some cases, the proprietary tools can't express everything that you can express by using SQL. If you need to perform an operation that the proprietary tool can't handle, you may need to use SQL. So becoming very familiar with SQL is a pretty good idea, even if you do use a proprietary tool most of the time. To successfully perform an operation that's too complex for your proprietary tool, you need a clear understanding of how SQL works and what it can do.

Retrieving Data

The data manipulation task that users perform most frequently is retrieving selected information from a database. You may want to retrieve the contents of one specific row out of thousands in a table. You may want to retrieve all the rows that satisfy a condition or a combination of conditions. You may even want to retrieve all the rows in the table. One particular SQL statement, the SELECT statement, performs all these tasks for you.

The simplest use of the SELECT statement is to retrieve all the data in all the rows of a specified table. To do so, use the following syntax:

```
SELECT * FROM CUSTOMER ;
```

The asterisk (*) is a wildcard character that means *everything*. In this context, the asterisk is a shorthand substitute for a listing of all the column names of the CUSTOMER table. As a result of this statement, all the data in all the rows and columns of the CUSTOMER table appear on-screen.

SELECT statements can be much more complicated than the statement in this example. In fact, some SELECT statements can be so complicated that they're virtually indecipherable. This potential complexity is a result of the fact that you can tack multiple modifying clauses onto the basic statement. Chapter 9 covers modifying clauses in detail. In this chapter, I briefly discuss the WHERE clause, which is the most commonly used method to restrict the rows that a SELECT statement returns.

A SELECT statement with a WHERE clause has the following general form:

```
SELECT column_list FROM table_name
   WHERE condition ;
```

The column list specifies which of the columns in the table you want to display. The statement displays only the columns that you list. The FROM clause specifies from which table you want to display columns. The WHERE clause excludes rows that do not satisfy a specified condition. The condition may be simple (for example, WHERE CUSTOMER_STATE = 'NH'), or it may be compound (for example, WHERE CUSTOMER_STATE='NH' AND STATUS='Active').

The following example shows what a compound condition looks like inside a SELECT statement:

```
SELECT CUSTOMER_NAME, CUSTOMER_PHONE FROM CUSTOMER
   WHERE CUSTOMER_STATE = 'NH'
   AND STATUS = 'Active' ;
```

This statement returns the names and phone numbers of all active customers living in New Hampshire. The AND keyword means that for a row to qualify for retrieval, that row must meet both conditions, CUSTOMER_STATE = 'NH' and STATUS = 'ACTIVE'.

Creating Views

The structure of a database that's designed according to sound principles — including appropriate normalization — maximizes the integrity of the data. This structure, however, is often not the best way to look at the data. Several different applications may all make use of the same data, but each application may have a different emphasis. One of the most powerful features of SQL is its capability to display views of the data that are structured differently from how the database tables actually store the data. The tables you use as sources for columns and rows in a view are the *base tables*. Chapter 3 discusses views as part of the Data Definition Language (DDL). This section looks at views in the context of retrieving and manipulating data.

A SELECT statement always returns a result in the form of a virtual table. A *view* is a special kind of virtual table. You can distinguish a view from other virtual tables because the database's metadata holds the definition of a view. This distinction gives view a degree of persistence that other virtual tables don't possess. You can manipulate a view just as you can manipulate a real table. The difference is that a view's data doesn't have an independent existence. The view derives its data from the table or tables from which you draw the view's columns. Each application can have its own unique views of the same data.

Consider the VetLab database described in Chapter 5. That database contains five tables: CLIENT, TESTS, EMPLOYEE, ORDERS, and RESULTS. Suppose the national marketing manager wants to see from which states the company's orders are coming: Part of this information lies in the CLIENT table; part lies in the ORDERS table. Suppose the quality-control officer wants to compare the order date of a test to the date on which the final test result came in. This comparison requires some data from the ORDERS table and some from the RESULTS table. To satisfy needs such as these, you can create views that give you exactly the data you want in each specific case.

From tables

For the marketing manager, you can create the view shown in Figure 6-1.

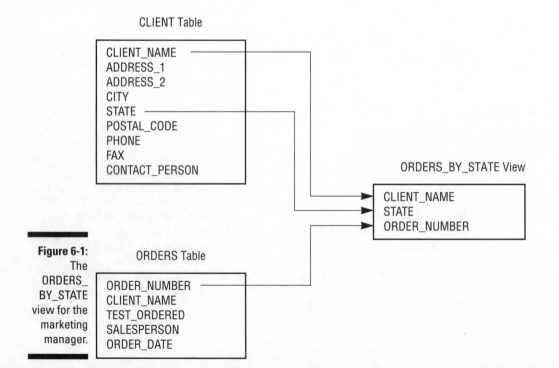

Figure 6-1:
The
ORDERS_
BY_STATE
view for the
marketing
manager.

The following statement creates the marketing manager's view:

```
CREATE VIEW ORDERS_BY_STATE
    (CLIENT_NAME, STATE, ORDER_NUMBER)
  AS SELECT CLIENT.CLIENT_NAME, STATE, ORDER_NUMBER
  FROM CLIENT, ORDERS
  WHERE CLIENT.CLIENT_NAME = ORDERS.CLIENT_NAME ;
```

The new view has three columns, CLIENT_NAME, STATE, and ORDER_NUMBER. CLIENT_NAME appears in both the CLIENT and the ORDERS table and serves as the link between the two tables. The new view draws STATE information from the CLIENT table and takes the ORDER_NUMBER of each order from the ORDERS table. In the preceding example, you explicitly declare the names of the columns in the new view. This declaration is not strictly necessary, however, if the names are the same as the names of the corresponding columns in the source tables. The example in the following section shows a similar CREATE VIEW statement but with the view column names implied rather than explicitly stated.

With a selection condition

The quality-control officer requires a different view from the one that the marketing manager uses, as shown by the example in Figure 6-2.

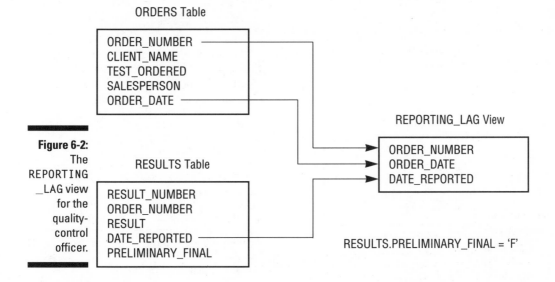

Figure 6-2:
The
REPORTING
_LAG view
for the
quality-
control
officer.

ORDERS Table

ORDER_NUMBER
CLIENT_NAME
TEST_ORDERED
SALESPERSON
ORDER_DATE

REPORTING_LAG View

ORDER_NUMBER
ORDER_DATE
DATE_REPORTED

RESULTS Table

RESULT_NUMBER
ORDER_NUMBER
RESULT
DATE_REPORTED
PRELIMINARY_FINAL

RESULTS.PRELIMINARY_FINAL = 'F'

Here's the code that creates the view in Figure 6-2:

```
CREATE VIEW REPORTING_LAG
    AS SELECT ORDERS.ORDER_NUMBER, ORDER_DATE, DATE_REPORTED
    FROM ORDERS, RESULTS
    WHERE ORDERS.ORDER_NUMBER = RESULTS.ORDER_NUMBER
    AND RESULTS.PRELIM_FINAL = 'F' ;
```

This view contains order-date information from the ORDERS table and final-report-date information from the RESULTS table. Only rows that have an `'F'` in the `PRELIM_FINAL` column of the RESULTS table appear in the `REPORTING_LAG` view.

With a modified attribute

The `SELECT` clauses in the examples in the two previous sections contain only column names. You can, however, include expressions in the `SELECT` clause as well. Suppose the owner of VetLab is having a birthday and wants to give all his customers a 10 percent discount to celebrate. He can create a view that he bases on the ORDERS table and the TESTS table. He may construct this table as shown in the following code example:

```
CREATE VIEW BIRTHDAY
    (CLIENT_NAME, TEST, ORDER_DATE, BIRTHDAY_CHARGE)
    AS SELECT CLIENT_NAME, TEST_ORDERED, ORDER_DATE,
        STANDARD_CHARGE * .9
    FROM ORDERS, TESTS
    WHERE TEST_ORDERED = TEST_NAME ;
```

Notice that the second column in the `BIRTHDAY` view — TEST — corresponds to the `TEST_ORDERED` column in the ORDERS table, which also corresponds to the `TEST_NAME` column in the TESTS table. Figure 6-3 shows how to create this view.

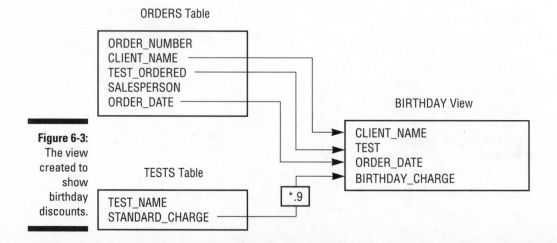

Figure 6-3:
The view created to show birthday discounts.

You can build a view that you base on multiple tables, as shown in the preceding examples, or you can build a view that you base on only one table. If you don't need some of the columns or rows in a table, create a view to remove these elements from sight and then deal with the view rather than the original table. This approach protects the user from confusion or distraction that may result from looking at parts of the table that aren't relevant to the task at hand.

Another reason for creating a view is to provide security for its underlying tables. You may want to make some of the columns in your tables available for inspection while hiding others. You can create a view that includes only the columns that you want to make available and then grant broad access to that view, while restricting access to the tables from which you draw the view. Chapter 13 explores database security and describes how to grant and revoke data-access privileges.

Updating Views

After you create a table, that table is automatically capable of accommodating insertions, updates, and deletions. Views, on the other hand, don't necessarily exhibit the same capability. If you update a view, you're actually updating its underlying table. Some views, however, may draw components from two or more tables. If you update such a view, how do you know which of its underlying tables gets updated? Another problem involves the SELECT list. A view may include an expression for a SELECT list. How do you update an expression? Suppose that you create a view by using the following statement:

```
CREATE VIEW COMP AS SELECT NAME, SALARY+COMM AS PAY
   FROM EMPLOYEE ;
```

Can you update PAY by using the following statement?

```
UPDATE COMP SET PAY = PAY + 100 ;
```

No, this approach doesn't make any sense — because the underlying table has no PAY column. You can't update something that doesn't exist in the base table.

Keep the following rule in mind whenever you consider updating views: You can't update a column of a view unless it corresponds to a column of an underlying base table.

Adding New Data

Every database table starts out empty. After you create a table, either by using SQL's DDL or a RAD tool, that table is nothing but a structured shell containing no data. To make the table useful, you must put some data into it. You may or may not have that data already stored in digital form.

If your data is not already in digital form, someone will probably have to use a keyboard and monitor to enter the data one record at a time. You can also enter data by using optical scanners and voice recognition systems, but the use of such devices for data entry is still relatively rare. If your data is already in digital form but perhaps not in the format of the database tables that you use, then you first need to translate the data into the appropriate format and then insert the data into the database. You may also want to transfer data that's already in the correct format to a new database. Depending on the current form of the data, you may be able to transfer it to your database in one operation, or you may need to enter the data one record at a time. Each data record that you enter corresponds to a single row in a database table.

Adding data one row at a time

Most DBMSs support form-based data entry. This feature enables you to create a screen form that has a field for every column in a database table. Field labels on the form enable you to determine easily what data goes into each field. The data-entry operator enters all the data for a single row into the form. After the DBMS accepts the new row, the system clears the form to accept another row. In this way, you can easily add data to a table one row at a time.

Form-based data entry is easy to use and is less susceptible to data-entry errors than is a list of comma-delimited values.. The main problem with form-based data entry is that it is nonstandard. Each different DBMS has its own method of creating forms. This diversity, however, is no problem for the data-entry operator. You can make the form look mostly the same from one DBMS to another. The application developer is the user who must return to the bottom of the learning curve every time he or she changes development tools. Another possible problem with form-based data entry is that some implementations may not permit a full range of validity checks on the data that you enter.

The best way to maintain a high level of data integrity in a database is to keep bad data out of the database in the first place. You can prevent the entry of some bad data by applying constraints to the fields on a data-entry form. This approach enables you to make sure that the database accepts only data values of the correct type and that fall within a predefined range. Of course, applying such constraints can't prevent all possible errors, but doing so does catch some of them.

If the form-design tool in your DBMS doesn't enable you to apply all the validity checks that you need to ensure data integrity, you may want to build your own screen, accept data entries into variables, and check the entries by using application program code. After you're sure that all the values entered for a table row are valid, you can then add that row by using the SQL INSERT command.

If you enter the data for a single row into a database table, the INSERT command uses the following syntax:

```
INSERT INTO table_1 [(column_1, column_2, ..., column_n)]
    VALUES (value_1, value_2, ..., value_n) ;
```

As indicated by the square brackets ([ ]), the listing of column names is optional. The default column list order is the order of the columns in the table. If you put the VALUES in the same order as the columns in the table, these elements go into the correct columns — whether you explicitly specify those columns or not. If you want to specify the VALUES in some order other than the order of the columns in the table, then you must list the column names, putting the columns in an order that corresponds to the order of the VALUES.

To enter a record into the CUSTOMER table, for example, use the following syntax:

```
INSERT INTO CUSTOMER (CUSTOMER_ID, FIRST_NAME, LAST_NAME,
    STREET, CITY, STATE, ZIPCODE, PHONE)
    VALUES (:vcustid, 'David', 'Taylor', '235 Nutley Ave.',
    'Nutley', 'NJ', '07110', '(201) 555-1963') ;
```

The first VALUE, vcustid, is a variable that you increment with your program code after you enter each new row of the table. This approach guarantees that you have no duplication of the CUSTOMER_ID. CUSTOMER_ID is the primary key for this table and, therefore, must remain unique. The rest of the values are data items rather than variables that contain data items. Of course, you can hold the data for these columns in variables, too, if you want. The INSERT statement works equally well either with variables or with an explicit copy of the data itself as arguments of the VALUES keyword.

Adding data only to selected columns

Sometimes you want to note the existence of an object, even if you don't have all the facts on it yet. If you have a database table for such objects, then you can insert a row for the new object without filling in the data in all the columns. If you want the table in *first normal form*, you must insert enough data to distinguish the new row from all the other rows in the table. (For a discussion of *first normal form*, see Chapter 5.) Inserting the new row's primary key is sufficient for this purpose. In addition to the primary key, insert any other data that you have about the object. Columns in which you enter no data contain nulls.

The following example shows such a partial row entry:

```
INSERT INTO CUSTOMER (CUSTOMER_ID, FIRST_NAME, LAST_NAME)
    VALUES (:vcustid, 'Tyson', 'Taylor') ;
```

You insert only the customer's unique identification number and name into the database table. The other columns in this row contain null values.

Adding a block of rows to a table

Loading a database table one row at a time by using INSERT statements can become awfully tedious, particularly if that's all you do all day. Even entering the data into a carefully human-engineered ergonomic screen form gets tiring after a while. Clearly, if you do have a reliable way to enter the data automatically, you're going to find occasions in which automatic entry is better than having a person sit at a keyboard and type.

Automatic data entry is feasible, for example, if the data already exists in electronic form because at some point in the past, somebody somewhere manually entered the data into a computer. If so, you have no compelling reason to repeat history. The transfer of data from one data file to another is a task that a computer can perform with a minimum of human involvement. If you know the characteristics of the source data and the desired form of the destination table, a computer can (in principle) perform the data transfer automatically.

Copying from a foreign data file

Suppose that you're building a database for a new application. Some of the data that you need already exists in a computer file. The file may be a flat file or a table in a database that operates in a DBMS different from the one you use. The data may be in ASCII or EBCDIC code or in some arcane proprietary format. What should you do?

The first thing you do is hope and pray that the data you want is in a format that has seen widespread use. If the data is in a popular format, you have a good chance of finding a format conversion utility that can translate the data into one or more other popular formats. Your development environment can probably import at least one of these formats. If you're really lucky, your development environment can handle the data's current format directly. On personal computers, the Access, dBASE, and Paradox formats are probably the most widely used. If the data that you want is in one of those formats, conversion should be easy. If the format of the data is something less common, you may need to go through a two-step conversion.

As a last resort, you can always turn to one of the professional data-translation services. These businesses specialize in translating computer data from one format to another. They have the capability of dealing with hundreds of different formats — most of which nobody has ever heard of. Give one of these services a tape or disk containing the data in its original format, and you get back the same data translated into whatever format you specify.

Transferring all rows between tables

A much less severe problem than dealing with foreign data is taking data that already exists in one table in your database and combining that data with the data in another table. This process works great if the structure of the second table is identical to the structure of the first table — that is, every column in the first table has a corresponding column in the second table, and the data types of the corresponding columns match. If so, you can combine the contents of the two tables by using the UNION relational operator. The result is a virtual table containing data from both source tables. I discuss the relational operators, including UNION, in Chapter 10.

Transferring selected columns and rows between tables

More often than not, however, the data in the source table doesn't exactly match the structure of the table into which you want to insert the data. Perhaps only some of the columns match — and these are the columns that you want to transfer. By combining SELECT statements with a UNION, you can specify which columns from the source tables to include in the virtual result table. By including WHERE clauses in the SELECT statements, you can restrict the rows that you place into the result table to those that satisfy specific conditions. I cover WHERE clauses extensively in Chapter 9.

Suppose that you have two tables, PROSPECT and CUSTOMER, and you want to list everyone living in the state of Maine who appears in either table. You can create a virtual result table with the desired information by using the following command:

```
SELECT FIRST_NAME, LAST_NAME
    FROM PROSPECT
    WHERE STATE = 'ME'
UNION
SELECT FIRST_NAME, LAST_NAME
    FROM CUSTOMER
    WHERE STATE = 'ME' ;
```

The SELECT statements specify that the columns included in the result table are FIRST_NAME and LAST_NAME. The WHERE clauses restrict the rows included to those with the value 'ME' in the STATE column. The STATE column isn't included in the result table but is present in both the PROSPECT and CUSTOMER tables. The UNION operator combines the results from the SELECT on PROSPECT with the results of the SELECT on CUSTOMER, deletes any duplicate rows, and then displays the result.

Another way to copy data from one table in a database to another is to nest a SELECT statement within an INSERT statement. This method (a *subselect*) doesn't create a virtual table but instead actually duplicates the selected data. You can take all the rows from the CUSTOMER table, for example, and insert those rows into the PROSPECT table. Of course, this only works if the structures of the CUSTOMER and PROSPECT tables are identical. Later, if you want to isolate those customers who live in Maine, a simple SELECT with one condition in the WHERE clause does the trick, as shown in the following example.

```
INSERT INTO PROSPECT
    SELECT * FROM CUSTOMER
    WHERE STATE = 'ME' ;
```

Even though this operation creates redundant data (you're now storing customer data in both the PROSPECT table and the CUSTOMER table), you may want to do it anyway to improve the performance of retrievals. Beware of the redundancy, however, and to maintain data consistency, make sure that you don't insert, update, or delete rows in one table without inserting, updating, or deleting the corresponding rows in the other table.

Updating Existing Data

You can count on one thing in this world — change. If you don't like the current state of affairs, just wait a while. Before long, things are different.

Because the world is constantly changing, the databases used to model aspects of the world need to change too. A customer may change his address. The quantity of a product in stock may change (because, you hope, someone buys one now and then). A basketball player's season performance statistics change each time he plays in another game. These are the kinds of typical events that require you to update a database.

SQL provides the UPDATE statement for changing data in a table. By using a single UPDATE statement, you can change one, some, or all the rows in a table. The UPDATE statement uses the following syntax:

```
UPDATE table_name
    SET column_1 = expression_1, column_2 = expression_2,
    ..., column_n = expression_n
    [WHERE predicates] ;
```

The WHERE clause is optional. This clause specifies the rows that you're updating. If you don't use a WHERE clause, all the rows in the table are updated. The SET clause specifies the new values for the columns that you're changing.

Consider the CUSTOMER table shown in Table 6-1.

Table 6-1	CUSTOMER Table		
Name	*City*	*Area-Code*	*Telephone*
Abe Abelson	Springfield	(714)	555-1111
Bill Bailey	Decatur	(714)	555-2222
Chuck Wood	Philo	(714)	555-3333
Don Stetson	Philo	(714)	555-4444
Dolph Stetson	Philo	(714)	555-5555

Customer lists change occasionally — as people move, change their phone number, and so on. Suppose that Abe Abelson moves from Springfield to Kankakee. You can update his record in the table by using the following UPDATE statement:

```
UPDATE CUSTOMER
    SET CITY = 'Kankakee', TELEPHONE = '666-6666'
    WHERE NAME = 'Abe Abelson' ;
```

This statement causes the changes shown in Table 6-2.

Table 6-2	CUSTOMER Table after UPDATE to One Row		
Name	**City**	**Area-Code**	**Telephone**
Abe Abelson	Kankakee	(714)	666-6666
Bill Bailey	Decatur	(714)	555-2222
Chuck Wood	Philo	(714)	555-3333
Don Stetson	Philo	(714)	555-4444
Dolph Stetson	Philo	(714)	555-5555

You can use a similar statement to update multiple rows. Assume that Philo is experiencing explosive population growth and now requires its own area code. You can change all rows for customers who live in Philo by using a single UPDATE statement, as follows:

```
UPDATE CUSTOMER
    SET AREA_CODE = '(619)'
    WHERE CITY = 'Philo' ;
```

The table now looks like the one shown in Table 6-3.

Table 6-3	CUSTOMER Table after UPDATE to Several Rows		
Name	**City**	**Area-Code**	**Telephone**
Abe Abelson	Kankakee	(714)	666-6666
Bill Bailey	Decatur	(714)	555-2222
Chuck Wood	Philo	(619)	555-3333
Don Stetson	Philo	(619)	555-4444
Dolph Stetson	Philo	(619)	555-5555

Updating all the rows of a table is even easier than updating only some of the rows. You don't need to use a WHERE clause to restrict the statement. Imagine that the city of Rantoul has acquired major political clout and has now annexed not only Kankakee, Decatur, and Philo, but also all the cities and towns in the database. You can update all the rows by using a single statement, as follows:

```
UPDATE CUSTOMER
   SET CITY = 'Rantoul' ;
```

Table 6-4 shows the result.

Table 6-4	CUSTOMER Table after UPDATE to All Rows		
Name	*City*	*Area-Code*	*Telephone*
Abe Abelson	Rantoul	(714)	666-6666
Bill Bailey	Rantoul	(714)	555-2222
Chuck Wood	Rantoul	(619)	555-3333
Don Stetson	Rantoul	(619)	555-4444
Dolph Stetson	Rantoul	(619)	555-5555

The WHERE clause that you use to restrict the rows to which an UPDATE statement applies can contain a *subselect*. A subselect enables you to update rows in one table based on the contents of another table.

For example, suppose that you're a wholesaler and your database includes a VENDOR table containing the names of all the manufacturers from whom you buy products. You also have a PRODUCT table containing the names of all the products that you sell and the prices that you charge for them. The VENDOR table has columns VENDOR_ID, VENDOR_NAME, STREET, CITY, STATE, and ZIP. The PRODUCT table has PRODUCT_ID, PRODUCT_NAME, VENDOR_ID, and SALE_PRICE.

Your vendor, Cumulonimbus Corporation, decides to raise the prices of all its products by 10 percent. To maintain your own profit margin, you must raise your prices on the products that you obtain from Cumulonimbus by 10 percent. You can do so by using the following UPDATE statement:

```
UPDATE PRODUCT
   SET SALE_PRICE = (SALE_PRICE * 1.1)
   WHERE VENDOR_ID IN
      (SELECT VENDOR_ID FROM VENDOR
      WHERE VENDOR_NAME = 'Cumulonimbus Corporation') ;
```

The subselect finds the VENDOR_ID that corresponds to Cumulonimbus. You can then use the VENDOR_ID field in the PRODUCT table to find the rows that you need to update. The prices on all Cumulonimbus products increase by 10 percent, while the prices on all other products stay the same. I discuss subselects more extensively in Chapter 11.

Deleting Obsolete Data

As time passes, data can get old and lose its usefulness. You may want to remove this outdated data from its table. Unneeded data in a table slows performance, consumes memory, and can confuse users. You may want to transfer older data to an archive table and then take the archive off-line. That way, in the unlikely event that you ever need to look at that data again, you can recover it. In the meantime, it doesn't slow down your everyday processing. Whether you decide that obsolete data is worth archiving or not, you eventually come to the point where you want to delete that data. SQL provides for the removal of rows from database tables by use of the DELETE statement.

You can delete all the rows in a table by using a single DELETE statement, or you can restrict the deletion to only selected rows by adding a WHERE clause. The syntax is similar to the syntax of a SELECT statement, except that you use no specification of columns. If you delete a table row, you remove all the data in that row's columns.

For example, suppose that your customer, David Taylor, just moved to Tahiti and isn't going to buy anything from you anymore. You can remove him from your CUSTOMER table by using the following statement:

```
DELETE FROM CUSTOMER
    WHERE FIRST_NAME = 'David' AND LAST_NAME = 'Taylor' ;
```

Assuming that you have only one customer named David Taylor, this statement makes the intended deletion. If any chance exists that you have two customers who share the name David Taylor, then you can add more conditions to the WHERE clause (such as STREET or PHONE or CUSTOMER_ID) to make sure that you delete only the one you want to remove.

Chapter 7

Specifying Values

- -

In This Chapter

▶ Using variables to eliminate redundant coding

▶ Extracting frequently-required information from a database table field

▶ Combining simple values to form complex expressions

- -

*T*hroughout this book, importance of database structure for maintaining database integrity is emphasized. Although the significance of database structure is often overlooked, you must never forget, however, that the most important thing is the data itself. After all, the values held in the cells that form the intersections of the rows and columns of a database table are the raw materials from which you can derive meaningful relationships and trends.

You can represent values in several ways. You can represent them directly, or you can derive them with functions or expressions. This chapter describes the various kinds of values, as well as functions and expressions.

Functions examine data and calculate a value based on the data. *Expressions* are combinations of data items that SQL evaluates to produce a single value.

Values

SQL recognizes several different kinds of values:

> ✔ Row values
>
> ✔ Literal values
>
> ✔ Variables
>
> ✔ Special variables
>
> ✔ Column references

Atoms aren't indivisible either

In the nineteenth century, scientists believed that an atom was the irreducible smallest possible piece of matter. That's why they named it *atom*, which comes from the Greek word *atomos*, which means *indivisible*. Now scientists know that atoms aren't indivisible — they're made up of protons, neutrons, and electrons. Protons and neutrons, in turn, are made up of quarks, gluons, and virtual quarks. Even these things may not be indivisible. Who knows?

The value of a field in a database table is called *atomic*, even though many fields aren't indivisible either. A DATE value has components of month, year, and day. A TIMESTAMP value has components of hour, minute, second, and so on. A REAL or FLOAT value has components of exponent and mantissa. A CHAR value has components that you can access by using SUBSTRING. Therefore, calling database field values *atomic* is true to the analogy of atoms of matter. Neither modern application of the term *atomic*, however, is true to the word's original meaning.

Row values

The most visible values in a database are table *row values*. These are the values that each row of a database table contains. A row value is typically made up of multiple components, because each column in a row contains a value. A *field* is the intersection of a single column with a single row. A field contains a *scalar,* or *atomic,* value. A value that's scalar or atomic has only a single component.

Literal values

In SQL, either a variable or a constant may represent a *value*. Logically enough, the value of a *variable* may change from time to time, but the value of a *constant* never changes. An important kind of constant is the *literal value*. You may consider a *literal* to be a *WYSIWYG* value, because *What You See Is What You Get*. The representation is itself the value.

Just as SQL has many different data types, it also has many different types of literals. Table 7-1 shows some examples of literals of the various data types.

Notice that single quotes enclose the literals of the nonnumeric types. These marks help to prevent confusion; they can, however, also cause problems.

Table 7-1	Example Literals of Various Data Types
Data Type	**Example Literal**
INTEGER	186282
SMALLINT	186
NUMERIC	186282.42
DECIMAL	186282.42
REAL	6.02257E-23
DOUBLE PRECISION	3.1415926535897E00
FLOAT	6.02257E-23
CHARACTER(15) Note: Fifteen total characters and spaces are between the quote marks above.	'GREECE '
VARCHAR (CHARACTER VARYING)	'lepton'
NATIONAL CHARACTER(15) Note: Fifteen total characters and spaces are between the quote marks above.	'ΕΛΛΑΣ '[1]
NATIONAL CHARACTER VARYING	'λεπτου'[2]
BIT(12)	B'100111001110'[3]
BIT(12)	X'9CE'[4]
BIT VARYING(16)	B'1001111000111'
BIT VARYING(16)	X'F7'
DATE	DATE '1969-07-20'
TIME(2)	TIME '13.41.32.50'
TIMESTAMP(0)	TIMESTAMP '1998-05-17-13.03.16.000000'
TIME WITH TIMEZONE(4)	TIME '13.41.32.5000-08.00'
TIMESTAMP WITH TIMEZONE(0)	TIMESTAMP '1998-05-17-13.03.16.0000+02.00'
INTERVAL DAY	INTERVAL '7' DAY

[1]This term is the word that Greeks use to name their own country in their own language. (The English equivalent is 'Hellas.')

[2]This term is the word 'lepton' in Greek national characters.

[3]BIT and BIT VARYING values that start with a 'B' are interpreted as binary numbers.

[4]BIT and BIT VARYING values that start with an 'X' are interpreted as hexadecimal numbers.

What if a literal is a character string that itself contains a single quote? In that case, you must type two single quotes to show that one of the quote marks that you're typing is a part of the character string and not an indicator of the end of the string. You'd type `'Earth''s atmosphere'`, for example, to represent the character literal `'Earth's atmosphere'`.

Variables

The ability to manipulate literals and other kinds of constants while dealing with a database is great, but it is helpful to have variables, too. In many cases, you'd need to do much more work if you didn't have variables. A *variable,* by the way, is a quantity that has a value that can change. Look at the following example to see why variables are valuable.

Suppose that you're a retailer who has several classes of customers. You give your high-volume customers the best price, your medium-volume customers the next best price, and your low-volume customers the highest price. You want to index all prices to your cost of goods. For your F-117A product, you decide to charge your high-volume customers (Class C) 1.4 times your cost of goods. You charge your medium-volume customers (Class B) 1.5 times your cost of goods, and you charge your low-volume customers (Class A) 1.6 times your cost of goods.

You store the cost of goods and the prices that you charge in a table you name PRICING. To implement your new pricing structure, you issue the following SQL commands:

```
UPDATE PRICING
   SET PRICE = COST * 1.4
   WHERE PRODUCT = 'F-117A'
      AND CLASS = 'C' ;
UPDATE PRICING
   SET PRICE = COST * 1.5
   WHERE PRODUCT = 'F-117A'
      AND CLASS = 'B' ;
UPDATE PRICING
   SET PRICE = COST * 1.6
   WHERE PRODUCT = 'F-117A'
      AND CLASS = 'A' ;
```

This code is fine and meets your needs — for now. But what if aggressive competition begins to eat into your market share? You may need to reduce your margins to remain competitive. You need to enter something along the lines of the following commands:

```
UPDATE PRICING
   SET PRICE = COST * 1.25
   WHERE PRODUCT = 'F-117A'
      AND CLASS = 'C' ;
UPDATE PRICING
   SET PRICE = COST * 1.35
   WHERE PRODUCT = 'F-117A'
      AND CLASS = 'B' ;
UPDATE PRICING
   SET PRICE = COST * 1.45
   WHERE PRODUCT = 'F-117A'
      AND CLASS = 'A' ;
```

If you're in a volatile market, you may need to rewrite your SQL code repeatedly. This task can become very tedious, particularly if prices appear in multiple places in your code. You can minimize this problem if you replace literals (such as 1.45) with variables (such as :multiplierA). Then you can perform your updates as follows:

```
UPDATE PRICING
   SET PRICE = COST * :multiplierC
   WHERE PRODUCT = 'F-117A'
      AND CLASS = 'C' ;
UPDATE PRICING
   SET PRICE = COST * :multiplierB
   WHERE PRODUCT = 'F-117A'
      AND CLASS = 'B' ;
UPDATE PRICING
   SET PRICE = COST * :multiplierA
   WHERE PRODUCT = 'F-117A'
      AND CLASS = 'A' ;
```

Now whenever market conditions force you to change your pricing, you need only change the values of the variables :multiplierC, :multiplierB, and :multiplierA. These variables are parameters that pass to the SQL code, which then uses the variables to compute new prices.

Sometimes you see variables that you use in this way called *parameters* and, at other times, *host variables*. Variables are called *parameters* if they are in applications written in SQL module language and *host variables* if they're used in embedded SQL.

Embedded SQL means that SQL statements are embedded into the code of an application written in a host language. Alternatively, you can use SQL module language to create an entire module of SQL code. The host language application then calls the module. Either method can give you the capabilities that you want. The approach that you use depends on your particular implementation of SQL.

Special variables

If a user on a client machine connects to a database on a server, this connection establishes a *session*. If the user connects to several databases, the session associated with the most recent connection is considered the *current session; previous sessions* are considered *dormant*. SQL:1999 defines several special variables that are valuable on multiuser systems. These variables keep track of the different users. The special variable SESSION_USER, for example, holds a value that's equal to the user authorization identifier of the current SQL session. If you write a program that performs a monitoring function, you can interrogate SESSION_USER to find out who is executing SQL statements.

An SQL module may have a user-specified authorization identifier associated with it. The CURRENT_USER variable stores this value. If a module has no such identifier, CURRENT_USER has the same value as SESSION_USER.

The SYSTEM_USER variable contains the operating system's identifier of a user. This identifier may differ from that user's identifier in an SQL module. A user may log onto the system as LARRY, for example, but identify himself to a module as PLANT_MGR. The value in SESSION_USER is PLANT_MGR. If he makes no explicit specification of the module identifier, and CURRENT_USER also contains PLANT_MGR. SYSTEM_USER holds the value LARRY.

One use of the SYSTEM_USER, SESSION_USER, and CURRENT_USER special variables is to track who is using the system. You can maintain a log table and periodically insert into that table the values that SYSTEM_USER, SESSION_USER, and CURRENT_USER contain. The following example shows how:

```
INSERT INTO USAGELOG (SNAPSHOT)
   VALUES ('User ' || SYSTEM_USER ||
      ' with ID ' || SESSION_USER ||
      ' active at ' || CURRENT_TIMESTAMP) ;
```

This statement produces log entries similar to the following example:

```
User LARRY with ID PLANT_MGR active at 1998-05-17-14.18.00
```

Column references

Columns contain values, one in each row of a table. SQL statements often refer to such values. A fully qualified column reference consists of the table name, a period, and then the column name (for example, PRICING.PRODUCT). Consider the following statement:

```
SELECT PRICING.COST
   FROM PRICING
   WHERE PRICING.PRODUCT = 'F-117A' ;
```

`PRICING.PRODUCT` is a column reference. This reference contains the value `'F-117A'`. `PRICING.COST` is also a column reference, but you don't know its value until after the preceding `SELECT` statement executes.

Because it only makes sense to reference columns in the current table, you don't generally need to use fully qualified column references. The following statement, for example, is completely equivalent to the previous one:

```
SELECT COST
   FROM PRICING
   WHERE PRODUCT = 'F-117A' ;
```

At times, however, you may be dealing with more than one table. Two tables in a database may contain one or more columns with the same name. If so, you must fully qualify column references for those columns to guarantee that the column you get is indeed the one you want.

For example, suppose that your company maintains facilities at Hollis and at Jefferson, and you maintain separate employee records for each site. You name the employee table at Hollis EMP_HOLLIS, and you name the Jefferson employee table EMP_JEFFERSON. You want a list of all employees who work at both sites, so you need to find all employees whose names appear in both tables. The following `SELECT` gives you what you want:

```
SELECT EMP_HOLLIS.F_NAME, EMP_HOLLIS.L_NAME
   FROM EMP_HOLLIS, EMP_JEFFERSON
   WHERE EMP_HOLLIS.EMP_ID = EMP_JEFFERSON.EMP_ID ;
```

Because the employee's ID number is unique and is the same regardless of work site, you can use this ID as a link between the two tables. This retrieval returns only the names of employees who appear in both tables.

Functions

A *function* is a simple-to-moderately complex operation that the usual SQL commands don't perform but that comes up fairly often in practice. SQL provides functions that perform tasks that the application code in the host language (within which you embed your SQL statements) would otherwise need to perform. SQL has two main categories of functions: *set* (or *aggregate*) functions and *value functions*.

Summarizing by using set functions

The set functions apply to *sets* of rows in a table rather than to a single row. These functions summarize some characteristic of the current set of rows. The set may include all the rows in the table or a subset of rows that a `WHERE` clause specifies. (I discuss WHERE clauses extensively in Chapter 9.) Programmers sometimes call set functions *aggregate functions* because these functions take information from multiple rows, process that information in some way, and deliver a single-row answer. That answer is an *aggregation* of the information in the rows making up the set.

To illustrate the use of the set functions, consider Table 7-2, a list of nutrition facts for 100 grams of certain selected foods.

Table 7-2	Nutrition Facts for 100 Grams of Selected Foods			
Food	*Calories*	*Protein (grams)*	*Fat (grams)*	*Carbohydrate (grams)*
Almonds, roasted	627	18.6	57.7	19.6
Asparagus	20	2.2	0.2	3.6
Bananas, raw	85	1.1	0.2	22.2
Beef, lean hamburger	219	27.4	11.3	
Chicken, light meat	166	31.6	3.4	
Opossum, roasted	221	30.2	10.2	
Pork, ham	394	21.9	33.3	
Beans, lima	111	7.6	0.5	19.8
Cola	39			10.0
Bread, white	269	8.7	3.2	50.4
Bread, whole wheat	243	10.5	3.0	47.7
Broccoli	26	3.1	0.3	4.5
Butter	716	0.6	81.0	0.4
Jelly beans	367		0.5	93.1
Peanut brittle	421	5.7	10.4	81.0

A database table named FOODS stores the information in Table 7-2. Blank fields contain the value NULL. The set functions COUNT, AVG, MAX, MIN, and SUM can tell you important facts about the data in this table.

COUNT

The COUNT function tells you how many rows are in the table or how many rows in the table meet certain conditions. The simplest usage of this function is as follows:

```
SELECT COUNT (*)
   FROM FOODS ;
```

This function yields a result of 15, because it counts all rows in the FOODS table. The following statement produces the same result:

```
SELECT COUNT (CALORIES)
   FROM FOODS ;
```

Because the CALORIES column in every row of the table has an entry, the count is the same. If a column contains nulls, however, the function doesn't count the rows corresponding to those nulls.

The following statement returns a value of 11, because 4 of the 15 rows in the table contain nulls in the CARBOHYDRATE column.

```
SELECT COUNT (CARBOHYDRATE)
   FROM FOODS ;
```

A field in a database table may contain a null value for a variety of reasons. A common reason for this is that the actual value is not known or not yet known. Or the value may be known but not yet entered. Sometimes, if a value is known to be zero, the data entry operator doesn't bother entering anything in a field — leaving that field a null. This is not a good practice because zero is a definite value, and you can include it in computations. Null is *not* a definite value, and SQL doesn't include null values in computations.

You can also use the COUNT function, in combination with DISTINCT, to determine how many distinct values exist in a column. Consider the following statement:

```
SELECT COUNT (DISTINCT FAT)
   FROM FOODS ;
```

The answer that this statement returns is 12. You can see that a 100-gram serving of asparagus has exactly the same fat content as 100 grams of bananas (0.2 grams) and that a 100-gram serving of lima beans has exactly the same fat content as 100 grams of jelly beans (0.5 grams). Thus the table has a total of only 12 distinct fat values.

AVG

The AVG function calculates and returns the average of the values in the specified column. Of course, you can use the AVG function only on columns that contain numeric data, as in the following example:

```
SELECT AVG (FAT)
   FROM FOODS ;
```

The result is 15.37. This number is so high primarily because of the presence of butter in the database. You may wonder what the average fat content may be if you didn't include butter. To find out, you can add a WHERE clause to your statement, as follows:

```
SELECT AVG (FAT)
   FROM FOODS
   WHERE FOOD <> 'Butter' ;
```

The average fat value drops all the way down to 10.32 grams per 100 grams of food.

MAX

The MAX function returns the maximum value found in the specified column. The following statement returns a value of 81 (the fat content in 100 grams of butter):

```
SELECT MAX (FAT)
   FROM FOODS ;
```

MIN

The MIN function returns the minimum value found in the specified column. The following statement returns a value of 0.4, because the function doesn't treat the nulls as zeros:

```
SELECT MIN (CARBOHYDRATE)
   FROM FOODS ;
```

SUM

The SUM function returns the sum of all the values found in the specified column. The following statement returns 3,924, which is the total calorie content of all 15 foods:

```
SELECT SUM (CALORIES)
   FROM FOODS ;
```

Value functions

A number of operations apply in a wide variety of contexts. Because you need to use these operations so often, incorporating them into SQL as value functions makes good sense. SQL offers relatively few value functions compared to PC database management systems such as Access or dBASE, but the few that SQL does have are probably the ones that you want to use most often. SQL uses the following three types of value functions:

✔ String value functions

✔ Numeric value functions

✔ Datetime value functions

String value functions

String value functions take one character string (or bit string) as an input and produce another character string (or bit string) as an output. SQL has six such functions:

✔ SUBSTRING

✔ UPPER

✔ LOWER

✔ TRIM

✔ TRANSLATE

✔ CONVERT

SUBSTRING

Use the SUBSTRING function to extract a substring from a source string. The source string may be either a character string or a bit string. The extracted substring is of the same type as the source string. If the source string is a character string, for example, the substring is also a character string. Following is the syntax of the SUBSTRING function:

```
SUBSTRING (string_value FROM start [FOR length])
```

The clause in square brackets ([ ]) is optional. The substring extracted from string_value begins with the character (or bit) that *start* represents and continues for *length* characters (or bits). If the FOR clause is absent, the substring extracted extends from the start character to the end of the string. Consider the following example:

```
SUBSTRING ('Bread, whole wheat' FROM 8 FOR 7)
```

The substring extracted is 'whole w'. This substring starts with the eighth character of the source string and has a length of seven characters. On the surface, SUBSTRING doesn't seem like a very valuable function. If I have a literal like 'Bread, whole wheat', I don't need a function to figure out what the eighth through the fourteenth characters are. SUBSTRING really is a valuable function, however, because the string value doesn't need to be a literal. The value can be any expression that evaluates to a character string. Thus, I could have a variable named fooditem that takes on different values at different times. The following expression would extract the desired substring regardless of what character string the fooditem variable currently represents:

```
SUBSTRING (:fooditem FROM 8 FOR 7)
```

All the value functions are similar in that these functions can operate on expressions that evaluate to values as well as on the literal values themselves.

You need to watch out for a couple of things if you use the SUBSTRING function. Make sure that the substring that you specify actually falls within the source string. If you ask for a substring starting at character eight but the source string is only four characters long, you get a null result. You must, therefore, have some idea of the form of your data before you specify a substring function. You also don't want to specify a negative substring length, because the end of a string can't precede the beginning.

If a column is of the VARCHAR type, you may not know how far the field extends for a particular row. This lack of knowledge, however, doesn't present a problem for the SUBSTRING function. If the length that you specify goes beyond the right edge of the field, SUBSTRING returns whatever it finds. It doesn't return an error.

Say that you have the following statement:

```
SELECT * FROM FOODS
    WHERE SUBSTRING (FOOD FROM 8 FOR 7) = 'white' ;
```

This statement returns the row for white bread from the FOODS table, even though the value in the FOOD column ('Bread, white') is less than 14 characters long.

If any operand in the substring function has a null value, SUBSTRING returns a null result.

To extract a substring from a bit string, incorporate a 'B' in the string value argument, such as in the following example:

```
SUBSTRING (B'0111000110101' FROM 4 FOR 6)
```

This example returns a value of B'100011'. The substring starts with the fourth bit of the source string and proceeds for six bits.

UPPER

The UPPER value function converts a character string to all uppercase characters, as in the examples shown in the following table.

This statement	Returns
UPPER ('e. e. cummings')	'E. E. CUMMINGS'
UPPER ('Isaac Newton, Ph.D')	'ISAAC NEWTON, PH.D.'

The UPPER function doesn't affect a string that's already in all uppercase characters.

LOWER

The LOWER value function converts a character string to all lowercase characters, as in the examples in the following table.

This statement	Returns
LOWER ('TAXES')	'taxes'
LOWER ('E. E. Cummings')	'e. e. cummings'

The LOWER function doesn't affect a string that's already in all lowercase characters.

TRIM

Use the TRIM function to trim off leading or trailing blanks (or other characters, for that matter) from a character string. The following examples show how to use TRIM.

This statement	Returns
TRIM (LEADING ' ' FROM ' treat ')	'treat '
TRIM (TRAILING ' ' FROM ' treat ')	' treat'
TRIM (BOTH ' ' FROM ' treat ')	'treat'
TRIM (BOTH 't' from 'treat')	'rea'

The default trim character is the blank, so the following syntax also is legal:

```
TRIM (BOTH FROM ' treat ')
```

This syntax gives you the same result as the third example in the table — `'treat'`.

TRANSLATE and CONVERT

The `TRANSLATE` and `CONVERT` functions take a source string in one character set and transform the original string into a string in another character set. Examples may be English to Kanji or Hebrew to French. The conversion functions that specify these transformations are implementation-specific. Consult the documentation of your implementation for details.

If translating from one language to another was as easy as invoking an SQL `TRANSLATE` function, that would be great. Unfortunately, the task is not that easy. All `TRANSLATE` does is translate a character in the first character set to the corresponding character in the second character set. The function can, for example, translate `'Ελλασ'` to `'Ellas'`. `TRANSLATE` can't, however, translate `'Ελλασ'` to `'Greece'`.

Numeric value functions

Numeric value functions may take data of a variety of types as input, but the output is always a numeric value. SQL has five numeric value functions:

- ✔ POSITION
- ✔ CHARACTER_LENGTH
- ✔ OCTET_LENGTH
- ✔ BIT_LENGTH
- ✔ EXTRACT

POSITION

`POSITION` searches for a specified target string within a specified source string and returns the character position where the target string begins. The syntax is as follows:

```
POSITION (target IN source)
```

The following table shows a few examples.

This statement	*Returns*
POSITION ('B' IN 'Bread, whole wheat')	1
POSITION ('Bre' IN 'Bread, whole wheat')	1
POSITION ('wh' IN 'Bread, whole wheat')	8
POSITION ('whi' IN 'Bread, whole wheat')	0
POSITION ('' IN 'Bread, whole wheat')	1

If the function doesn't find the target string, the POSITION function returns a zero value. If the target string has zero length (as in the last example), the POSITION function always returns a value of one. If any operand in the function has a null value, the result is a null value.

CHARACTER_LENGTH

The CHARACTER_LENGTH function returns the number of characters in a character string. The following statement, for example, returns 16:

```
CHARACTER_LENGTH ('Opossum, roasted')
```

As I note in regard to the SUBSTRING function (in the "Substring" section earlier in the chapter), this function is not particularly useful if its argument is a literal like 'Opossum, roasted'. I can just as easily write 16 as I can CHARACTER_LENGTH ('Opossum, roasted'). In fact, writing 16 is easier. This function becomes more useful if its argument is an expression rather than a literal value.

OCTET_LENGTH

In music, a vocal ensemble made up of eight singers is called an *octet*. Typically, the parts that the ensemble represents are first and second soprano, first and second alto, first and second tenor, and first and second bass. In computer terminology, an ensemble of eight data bits is called a *byte*. The word *byte* is clever in that the term clearly relates to *bit* but implies something larger than a bit. A nice word play — but, unfortunately, nothing in the word *byte* conveys the concept of "eightness." By borrowing the musical term, a more apt description of a collection of eight bits becomes possible.

Practically all modern computers use eight bits to represent a single alphanumeric character. More complex character sets (such as Chinese) require 16 bits to represent a single character. The OCTET_LENGTH function counts and returns the number of octets (bytes) in a string. If the string is a bit string, OCTET_LENGTH returns the number of octets you need to hold that number of bits. If the string is an English-language character string (with one octet per character), the function returns the number of characters in the string. If the string is a Chinese-character string, the number the function returns is twice the number of Chinese characters. The following strings offer some examples:

```
OCTET_LENGTH ('Beans, lima')returns 11
OCTET_LENGTH (B'10111010011')    returns 2
```

The second string is 11 bits long, so you'd need two octets to hold the entire string.

Some character sets use a variable number of octets for different characters. In particular, some character sets that support mixtures of Kanji and Latin characters use *escape* characters to switch between the two character sets. A string that contains both Latin and Kanji may have, for example, 30 characters and require 30 octets if all the characters are Latin; 62 characters if all the characters are Kanji (60 characters plus a leading and trailing shift character); and 150 characters if the characters alternate between Latin and Kanji (because each Kanji character needs two octets for the character and one octet each for the leading and trailing shift characters). The OCTET_LENGTH function returns the number of octets you need for the current value of the string.

BIT_LENGTH

If you understand CHARACTER_LENGTH and OCTET_LENGTH, the BIT_LENGTH function should be easy for you. BIT_LENGTH returns the length of a bit string. If the string is six bits long, the function returns a 6. If the string is 15 bits long, the function returns a 15. The following statement, for example, returns 8:

```
BIT_LENGTH (B'01100111')
```

EXTRACT

The EXTRACT function extracts a single field from a datetime or an interval. The following statement, for example, returns 08:

```
EXTRACT (MONTH FROM DATE '2000-08-20')
```

Datetime value functions

SQL includes three functions that return information about the current date, current time, or both. CURRENT_DATE returns the current date; CURRENT_TIME returns the current time; and CURRENT_TIMESTAMP returns (surprise!) both the current date and the current time. CURRENT_DATE doesn't take an argument, but CURRENT_TIME and CURRENT_TIMESTAMP both take a single argument. The argument specifies the precision for the seconds part of the time value that the function returns. *Datetime* data types are described in Chapter 2 and the concept of precision is explained there as well.

The following table offers some examples of these datetime value functions.

This statement	Returns
CURRENT_DATE	2000-12-31
CURRENT_TIME (1)	08:36:57.3
CURRENT_TIMESTAMP (2)	2000-12-31 08:36:57.38

The date that CURRENT_DATE returns is DATE type data, not CHARACTER. The time that CURRENT_TIME (p) returns is TIME type data, and the timestamp that CURRENT_TIMESTAMP(p) returns is TIMESTAMP type data. Because SQL retrieves date and time information from your computer's system clock, the information is correct for the time zone in which the computer resides.

In some applications, you may want to deal with dates, times, or timestamps as character strings to take advantage of the functions that operate on character data. You can perform a type conversion by using the CAST expression, which is described in Chapter 8.

Value Expressions

An expression may be simple or very complex. The expression can contain literal values, column names, parameters, host variables, subqueries, logical connectives, and arithmetic operators. Regardless of its complexity, however, an expression must reduce to a single value.

For this reason, SQL expressions are commonly known as *value expressions*. Combining multiple value expressions into a single expression is possible, as long as the component value expressions reduce to values of compatible data types.

SQL:1999 has five different kinds of value expressions:

- ✔ String value expressions
- ✔ Numeric value expressions
- ✔ Datetime value expressions
- ✔ Interval value expressions
- ✔ Conditional value expressions

String value expressions

The simplest *string value expression* is a single string value specification. Other possibilities include a column reference, a set function, a scalar sub-query, a CASE expression, a CAST expression, or a complex string value expression. I discuss CASE and CAST value expressions in Chapter 8. Only one operator is possible in a string value expression: the *concatenation operator.* You may concatenate any of the expressions I mention in the bulleted list prior to this paragraph with another expression to create a more complex string value expression. A pair of vertical lines (||) represents the concatenation operator. The following table shows some examples of string value expressions.

Expression	Produces
'Peanut ' || 'brittle'	'Peanut brittle'
'Jelly' || ' ' || 'beans'	'Jelly beans'
FIRST_NAME || ' ' || LAST_NAME	'Joe Smith'
B'1100111' || B'01010011'	B'110011101010011'
'' || 'Asparagus'	'Asparagus'
'Asparagus' || ''	'Asparagus'
'As' || '' || 'par' || '' || 'agus'	'Asparagus'

As the table shows, if you concatenate a string to a zero-length string, the result is the same as the original string.

Numeric value expressions

In *numeric value expressions,* you can apply the addition, subtraction, multi-plication, and division operators to numeric-type data. The expression must reduce to a numeric value. The components of a numeric value expression may be of different data types as long as all are numeric. The data type of the result depends on the data types of the components from which you derive the result. The SQL:1999 standard doesn't rigidly specify the type that results from any specific combination of source expression components because of differences among hardware platforms. Check the documentation for your specific platform when mixing numeric data types.

Following are some examples of numeric value expressions:

- ✔ -27
- ✔ 49 + 83
- ✔ 5 * (12 - 3)
- ✔ PROTEIN + FAT + CARBOHYDRATE
- ✔ FEET/5280
- ✔ COST * :multiplierA

Datetime value expressions

Datetime value expressions perform operations on data that deal with dates and timesThese value expressions can contain components that are of the types DATE, TIME, TIMESTAMP, or INTERVAL. The result of a datetime value expression is always of a datetime type (either DATE, TIME, or TIMESTAMP). The following expression, for example, gives the date of one week from today:

```
CURRENT_DATE + INTERVAL '7' DAY
```

Times are maintained in Universal Time Coordinated (UTC) — formerly known as Greenwich Mean Time — but you can specify an offset to make the time correct for any particular time zone. For your system's local time zone, you can use the simple syntax given in the following example:

```
TIME '22:55:00' AT LOCAL
```

Alternatively, you can specify this value the long way:

```
TIME '22:55:00' AT TIME ZONE INTERVAL '-08.00' HOUR TO MINUTE
```

This expression defines the local time as the time zone for Portland, Oregon, which is eight hours earlier than that of Greenwich, England.

Interval value expressions

If you subtract one datetime from another, you get an *interval*. Adding one datetime to another makes no sense, so SQL doesn't permit you to do so. If you add two intervals together or subtract one interval from another interval, the result is an interval. You can also either multiply or divide an interval by a numeric constant.

Recall that SQL has two types of intervals: *year-month* and *day-time*. To avoid ambiguities, you must specify which to use in an interval expression. The following expression, for example, gives the interval in years and months until you reach retirement age:

```
(BIRTHDAY_65 - CURRENT_DATE) YEAR TO MONTH
```

The following example, on the other hand, gives an interval of 40 days:

```
INTERVAL '17' DAY + INTERVAL '23' DAY
```

The example that follows approximates the total number of months that a mother of five has been pregnant (assuming that she's not currently expecting number six!):

```
INTERVAL '9' MONTH * 5
```

Intervals can be negative as well as positive and may consist of any value expression or combination of value expressions that evaluates to an interval.

Conditional value expressions

The value of a *conditional value expression* depends on a condition. The conditional value expressions CASE, NULLIF, and COALESCE are significantly more complex than the other kinds of value expressions. In fact, these three conditional value expressions are so complex that I don't have enough room to talk about them here. I give conditional value expressions extensive coverage, therefore, in Chapter 8.

How do you enter SQL statements into an Access 2000 database?

Access 2000 does not make it easy to enter SQL statements. You have to enter all SQL statements as queries, regardless of whether they are really queries. Other products such as SQL Server, Oracle, MySQL, or PostgreSQL provide editors you can use to enter SQL statements. In SQL Server you can use the Query Analyzer. For others, consult their documentation.

You can enter SQL statements into Access, but the path to doing so is obscure. Once you open a database, select Queries from the Window displaying your database. Next, create a query in Design View or with a wizard. It doesn't matter what query you create. Once the query exists, double click on it to select it. Now you can click on View from the main menu. One of the choices is SQL View. Click on that. It will show the SQL code of the query you entered. You can now erase that query and enter SQL Code for a new 'query'. The query could be a CREATE TABLE statement or some other decidedly non-query statement. Execute your new query by clicking on the exclamation point in the menu bar or by selecting Query then Run from the main menu.

Chapter 8

Advanced SQL Value Expressions

● ●

● ●

SQL is described in Chapter 2 as a *data sub-language*. In fact, the sole function of SQL is to operate on data in a database. SQL lacks many of the features of a conventional procedural language. As a result, developers who use SQL must switch back and forth between SQL and its host language to control the flow of execution. This repeated switching complicates matters at development time and negatively affects performance at run time.

The performance penalty exacted by the limitations of SQL prompted the addition of new features to SQL-92 in order to reduce an application's reliance on its host language. New features in SQL:1999 move SQL even further in the direction of a complete language. However, many applications still require a host language "wrapper" around the SQL code. One of the new features that appeared in SQL-92, the CASE expression, provides a long-sought conditional structure. A second SQL-92 feature, the CAST expression, facilitates data conversion in a table from one type of data to another. A third SQL-92 feature, the row value expression, enables you to operate on a list of values where, previously, only a single value was possible. For example, if your list of values is a list of columns in a table, you can now perform an operation on all those columns by using a very simple syntax.

CASE Conditional Expressions

Every complete computer language has some kind of conditional statement or command. In fact, most have several kinds. Probably the most common conditional statement or command is the IF...THEN...ELSE...ENDIF structure. If the condition following the IF keyword evaluates to True, the block of commands following the THEN keyword executes. If the condition doesn't evaluate to True, the block of commands after the ELSE keyword executes. The ENDIF keyword signals the end of the structure. This structure is great for any decision that goes one of two ways. The structure is less applicable to decisions that can have more than two outcomes.

Most complete languages have a CASE statement that handles situations in which you may want to perform more than two different tasks based on more than two conditions.

SQL differs from other languages in that CASE is an *expression* in SQL rather than a statement. As such, CASE is only part of a statement — not a statement in its own right. In SQL, you can place a CASE expression almost any place where a value is legal. At run time, a CASE expression evaluates to a value. The CASE statements that you find in other languages don't evaluate to a value; rather, they execute a block of statements.

You can use the CASE expression in the following two ways:

- ✔ Use the expression with search conditions. CASE searches for rows in a table where specified conditions are True. If CASE finds a search condition to be True for a table row, the statement containing the CASE expression makes a specified change to that row.

- ✔ Use a CASE expression to compare a table field to a value that you specify in the CASE expression. The outcome of the statement containing the CASE expression depends on which value of several specified values in the table field is equal to each table row.

The sections "Using CASE with search conditions" and "Using CASE with values" help make these concepts more clear. In the first of these sections, two examples use CASE with search conditions. One example searches a table and makes different changes to table values, based on a condition. The second section "Using CASE with values" explores two examples of the value form of CASE.

Using CASE with search conditions

One powerful way to use the CASE expression is to search a table for rows in which a specified search condition is True. If you use CASE this way, the expression uses the following syntax:

```
CASE
    WHEN condition1 THEN result1
    WHEN condition2 THEN result2
    ...
    WHEN conditionn THEN resultn
    ELSE resultx
END
```

CASE examines the first *qualifying row* (the first row that meets the conditions of the enclosing WHERE clause, if any) to see whether condition1 is True. If it is, the CASE expression receives a value of result1. If condition1 is not True, CASE evaluates the row for condition2. If condition2 is True, the CASE expression receives the value of result2, and so on. If none of the stated conditions are True, the CASE expression receives the value of resultx. The ELSE clause is optional. If the expression has no ELSE clause and none of the specified conditions are True, the expression receives a null value. After the SQL statement containing the CASE expression applies itself to the first qualifying row in a table and takes the appropriate action, it then processes the next row. This sequence continues until the SQL statement finishes processing the entire table.

Updating values based on a condition

Because you can embed a CASE expression within an SQL statement in almost any place where a value is possible, this expression gives you tremendous flexibility. You can use CASE within an UPDATE statement, for example, to make different changes to table values — based on a certain condition. Consider the following example:

```
UPDATE FOODS
    SET RATING = CASE
                    WHEN FAT < 1
                        THEN 'very low fat'
                    WHEN FAT < 5
                        THEN 'low fat'
                    WHEN FAT < 20
                        THEN 'moderate fat'
                    WHEN FAT < 50
                        THEN 'high fat'
                    ELSE 'heart attack city'
                 END ;
```

This statement evaluates the WHEN conditions in order until the first True value is returned, after which the statement ignores the rest of the conditions. For this reason, you don't need to code the preceding example as follows:

```
WHEN FAT < 1
     THEN 'very low fat'
WHEN FAT >= 1 AND FAT < 5
     THEN 'low fat'
WHEN FAT >= 5 AND FAT < 20
     THEN 'moderate fat'
WHEN FAT >= 20 AND < 50
     THEN 'high fat'
ELSE 'heart attack city'
```

Table 7-2 in Chapter 7 shows the fat content of 100 grams of certain foods. A database table holding this information can contain a RATING column that gives a quick assessment of the meaning of the fat content. If you run the preceding UPDATE on the FOODS table in Chapter 7, the statement assigns asparagus a value of very low fat, gives chicken a value of low fat, and puts roasted almonds into the heart attack city category.

Avoiding conditions that cause errors

Another valuable use of CASE is *exception avoidance* — checking for conditions that cause errors.

Consider a case that determines compensation for salespeople. Companies that compensate their salespeople by straight commission often pay their new employees by giving them a "draw" against commission. In the following example, new salespeople receive a draw against commission that's phased out gradually as their commissions rise:

```
UPDATE SALES_COMP
   SET COMP = COMMISSION + CASE
                           WHEN COMMISSION <> 0
                               THEN DRAW/COMMISSION
                           WHEN COMMISSION = 0
                               THEN DRAW
                   END ;
```

If the salesperson's commission is zero, the structure in this example avoids a division by zero operation, which causes an error. If the salesperson has a nonzero commission, total compensation is the commission plus a draw that is reduced proportionately to the size of the commission.

All of the THEN expressions in a CASE expression must be of the same type — all numeric, all character, or all date. The result of the CASE expression is also of the same type.

Using CASE with values

You can use a more compact form of the CASE expression if you're comparing a test value for equality with a series of other values. This form is useful within a SELECT or UPDATE statement if a table contains a limited number of values in a column and you want to associate a corresponding result value to each of those column values. If you use CASE in this way, the expression has the following syntax:

```
CASE valuet
    WHEN value1 THEN result1
    WHEN value2 THEN result2
    ...
    WHEN valuen THEN resultn
    ELSE resultx
END
```

If the test value (*valuet*) is equal to *value1*, the expression takes on the value *result1*. If *valuet* isn't equal to *value1* but is equal to *value2*, the expression takes on the value *result2*. The expression tries each comparison value in turn, all the way down to *valuen*, until it achieves a match. If none of the comparison values equals the test value, the expression takes on the value *resultx*. Again, if the optional ELSE clause isn't present and none of the comparison values match the test value, the expression receives a null value.

To understand how the value form works, consider a case in which you have a table containing the names and ranks of various military officers. You want to list the names preceded by the correct abbreviation for each rank. The following statement does the job:

```
SELECT CASE RANK
        WHEN 'general'            THEN 'Gen.'
        WHEN 'colonel'            THEN 'Col.'
        WHEN 'lieutenant colonel' THEN 'Lt. Col.'
        WHEN 'major'              THEN 'Maj.'
        WHEN 'captain'            THEN 'Capt.'
        WHEN 'first lieutenant'   THEN '1st. Lt.'
        WHEN 'second lieutenant'  THEN '2nd. Lt.'
        ELSE 'Mr.'
    END,
        LAST_NAME
    FROM OFFICERS ;
```

The result is a list similar to the following example:

```
Capt.  Midnight
Col.   Sanders
Gen.   Schwarzkopf
Maj.   Disaster
Mr.    Nimitz
```

Chester Nimitz was an admiral in the United States Navy during World War II. Because his rank isn't one of those listed in the CASE expression, the ELSE clause determines his title.

For another example, suppose that Captain Midnight gets a promotion to major and you want to update the OFFICERS database accordingly. Assume that the variable *officer_last_name* contains the value 'Midnight' and that the variable *new_rank* contains an integer (4) that corresponds to Midnight's new rank, according to the following table.

new_rank	Rank
1	general
2	colonel
3	lieutenant colonel
4	major
5	captain
6	first lieutenant
7	second lieutenant
8	Mr.

You can record the promotion by using the following SQL code:

```
UPDATE OFFICERS
   SET RANK = CASE :new_rank
                 WHEN 1 THEN 'general'
                 WHEN 2 THEN 'colonel'
                 WHEN 3 THEN 'lieutenant colonel'
                 WHEN 4 THEN 'major'
                 WHEN 5 THEN 'captain'
                 WHEN 6 THEN 'first lieutenant'
                 WHEN 7 THEN 'second lieutenant'
                 WHEN 8 THEN 'Mr.'
              END
   WHERE LAST_NAME = :officer_last_name ;
```

An alternative syntax for the CASE with values is as follows:

```
CASE
    WHEN valuet = value1 THEN result1
    WHEN valuet = value2 THEN result2
    ...
    WHEN valuet = valuen THEN resultn
    ELSE resultx
END
```

A special CASE — NULLIF

The one thing you can be sure of in this world is change. Sometimes things change from one known state to another. Other times, you think that you know something but later you find out that you didn't know it after all. Classical thermodynamics, as well as modern chaos theory, tells us that systems naturally migrate from a well-known, ordered state into a disordered state that no one can predict. Anyone who has ever monitored the status of a teenager's room for a one-week period after the room is cleaned can vouch for the accuracy of these theories.

Database tables have definite values in fields containing known contents. Usually, if the value of a field is unknown, the field contains the null value. In SQL, you can use a CASE expression to change the contents of a table field from a definite value to a null. The null indicates that you no longer know the value of the field. Consider the following example.

Imagine that you own a small airline that offers flights between Southern California and Washington State. Until recently, some of your flights stopped at San Jose International Airport to refuel before continuing on. Unfortunately, you just lost your right to fly into San Jose. From now on, you must make your refueling stop at either San Francisco International or Oakland International. At this point, you don't yet know which flights stop at which airport, but you definitely know that none of the flights are stopping at San Jose. You have a FLIGHT database that contains important information about each of your routes, and now you want to update the database to remove all references to San Jose. The following example shows one way to do this:

```
UPDATE FLIGHT
    SET REFUEL_STOP = CASE
                        WHEN REFUEL_STOP = 'San Jose'
                            THEN NULL
                        ELSE REFUEL_STOP
                      END ;
```

Because occasions like this one frequently arise in which you want to replace a known value with a null, SQL:1999 offers a shorthand notation to accomplish this task. The preceding example, expressed in this shorthand form, appears as follows:

```
UPDATE FLIGHT
    SET REFUEL_STOP = NULLIF(REFUEL_STOP, 'San Jose') ;
```

You can read this expression as, "Update the FLIGHT database by setting column REFUEL_STOP to null if the existing value of REFUEL_STOP is 'San Jose'. Otherwise, make no change."

NULLIF comes in even handier if you're converting data that you originally accumulated for use with a program written in a standard programming language such as COBOL or Fortran. Standard programming languages don't have nulls, so a common practice is to represent the "not known" or "not applicable" concept by using special values. A numeric -1 may represent a "not known" value for SALARY, for example, and a character string "***" may represent a "not known" or "not applicable" value for JOBCODE. If you want to represent these "not known" and "not applicable" states in an SQL-compatible database by using nulls, you need to convert the special values to nulls. The following example makes this conversion for an employee table, in which some salary values are unknown:

```
UPDATE EMP
    SET SALARY = CASE SALARY
                      WHEN -1 THEN NULL
                      ELSE SALARY
                 END ;
```

You can perform this conversion more conveniently by using NULLIF, as follows:

```
UPDATE EMP
    SET SALARY = NULLIF(SALARY, -1) ;
```

Another special CASE — COALESCE

COALESCE, like NULLIF, is a shorthand form of a particular CASE expression. COALESCE deals with a list of values that may or may not be null. If one of the values in the list is nonnull, the COALESCE expression takes on that value. If more than one value in the list is nonnull, the expression takes on the value of the first nonnull item in the list. If all the values in the list are null, the expression takes on the null value.

A CASE expression with this function has the following form:

```
CASE
    WHEN value1 IS NOT NULL
        THEN value1
    WHEN value2 IS NOT NULL
        THEN value2
    ...
    WHEN valuen IS NOT NULL
        THEN valuen
    ELSE NULL
END
```

The corresponding COALESCE shorthand appears as follows:

```
COALESCE(value1, value2, ..., valuen)
```

You may want to use a COALESCE expression after you perform an OUTER JOIN operation (discussed in Chapter 10). In such cases, COALESCE can save you a lot of typing.

CAST Data-Type Conversions

Chapter 2 covers the different data types that SQL recognizes and supports. Ideally, each column in a database table has a perfect choice of data type. In this non-ideal world, however, exactly what that perfect choice may be isn't always clear. In defining a database table, suppose you assign a data type to a column that works perfectly for your current application. Later, however, you might want to expand the scope of your application or write an entirely new application that makes a different use of the data. This new use could require a data type different from the one you originally chose.

You may want to compare a column of one type in one table with a column of a different type in a different table. You could, for example, have dates stored as character data in one table and as date data in another table. Even if both columns contain the same things (dates, for example) the fact that the types are different may prevent you from making the comparison. In SQL-86 and SQL-89, type incompatibility posed a big problem. SQL-92, however, introduced an easy-to-use solution in the CAST expression.

The CAST expression converts table data or host variables of one type to another type. After you make the conversion, you can proceed with the operation or analysis that you originally envisioned.

Naturally, you face some restrictions when using the CAST expression. You can't just indiscriminately convert data of any type into any other type. The data that you're converting must be compatible with the new data type. You can, for example, use CAST to convert the CHAR(10) character string '1998-04-26' to the DATE type. You can't, however, use CAST to convert the CHAR(10) character string 'rhinoceros' to the DATE type. You can't convert an INTEGER to the SMALLINT type if the former exceeds the maximum size of a SMALLINT.

You can convert an item of any of the character types to any other type (such as numeric or date) provided that the value of the item has the form of a literal of the new type. Conversely, you can convert an item of any type to any of the character types, provided that the value of the item has the form of a literal of the original type.

The following list describes some additional possible conversions you can make:

- ✔ *Any bit string to a character string.* The bits function like the bits that make up characters.

- ✔ *Any numeric type to any other numeric type.* If converting to a type of less fractional precision, the system rounds or truncates the result.

- ✔ *Any exact numeric type to a single component interval,* such as INTERVAL DAY or INTERVAL SECOND.

- ✔ *Any* DATE *to a* TIMESTAMP. The time part of the TIMESTAMP fills in with zeros.

- ✔ *Any* TIME *to a* TIME *with a different fractional-seconds precision or a* TIMESTAMP. The date part of the TIMESTAMP fills in with the current date.

- ✔ *Any* TIMESTAMP *to either a* DATE, *a* TIME, *or a* TIMESTAMP *with a different fractional-seconds precision.*

- ✔ *Any year-month* INTERVAL *to an exact numeric type or another year-month* INTERVAL *with different leading-field precision.*

- ✔ *Any day-time* INTERVAL *to an exact numeric type or another day-time* INTERVAL *with different leading-field precision.*

Using CAST within SQL

Suppose that you work for a sales company that keeps track of prospective employees as well as employees whom you've actually hired. You list the prospective employees in a table named PROSPECT, and you distinguish each one by their Social Security number, which you store as a CHAR(9) type. You list the employees in a table named EMPLOYEE, and you distinguish them by their Social Security number, which is of INTEGER type. You now want to generate a list of all people who appear in both tables. You can use CAST to perform the task, as follows:

```
SELECT * FROM EMPLOYEE
    WHERE EMPLOYEE.SSN =
        CAST(PROSPECT.SSN AS INTEGER) ;
```

Using CAST between SQL and the host language

The key use of CAST is to deal with data types that are in SQL, but not in the host language that you use. The following list offers some examples of these data types:

- ✔ SQL has DECIMAL and NUMERIC, but Fortran and Pascal don't.
- ✔ SQL has FLOAT and REAL, but standard COBOL doesn't.
- ✔ SQL has DATETIME, which no other language has.

Suppose that you want to use Fortran or Pascal to access tables with DECIMAL(5,3) columns, and you don't want the inaccuracies that result from converting those values to the REAL data type of Fortran and Pascal. You can perform this task by CASTing the data to and from character-string host variables. You retrieve a numeric salary of 198.37 as a CHAR(10) value of '0000198.37'. Then if you want to update that salary to 203.74, you can place that value in a CHAR(10) as '0000203.74'. First, you use CAST to change the SQL DECIMAL (5,3) data type to the CHAR (10) type for the specific employee whose ID number you're storing in the host variable :emp_id_var, as follows:

```
SELECT CAST(SALARY AS CHAR(10)) INTO :salary_var
        FROM EMP
        WHERE EMPID = :emp_id_var ;
```

Then the application examines the resulting character string value in :salary_var, possibly sets the string to a new value of '000203.74', and then updates the database by using the following SQL code:

```
UPDATE EMP
    SET SALARY = CAST(:salary_var AS DECIMAL(5,3))
        WHERE EMPID = :emp_id_var ;
```

Dealing with character-string values like '000198.37' is awkward in Fortran or Pascal, but you can write a set of subroutines to do the necessary manipulations. You can then retrieve and update any SQL data from any host language and get and set exact values.

The general idea is that CAST is most valuable for converting between host types and the database rather than for converting within the database.

Row Value Expressions

In SQL-86 and SQL-89, most operations deal with a single value or a single column in a table row. To operate on multiple values, you must build complex expressions by using logical connectives (which I discuss in Chapter 9).

SQL-92 introduced *row value expressions,* which operate on a list of values or columns rather than a single value or column. A row value expression is a list of value expressions that you enclose in parentheses and separate by commas. You can operate on an entire row at once or on a selected subset of the row.

Chapter 6 covers how to use the INSERT statement to add a new row to an existing table. To do so, the statement uses a row value expression. Consider the following example:

```
INSERT INTO FOODS
    (FOODNAME, CALORIES, PROTEIN, FAT, CARBOHYDRATE)
    VALUES
    ('Cheese, cheddar', 398, 25, 32.2, 2.1) ;
```

In this example, ('Cheese, cheddar', 398, 25, 32.2, 2.1) is a row value expression. If you use a row value expression in an INSERT statement this way, it can contain null and default values. (A *default value* is the value that a table column assumes if you specify no other value.) The following line, for example, is a legal row value expression:

```
('Cheese, cheddar', 398, NULL, 32.2, DEFAULT)
```

You can add multiple rows to a table by putting multiple row value expressions in the VALUES clause, as follows:

```
INSERT INTO FOODS
    (FOODNAME, CALORIES, PROTEIN, FAT, CARBOHYDRATE)
    VALUES
    ('Lettuce', 14, 1.2, 0.2, 2.5),
    ('Margarine', 720, 0.6, 81.0, 0.4),
    ('Mustard', 75, 4.7, 4.4, 6.4),
    ('Spaghetti', 148, 5.0, 0.5, 30.1) ;
```

You can use row value expressions to save typing in comparisons. Suppose you have two tables of nutritional values, one compiled in English and the other in Spanish. You want to find those rows in the English language table which correspond exactly to the rows in the Spanish language table. Without a row value expression, you may need to formulate something like the following example:

```
SELECT * FROM FOODS
   WHERE FOODS.CALORIES = COMIDA.CALORIA
      AND FOODS.PROTEIN = COMIDA.PROTEINA
      AND FOODS.FAT = COMIDA.GORDO
      AND FOODS.CARBOHYDRATE = COMIDA.CARBOHIDRATO ;
```

Row value expressions enable you to code the same logic as follows:

```
SELECT * FROM FOODS
   WHERE (FOODS.CALORIES, FOODS.PROTEIN, FOODS.FAT,
         FOODS.CARBOHYDRATE)
      =
         (COMIDA.CALORIA, COMIDA.PROTEINA, COMIDA.GORDO,
         COMIDA.CARBOHIDRATO) ;
```

In this example, you don't save much typing. You would benefit slightly more if you were comparing more columns. In cases of marginal benefit like this example, you may be better off sticking with the older syntax because its meaning is clearer.

You gain one benefit by using a row value expression instead of its coded equivalent — the row value expression is much faster. In principle, a very clever implementation can analyze the coded version and implement it as the row value version, but in practice, this operation is a difficult optimization that no DBMS currently on the market can perform.

Chapter 9

Zeroing in on the Data You Want

A database management system has two main functions: storing data and providing easy access to that data. Storing data is nothing special; a file cabinet can perform that chore. The hard part of data management is providing easy access. For data to be useful, you must be able to separate the (usually) small amount you do want from the huge amount you don't want.

SQL enables you to use some characteristic of the data itself to determine whether or not a particular table row is of interest to you. The SELECT, DELETE, and UPDATE statements convey to the database *engine* (that part of the DBMS that actually interacts with the data) which rows to select, delete, or update. Modifying clauses are added to the SELECT, DELETE, and UPDATE statements to refine the search to your specifications.

Modifying Clauses

The modifying clauses available in SQL are FROM, WHERE, HAVING, GROUP BY, and ORDER BY. The FROM clause tells the database engine which table or tables to operate on. The WHERE and HAVING clauses specify a characteristic of the data that determines whether or not to include a particular row in the current operation. The GROUP BY and ORDER BY clauses specify how to display the retrieved rows. Table 9-1 provides a summary.

Table 9-1	Modifying Clauses and Functions
Modifying Clause	*Function*
FROM	Specifies from which tables to take data.
WHERE	Filters out rows that don't satisfy the search condition.
GROUP BY	Separates rows into groups based on the values in the grouping columns.
HAVING	Filters out groups that don't satisfy the search condition.
ORDER BY	Sorts the results of prior clauses to produce final output.

If you use more than one of these clauses, then they must appear in the following order:

```
SELECT column_list
    FROM table_list
    [WHERE search_condition]
    [GROUP BY grouping_column]
    [HAVING search_condition]
    [ORDER BY ordering_condition] ;
```

The WHERE clause is a filter that passes rows that meet the search condition and rejects those that don't meet the condition. The GROUP BY clause rearranges the rows that the WHERE clause passes according to the value of the grouping column. The HAVING clause is another filter that takes each group that the GROUP BY clause forms and passes those groups that meet the search condition, rejecting the rest. The ORDER BY clause sorts whatever remains after all the preceding clauses process the table. As the square brackets ([ ]) indicate, the WHERE, GROUP BY, HAVING, and ORDER BY clauses are optional.

SQL evaluates these clauses in the order FROM, WHERE, GROUP BY, HAVING, and finally SELECT, with the clauses operating in a "pipeline" manner, in which each clause receives the result of the prior clause and produces an output for the next clause. In functional notation, this order of evaluation appears as follows:

```
SELECT(HAVING(GROUP BY(WHERE(FROM...))))
```

ORDER BY operates after SELECT, which explains why ORDER BY can only reference columns in the SELECT list. ORDER BY can't reference other columns in the FROM table(s).

FROM Clauses

The FROM clause is easy to understand if you specify only one table, as in the following example:

```
SELECT * FROM SALES ;
```

This statement returns all the data in all the rows of every column in the SALES table. You can, however, specify more than one table in a FROM clause. Consider the following example:

```
SELECT *
   FROM CUSTOMER, SALES ;
```

This statement forms a virtual table that combines the data from the CUSTOMER table with the data from the SALES table. Each row in the CUSTOMER table combines with every row in the SALES table to form the new table. The new virtual table that this combination forms, therefore, contains the number of rows in the CUSTOMER table multiplied by the number of rows in the SALES table. If the CUSTOMER table has ten rows and the SALES table has one hundred, then the new virtual table has a thousand rows.

This operation is called the *Cartesian product* of the two source tables. The Cartesian product is actually a type of JOIN. I cover JOIN operations in detail in Chapter 10.

In most applications, the majority of the rows that form as a result of taking the Cartesian product of two tables are meaningless. In the case of the virtual table that forms from the CUSTOMER and SALES tables, only the rows where the CUSTOMER_ID from the CUSTOMER table matches the CUSTOMER_ID from the SALES table are of interest. You can filter out the rest of the rows by using a WHERE clause.

WHERE Clauses

I use the WHERE clause many times throughout this book without really explaining it because its meaning and use are obvious: A statement performs an operation (such as a SELECT, DELETE, or UPDATE) only on table rows WHERE a stated condition is True. The syntax of the WHERE clause is as follows:

```
SELECT column_list
   FROM table_name
   WHERE condition ;

DELETE FROM table_name
   WHERE condition ;
```

```
UPDATE table_name
    SET column1=value1, column2=value2, ..., columnn=valuen
    WHERE condition ;
```

In all cases, the condition in the WHERE clause may be simple or arbitrarily complex. You may join multiple conditions together by using the logical connectives AND, OR, and NOT (which I discuss later in this chapter) to create a single condition.

The following statements show you some typical examples of WHERE clauses:

```
WHERE CUSTOMER.CUSTOMER_ID = SALES.CUSTOMER_ID
WHERE FOODS.CALORIES = COMIDA.CALORIA
WHERE FOODS.CALORIES < 219
WHERE FOODS.CALORIES > 3 * base_value
WHERE FOODS.CALORIES < 219 AND FOODS.PROTEIN > 27.4
```

The conditions that these WHERE clauses express are known as predicates. A *predicate* is an expression that asserts a fact about values.

The predicate FOODS.CALORIES < 219, for example, is True if the value for the current row of the column FOODS.CALORIES is less than 219. If the assertion is True, it satisfies the condition. An assertion may be True, False, or unknown. The unknown case arises if one or more elements in the assertion are null. The *comparison predicates* (=, <, >, <>, <=, and >=) are the most common, but SQL offers a number of others that greatly increase your capability to distinguish, or "filter out," a desired data item from others in the same column. The following list notes the predicates that give you that filtering capability:

- Comparison Predicates
- BETWEEN
- IN [NOT IN]
- LIKE [NOT LIKE]
- NULL
- ALL, SOME, ANY
- EXISTS
- UNIQUE
- OVERLAPS
- MATCH
- SIMILAR
- DISTINCT

Comparison predicates

The examples in the preceding section show typical uses of comparison predicates in which you compare one value to another. For every row in which the comparison evaluates to a True value, that value satisfies the WHERE clause and the operation (SELECT, UPDATE, DELETE, or whatever) executes upon that row. Rows that the comparison evaluates to FALSE are skipped. Consider, for example, the following SQL statement:

```
SELECT * FROM FOODS
   WHERE CALORIES < 219 ;
```

This statement displays all rows from the FOODS table that have a value of less than 219 in the CALORIES column.

Six comparison predicates are listed in Table 9-2.

Table 9-2	SQL's Comparison Predicates
Comparison	*Symbol*
Equal	=
Not equal	<>
Less than	<
Less than or equal	<=
Greater than	>
Greater than or equal	>=

BETWEEN

Sometimes, you want to select a row if the value in a column falls within a specified range. One way to make this selection is by using comparison predicates. You can, for example, formulate a WHERE clause to select all the rows in the FOODS table that have a value in the CALORIES column greater than 100 and less than 300, as follows:

```
WHERE FOODS.CALORIES > 100 AND FOODS.CALORIES < 300
```

This comparison doesn't include foods with a calorie count of exactly 100 or 300 — only those values that fall in between these two numbers. To include the end points, you can write the statement as follows:

```
WHERE FOODS.CALORIES >= 100 AND FOODS.CALORIES <= 300
```

Another way of specifying a range that includes the end points is to use a BETWEEN predicate in the following manner:

```
WHERE FOODS.CALORIES BETWEEN 100 AND 300
```

This clause is functionally identical to the preceding example, which uses comparison predicates. As you can see, this formulation saves some typing and is also a little more intuitive than the one that uses two comparison predicates joined by the logical connective AND.

The BETWEEN keyword may be confusing because it doesn't tell you explicitly whether the clause includes the end points. In fact, the clause does include these end points. BETWEEN also fails to tell you explicitly that the first term in the comparison must be equal to or less than the second. If, for example, FOODS.CALORIES contains a value of 200, the following clause returns a True value:

```
WHERE FOODS.CALORIES BETWEEN 100 AND 300
```

However, a clause that you may think is equivalent to the preceding example returns the opposite result, False:

```
WHERE FOODS.CALORIES BETWEEN 300 AND 100
```

If you use BETWEEN, you must be able to guarantee that the first term in your comparison is always equal to or less than the second term.

You can use the BETWEEN predicate with character, bit, and datetime data types as well as with the numeric types. You may see something like the following example:

```
SELECT FIRST_NAME, LAST_NAME
    FROM CUSTOMER
    WHERE CUSTOMER.LAST_NAME BETWEEN 'A' AND 'Mzzz' ;
```

This example returns all customers whose last name is in the first half of the alphabet.

IN and NOT IN

The IN and NOT IN predicates deal with whether specified values, such as OR, WA, and ID, are contained within a particular set of values, such as the states of the United States. You may, for example, have a table that lists suppliers of a commodity that your company purchases on a regular basis. You want to know the phone numbers of those suppliers located in the Pacific

Northwest. You can find these numbers by using comparison predicates, such as those shown in the following example:

```
SELECT company, phone
    FROM SUPPLIER
    WHERE state = 'OR' OR state = 'WA' OR state = 'ID' ;
```

You can, however, also use the IN predicate to perform the same task, as follows:

```
SELECT company, phone
    FROM SUPPLIER
    WHERE state IN ('OR', 'WA', 'ID') ;
```

This formulation is a little more compact than the one using comparison predicates and logical OR.

The NOT IN version of this predicate works the same way. Say that you have locations in California, Arizona, and New Mexico, and to avoid paying sales tax, you want to consider using suppliers located anywhere except in those states. Use the following construction:

```
SELECT company, phone
    FROM SUPPLIER
    WHERE state NOT IN ('CA', 'AZ', 'NM') ;
```

Using the IN keyword this way saves you a little typing. Saving a little typing, however, isn't that great of an advantage. You can do the same job by using comparison predicates as shown in the first example of this section.

You may have another good reason to use the IN predicate rather than comparison predicates, even if using IN doesn't save much typing. Your DBMS probably implements the two methods differently, and one of the methods may be significantly faster than the other on your system. You may want to run a performance comparison on the two ways of expressing inclusion in (or exclusion from) a group and then use the technique that produces the quicker result. A DBMS with a good optimizer will probably choose the more efficient method, regardless of which kind of predicate you use. A performance comparison will give you some idea of how good your DBMS's optimizer is. If a significant difference between the run times of the two statements exists, then the quality of your DBMS's optimizer is called into question.

The IN keyword is valuable in another area, too. If IN is part of a subquery, the keyword enables you to pull information from two tables to obtain results that you can't derive from a single table. I cover subqueries in Chapter 11, but following is an example that shows how a subquery uses the IN keyword.

Suppose that you want to display the names of all customers who've bought the F-117A product in the last 30 days. Customer names are in the CUSTOMER table and sales transaction data is in the TRANSACT table. You can use the following query:

```
SELECT FIRST_NAME, LAST_NAME
   FROM CUSTOMER
   WHERE CUSTOMER_ID IN
     (SELECT CUSTOMER_ID
        FROM TRANSACT
        WHERE PRODUCT_ID = 'F-117A'
        AND TRANS_DATE >= (CURRENT_DATE - 30)) ;
```

The inner SELECT of the TRANSACT table nests within the outer SELECT of the CUSTOMER table. The inner SELECT finds the CUSTOMER_ID numbers of all customers who bought the F-117A product in the last 30 days. The outer SELECT displays the first and last names of all customers whose CUSTOMER_ID is retrieved by the inner SELECT.

LIKE and NOT LIKE

You can use the LIKE predicate to compare two character strings for a partial match. Partial matches are valuable if you have some idea of the string for which you're searching but don't know its exact form. You can also use partial matches to retrieve multiple rows that contain similar strings in one of the table's columns.

To identify partial matches, SQL makes use of two wildcard characters. The percent sign (%) can stand for any string of characters that have zero or more characters. The underscore (_) stands for any single character. Table 9-3 provides some examples that show how to use LIKE.

Table 9-3	SQL's LIKE Predicate
Statement	*Values Returned*
WHERE WORD LIKE 'intern%'	intern internal international internet interns
WHERE WORD LIKE '%Peace%'	Justice of the Peace Peaceful Warrior
WHERE WORD LIKE 't_p_'	tape taps tipi tips tops type

The NOT LIKE predicate retrieves all rows that don't satisfy a partial match, including one or more wildcard characters, as in the following example:

```
WHERE PHONE NOT LIKE '503%'
```

This example returns all the rows in the table for which the phone number starts with something other than 503.

You may want to search for a string that includes a percent sign or an underscore. In this case, you want SQL to interpret the percent sign *as* a percent sign and not as a wildcard character. You can conduct such a search by typing an escape character just prior to the character you want SQL to take literally. You can choose any character as the escape character, as long as that character doesn't appear in the string that you're testing, as shown in the following example:

```
SELECT QUOTE
   FROM BARTLETTS
   WHERE QUOTE LIKE '20#%'
      ESCAPE '#' ;
```

The % character is escaped by the preceding # sign, so the statement actually interprets this symbol as a percent sign rather than as a wildcard. You can escape an underscore or the escape character itself, in the same way. The preceding query, for example, would find the following quotation in *Bartlett's Familiar Quotations:*

```
20% of the salespeople produce 80% of the results
```

The query would also find the following:

```
20%
```

SIMILAR

SQL:1999 adds the SIMILAR predicate, which offers a more powerful way of finding partial matches than the LIKE predicate provides. With the SIMILAR predicate, you can compare a character string to a regular expression. For example, say you're searching the OPERATING_SYSTEM column of a software compatibility table to look for Microsoft Windows compatibility. You could construct a WHERE clause such as the following:

```
WHERE OPERATING_SYSTEM SIMILAR TO
'('Windows '(3.1|95|98|'Millenium Edition'|CE|NT|2000))'
```

This predicate retrieves all rows that contain any of the specified Microsoft operating systems.

NULL

The NULL predicate finds all rows where the value in the selected column is null. In the FOODS table in Chapter 7, several rows have null values in the CARBOHYDRATE column. You can retrieve their names by using a statement such as the following:

```
SELECT (FOOD)
   FROM FOODS
   WHERE CARBOHYDRATE IS NULL ;
```

This query returns the following values:

```
Beef, lean hamburger
Chicken, light meat
Opossum, roasted
Pork, ham
```

As you may expect, including the NOT keyword reverses the result, as in the following example:

```
SELECT (FOOD)
   FROM FOODS
   WHERE CARBOHYDRATE IS NOT NULL ;
```

This query returns all the rows in the table except the four that the preceding query returns.

The statement CARBOHYDRATE IS NULL is not the same as CARBOHYDRATE = NULL. To illustrate this point, assume that, in the current row of the FOODS table, both CARBOHYDRATE and PROTEIN are null. From this fact, you can draw the following conclusions:

- CARBOHYDRATE IS NULL is True.
- PROTEIN IS NULL is True.
- CARBOHYDRATE IS NULL AND PROTEIN IS NULL is True.
- CARBOHYDRATE = PROTEIN is unknown.
- CARBOHYDRATE = NULL is an illegal expression.

Using the keyword NULL in a comparison is meaningless, because the answer always returns as "unknown."

Why is CARBOHYDRATE = PROTEIN defined as unknown, even though CARBO-HYDRATE and PROTEIN have the same (null) value? Because NULL simply means "I don't know." You don't know what CARBOHYDRATE is, and you don't know what PROTEIN is; therefore, you don't know whether those (unknown) values are the same. Maybe CARBOHYDRATE is 37 and PROTEIN is 14, or maybe

CARBOHYDRATE is 93 and PROTEIN is 93. If you don't know either the carbohydrate value or the protein value, you can't say whether or not the two are the same.

ALL, SOME, ANY

Thousands of years ago, the Greek philosopher Aristotle formulated a system of logic that became the basis for much of Western thought. The essence of this logic is to start with a set of premises that you know to be true, apply valid operations to these premises, and, thereby, arrive at new truths. An example of this procedure is as follows:

> *Premise 1:* All Greeks are human.
>
> *Premise 2:* All humans are mortal.
>
> *Conclusion:* All Greeks are mortal.

Another example:

> *Premise 1:* Some Greeks are women.
>
> *Premise 2:* All women are human.
>
> *Conclusion:* Some Greeks are human.

Another way of stating the same logical idea of this second example is as follows:

> If any Greeks are women and all women are human, then some Greeks are human.

The first example uses the universal quantifier ALL in both premises, enabling you to make a sound deduction about all Greeks in the conclusion. The second example uses the existential quantifier SOME in one premise, enabling you to make a deduction about some Greeks in the conclusion. The third example uses the existential quantifier ANY, which is a synonym for SOME, to reach the same conclusion you reach in the second example.

Look at how SOME, ANY, and ALL apply in SQL.

Consider an example in baseball statistics. Baseball is a physically demanding sport, especially for pitchers. A pitcher must throw the baseball from the pitcher's mound to home plate between 90 and 150 times in the course of a game. This effort can be very tiring, and many times, the pitcher becomes ineffective and a relief pitcher must replace him before the game ends. Pitching an entire game is an outstanding achievement, regardless of whether the effort results in a victory.

ANY can be ambiguous

The original SQL used the word ANY for exis-tential quantification. This usage turned out to be confusing and error-prone, because the English language connotations of *any* are some-times universal and sometimes existential:

✔ "Do any of you know where Baker Street is?"

✔ "I can eat more eggs than any of you."

The first sentence is probably asking whether at least one person knows where Baker Street is.

Any is used as an existential quantifier. The second sentence, however, is a boast that's stating that I can eat more eggs than the biggest eater among all you people can eat. In this case, *any* is used as a universal quantifier.

Thus, for the SQL-92 standard, the developers retained the word ANY for compatibility with early products but added the word SOME as a less confusing synonym. SQL:1999 continues to support both existential quantifiers.

Suppose that you're keeping track of the number of complete games that all major-league pitchers pitch. In one table, you list all the American League pitchers, and in another table, you list all the National League pitchers. Both tables contain the players' first names, last names, and number of complete games pitched.

The American League permits a designated hitter (DH) (who isn't required to play a defensive position) to bat in place of any of the nine players who play defense. Usually the DH bats for the pitcher, because pitchers are notoriously poor hitters. They must spend so much time and effort on perfecting their pitching that they do not have as much time to practice batting as the other players do.

Say that you have a theory that, on average, American League starting pitch-ers throw more complete games than do National League starting pitchers. This is based on your observation that designated hitters enable hard-throw-ing but weak-hitting American League pitchers to stay in close games. Since the DH is already batting for them, the fact that they are poor hitters is not a liability. In the National League, however, a pinch hitter would replace a com-parable National League pitcher in a close game, because he would have a better chance at getting a hit. To test your theory, you formulate the follow-ing query:

```
SELECT FIRST_NAME, LAST_NAME
    FROM AMERICAN_LEAGUER
    WHERE COMPLETE_GAMES > ALL
        (SELECT COMPLETE_GAMES
            FROM NATIONAL_LEAGUER) ;
```

The subquery (the inner SELECT) returns a list, showing for every National League pitcher, the number of complete games he pitched. The outer query returns the first and last names of all American Leaguers who pitched more complete games than ALL of the National Leaguers. The query returns the names of those American League pitchers who pitched more complete games than the pitcher who has thrown the most complete games in the National League.

Consider the following similar statement:

```
SELECT FIRST_NAME, LAST_NAME
   FROM AMERICAN_LEAGUER
   WHERE COMPLETE_GAMES > ANY
      (SELECT COMPLETE_GAMES
         FROM NATIONAL_LEAGUER) ;
```

In this case, you use the existential quantifier ANY instead of the universal quantifier ALL. The subquery (the inner, nested query) is identical to the sub-query in the previous example. This subquery retrieves a complete list of the complete game statistics for all the National League pitchers. The outer query returns the first and last names of all American League pitchers who pitched more complete games than ANY National League pitcher. Because you can be virtually certain that at least one National League pitcher hasn't pitched a complete game, the result probably includes all American League pitchers who've pitched at least one complete game.

If you replace the keyword ANY with the equivalent keyword SOME, the result is the same. If the statement that at least one National League pitcher hasn't pitched a complete game is a true statement, you can then say that SOME National League pitcher hasn't pitched a complete game.

EXISTS

You can use the EXISTS predicate in conjunction with a subquery to deter-mine whether the subquery returns any rows at all. If the subquery returns at least one row, that result satisfies the EXISTS condition, and the outer query executes. Consider the following example:

```
SELECT FIRST_NAME, LAST_NAME
   FROM CUSTOMER
   WHERE EXISTS
      (SELECT DISTINCT CUSTOMER_ID
         FROM SALES
         WHERE SALES.CUSTOMER_ID = CUSTOMER.CUSTOMER_ID);
```

The SALES table contains a record of all of a company's sales. The table includes the CUSTOMER_ID of the customer who makes each purchase, as well as other pertinent information. The CUSTOMER table contains each cus-tomer's first and last names, but no information about specific transactions.

The subquery in the preceding example returns a row for every customer who has made at least one purchase. The outer query returns the first and last names of the customers who made the purchases that the SALES table records.

EXISTS is equivalent to a comparison of COUNT with zero, as the following query shows:

```
SELECT FIRST_NAME, LAST_NAME
    FROM CUSTOMER
    WHERE 0 <>
      (SELECT COUNT(*)
        FROM SALES
        WHERE SALES.CUSTOMER_ID = CUSTOMER.CUSTOMER_ID);
```

For every row in the SALES table that contains a CUSTOMER_ID that's equal to a CUSTOMER_ID in the CUSTOMER table, this statement displays the FIRST_NAME and LAST_NAME columns in the CUSTOMER table. For every sale in the SALES table, therefore, the statement displays the name of the customer who made the purchase.

UNIQUE

As you do with the EXISTS predicate, you use the UNIQUE predicate with a subquery. Although the EXISTS predicate evaluates to True only if the subquery returns at least one row, the UNIQUE predicate evaluates to True only if no two rows that the subquery returns are identical. In other words, the UNIQUE predicate evaluates to True only if all rows that its subquery returns are unique. Consider the following example:

```
SELECT FIRST_NAME, LAST_NAME
    FROM CUSTOMER
    WHERE UNIQUE
      (SELECT CUSTOMER_ID FROM SALES
        WHERE SALES.CUSTOMER_ID = CUSTOMER.CUSTOMER_ID);
```

This statement retrieves the names of all new customers for whom the SALES table records only one sale. Two null values are considered to be not equal to each other and thus unique. When the UNIQUE keyword is applied to a result table that only contains two null rows, the UNIQUE predicate evaluates to True.

DISTINCT

The DISTINCT predicate is similar to the UNIQUE predicate, except in the way it treats nulls. If all the values in a result table are UNIQUE, then they're also

DISTINCT from each other. However, unlike the result for the UNIQUE predicate, if the DISTINCT keyword is applied to a result table that contains only two null rows, then the DISTINCT predicate evaluates to False. Two null values are *not* considered distinct from each other, while at the same time they are considered to be unique. This strange situation seems contradictory, but there's a reason for it. In some situations, you may want to treat two null values as different from each other, while in other situations, you want to treat them as if they're the same. In the first case, use the UNIQUE predicate. In the second case, use the DISTINCT predicate.

OVERLAPS

You use the OVERLAPS predicate to determine whether two intervals of time overlap each other. This predicate is useful for avoiding scheduling conflicts. If the two intervals overlap, the predicate returns a True value. If they don't overlap, the predicate returns a False value.

You can specify an interval in two ways: either as a start time and an end time or as a start time and a duration. Following are a few examples:

```
(TIME '2:55:00', INTERVAL '1' HOUR)
OVERLAPS
(TIME '3:30:00', INTERVAL '2' HOUR)
```

The preceding example returns a True, because 3:30 is less than one hour after 2:55.

```
(TIME '9:00:00', TIME '9:30:00')
OVERLAPS
(TIME '9:29:00', TIME '9:31:00')
```

The preceding example returns a True, because you have one minute of overlap between the two intervals.

```
(TIME '9:00:00', TIME '10:00:00')
OVERLAPS
(TIME '10:15:00', INTERVAL '3' HOUR)
```

The preceding example returns a False, because the two intervals don't overlap.

```
(TIME '9:00:00', TIME '9:30:00')
OVERLAPS
(TIME '9:30:00', TIME '9:35:00')
```

This example returns a False, because even though the two intervals are contiguous, they don't overlap.

MATCH

In Chapter 5, I discuss referential integrity, which involves maintaining consistency in a multitable database. You can lose integrity by adding a row to a child table that doesn't have a corresponding row in the child's parent table. You can cause similar problems by deleting a row from a parent table if rows corresponding to that row exist in a child table.

Say that your business has a CUSTOMER table that keeps track of all your customers and a SALES table that records all sales transactions. You don't want to add a row to SALES until after you enter the customer making the purchase into the CUSTOMER table. You also don't want to delete a customer from the CUSTOMER table if that customer made purchases that exist in the SALES table. Before you perform an insertion or deletion, you may want to check the candidate row to make sure that inserting or deleting that row doesn't cause integrity problems. The MATCH predicate can perform such a check.

Examine the use of the MATCH predicate through an example that employs the CUSTOMER and SALES tables. CUSTOMER_ID is the primary key of the CUSTOMER table and acts as a foreign key in the SALES table. Every row in the CUSTOMER table must have a unique, nonnull CUSTOMER_ID. CUSTOMER_ID isn't unique in the SALES table, because repeat customers buy more than once. This situation is fine and does not threaten integrity, because CUSTOMER_ID is a foreign key rather than a primary key in that table.

Seemingly, CUSTOMER_ID can be null in the SALES table, because someone can walk in off the street, buy something, and walk out again before you get a chance to enter his or her name and address into the CUSTOMER table. This situation can create a row in the child table with no corresponding row in the parent table. To overcome this problem, you can create a generic customer in the CUSTOMER table and assign all such anonymous sales to that customer.

Say that a customer steps up to the cash register and claims that she bought an F-117A Stealth fighter on May 18, 1998. She now wants to return the plane because it shows up like an aircraft carrier on opponent radar screens. You can verify her claim by searching your SALES database for a match. First, you must retrieve her CUSTOMER_ID into the variable vcustid; then you can use the following syntax:

```
... WHERE (:vcustid, 'F-117A', '1998-05-18')
        MATCH
        (SELECT CUSTOMER_ID, PRODUCT_ID, SALE_DATE
            FROM SALES)
```

If a sale exists for that customer ID for that product on that date, the MATCH predicate returns a True value. Give the customer her money back. (*Note:* If any of the values in the first argument of the MATCH predicate are null, a True value always returns.)

SQL's developers added the MATCH predicate and the UNIQUE predicate for the same reason — they provide a way to explicitly perform the tests defined for the implicit referential integrity (RI) and UNIQUE constraints.

The general form of the MATCH predicate is as follows:

```
Row_value MATCH  [UNIQUE] [SIMPLE| PARTIAL | FULL ] Subquery
```

The UNIQUE, SIMPLE, PARTIAL, and FULL options relate to rules that come into play if the row value expression R has one or more columns that are null. The rules for the MATCH predicate are a copy of corresponding referential integrity rules.

Referential integrity rules

Referential integrity rules require that the values of a column or columns in one table match the values of a column or columns in another table. You refer to the columns in the first table as the *foreign key* and the columns in the second table as the *primary key* or *unique key*. You may, for example, declare the column EMP_DEPTNO in an EMPLOYEE table as a foreign key that references the DEPTNO column of a DEPT table. This matchup ensures that if you record an employee in the EMPLOYEE table as working in department 123, a row appears in the DEPT table where DEPTNO is 123.

This situation is fairly straightforward if the foreign key and primary key both consist of a single column. The two keys can, however, consist of multiple columns. The DEPTNO value, for example, may be unique only within a LOCATION; therefore, to uniquely identify a DEPT row, you must specify both a LOCATION and a DEPTNO. If, for example, both the Boston and Tampa offices have a department 123, you need to identify the departments as ('Boston', '123') and ('Tampa', '123'). In this case, the EMPLOYEE table needs two columns to identify a DEPT. Call those columns EMP_LOC and EMP_DEPTNO. If an employee works in department 123 in Boston, the EMP_LOC and EMP_DEPTNO values are 'Boston' and '123'. And the foreign key declaration in EMPLOYEE is as follows:

```
FOREIGN KEY (EMP_LOC, EMP_DEPTNO)
   REFERENCES DEPT (LOCATION, DEPTNO)
```

Drawing valid conclusions from your data is complicated immensely if the data contains nulls. Sometimes you want to treat null-containing data one way and sometimes you want to treat it another way. The UNIQUE, SIMPLE, PARTIAL, and FULL keywords specify different ways of treating data that contains nulls. If your data does not contain any null values, you can save yourself a lot of head scratching by merely skipping from here to the next section of this book, "Logical Connectives." If your data *does* contain null values, drop out of Evelyn Woods speed reading mode now and read the following paragraphs slowly and carefully. Each paragraph presents a different situation with respect to null values and tells how the MATCH predicate handles it.

If the values of EMP_LOC and EMP_DEPTNO are both nonnull or both null, the referential integrity rules are the same as for single-column keys with values that are null or nonnull. But if EMP_LOC is null and EMP_DEPTNO is nonnull — or EMP_LOC is nonnull and EMP_DEPTNO is null — you need new rules. What should the rules be if you insert or update the EMPLOYEE table with EMP_LOC and EMP_DEPTNO values of (NULL, '123') or ('Boston', NULL)? You have six main alternatives, SIMPLE, PARTIAL, and FULL, each either with or without the UNIQUE keyword. The UNIQUE keyword, if present, means that a matching row in the subquery result table must be unique in order for the predicate to evaluate to a True value. If both components of the row value expression R are null, then the MATCH predicate returns a True value regardless of the contents of the subquery result table being compared.

If neither component of the row value expression R is null, SIMPLE is specified, UNIQUE is not specified, and at least one row in the subquery result table matches R, then the MATCH predicate returns a True value. Otherwise, it returns a False value.

If neither component of the row value expression R is null, SIMPLE is specified, UNIQUE is specified, and at least one row in the subquery result table is both unique and matches R, then the MATCH predicate returns a True value. Otherwise, it returns a False value.

If any component of the row value expression R is null and SIMPLE is specified, then the MATCH predicate returns a True value.

If any component of the row value expression R is nonnull, PARTIAL is specified, UNIQUE is not specified, and the nonnull parts of at least one row in the subquery result table matches R, then the MATCH predicate returns a True value. Otherwise, it returns a False value.

If any component of the row value expression R is nonnull, PARTIAL is specified, UNIQUE is specified, and the nonnull parts of R match the nonnull parts of at least one unique row in the subquery result table, then the MATCH predicate returns a True value. Otherwise, it returns a False value.

If neither component of the row value expression R is null, FULL is specified, UNIQUE is not specified, and at least one row in the subquery result table matches R, then the MATCH predicate returns a True value. Otherwise, it returns a False value.

If neither component of the row value expression R is null, FULL is specified, UNIQUE is specified, and at least one row in the subquery result table is both unique and matches R, then the MATCH predicate returns a True value. Otherwise, it returns a False value.

Rule by committee

The SQL-89 version of the standard specified the `UNIQUE` rule as the default, before anyone proposed or debated the other alternatives. During development of the SQL-92 version of the standard, proposals appeared for the other alternatives. Some people strongly preferred the PARTIAL rules and argued that they should be the only rules. These people thought that the SQL-89 (`UNIQUE`) rules were so undesirable that they wanted those rules considered a bug and the `PARTIAL` rules specified as a correction. Other people preferred the `UNIQUE` rules and thought that the `PARTIAL` rules were obscure, error-prone, and inefficient. Still other people preferred the additional discipline of the `FULL` rules. The issue was finally settled by providing all three keywords so that the user could choose whichever approach she preferred. SQL:1999 added the `SIMPLE` rules. The proliferation of rules makes dealing with nulls anything but simple. If neither `SIMPLE`, `PARTIAL`, nor `FULL` is specified, the `SIMPLE` rules are followed.

If any component of the row value expression R is null and `FULL` is specified, then the `MATCH` predicate returns a False value.

Logical Connectives

Often, as a number of previous examples show, applying one condition in a query isn't enough to return the rows that you want from a table. In some cases, the rows must satisfy two or more conditions. In other cases, if a row satisfies any of two or more conditions, it qualifies for retrieval. On other occasions, you want to retrieve only rows that don't satisfy a specified condition. To meet these needs, SQL offers the logical connectives `AND`, `OR`, and `NOT`.

AND

If multiple conditions must all be True before you can retrieve a row, use the `AND` logical connective. Consider the following example:

```
SELECT INVOICE_NO, SALE_DATE, SALESPERSON, TOTAL_SALE
    FROM SALES
    WHERE SALE_DATE >= '1998-05-18'
        AND SALE_DATE <= '1998-05-24' ;
```

The `WHERE` clause must meet the following two conditions:

- ✔ `SALE_DATE` must be greater than or equal to May 18, 1998.
- ✔ `SALE_DATE` must be less than or equal to May 24, 1998.

Only rows that record sales occurring during the week of May 18 meet both conditions. The query returns only these rows.

Notice that the AND connective is strictly logical. This restriction can sometimes be confusing because people commonly use the word *and* with a looser meaning. Suppose, for example, that your boss says to you, "I'd like to see the sales for Ferguson and Ford." He said, "Ferguson and Ford," so you may write the following SQL query:

```
SELECT *
    FROM SALES
    WHERE SALESPERSON = 'Ferguson'
        AND SALESPERSON = 'Ford';
```

Well, don't take that answer back to your boss. The following query is more what he had in mind:

```
SELECT *
    FROM SALES
    WHERE SALESPERSON IN ('Ferguson', 'Ford') ;
```

The first query won't return anything, because none of the sales in the SALES table were made by *both* Ferguson and Ford. The second query will return the information on all sales made by either Ferguson or Ford, which is probably what the boss wanted.

OR

If any one of two or more conditions must be True to qualify a row for retrieval, use the OR logical connective, as in the following example:

```
SELECT INVOICE_NO, SALE_DATE, SALESPERSON, TOTAL_SALE
    FROM SALES
        WHERE SALESPERSON = 'Ford'
            OR TOTAL_SALE > 200 ;
```

This query retrieves all of Ford's sales, regardless of how large, as well as all sales of more than $200, regardless of who made the sales.

NOT

The NOT connective negates a condition. If the condition normally returns a True value, adding NOT causes the same condition to return a False value. If a condition normally returns a False value, adding NOT causes the condition to return a True value. Consider the following example:

```
SELECT INVOICE_NO, SALE_DATE, SALESPERSON, TOTAL_SALE
    FROM SALES
        WHERE NOT (SALESPERSON = 'Ford') ;
```

This query returns rows for all sales transactions that salespeople other than Ford completed.

When you use AND, OR, or NOT, sometimes the scope of the connective isn't clear. To be safe, use parentheses to make sure that SQL applies the connective to the predicate you want. In the preceding example, the NOT connective applies to the entire predicate (SALESPERSON = 'Ford').

GROUP BY Clauses

Sometimes, rather than retrieving individual records, you want to know something about a group of records. The GROUP BY clause is the tool you need.

Suppose you're the sales manager and you want to look at the performance of your sales force. You could do a simple SELECT such as the following:

```
SELECT INVOICE_NO, SALE_DATE, SALESPERSON, TOTAL_SALE
    FROM SALES;
```

You would receive a result similar to that shown in Figure 9-1.

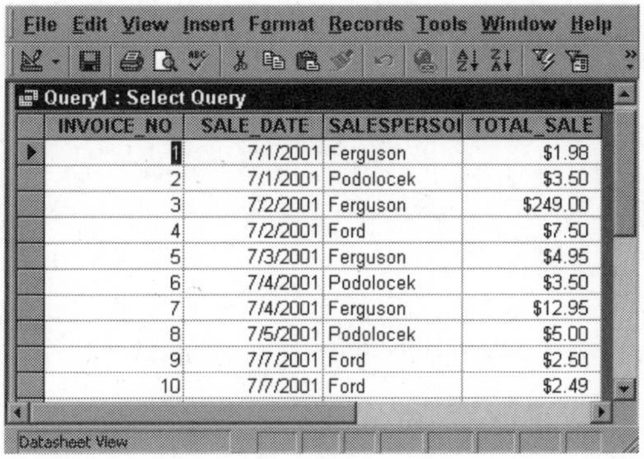

Figure 9-1:
Result set for retrieval of sales from 07/01/2001 to 07/07/2001.

File Edit View Insert Format Records Tools Window Help

Query1 : Select Query

INVOICE_NO	SALE_DATE	SALESPERSON	TOTAL_SALE
1	7/1/2001	Ferguson	$1.98
2	7/1/2001	Podolocek	$3.50
3	7/2/2001	Ferguson	$249.00
4	7/2/2001	Ford	$7.50
5	7/3/2001	Ferguson	$4.95
6	7/4/2001	Podolocek	$3.50
7	7/4/2001	Ferguson	$12.95
8	7/5/2001	Podolocek	$5.00
9	7/7/2001	Ford	$2.50
10	7/7/2001	Ford	$2.49

Datasheet View

This result gives you some idea of how well your salespeople are doing since there are so few total sales involved. However in a real company there would be many more sales and it wouldn't be as easy to tell whether sales objectives were being met. To do that you can combine the GROUP BY clause with one of the aggregate functions (also called set functions) to get a quantitative picture of sales performance. You could, for instance, see who is selling more of the profitable high-ticket items using the average (AVG) function as follows:

```
SELECT SALESPERSON, AVG(TOTAL_SALE)
    FROM SALES
    GROUP BY SALESPERSON;
```

You would receive a result similar to that shown in Figure 9-2.

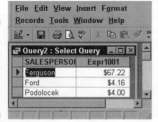

Figure 9-2:
Average
sales for
each
salesperson.

We see from the result in Figure 9-2 that Ferguson's average sale is considerably higher than that of the other two salespeople. You compare total sales with a very similar query:

```
SELECT SALESPERSON, SUM(TOTAL_SALE)
    FROM SALES
    GROUP BY SALESPERSON;
```

This gives the result shown in Figure 9-3.

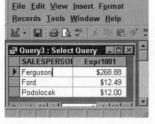

Figure 9-3:
Total sales
for each
salesperson.

Ferguson has the highest total sales also, which is consistent with having the highest average sales.

HAVING Clauses

You can analyze the grouped data further, using the HAVING Clause. The HAVING clause is a filter that acts something like a WHERE clause, but on groups of rows rather than on individual rows. To illustrate the function of the HAVING clause, suppose the sales manager considers Ferguson to be in a class by himself. His performance distorts the overall data for the other sales people. You can exclude Ferguson's sales from the grouped data using a HAVING clause as follows:

```
SELECT SALESPERSON, SUM(TOTAL_SALE)
    FROM SALES
    GROUP BY SALESPERSON
    HAVING SALESPERSON <> 'Ferguson';
```

This gives the result shown in Figure 9-4.

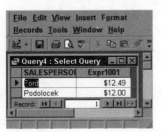

Figure 9-4:
Total sales
for all
salespeople
except
Ferguson.

Only rows where the salesperson is not Ferguson are considered.

ORDER BY Clauses

Use the ORDER BY clause to display the output table of a query in either ascending or descending alphabetical order. While the GROUP BY clause gathers rows into groups and sorts the groups into alphabetical order, ORDER BY sorts individual rows. The ORDER BY clause must be the last clause that you specify in a query. If the query also contains a GROUP BY clause, the clause first arranges the output rows into groups. The ORDER BY clause then sorts the rows within each group. If you have no GROUP BY clause, then the statement considers the entire table as a group, and the ORDER BY clause sorts all its rows according to the column (or columns) that the ORDER BY clause specifies.

To illustrate this point, consider the data in the SALES table. The SALES table contains columns for INVOICE_NO, SALE_DATE, SALESPERSON, and TOTAL_SALE. If you simply use the following example, you see all the SALES data, but in an arbitrary order:

```
SELECT * FROM SALES ;
```

On one implementation, this order may be the one in which you inserted the rows in the table, and on another implementation, the order may be that of the most recent updates. The order can also change unexpectedly if anyone physically reorganizes the database. Most of the time, you want to specify the order in which you want the rows. You may, for example, want to see the rows in order by the SALE_DATE, as follows:

```
SELECT * FROM SALES ORDER BY SALE_DATE ;
```

This example returns all the rows in the SALES table, in order by SALE_DATE.

For rows with the same SALE_DATE, the default order depends on the implementation. You can, however, specify how to sort the rows that share the same SALE_DATE. You may, for example, want to see the SALES for each SALE_DATE in order by INVOICE_NO, as follows:

```
SELECT * FROM SALES ORDER BY SALE_DATE, INVOICE_NO ;
```

This example first orders the SALES by SALE_DATE; then for each SALE_DATE, it orders the SALES by INVOICE_NO. Don't confuse that example, however, with the following query:

```
SELECT * FROM SALES ORDER BY INVOICE_NO, SALE_DATE ;
```

This query first orders the SALES by INVOICE_NO. Then for each different INVOICE_NO, the query orders the SALES by SALE_DATE. This will probably not yield the result you want, because it is unlikely that multiple sale dates will exist for a single invoice number.

The following query is another example of how SQL can return data:

```
SELECT * FROM SALES ORDER BY SALESPERSON, SALE_DATE ;
```

This example first orders by SALESPERSON and then by SALE_DATE. After you look at the data in that order, you may want to invert it, as follows:

```
SELECT * FROM SALES ORDER BY SALE_DATE, SALESPERSON ;
```

This example orders the rows first by SALE_DATE and then by SALESPERSON.

All these ordering examples are ascending (ASC), which is the default sort order. The last SELECT shows earlier SALES first and, within a given date, shows SALES for 'Adams' before 'Baker'. If you prefer descending (DESC) order, you can specify this order for one or more of the order columns, as follows:

```
SELECT * FROM SALES
ORDER BY SALE_DATE DESC, SALESPERSON ASC ;
```

This example specifies a descending order for sales date, showing the more recent sales first, but an ascending order for salespeople, putting them in normal alphabetical order.

Chapter 10

Relational Operators

. . . .

. . . .

*S*QL is a query language for relational databases. In chapters before this one, I present simple databases, and in most cases, my examples deal with only one table. It's now time to put the *relational* in relational database. After all, relational databases are so named because they consist of multiple, related tables.

Because the data in a relational database is distributed across multiple tables, a query usually draws data from more than one table. SQL:1999 has operators that combine data from multiple sources into a single result table. These are the UNION, INTERSECTION, and EXCEPT operators, as well as a family of JOIN operators. Each combines data from multiple tables in a different way.

UNION

The UNION operator is the SQL implementation of relational algebra's union operator. The UNION operator enables you to draw information from two or more tables that have the same structure.

Same structure means that the tables must all have the same number of columns, and that corresponding columns all have identical data types and lengths. When these criteria are met, the tables are union compatible. The union of two tables returns all the rows that appear in either table and eliminates duplicates.

Say that you create a baseball statistics database (like the one in Chapter 9). It contains two union-compatible tables named AMERICAN and NATIONAL. Both tables have three columns, and corresponding columns are all the same type. In fact, corresponding columns have identical column names (although this condition isn't required for union compatibility).

NATIONAL lists the names and number of complete games pitched by National League pitchers. AMERICAN lists the same information about pitchers in the American League. The UNION of the two tables gives you a virtual result table containing all the rows in the first table plus all the rows in the second table. For this example, I put just a few rows in each table to illustrate the operation:

```
SELECT * FROM NATIONAL ;
FIRST_NAME   LAST_NAME   COMPLETE_GAMES
----------   ---------   --------------
Sal          Maglie                  11
Don          Newcombe                 9
Sandy        Koufax                  13
Don          Drysdale                12

SELECT * FROM AMERICAN ;

FIRST_NAME   LAST_NAME   COMPLETE_GAMES
----------   ---------   --------------
Whitey       Ford                    12
Don          Larson                  10
Bob          Turley                   8
Allie        Reynolds                14

SELECT * FROM NATIONAL
UNION
SELECT * FROM AMERICAN ;

FIRST_NAME   LAST_NAME   COMPLETE_GAMES
----------   ---------   --------------
Allie        Reynolds                14
Bob          Turley                   8
Don          Drysdale                12
Don          Larson                  10
Don          Newcombe                 9
Sal          Maglie                  11
Sandy        Koufax                  13
Whitey       Ford                    12
```

I've been using the asterisk (*) as shorthand for all the columns in a table. This shortcut is fine most of the time, but it can get you into trouble when you use relational operators in embedded or module-language SQL. What if you add one or more new columns to one table and not to another, or you add different columns to the two tables? The two tables are then no longer union-compatible, and your program will be invalid the next time it's recompiled. Even if the same new columns are added to both tables so that they are still union-compatible, your program is probably not prepared to deal with this additional data. So, explicitly listing the columns that you want rather than relying on the * shorthand is generally a good idea. When you're entering ad hoc SQL from the console, the asterisk will probably work fine because you can quickly display table structure to verify union compatibility if your query isn't successful.

The UNION operation normally eliminates any duplicate rows that result from its operation, which is the desired result most of the time. Sometimes, however, you may want to preserve duplicate rows. On those occasions, use UNION ALL.

Referring to the example, suppose that "Bullet" Bob Turley had been traded in midseason from the New York Yankees in the American League to the Brooklyn Dodgers in the National League. Now suppose that during the season, he pitched eight complete games for each team. The ordinary UNION displayed in the example throws away one of the two lines containing Turley's data. Although he seemed to pitch only eight complete games in the season, he actually hurled a remarkable 16 complete games. The following query gives you the true facts:

```
SELECT * FROM NATIONAL
UNION ALL
SELECT * FROM AMERICAN ;
```

You can sometimes form the UNION of two tables even if they are not union-compatible. If the columns you want in your result table are present and compatible in both tables, you can perform a UNION CORRESPONDING operation. Only the specified columns are considered and they are the only columns displayed in the result table.

Baseball statisticians keep entirely different statistics on pitchers than they keep on outfielders. Although in both cases, first name, last name, putouts, errors, and fielding percentage are recorded. Outfielders, of course, don't have a won/lost record, a saves record, or a number of other things that pertain only to pitching. You can still perform a UNION that takes data from the OUTFIELDER table and from the PITCHER table to give you some overall information about defensive skill:

```
SELECT *
   FROM OUTFIELDER
UNION CORRESPONDING
   (FIRST_NAME, LAST_NAME, PUTOUTS, ERRORS, FIELD_PCT)
SELECT *
   FROM PITCHER ;
```

The result table holds the first and last names of all the outfielders and pitchers, along with the number of putouts, errors, and the fielding percentage of each player. As with the simple UNION, duplicates are eliminated. Thus, if a player spent some time in the outfield as well as being a pitcher, the UNION CORRESPONDING operation loses some of his statistics. To avoid this problem, use UNION ALL CORRESPONDING.

Each column name in the list following the CORRESPONDING keyword must be a name that exists in both of the unioned tables. If you omit this list of names, an implicit list of all names that appear in both tables is used. This implicit list of names may change, however, when new columns are added to one or both of the tables. Therefore, explicitly listing the column names is better than omitting them.

INTERSECT

The UNION operation produces a result table containing all rows that appear in any of the source tables. If you want only rows that appear in all the source tables, you can use the INTERSECT operation, which is the SQL implementation of relational algebra's intersect operation. I illustrate INTERSECT by returning to the fantasy world in which Bob Turley was traded to the Dodgers in midseason:

```
SELECT * FROM NATIONAL;
FIRST_NAME   LAST_NAME   COMPLETE_GAMES
---------    ---------   --------------
Sal          Maglie                  11
Don          Newcombe                 9
Sandy        Koufax                  13
Don          Drysdale                12
Bob          Turley                   8

SELECT * FROM AMERICAN;
FIRST_NAME   LAST_NAME   COMPLETE_GAMES
---------    ---------   --------------
Whitey       Ford                    12
Don          Larson                  10
Bob          Turley                   8
Allie        Reynolds                14
```

Only rows that appear in all source tables show up in the INTERSECT operation's result table:

```
SELECT *
    FROM NATIONAL
INTERSECT
SELECT *
    FROM AMERICAN;
FIRST_NAME   LAST_NAME   COMPLETE_GAMES
---------    ---------   --------------
Bob          Turley                   8
```

The result table tells us that Bob Turley was the only pitcher to throw the same number of complete games in both leagues. (A rather obscure distinction for old Bullet Bob.)

The ALL and CORRESPONDING keywords function in an INTERSECT operation the same way they do in a UNION operation. If you use ALL, duplicates are retained in the result table. If you use CORRESPONDING, the intersected tables need not be union-compatible, although the corresponding columns need to have matching types and lengths.

Consider another example: A municipality keeps track of the pagers carried by police officers, fire fighters, street sweepers, and other city employees. A database table called PAGERS contains data on all pagers in active use. Another table named OUT, with an identical structure, contains data on all pagers that for one reason or another have been taken out of service. No pager should ever exist in both tables. With an INTERSECT operation, you can test to see whether such an unwanted duplication has occurred:

```
SELECT *
   FROM PAGERS
INTERSECT CORRESPONDING (PAGER_ID)
SELECT *
   FROM OUT ;
```

If the result table contains any rows at all, you know you have a problem. You should investigate any PAGER_ID entries that appear in the result table. The corresponding pager is either active or out of service. It can't be both. After you detect the problem, you can perform a DELETE operation on one of the two tables to restore database integrity.

EXCEPT

The UNION operation acts on two source tables and returns all rows that appear in either table. The INTERSECT operation returns all rows that appear in both the first and the second table. In contrast, the EXCEPT operation returns all rows that appear in the first table but that do not also appear in the second table.

Returning to the municipal pager database example, say that a group of pagers that had been declared out of service and returned to the vendor for repairs have now been fixed and placed back into service. The PAGERS table was updated to reflect the returned pagers, but for some reason the returned pagers were not removed from the OUT table as they should have been. You can display the PAGER_ID numbers of the pagers in the OUT table, with the reactivated ones eliminated, using an EXCEPT operation:

```
SELECT *
   FROM OUT
EXCEPT CORRESPONDING (PAGER_ID)
SELECT *
   FROM PAGERS;
```

This query returns all the rows in the OUT table whose PAGER_ID is not also present in the PAGERS table.

JOINS

The UNION, INTERSECT, and EXCEPT operators are valuable in multitable databases in which the tables are union-compatible. In many cases, however, you want to draw data from multiple tables that have very little in common. JOINs are powerful relational operators that combine data from multiple tables into a single result table. The source tables may have little (or even nothing) in common with each other.

SQL:1999 supports a number of different types of JOINs. The best one to choose in a given situation depends on the result you're trying to achieve.

Basic JOIN

Any multitable query is a type of JOIN. The source tables are joined in the sense that the result table includes information taken from all the source tables. The simplest JOIN is a two-table SELECT that has no WHERE clause qualifiers. Every row of the first table is joined to every row of the second table. The result table is the Cartesian product of the two-source tables. (I discuss the notion of Cartesian product in Chapter 9, in connection with the FROM clause.) The number of rows in the result table is equal to the number of rows in the first source table multiplied by the number of rows in the second source table.

For example, imagine that you're the personnel manager for a company and that part of your job is to maintain records on the employees. Most of the data for an employee, such as home address and telephone number, is not particularly sensitive. Some data, however, such as current salary, should be available only to authorized personnel. To maintain security of the sensitive information, keep it in a separate table that is password protected. Consider the following pair of tables:

```
EMPLOYEE                        COMPENSATION
--------                        ------------
EMP_ID                          EMPLOY
F_NAME                          SALARY
L_NAME                          BONUS
CITY
PHONE
```

Fill the tables with some sample data:

```
EMP_ID     F_NAME     L_NAME     CITY        PHONE
------     ------     ------     ----        -----
     1     Whitey     Ford       Orange      555-1001
     2     Don        Larson     Newark      555-3221
     3     Sal        Maglie     Nutley      555-6905
     4     Bob        Turley     Passaic     555-8908

EMPLOY     SALARY     BONUS
------     ------     -----
     1     33000      10000
     2     18000      2000
     3     24000      5000
     4     22000      7000
```

Create a virtual result table with the following query:

```
SELECT *
   FROM EMPLOYEE, COMPENSATION ;
```

Producing:

```
EMP_ID F_NAME L_NAME CITY     PHONE       EMPLOY SALARY BONUS
------ ------ ------ ----     -----       ------ ------ -----
     1 Whitey Ford   Orange   555-1001         1 33000  10000
     1 Whitey Ford   Orange   555-1001         2 18000  2000
     1 Whitey Ford   Orange   555-1001         3 24000  5000
     1 Whitey Ford   Orange   555-1001         4 22000  7000
     2 Don    Larson Newark   555-3221         1 33000  10000
     2 Don    Larson Newark   555-3221         2 18000  2000
     2 Don    Larson Newark   555-3221         3 24000  5000
     2 Don    Larson Newark   555-3221         4 22000  7000
     3 Sal    Maglie Nutley   555-6905         1 33000  10000
     3 Sal    Maglie Nutley   555-6905         2 18000  2000
     3 Sal    Maglie Nutley   555-6905         3 24000  5000
     3 Sal    Maglie Nutley   555-6905         4 22000  7000
     4 Bob    Turley Passaic  555-8908         1 33000  10000
     4 Bob    Turley Passaic  555-8908         2 18000  2000
     4 Bob    Turley Passaic  555-8908         3 24000  5000
     4 Bob    Turley Passaic  555-8908         4 22000  7000
```

The result table, which is the Cartesian product of the EMPLOYEE and the COMPENSATION tables, contains considerable redundancy. Furthermore, it doesn't make much sense. It combines every row of EMPLOYEE with every row of COMPENSATION. Of these, the only rows that convey meaningful information are those in which the EMP_ID number that came from EMPLOYEE matches the EMPLOY number that came from COMPENSATION. In those rows, an employee's name and address are associated with that same employee's compensation.

When you're trying to get useful information out of a multitable database, the Cartesian product produced by a basic JOIN is almost never what you want, but it's almost always the first step toward what you want, however. By applying constraints to the JOIN with a WHERE clause, you can filter out the unwanted rows. The most common JOIN that uses the WHERE clause filter is the equi-join.

Equi-join

An *equi-join* is a basic join with a WHERE clause containing a condition specifying that the value in one column in the first table must be equal to the value of a corresponding column in the second table. Applying an equi-join to the example tables from the previous section brings a much more meaningful result:

```
SELECT *
   FROM EMPLOYEE, COMPENSATION
   WHERE EMPLOYEE.EMP_ID = COMPENSATION.EMPLOY ;
```

This produces:

EMP_ID	F_NAME	L_NAME	CITY	PHONE	EMPLOY	SALARY	BONUS
1	Whitey	Ford	Orange	555-1001	1	33000	10000
2	Don	Larson	Newark	555-3221	2	18000	2000
3	Sal	Maglie	Nutley	555-6905	3	24000	5000
4	Bob	Turley	Passaic	555-8908	4	22000	7000

In this result table, the salaries and bonuses on the right apply to the employees named on the left. The table still has some redundancy, however, because the EMP_ID column duplicates the EMPLOY column. You can fix this problem with a slight reformulation of the query:

```
SELECT EMPLOYEE.*,COMPENSATION.SALARY,COMPENSATION.BONUS
   FROM EMPLOYEE, COMPENSATION
   WHERE EMPLOYEE.EMP_ID = COMPENSATION.EMPLOY ;
```

This produces:

EMP_ID	F_NAME	L_NAME	CITY	PHONE	SALARY	BONUS
1	Whitey	Ford	Orange	555-1001	33000	10000
2	Don	Larson	Newark	555-3221	18000	2000
3	Sal	Maglie	Nutley	555-6905	24000	5000
4	Bob	Turley	Passaic	555-8908	22000	7000

This table tells you what you want to know, but doesn't burden you with any extraneous data. The query was somewhat tedious to write, however. To avoid ambiguity, qualify the column names with the names of the tables they came from. Writing those table names repeatedly provides good exercise for the fingers but has no merit otherwise.

You can cut down on the amount of typing by using aliases (or *correlation names*). An *alias* is a short name that stands for a table name. If you use aliases in recasting the preceding query, it comes out like this:

```
SELECT E.*, C.SALARY, C.BONUS
    FROM EMPLOYEE E, COMPENSATION C
    WHERE E.EMP_ID = C.EMPLOY ;
```

In this example, E is the alias for EMPLOYEE and C is the alias for COMPENSATION. The alias is local to the statement it is in. After you declare an alias (in the FROM clause), you must use it throughout the statement. You can't use both the alias and the long form of the table name.

Mixing the long form of table names with aliases creates confusion. Consider the following example, which is confusing:

```
SELECT T1.C, T2.C
    FROM T1 T2, T2 T1
    WHERE T1.C > T2.C ;
```

In this example, the alias for T1 is T2 and the alias for T2 is T1. Admittedly, this isn't a smart selection of aliases, but it isn't forbidden by the rules. If you can mix aliases with long form table names, you can't tell which table is which.

The preceding example with aliases is equivalent to the following SELECT with no aliases:

```
SELECT T2.C, T1.C
    FROM T1 , T2
    WHERE T2.C > T1.C ;
```

SQL:1999 enables you to join more than two tables. The maximum number varies from one implementation to another. The syntax is analogous to the two-table case:

```
SELECT E.*, C.SALARY, C.BONUS, Y.TOTAL_SALES
    FROM EMPLOYEE E, COMPENSATION C, YTD_SALES Y
    WHERE E.EMP_ID = C.EMPLOY
        AND C.EMPLOY = Y.EMPNO ;
```

This statement performs an equi-join on three tables, pulling data from corresponding rows of each one to produce a result table that shows the salespeople's names, the amount of sales they are responsible for, and their compensation. The sales manager can quickly see whether compensation is in line with production.

Storing a salesperson's year-to-date sales in a separate YTD_SALES table ensures better performance and reliability than keeping that data in the EMPLOYEE table. The data in the EMPLOYEE table is relatively static. A person's name, address, and telephone number don't change very often. In contrast, the year-to-date sales change frequently (you hope). Because YTD_SALES has fewer columns than EMPLOYEE, you may be able to update it more quickly. If, in the course of updating sales totals, you don't touch the EMPLOYEE table, you decrease the risk of accidentally modifying EMPLOYEE information that should stay the same.

Cross join

CROSS JOIN is the keyword for the basic join without a WHERE clause. Therefore,

```
SELECT *
FROM EMPLOYEE, COMPENSATION ;
```

can also be written as:

```
SELECT *
FROM EMPLOYEE CROSS JOIN COMPENSATION ;
```

The result is the Cartesian product (also called the *cross product*) of the two source tables. CROSS JOIN rarely gives you the final result you want, but it can be useful as the first step in a chain of data manipulation operations that ultimately produce the desired result.

Natural join

The *natural join* is a special case of an equi-join. In the WHERE clause of an equi-join, a column from one source table is compared with a column of a second source table for equality. The two columns must be the same type and length, however, the columns being compared must have the same name. In fact, in a natural join, all columns in one table that have the same names as corresponding columns in the second table are compared for equality.

Imagine that the COMPENSATION table from the preceding example has columns EMP_ID, SALARY, and BONUS rather than EMPLOY, SALARY, and BONUS. In that case, you could perform a natural join of the COMPENSATION table with the EMPLOYEE table. The traditional JOIN syntax would look like this:

```
SELECT E.*, C.SALARY, C.BONUS
    FROM EMPLOYEE E, COMPENSATION C
    WHERE E.EMP_ID = C.EMP_ID ;
```

This query is a natural join. An alternate syntax for the same operation is the following:

```
SELECT E.*, C.SALARY, C.BONUS
    FROM EMPLOYEE E NATURAL JOIN COMPENSATION C ;
```

Condition join

A *condition join* is like an equi-join, except the condition being tested doesn't have to be equal (although it can be). It can be any well-formed predicate. If the condition is satisfied, the corresponding row becomes part of the result table. The syntax is a little different from what you have seen so far, in that the condition is contained in an ON clause rather than a WHERE clause.

Say that a baseball statistician wants to know which National League pitchers have pitched exactly the same number of complete games as one or more American League pitchers. This question is a job for an equi-join, which can also be expressed with condition join syntax:

```
SELECT *
    FROM NATIONAL JOIN AMERICAN
    ON NATIONAL.COMPLETE_GAMES = AMERICAN.COMPLETE_GAMES ;
```

Column-name join

The *column-name join* is like a natural join, but it's more flexible. In a natural join, all columns in the source tables that have the same name are compared with each other for equality. With the column-name join, you select which same-name columns are to be compared and which are not. You can choose them all if you want, making the column-name join effectively a natural join. Or you may choose fewer than all same-name columns. In this way, you have a great degree of control over which cross product rows qualify to be placed into your result table.

Say that you're a chess set manufacturer who has one inventory table that keeps track of your stock of white pieces and another that keeps track of black pieces. The tables contain data as follows:

```
WHITE                           BLACK
-----                           -----

Piece Quant Wood                Piece Quant Wood
----- ----- ----                ----- ----- ----
King    502 Oak                 King    502 Ebony
Queen   398 Oak                 Queen   397 Ebony
Rook   1020 Oak                 Rook   1020 Ebony
Bishop  985 Oak                 Bishop  985 Ebony
Knight  950 Oak                 Knight  950 Ebony
Pawn    431 Oak                 Pawn    453 Ebony
```

For each type of piece, the number of white pieces should match the number of black pieces. If they don't match, some chessmen are being lost or stolen, and you need to tighten up security measures.

A natural join compares all columns with the same name for equality. In this case, a result table with no rows is produced because no rows in the WOOD column in the WHITE table match any of the rows in the WOOD column in the BLACK table. This result table doesn't help you determine whether any merchandise is missing. Instead, do a column-name join that excludes the WOOD column from consideration. It can take the following form:

```
SELECT *
    FROM WHITE JOIN BLACK
    USING (PIECE, QUANT) ;
```

The result table shows only the rows for which the number of white pieces in stock equals the number of black pieces:

```
Piece Quant Wood Piece Quant Wood
----- ----- ---- ----- ----- ----
King    502 Oak  King    502 Ebony
Rook   1020 Oak  Rook   1020 Ebony
Bishop  985 Oak  Bishop  985 Ebony
Knight  950 Oak  Knight  950 Ebony
```

The shrewd person can deduce that Queen and Pawn are missing from the list, indicating a shortage somewhere for those piece types.

Inner join

By now, you're probably getting the idea that joins are pretty esoteric and that it takes an uncommon level of spiritual discernment to deal with them adequately. You may have even heard of the mysterious *inner join* and speculated that it probably represents the very core or essence of relational operations. Well, ha!

The joke is on you. Nothing's mysterious about inner joins at all. In fact, all the joins covered so far in this chapter are inner joins. I could have formulated the column-name join in the last example as an inner join by using the following syntax:

```
SELECT *
    FROM WHITE INNER JOIN BLACK
    USING (PIECE, QUANT) ;
```

The result is exactly the same.

The inner join is so named to distinguish it from the outer join. An inner join discards all rows from the result table that don't have corresponding rows in both source tables. An outer join preserves unmatched rows. That is the difference. There is nothing metaphysical about it.

Outer join

When you're joining two tables, the first one (call it the one on the left) may have rows that don't have matching counterparts in the second table (the one on the right). Conversely, the table on the right may have rows that don't have matching counterparts in the table on the left. If you perform an inner join on those tables, all the unmatched rows are excluded from the output. *Outer joins,* however, don't exclude the unmatched rows. Actually, outer joins come in three types: the left outer join, the right outer join, and the full outer join.

Left outer join

In a query that includes a join, the left table is the one that precedes the keyword JOIN and the right table is the one that follows it. The *left outer join* preserves unmatched rows from the left table but discards unmatched rows from the right table.

To understand outer joins, consider a corporate database that maintains records of the company's employees, departments, and locations. The following lists contain the database's example data:

LOCATION	
LOCATION_ID	*CITY*
1	Boston
3	Tampa
5	Chicago

DEPT		
DEPT_ID	*LOCATION_ID*	*NAME*
21	1	Sales
24	1	Admin
27	5	Repair
29	5	Stock

EMPLOYEE		
EMP_ID	*DEPT_ID*	*NAME*
61	24	Kirk
63	27	McCoy

Now suppose that you want to see all the data for all employees, including department and location. You get this with an equi-join:

```
SELECT *
   FROM LOCATION L, DEPT D, EMPLOYEE E
   WHERE L.LOCATION_ID = D.LOCATION_ID
      AND D.DEPT_ID = E.DEPT_ID ;
```

This statement produces the following result:

```
1    Boston    24   1    Admin    61   24   Kirk
5    Chicago   27   5    Repair   63   27   McCoy
```

This result table gives all the data for all the employees, including their location and department. The equi-join works because every employee has a location and a department.

Suppose now that you want the data on the locations, with the related department and employee data. This is a different problem because a location without any associated departments may exist. To get what you want, you have to use an outer join, as in the following example:

```
SELECT *
   FROM LOCATION L LEFT OUTER JOIN DEPT D
      ON (L.LOCATION_ID = D.LOCATION_ID)
   LEFT OUTER JOIN EMPLOYEE E
      ON (D.DEPT_ID = E.DEPT_ID);
```

This join pulls data from three tables. First, the LOCATION table is joined to the DEPT table. The resulting table is then joined to the EMPLOYEE table. Rows from the table on the left of the LEFT OUTER JOIN operator that have no corresponding row in the table on the right are included in the result. Thus, in the first join, all locations are included, even if no department associated with them exists. In the second join, all departments are included, even if no employee associated with them exists. The result is as follows:

```
1    Boston    24    1    Admin    61    24    Kirk
5    Chicago   27    5    Repair   63    27    McCoy
3    Tampa     NULL  NULL NULL     NULL  NULL  NULL
5    Chicago   29    5    Stock    NULL  NULL  NULL
1    Boston    21    1    Sales    NULL  NULL  NULL
```

The first two rows are the same as the two result rows in the previous example. The third row (3 Tampa) has nulls in the department and employee columns because no departments are defined for Tampa and no employees are stationed there. The fourth and fifth rows (5 Chicago and 1 Boston) contain data about the Stock and the Sales departments, but the employee columns for these rows contain nulls because these two departments have no employees. This outer join tells you everything that the equi-join told you plus the following:

- ✔ All the company's locations, whether they have any departments or not

- ✔ All the company's departments, whether they have any employees or not

The rows returned in the preceding example aren't guaranteed to be in the order you want. The order may vary from one implementation to the next. To make sure that the rows returned are in the order you want, add an ORDER BY clause to your SELECT statement, like this:

```
SELECT *
    FROM LOCATION L LEFT OUTER JOIN DEPT D
        ON (L.LOCATION_ID = D.LOCATION_ID)
    LEFT OUTER JOIN EMPLOYEE E
        ON (D.DEPT_ID = E.DEPT_ID)
    ORDER BY L.LOCATION_ID, D.DEPT_ID, E.EMP_ID;
```

The left outer join language may be abbreviated as LEFT JOIN because there's no such thing as a left inner join.

Right outer join

I bet you figured out how the right outer join behaves. Right! The *right outer join* preserves unmatched rows from the right table but discards unmatched rows from the left table. You can use it on the same tables and get the same result by reversing the order in which you present tables to the join:

```
SELECT *
    FROM EMPLOYEE E RIGHT OUTER JOIN DEPT D
        ON (D.DEPT_ID = E.DEPT_ID)
    RIGHT OUTER JOIN LOCATION L
        ON (L.LOCATION_ID = D.LOCATION_ID) ;
```

In this formulation, the first join produces a table that contains all departments, whether they have an associated employee or not. The second join produces a table that contains all locations, whether they have an associated department or not.

The right outer join language can be abbreviated as RIGHT JOIN because there's no such thing as a right inner join.

Full outer join

The *full outer join* combines the functions of the left outer join and the right outer join. It retains the unmatched rows from both the left and the right tables. Consider the most general case of the company database used in the preceding examples. It could have:

- ✔ Locations with no departments
- ✔ Departments with no locations
- ✔ Departments with no employees
- ✔ Employees with no departments

To show all locations, departments, and employees, regardless of whether they have corresponding rows in the other tables, use a full outer join in the following form:

```
SELECT *
    FROM LOCATION L FULL JOIN DEPT D
        ON (L.LOCATION_ID = D.LOCATION_ID)
    FULL JOIN EMPLOYEE E
        ON (D.DEPT_ID = E.DEPT_ID) ;
```

The full outer join language can be abbreviated as FULL JOIN because there's no such thing as a full inner join.

Union join

Unlike the other kinds of join, the *union join* makes no attempt to match a row from the left source table with any of the rows in the right source table. It creates a new virtual table that contains the union of all the columns in both source tables. In the virtual result table, the columns that came from the left source table contain all the rows that were in the left source table. For those rows, the columns that came from the right source table all have the null value. Similarly, the columns that came from the right source table contain all the rows that were in the right source table. For those rows, the columns that came from the left source table all have the null value. Thus, the table resulting from a union join contains all the columns of both source tables, and the number of rows that it contains is the sum of the number of rows in the two source tables.

The result of a union join by itself is not immediately useful in most cases. It produces a result table with many nulls in it. You can use it, however, in conjunction with the COALESCE expression I discuss in Chapter 8 to give you useful information. Look at an example.

Suppose that you work for a company that designs and builds experimental rockets. You have several projects in the works. You also have several design engineers who have skills in multiple areas. As a manager, you want to know which employees, having which skills, have worked on which projects. Currently, this data is scattered among the EMPLOYEE table, the PROJECTS table, and the SKILLS table.

The EMPLOYEE table carries data about employees, and EMPLOYEE.EMP_ID is its primary key. The PROJECTS table has a row for each project that an employee has worked on. PROJECTS.EMP_ID is a foreign key that references the EMPLOYEE table. The SKILLS table shows the expertise of each employee. SKILLS.EMP_ID is a foreign key that references the EMPLOYEE table.

The EMPLOYEE table has exactly one row for each employee; the PROJECTS table and the SKILLS table have zero or more rows.

Tables 10-1, 10-2, and 10-3 show example data in the three tables.

Table 10-1	EMPLOYEE Table
EMP_ID	*NAME*
1	Ferguson
2	Frost
3	Toyon

Table 10-2	PROJECTS Table
PROJECT_NAME	*EMP_ID*
X-63 Structure	1
X-64 Structure	1
X-63 Guidance	2
X-64 Guidance	2
X-63 Telemetry	3
X-64 Telemetry	3

Table 10-3	SKILLS Table
SKILL	*EMP_ID*
Mechanical Design	1
Aerodynamic Loading	1
Analog Design	2
Gyroscope Design	2
Digital Design	3
R/F Design	3

From the tables, you can see that Ferguson has worked on X-63 and X-64 structure design and has expertise in mechanical design and aerodynamic loading.

Now suppose that, as a manager, you want to see all the information about all the employees. You decide to apply an equi-join to the EMPLOYEE, PROJECTS, and SKILLS tables:

```
SELECT *
  FROM EMPLOYEE E, PROJECTS P, SKILLS S
  WHERE E.EMP_ID = P.EMP_ID
    AND E.EMP_ID = S.EMP_ID ;
```

You can express this same operation as an inner join by using the following syntax:

```
SELECT *
    FROM EMPLOYEE E INNER JOIN PROJECTS P
        ON (E.EMP_ID = P.EMP_ID)
    INNER JOIN SKILLS S
        ON (E.EMP_ID = S.EMP_ID) ;
```

Both formulations give the same result, as shown in Table 10-4.

Table 10-4			Result of Inner Join		
E.EMP_ID	**E.NAME**	**P.EMP_ID**	**PROJECT_NAME**	**S.EMP_ID**	**S.SKILL**
1	Ferguson	1	X-63 Structure	1	Mechanical Design
1	Ferguson	1	X-63 Structure	1	Aerodynamic Loading
1	Ferguson	1	X-64 Structure	1	Mechanical Design
1	Ferguson	1	X-64 Structure	1	Aerodynamic Loading
2	Frost	2	X-63 Guidance	2	Analog Design
2	Frost	2	X-63 Guidance	2	Gyroscope Design
2	Frost	2	X-64 Guidance	2	Analog Design
2	Frost	2	X-64 Guidance	2	Gyroscope Design
3	Toyon	3	X-63 Telemetry	3	Digital Design
3	Toyon	3	X-63 Telemetry	3	R/F Design
3	Toyon	3	X-64 Telemetry	3	Digital Design
3	Toyon	3	X-64 Telemetry	3	R/F Design

This arrangement of the data is not particularly enlightening. The employee ID numbers appear three times and the projects and skills are duplicated for each employee. The inner joins are not well suited to answering this type of question. You can put the union join to work here, along with some strategi-cally chosen SELECT statements, to produce a more suitable result. You begin with the basic union join:

```
SELECT *
    FROM EMPLOYEE E UNION JOIN PROJECTS P
        UNION JOIN SKILLS S ;
```

Notice that the union join has no ON clause. It doesn't filter the data, so an ON clause isn't needed. This statement produces the result shown in Table 10-5.

Table 10-5			Result of UNION JOIN		
E.EMP_ID	*E.NAME*	*P.EMP_ID*	*P.PROJECT_NAME*	*S.EMP_ID*	*S.SKILL*
1	Ferguson	NULL	NULL	NULL	NULL
NULL	NULL	1	X-63 Structure	NULL	NULL
NULL	NULL	1	X-64 Structure	NULL	NULL
NULL	NULL	NULL	NULL	1	Mechanical Design
NULL	NULL	NULL	NULL	1	Aerodynamic Loading
2	Frost	NULL	NULL	NULL	NULL
NULL	NULL	2	X-63 Guidance	NULL	NULL
NULL	NULL	2	X-64 Guidance	NULL	NULL
NULL	NULL	NULL	NULL	2	Analog Design
NULL	NULL	NULL	NULL	2	Gyroscope Design
3	Toyon	NULL	NULL	NULL	NULL
NULL	NULL	3	X-63 Telemetry	NULL	NULL
NULL	NULL	3	X-64 Telemetry	NULL	NULL
NULL	NULL	NULL	NULL	3	Digital Design
NULL	NULL	NULL	NULL	3	R/F Design

Each table has been extended to the right or left with nulls, and those null-extended rows have been unioned. The order of the rows is arbitrary and depends on the implementation. Now you can "massage" the data to put it in a more useful form.

First, notice that the table has three ID columns, only one of which is nonnull in any row. You can improve the display by coalescing the ID columns. As I note in Chapter 8, the COALESCE expression takes on the value of the first nonnull value in a list of values. In the present case, it takes on the value of the only nonnull value in a column list:

```
SELECT COALESCE (E.EMP_ID, P.EMP_ID, S.EMP_ID) AS ID,
    E.NAME, P.PROJECT_NAME, S.SKILL
  FROM EMPLOYEE E UNION JOIN PROJECTS P
    UNION JOIN SKILLS S
  ORDER BY ID ;
```

The FROM clause is the same as in the previous example, but now you're coalescing the three EMP_ID columns into a single column named ID. You're also ordering the result by ID. Table 10-6 shows the result.

Table 10-6   Result of Union Join with COALESCE Expression

ID	E.NAME	P.PROJECT_NAME	S.SKILL
1	Ferguson	X-63 Structure	NULL
1	Ferguson	X-64 Structure	NULL
1	Ferguson	NULL	Mechanical Design
1	Ferguson	NULL	Aerodynamic Loading
2	Frost	X-63 Guidance	NULL
2	Frost	X-64 Guidance	NULL
2	Frost	NULL	Analog Design
2	Frost	NULL	Gyroscope Design
3	Toyon	X-63 Telemetry	NULL
3	Toyon	X-64 Telemetry	NULL
3	Toyon	NULL	Digital Design
3	Toyon	NULL	R/F Design

Each row in this result has data about a project or a skill, but not both. When you read the result, you have to first determine what type of information is in each row (project or skill). If the PROJECT_NAME column has a nonnull value, the row names a project the employee has worked on. If the SKILL column is nonnull, the row names one of the employee's skills.

You can make the result a little clearer by adding another COALESCE to the SELECT statement, as follows:

```
SELECT COALESCE (E.EMP_ID, P.EMP_ID, S.EMP_ID) AS ID,
       E.NAME, COALESCE (P.TYPE, S.TYPE) AS TYPE,
       PROJECT_NAME, S.SKILL
   FROM EMPLOYEE E
      UNION JOIN (SELECT "Project" AS TYPE, P.*
                     FROM PROJECTS) P
      UNION JOIN (SELECT "Skill" AS TYPE, S.*
                     FROM SKILLS) S
   ORDER BY ID, TYPE ;
```

In the union join, the PROJECTS table has been replaced with a nested SELECT that appends a column named P.TYPE with a constant value "Project" to the columns coming from the PROJECTS table. Similarly, the SKILLS table has been replaced with a nested SELECT that appends a column named S.TYPE with a constant value "Skill" to the columns coming from the SKILLS table. In each row, P.TYPE is either null or "Project", and S.TYPE is either null or "Skill".

The outer SELECT list specifies a COALESCE of those two TYPE columns into a single column named TYPE. You then specify TYPE in the ORDER BY clause, which sorts the rows that all have the same ID so that all projects are first, followed by all the skills. The result is shown in Table 10-7.

Table 10-7		Refined Result of Union Join with COALESCE Expressions		
ID	*E.NAME*	*TYPE*	*PROJECT_NAME*	*SKILL*
1	Ferguson	Project	X-63 Structure	NULL
1	Ferguson	Project	X-64 Structure	NULL
1	Ferguson	Skill	NULL	Mechanical Design
1	Ferguson	Skill	NULL	Aerodynamic Loading
2	Frost	Project	X-63 Guidance	NULL

ID	E.NAME	TYPE	PROJECT_NAME	SKILL
2	Frost	Project	X-64 Guidance	NULL
2	Frost	Skill	NULL	Analog Design
2	Frost	Skill	NULL	Gyroscope Design
3	Toyon	Project	X-63 Telemetry	NULL
3	Toyon	Project	X-64 Telemetry	NULL
3	Toyon	Skill	NULL	Digital Design
3	Toyon	Skill	NULL	R/F Design

The result table now presents a very readable account of the project experience and the skill sets of all the employees in the EMPLOYEE table.

Considering the number of different JOIN operations available, relating data from different tables shouldn't be a problem, regardless of the structure of those tables. Trust that if the raw data exists in your database, SQL:1999 has the means to get it out and display it in a meaningful form.

ON versus WHERE

The function of the ON and WHERE clauses in the various types of joins is potentially confusing. These facts may help you keep things straight:

- ✔ The ON clause is part of the inner, left, right, and full joins. The cross join and union join don't have an ON clause because neither of them does any filtering of the data.

- ✔ The ON clause in an inner join is logically equivalent to a WHERE clause; the same condition could be specified either in the ON clause or a WHERE clause.

- ✔ The ON clauses in outer joins (left, right, and full joins) are different from WHERE clauses. The WHERE clause simply filters the rows that are returned by the FROM clause. Rows that are rejected by the filter are simply not included in the result. The ON clause in an outer join first filters the rows of a cross product and then includes the rejected rows, extended with nulls.

Chapter 11

Delving Deep with Nested Queries

● ●

In This Chapter

▶ Pulling data from multiple tables with a single SQL statement

▶ Finding data items by comparing a value taken from one table with a set of values taken from another table

▶ Finding data items by comparing a value taken from one table with a single value SELECTed from another table

▶ Finding data items by comparing a value taken from one table with all the corresponding values in another table

▶ Making queries that correlate rows in one table with corresponding rows in another table

▶ Determining which rows to update, delete, or insert by using a subquery

● ●

*O*ne of the best ways to protect the integrity of your data is to avoid modification anomalies by normalizing your database. *Normalization* involves breaking up a single table into multiple tables, each of which has a single theme. You don't want product information in the same table with customer information, for example, even if the customers have bought products.

If you normalize a database properly, the data is scattered across multiple tables. Most queries that you want to make need to pull data from two or more tables. One way to do this is to use a JOIN operator or one of the other relational operators (UNION, INTERSECT, or EXCEPT). The relational operators take information from multiple tables and combine it all into a single table. Different operators combine the data in different ways. Another way to pull data from two or more tables is to use a nested query.

In SQL, a *nested query* is one in which an outer enclosing statement contains within it a subquery. That subquery may itself serve as an enclosing statement for a lower-level subquery that is nested within it. There are no theoretical limits to the number of nesting levels that a nested query may have, although implementation-dependent practical limits do exist.

Subqueries are invariably SELECT statements, but the outermost enclosing statement may also be an INSERT, UPDATE, or DELETE.

Because a subquery can operate on a different table than the table operated on by its enclosing statement, nested queries give you another way to extract information from multiple tables.

For example, suppose that you want to query your corporate database to find all department managers who are more than 50 years old. With the JOINs I discuss in Chapter 10, you may use a query like this:

```
SELECT D.DEPTNO, D.NAME, E.NAME, E.AGE
    FROM DEPT D, EMPLOYEE E
    WHERE D.MANAGER_ID = E.ID AND E.AGE > 50 ;
```

D is the alias for the DEPT table and E is the alias for the EMPLOYEE table. The EMPLOYEE table has an ID column that is the primary key, and the DEPT table has a column MANAGER_ID that is the ID value of the employee who is the manager of the department. I use a simple JOIN (the list of tables in the FROM clause) to pair related tables, and a WHERE to filter all rows except those that meet the criterion. Note that the SELECT statement's parameter list includes the DEPTNO and NAME columns from the DEPT table and the NAME and AGE columns from the EMPLOYEE table.

Next, suppose that you are interested in the same set of rows but you want only the columns from the DEPT table — in other words, you are interested in the departments whose manager is 50 or older, but you don't care who that manager is or exactly how old he or she is. You could then write the query with a *subquery* rather than a join:

```
SELECT D.DEPTNO, D.NAME
    FROM DEPT D
    WHERE EXISTS (SELECT * FROM EMPLOYEE E
      WHERE E.ID = D.MANAGERID AND E.AGE > 50) ;
```

This query has two new elements: the EXISTS keyword and the SELECT * in the WHERE clause of the first SELECT. The second SELECT is a subquery (or *subselect*) and the EXISTS keyword is one of several tools for use with a subquery that is described in this chapter.

Why Use a Subquery?

In many instances, you can accomplish the same result with a subquery as you can with a JOIN. In most cases, the complexity of the subquery syntax is comparable to the complexity of the corresponding JOIN operation. It comes down to a matter of personal preference. Some people prefer formulating a retrieval in terms of JOIN operations, whereas others prefer nested queries. Sometimes, however, obtaining the results that you want isn't possible by using JOIN. In those cases, you must either use a nested query or break the problem up into multiple SQL statements and execute them one at a time.

What Subqueries Do

Subqueries are located within the WHERE clause of their enclosing statement. Their function is to set the search conditions for the WHERE clause. Different kinds of subqueries produce different results. Some subqueries produce a list of values that is then used as input by the enclosing statement. Other subqueries produce a single value that the enclosing statement then evaluates with a comparison operator. A third kind of subquery returns a value of True or False.

Nested queries that return sets of rows

To illustrate how a nested query returns a set of rows, suppose that you work for a system integrator of computer equipment. Your company, Zetec Corporation, assembles systems from components that you buy, and then it sells them to companies and government agencies. You keep track of your business with a relational database. The database consists of many tables, but right now you are concerned with only three of them: the PRODUCT table, the COMP_USED table, and the COMPONENT table. The PRODUCT table (shown in Table 11-1) contains a list of all your standard products. The COMPONENT table (shown in Table 11-2) lists components that go into your products, and the COMP_USED table (shown in Table 11-3) tracks which components go into each product. The tables are defined as follows:

Table 11-1	PRODUCT Table	
Column	*Type*	*Constraints*
MODEL	Char (6)	PRIMARY KEY
PRODNAME	Char (35)	
PRODDESC	Char (31)	
LISTPRICE	Numeric (9,2)	

Table 11-2	COMPONENT Table	
Column	*Type*	*Constraints*
COMPID	CHAR (6)	PRIMARY KEY
COMPTYPE	CHAR (10)	
COMPDESC	CHAR (31)	

Table 11-3	COMP_USED Table	
Column	*Type*	*Constraints*
MODEL	CHAR (6)	FOREIGN KEY (for PRODUCT)
COMPID	CHAR (6)	FOREIGN KEY (for COMPONENT)

A component may be used in multiple products, and a product can contain multiple components (a many-to-many relationship). This situation can cause integrity problems. To circumvent the problems, create the linking table COMP_USED to relate COMPONENT to PRODUCT. A component may appear in many COMP_USED rows, but each COMP_USED row references only one component (a one-to-many relationship). Similarly, a product may appear in many COMP_USED rows, but each COMP_USED row references only one product (another one-to-many relationship). By adding the linking table, a troublesome many-to-many relationship has been transformed into two relatively simple one-to-many relationships. This process of reducing the complexity of relationships is one example of normalization.

Subqueries introduced by the keyword IN

One form of a nested query compares a single value with the set of values returned by a SELECT. It uses the IN predicate with the following syntax:

```
SELECT column_list
    FROM table
    WHERE expression IN (subquery) ;
```

The expression in the WHERE clause evaluates to a value. If that value is IN the list returned by the subquery, then the WHERE clause returns a True value and the specified columns from the table row being processed are added to the result table. The subquery may reference the same table referenced by the outer query, or it may reference a different table.

I use Zetec's database to demonstrate this type of query. Assume that there is a shortage of computer monitors in the computer industry. When you run out of monitors, you can no longer deliver products that include them. You want to know which products are affected. Enter the following query:

```
SELECT MODEL
    FROM COMP_USED
    WHERE COMPID IN
        (SELECT COMPID
            FROM COMPONENT
            WHERE COMPTYPE = 'Monitor') ;
```

SQL processes the innermost query first, so it processes the COMPONENT table, returning the value of `COMPID` for every row where `COMPTYPE` is `'Monitor'`. The result is a list of the `ID` numbers of all monitors. The outer query then compares the value of `COMPID` in every row in the COMP_USED table against the list. If the comparison is successful, the value of the `MODEL` column for that row is added to the outer `SELECT`'s result table. The result is a list of all product models that include a monitor. The following example shows what happens when you actually run the query:

```
MODEL
-----
CX3000
CX3010
CX3020
MB3030
MX3020
MX3030
```

You now know which products will soon be out of stock. It's time to go to the sales force and tell them to slow down on promoting these particular products.

When you use this form of nested query, the subquery must specify a single column, and the data type of that column must match the data type of the argument preceding the `IN` keyword.

Subqueries introduced by the keyword NOT IN

Just as you can introduce a subquery with the `IN` keyword, you can do the opposite and introduce it with the `NOT IN` keyword. In fact, now is a great time for the management of Zetec to make such a query. By using the query in the preceding section, Zetec management found out what products not to sell. That is valuable information, but it doesn't pay the rent. What Zetec management really wants to know is what products *to* sell. Management wants to emphasize the sale of products that *don't* contain monitors. A nested query featuring a subquery introduced by the `NOT IN` keyword provides the requested information:

```
SELECT MODEL
   FROM COMP_USED
   WHERE MODEL NOT IN
      (SELECT MODEL
            FROM COMP_USED
            WHERE COMPID IN
               (SELECT COMPID
                     FROM COMPONENT
                     WHERE COMPTYPE = 'Monitor')) ;
```

This query produces the following result:

```
MODEL
-----
PX3040
PB3050
PX3040
PB3050
```

A couple of things are worth noting here. First, this query has two levels of nesting. The two subqueries are identical to the previous query statement. The only difference is that a new enclosing statement has been wrapped around them. The enclosing statement takes the list of products that contain monitors and applies a SELECT introduced by the NOT IN keyword to that list. The result is another list that contains all product models except those that have monitors.

Second, the result table does contain duplicates. The duplication occurs because a product containing several components that are not monitors has a row in the COMP_USED table for each component. The query creates an entry in the result table for each of those rows.

In the example, the number of rows does not create a problem because the result table is short. In the real world, however, such a result table may have hundreds or thousands of rows. To avoid confusion, you need to eliminate the duplicates. You can do so easily by adding the DISTINCT keyword to the query. Only rows that are distinct (different) from all previously retrieved rows are then added to the result table:

```
SELECT DISTINCT MODEL
   FROM COMP_USED
   WHERE MODEL NOT IN
      (SELECT MODEL
            FROM COMP_USED
            WHERE COMPID IN
               (SELECT COMPID
                     FROM COMPONENT
                     WHERE COMPTYPE = 'Monitor')) ;
```

As expected, the result is as follows:

```
MODEL
-----
PX3040
PB3050
```

Nested queries that return a single value

Introducing a subquery with one of the six comparison operators (=, <>, <, <=, >, >=) is often useful. In such a case, the expression preceding the operator evaluates to a single value, and the subquery following the operator must also evaluate to a single value. An exception is the case of the *quantified comparison operator,* which is a comparison operator followed by a quantifier (ANY, SOME, or ALL).

To illustrate a case in which a subquery returns a single value, look at another piece of Zetec Corporation's database. It contains a CUSTOMER table that holds information about the companies that buy Zetec products. It also contains a CONTACT table that holds personal data about individuals at each of Zetec's customer organizations. The tables are structured as shown in Tables 11-4 and 11-5:

Table 11-4	CUSTOMER Table	
Column	*Type*	*Constraints*
CUSTID	INTEGER	PRIMARY KEY
COMPANY	CHAR (40)	
CUSTADDRESS	CHAR (30)	
CUSTCITY	CHAR (20)	
CUSTSTATE	CHAR (2)	
CUSTZIP	CHAR (10)	
CUSTPHONE	CHAR (12)	
MODLEVEL	INTEGER	

Table 11-5	CONTACT Table	
Column	*Type*	*Constraints*
CUSTID	INTEGER	FOREIGN KEY
CONTFNAME	CHAR (10)	
CONTLNAME	CHAR (16)	
CONTPHONE	CHAR (12)	
CONTINFO	CHAR (50)	

Say that you want to look at the contact information for Olympic Sales, but you don't remember that company's CUSTID. Use a nested query like this one to recover the information you want:

```
SELECT *
   FROM CONTACT
      WHERE CONTID =
         (SELECT CONTID
            FROM CUSTOMER
               WHERE COMPANY = 'Olympic Sales') ;
```

The result looks something like this:

```
CUSTID CONTFNAME  CONTLNAME   CONTPHONE    CONTINFO
------ ---------  ---------   ---------    --------
   118 Jerry      Attwater    505-876-3456 Will play
                                           major role in
                                           coordinating
                                           the
                                           wireless
                                           Web.
```

You can now call Jerry at Olympic and tell him about this month's special sale on Web-enabled cell phones.

When you use a subquery in an "=" comparison, the SELECT list of the subquery must specify a single column (CONTID in the example). When the subquery is executed, it must return a single row in order to have a single value for the comparison.

In this example, I assume that the CUSTOMER table has only one row with a COMPANY value of 'Olympic Sales'. If the CREATE TABLE statement for CUSTOMER specified a UNIQUE constraint for COMPANY, such a statement guarantees that the subquery in the preceding example returns a single value (or no value). Subqueries like the one in the example, however, are commonly used on columns that are not specified to be UNIQUE. In such cases, you are relying on some other reasons for believing that the column has no duplicates.

If it turns out that more than one CUSTOMER has a value of 'Olympic Sales' in the COMPANY column, (perhaps in different states) then the subquery raises an error.

On the other hand, if no CUSTOMER with such a company name exists, then the subquery is treated as if it were null, and the comparison becomes "unknown." In this case, the WHERE clause returns no row (because it returns only rows with the condition True and filters rows with the condition False or "unknown"). This would probably happen, for example, if someone mis-spelled the COMPANY as 'Olumpic Sales'.

Although the equals operator (=) may be the most common, you can use any of the other five comparison operators in a similar structure. For every row in the table specified in the enclosing statement's FROM clause, the single value returned by the subquery is compared to the expression in the enclos-ing statement's WHERE clause. If the comparison gives a True value, a row is added to the result table.

You can guarantee that a subquery will return a single value if you include an aggregate function in it. Aggregate functions always return a single value. (Aggregate functions are described in Chapter 3.) Of course, this way of returning a single value is helpful only if you want the result of an aggregate function.

Say that you are a Zetec salesperson and you need to earn a big commission check to pay for some unexpected bills. You decide to concentrate on selling Zetec's most expensive product. You can find out what that product is with a nested query:

```
SELECT MODEL, PRODNAME, LISTPRICE
    FROM PRODUCT
        WHERE LISTPRICE =
            (SELECT MAX(LISTPRICE)
                FROM PRODUCT) ;
```

This is an example of a nested query where both the subquery and the enclosing statement operate on the same table. The subquery returns a single value: the maximum list price in the PRODUCT table. The outer query retrieves all rows from the PRODUCT table that have that list price.

The next example shows a comparison subquery that uses a comparison operator other than =:

```
SELECT MODEL, PRODNAME, LISTPRICE
    FROM PRODUCT
        WHERE LISTPRICE <
            (SELECT AVG(LISTPRICE)
                FROM PRODUCT) ;
```

The subquery returns a single value: the average list price in the PRODUCT table. The outer query retrieves all rows from the PRODUCT table that have a list price less than the average list price.

In the original SQL standard, a comparison could have only one subquery and it had to be on the right side of the comparison. SQL:1999 allows either or both operands of the comparison to be subqueries.

The ALL, SOME, and ANY quantifiers

Another way to make sure that a subquery returns a single value is to introduce it with a quantified comparison operator. The universal quantifier ALL and the existential quantifiers SOME and ANY, when combined with a comparison operator, process the list returned by a subquery, reducing it to a single value.

You'll see how these quantifiers affect a comparison by looking at the baseball pitchers complete game database from Chapter 10, which is listed next.

The contents of the two tables are given by the following two queries:

```
SELECT * FROM NATIONAL

FIRST_NAME   LAST_NAME   COMPLETE_GAMES
----------   ----------  --------------
Sal          Maglie                  11
Don          Newcombe                 9
Sandy        Koufax                  13
Don          Drysdale                12
Bob          Turley                   8

SELECT * FROM AMERICAN

FIRST_NAME   LAST_NAME   COMPLETE_GAMES
----------   ----------  --------------
Whitey       Ford                    12
Don          Larson                  10
Bob          Turley                   8
Allie        Reynolds                14
```

The theory is that the pitchers with the most complete games should be in the American League because of the presence of designated hitters in that league. One way to verify this theory is to build a query that returns all American League pitchers who have thrown more complete games than all the National League pitchers. The query can be formulated as follows:

```
SELECT *
   FROM AMERICAN
   WHERE COMPLETE_GAMES > ALL
      (SELECT COMPLETE_GAMES FROM NATIONAL) ;
```

This is the result:

```
FIRST_NAME   LAST_NAME   COMPLETE_GAMES
----------   ---------   --------------
Allie        Reynolds    14
```

The subquery (SELECT COMPLETE_GAMES FROM NATIONAL) returns the
values in the COMPLETE_GAMES column for all National League pitchers. The >
ALL quantifier says to return only those values of COMPLETE_GAMES in the
AMERICAN table that are greater than each of the values returned by the subquery. This condition translates into "greater than the highest value returned
by the subquery." In this case, the highest value returned by the subquery is
13 (Sandy Koufax). The only row in the American table higher than that is
Allie Reynolds's record, with 14 complete games.

What if your initial assumption was wrong? What if the major league leader in
complete games was a National League pitcher, in spite of the fact that the
National League has no designated hitter? If that were the case, the query

```
SELECT *
   FROM AMERICAN
   WHERE COMPLETE_GAMES > ALL
      (SELECT COMPLETE_GAMES FROM NATIONAL) ;
```

returns a warning stating that no rows satisfy the conditions of the query,
meaning that no American League pitcher has thrown more complete games
than the pitcher who has thrown the most complete games in the National
League.

Nested queries that are an existence test

A query returns data from all table rows that satisfy the conditions of the
query. Sometimes many rows are returned; sometimes only one. Sometimes
none of the rows in the table satisfy the conditions, and no rows are returned.
You can use the EXISTS and NOT EXISTS predicates to introduce a subquery.
That structure tells you whether any rows in the table located in the subquery's FROM clause meet the conditions in its WHERE clause.

Subqueries introduced with EXISTS and NOT EXISTS are fundamentally different from the subqueries in this chapter so far. In all the previous cases,
SQL first executes the subquery and then applies the result of that operation
to the enclosing statement. EXISTS and NOT EXISTS subqueries, on the
other hand, are examples of correlated subqueries.

A *correlated subquery* first finds the table and row specified by the enclosing
statement and then executes the subquery on the row in the subquery's table
that correlates with the current row of the enclosing statement's table.

The subquery either returns one or more rows or it returns none. If it returns at least one row, the `EXISTS` predicate succeeds, and the enclosing statement performs its action. In the same circumstances, the `NOT EXISTS` predicate fails, and the enclosing statement does not perform its action. After one row of the enclosing statement's table is processed, the same operation is performed on the next row. This action is repeated until every row in the enclosing statement's table has been processed.

EXISTS

Say that you are a salesperson for Zetec Corporation and you want to call your primary contact people at all of Zetec's customer organizations in California. Try the following query:

```
SELECT *
    FROM CONTACT
    WHERE EXISTS
        (SELECT *
            FROM CUSTOMER
            WHERE CUSTSTATE = 'CA'
                AND CONTACT.CUSTID = CUSTOMER.CUSTID) ;
```

Notice the reference to `CONTACT.CUSTID`, which is referencing a column from the outer query and comparing it with another column, `CUSTOMER.CUSTID` from the inner query. For each candidate row of the outer query, you evaluate the inner query, using the `CUSTID` value from the current `CONTACT` row of the outer query in the WHERE clause of the inner query.

The `CUSTID` column links the CONTACT table to the CUSTOMER table. SQL looks at the first record in the CONTACT table, finds the row in the CUSTOMER table that has the same `CUSTID`, and checks that row's `CUSTSTATE` field. If `CUSTOMER.CUSTSTATE = 'CA'`, then the current `CONTACT` row is added to the result table. The next `CONTACT` record is then processed in the same way, and so on until the entire CONTACT table has been processed. Since the query specifies `SELECT * FROM CONTACT`, all the fields of the contact table are returned, including the contact's name and phone number.

NOT EXISTS

In the previous example, the Zetec salesperson wanted to know the names and numbers of the contact people of all the customers in California. Imagine that a second salesperson is responsible for all of the U.S. except California. She can retrieve her contact people by using `NOT EXISTS` in a query similar to the preceding one:

```
SELECT *
    FROM CONTACT
    WHERE NOT EXISTS
        (SELECT *
            FROM CUSTOMER
            WHERE CUSTSTATE = 'CA'
                AND CONTACT.CUSTID = CUSTOMER.CUSTID) ;
```

Every row in CONTACT for which the subquery does not return a row is added to the result table.

Other correlated subqueries

As noted in a previous section of this chapter, subqueries introduced by IN or by a comparison operator need not be correlated queries, but they can be.

Correlated subqueries introduced with IN

In the section titled "Subqeries introduced by the keyword IN," earlier in this chapter, I discuss how a noncorrelated subquery can be used with the IN predicate. To show how a correlated subquery may use the IN predicate, ask the same question that came up with the EXISTS predicate. "What are the names and phone numbers of the contacts at all of Zetec's customers in California?" You can answer this question with a correlated IN subquery:

```
SELECT *
   FROM CONTACT
   WHERE 'CA' IN
      (SELECT CUSTSTATE
          FROM CUSTOMER
          WHERE CONTACT.CUSTID = CUSTOMER.CUSTID) ;
```

The statement is evaluated for each record in the CONTACT table. If, for that record, the CUSTID numbers in CONTACT and CUSTOMER match, then the value of CUSTOMER.CUSTSTATE is compared to 'CA'. The result of the subquery is a list that contains, at most, one element. If that one element is 'CA', the WHERE clause of the enclosing statement is satisfied, and a row is added to the query's result table.

Subqueries introduced with comparison operators

A correlated subquery can also be introduced by one of the six comparison operators, as shown in the next example.

Zetec pays bonuses to its salespeople based on their total monthly sales volume. The higher the volume is, the higher the bonus percentage is. The bonus percentage list is kept in a table named BONUSRATE:

MIN_AMOUNT	MAX_AMOUNT	BONUS_PCT
0.00	24999.99	0.
25000.00	49999.99	0.001
50000.00	99999.99	0.002
100000.00	249999.99	0.003
250000.00	499999.99	0.004
500000.00	749999.99	0.005
750000.00	999999.99	0.006

If a person's monthly sales are between $100,000.00 and $249,999.99, the bonus is 0.3 percent of sales.

Sales are recorded in a transaction master table named TRANSMASTER:

```
TRANSMASTER
-----------
Column          Type         Constraints
------          ----         -----------
TRANSID         INTEGER      PRIMARY KEY
CUSTID          INTEGER      FOREIGN KEY
EMPID           INTEGER      FOREIGN KEY
TRANSDATE       DATE
NET_AMOUNT      NUMERIC
FREIGHT         NUMERIC
TAX             NUMERIC
INVOICETOTAL    NUMERIC
```

Sales bonuses are based on the sum of the NET_AMOUNT field for all of a person's transactions in the month. You can find any particular person's bonus rate with a correlated subquery that uses comparison operators:

```
SELECT BONUS_PCT
    FROM BONUSRATE
        WHERE MIN_AMOUNT <=
            (SELECT SUM (NET_AMOUNT)
                FROM TRANSMASTER
                    WHERE EMPID = 133)
        AND MAX_AMOUNT >=
            (SELECT SUM (NET_AMOUNT)
                FROM TRANSMASTER
                    WHERE EMPID = 133) ;
```

This query is interesting in that it contains two subqueries, making use of the logical connective AND. The subqueries use the SUM aggregate operator, which returns a single value: the total monthly sales of employee number 133. That value is then compared against the MIN_AMOUNT and the MAX_AMOUNT columns in the BONUSRATE table, producing the bonus rate for that employee.

If you had not known the EMPID but had known the name of the person, you could arrive at the same answer with a more complex query:

```
SELECT BONUS_PCT
    FROM BONUSRATE
        WHERE MIN_AMOUNT <=
            (SELECT SUM (NET_AMOUNT)
                FROM TRANSMASTER
                    WHERE EMPID =
                        (SELECT EMPID
```

```
              FROM EMPLOYEE
                WHERE EMPLNAME = 'Coffin'))
    AND MAX_AMOUNT >=
        (SELECT SUM (NET_AMOUNT)
            FROM TRANSMASTER
              WHERE EMPID =
                  (SELECT EMPID
                      FROM EMPLOYEE
                        WHERE EMPLNAME = 'Coffin'));
```

This example uses subqueries nested within subqueries, which in turn are nested within an enclosing query, to arrive at the bonus rate for the employee named Coffin. This structure works only if you know for sure that the company has one, and only one, employee whose last name is Coffin. If you know that more than one employee is named Coffin, you can add terms to the WHERE clause of the innermost subquery until you are sure that only one row of the EMPLOYEE table is selected.

Subqueries in a HAVING clause

You can have a correlated subquery in a HAVING clause just as you can in a WHERE clause. As I mention in Chapter 9, a HAVING clause is normally preceded by a GROUP BY clause. The HAVING clause acts as a filter to restrict the groups created by the GROUP BY clause. Groups that don't satisfy the condition of the HAVING clause are not included in the result. When used in this way, the HAVING clause is evaluated for each group created by the GROUP BY clause. In the absence of a GROUP BY clause, the HAVING clause is evaluated for the set of rows passed by the WHERE clause, which is considered to be a single group. If neither a WHERE clause nor a GROUP BY clause is present, the HAVING clause is evaluated for the entire table:

```
SELECT TM1.EMPID
    FROM TRANSMASTER TM1
        GROUP BY TM1.EMPID
        HAVING MAX (TM1.NET_AMOUNT) >= ALL
            (SELECT 2 * AVG (TM2.NET_AMOUNT)
                FROM TRANSMASTER TM2
                    WHERE TM1.EMPID <> TM2.EMPID) ;
```

This query uses two aliases for the same table, enabling you to retrieve the employee ID number of all salespeople who had a sale of at least twice the average sale of all the other salespeople. The query works as follows:

1. The outer query groups TRANSMASTER rows by the EMPID. This is done with the SELECT, FROM, and GROUP BY clauses.

2. The HAVING clause filters these groups. For each group, it calculates the MAX of the NET_AMOUNT column for the rows in that group.

3. The inner query evaluates twice the average NET_AMOUNT from all rows of TRANSMASTER whose EMPID is different from the EMPID of the current group of the outer query. Note that in the last line you need to reference two different EMPID values, so in the FROM clauses of the outer and inner queries, you use different aliases for TRANSMASTER.

4. You then use those aliases in the comparison of the last line of the query to indicate that you are referencing both the EMPID from the current row of the inner subquery (TM2.EMPID) and the EMPID from the current group of the outer subquery (TM1.EMPID).

UPDATE, DELETE, and INSERT statements

In addition to SELECT statements, UPDATE, DELETE, and INSERT statements can also include WHERE clauses. Those WHERE clauses can contain subqueries in the same way that SELECT statement WHERE clauses do.

For example, Zetec has just made a volume purchase deal with Olympic Sales and wants to retroactively provide Olympic with a 10 percent credit for all its purchases in the last month. You can give this credit with an UPDATE statement:

```
UPDATE TRANSMASTER
    SET NET_AMOUNT = NET_AMOUNT * 0.9
    WHERE CUSTID =
        (SELECT CUSTID
            FROM CUSTOMER
            WHERE COMPANY = 'Olympic Sales') ;
```

You can also have a correlated subquery in an UPDATE statement. Suppose the CUSTOMER table has a column LAST_MONTHS_MAX, and Zetec wants to give such a credit for purchases that exceed LAST_MONTHS_MAX for the customer:

```
UPDATE TRANSMASTER TM
    SET NET_AMOUNT = NET_AMOUNT * 0.9
    WHERE NET_AMOUNT >
        (SELECT LAST_MONTHS_MAX
            FROM CUSTOMER C
            WHERE C.CUSTID = TM.CUSTID) ;
```

Note that this subquery is correlated: The WHERE clause in the last line references both the CUSTID of the CUSTOMER row from the subquery and the CUSTID of the current TRANSMASTER row that is a candidate for updating.

A subquery in an UPDATE statement can also reference the table that is being updated. Suppose that Zetec wants to give a 10 percent credit to customers whose purchases have exceeded $10,000:

```
UPDATE TRANSMASTER TM1
   SET NET_AMOUNT = NET_AMOUNT * 0.9
   WHERE 10000 < (SELECT SUM(NET_AMOUNT)
     FROM TRANSMASTER TM2
              WHERE TM1.CUSTID = TM2.CUSTID);
```

The inner subquery calculates the SUM of the NET_AMOUNT column for all TRANSMASTER rows for the same customer. What does this mean? Suppose that customer CUSTID 37 has four rows in TRANSMASTER with values for NET_AMOUNT: 3000, 5000, 2000, and 1000. The SUM of NET_AMOUNT for this CUSTID is 11000.

Note that the order in which the UPDATE statement processes the rows is defined by your implementation and is generally not predictable. The order may differ depending on how the rows are actually arranged on the disk. Assume that the implementation processes the rows for this CUSTID are in this order: first the TRANSMASTER with NET_AMOUNT 3000; then the one with NET_AMOUNT 5000; and so on. After the first three rows for CUSTID 37 have been updated, their NET_AMOUNT values are 2700 (90 percent of 3000), 4500 (90 percent of 5000), and 1800 (90 percent of 2000). Then when you process the last TRANSMASTER row for CUSTID 37, whose NET_AMOUNT is 1000, the SUM returned by the subquery would seem to be 10000 — that is, the SUM of the new NET_AMOUNT values of the first three rows for CUSTID 37, and the old NET_AMOUNT value of the last row for CUSTID 37. Thus it would seem that the last row for CUSTID 37 isn't updated, because the comparison with that SUM is not True (10000 is not less than SELECT SUM (NET_AMOUNT)). But that is not how the UPDATE statement is defined when a subquery references the table that is being updated. *All* evaluations of subqueries in an UPDATE statement reference the old values of the table being updated. In the preceding UPDATE for CUSTID 37, the subquery returns 11000 — the original SUM.

The subquery in a WHERE clause operates exactly the same as a SELECT statement or an UPDATE statement. The same is true for DELETE and INSERT. To delete all of Olympic's transactions, use this statement:

```
DELETE TRANSMASTER
   WHERE CUSTID =
      (SELECT CUSTID
          FROM CUSTOMER
          WHERE COMPANY = 'Olympic Sales') ;
```

As with UPDATE, DELETE subqueries can also be correlated and can also reference the table being deleted. The rules are similar to the rules for UPDATE subqueries. Suppose you want to delete all rows from TRANSMASTER for customers whose total NET_AMOUNT is larger than $10,000:

```
DELETE TRANSMASTER TM1
   WHERE 10000 < (SELECT SUM(NET_AMOUNT)
     FROM TRANSMASTER TM2
          WHERE TM1.CUSTID = TM2.CUSTID) ;
```

This query deletes all rows from TRANSMASTER that have CUSTID 37, as well as any other customers with purchases exceeding $10,000. All references to TRANSMASTER in the subquery denote the contents of TRANSMASTER before any deletes by the current statement. So even when you are deleting the last TRANSMASTER row for CUSTID 37, the subquery is evaluated on the original TRANSMASTER table and returns 11000.

When you update, delete, or insert database records, you risk making a table's data inconsistent with other tables in the database. Such an inconsistency is called a *modification anomaly,* discussed in Chapter 5. If you delete TRANSMAS-TER records and a TRANSDETAIL table depends on TRANSMASTER, you must delete the corresponding records from TRANSDETAIL, too. This operation is called a *cascading delete,* because the deletion of a parent record must cascade to its associated child records. Otherwise, the undeleted child records become orphans. In this case, they would be invoice detail lines that are in limbo because they are no longer connected to an invoice record.

INSERT can include a SELECT clause. A use for this statement is filling "snap-shot" tables. For a table with the contents of TRANSMASTER for October 27, do this:

```
CREATE TABLE TRANSMASTER_1027
    (TRANSID INTEGER, TRANSDATE DATE,
    ...) ;
INSERT INTO TRANSMASTER_1027
    (SELECT * FROM TRANSMASTER
        WHERE TRANSDATE = 2000-10-27) ;
```

Or you may want to save rows only for large NET_AMOUNTs:

```
INSERT INTO TRANSMASTER_1027
    (SELECT * FROM TRANSMASTER TM
    WHERE TM.NET_AMOUNT > 10000
        AND TRANSDATE = 2000-10-27) ;
```

Chapter 12

Recursive Queries

• •

• •

*O*ne of the major criticisms of SQL, up through and including SQL-92, was its inability to implement recursive processing. Many important problems that are difficult to solve by other means yield readily to recursive solutions. Extensions included in SQL:1999 allow recursive queries, greatly expanding the power of the language. If the implementation of SQL that you are using includes the recursion extensions, you will be able to efficiently solve a large new class of problems. However, since recursion is not a part of core SQL:1999, many implementations currently available do not include it.

What Is Recursion?

Well, for one thing, it's a feature that's been around for years in programming languages such as Logo, LISP, and C++. In these languages, you can define a *function* (a set of one or more commands) that performs a specific operation. The main program invokes the function by issuing a command called a *function call*. If the function calls itself as a part of its operation, you have the simplest form of recursion.

A simple program that uses recursion in one of its functions provides an illustration of the joys and pitfalls of recursion. The following program, written in C++, draws a spiral on the computer screen. It assumes that the drawing tool is initially pointing toward the top of the screen, and includes three functions:

✔ The function `line(n)` draws a line *n* units long.

✔ The function `left_turn(d)` rotates the drawing tool *d* degrees counterclockwise.

✔ We can also define the function `spiral(segment)` as follows:

```
void spiral(int segment)
{
    line(segment)
    left_turn(90)
    spiral(segment + 1)
} ;
```

If we call spiral(1) from the main program, the following actions take place:

spiral(1) draws a line one unit long toward the top of the screen.

spiral(1) turns left 90 degrees.

spiral(1) calls spiral(2).

spiral(2) draws a line 2 units long toward the left side of the screen.

spiral(2) turns left 90 degrees.

spiral(2) calls spiral(3).

And so on . . .

Eventually the program generates the spiral curve shown in Figure 12-1.

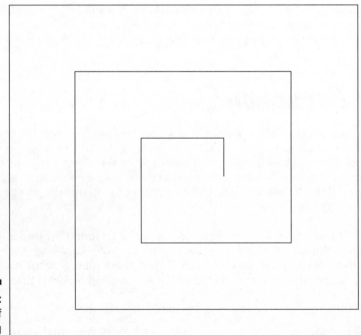

Figure 12-1:
Result of
calling
spiral
(1).

Houston, we have a problem

Well, okay. The situation here is not as serious as it was for Apollo 13 when their main oxygen tank exploded into space while they were en route to the moon. However, we still have a problem: Our little program is running away from us. It keeps calling itself and drawing longer and longer lines. It will continue to do that until the computer trying to execute it runs out of resources and (if we're lucky) puts an obnoxious error message up on the screen. If we're unlucky, the computer just crashes.

Failure is not an option

This scenario shows one of the dangers of using recursion. A program written to call itself invokes a new instance of itself — which in turn calls yet another instance, ad infinitum. This is generally not what you want. To address this problem, programmers include a *termination condition* within the recursive function — a limit on how deep the recursion can go — so the program performs the desired action and then terminates gracefully. We can include a termination condition in our spiral-drawing program to save computer resources and prevent dizziness in programmers:

```
void spiral2(int segment)
{
    if (segment <= 10)
    {
        line(segment)
        left_turn(90)
        spiral2(segment + 1)
    }
} ;
```

When you call spiral2(1), it executes and then (recursively) calls itself until the value of segment exceeds 10. At the point where segment = 11, the if (segment <=10) construct returns a False value and the code within the interior braces gets skipped. Control returns to the previous invocation of spiral2, and from there returns all the way up to the first invocation, after which the program terminates. Figure 12-2 shows the sequence of calls and returns that occurs.

Every time a function calls itself, it takes you one level farther away from the main program that was the starting point of the operation. For the main program to continue, the deepest iteration must return control to the iteration that called it. That iteration will have to do likewise, continuing all the way back to the main program that made the first call to the recursive function.

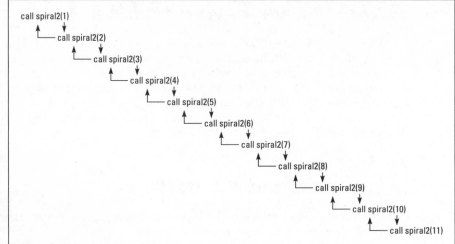

Figure 12-2:
Descending
through
recursive
calls, and
then
climbing
back up to
terminate.

Recursion is a powerful tool for repeatedly executing code when you don't know at the outset how many times the code should be repeated. It is also ideal for searching through tree-shaped structures such as family trees, complex electronic circuits, or multilevel distribution networks.

What Is a Recursive Query?

A recursive query is a query that is functionally dependent on itself. The simplest form of such functional dependence is the case where a query Q1 includes an invocation of itself in the query expression body. A more complex case would be where query Q1 depends on query Q2, which it turn depends on query Q1. There is still a functional dependency, and recursion is still involved, no matter how many queries lie in between the first and the second invocation of the same query.

Where Might I Use a Recursive Query?

Recursive queries might help save time and frustration in various kinds of problems. Suppose, for example, that you have a pass that gives you free air travel on any flight of the (fictional) Vannevar Airlines. Way cool — the next question is: *Where can I go for free?* The FLIGHT table contains all the flights that Vannevar runs. Table 12-1 shows the flight number and the source and destination of each flight.

Table 12-1	Flights Offered by Vannevar Airlines	
Flight No.	*Source*	*Destination*
3141	Portland	Orange County
2173	Portland	Charlotte
623	Portland	Daytona Beach
5440	Orange County	Montgomery
221	Charlotte	Memphis
32	Memphis	Champaign
981	Montgomery	Memphis

Figure 12-3 illustrates the routes on a map of the United States.

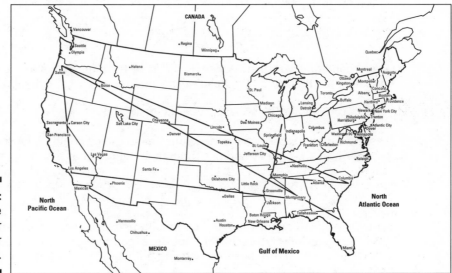

Figure 12-3:
Route
map for
Vannevar
Airlines.

Okay, to get that vacation plan started, you can create a database table for FLIGHT by using SQL as follows:

```
CREATE TABLE FLIGHT (
    FlightNo          INTEGER              NOT NULL,
    Source        CHARACTER (30),
    Destination       CHARACTER (30)
);
```

Once the table is created, you can populate it with the data shown in Table 12-1.

Suppose you're starting from Portland and you'd like to visit a friend in Montgomery. Naturally you'd wonder, *What cities can I reach via Vannevar if I start from Portland?* and *What cities can I reach via the same airline if I start from Montgomery?* Some cities are reachable in one hop, others are not. Some might require two or more hops. You can find all the cities that Vannevar will take you to, starting from any given city on their route map — but if you do it one query at a time, you're . . . .

Querying the hard way

To find out what you want to know — provided you have the time and patience — you could make a series of queries, starting with `Portland` as the starting city:

```
SELECT Destination FROM FLIGHT WHERE Source = "Portland";
```

The first query returns `Orange County`, `Charlotte`, and `Daytona Beach`. Your second query could use the first of these results as a starting point:

```
SELECT Destination FROM FLIGHT WHERE Source = "Orange
          County";
```

The second query returns `Montgomery`. Your third query could return to the results of the first query, and use the second result as a starting point:

```
SELECT Destination FROM FLIGHT WHERE Source = "Charlotte";
```

The third query returns `Memphis`. Your fourth query could go back to the results of the first query and use the remaining result as a starting point:

```
SELECT Destination FROM FLIGHT WHERE Source = "Daytona
          Beach";
```

Sorry, the fourth query returns a null result because Vannevar offers no outgoing flights from Daytona Beach. But the second query returned another city (`Montgomery`) as a possible starting point, so your fifth query could use that result:

```
SELECT Destination FROM FLIGHT WHERE Source = "Montgomery";
```

This query returns `Memphis`, but that doesn't matter; you already know it's among the cities you can get to (in this case, via Charlotte). But you might as well try this latest result as a starting point for another query:

```
SELECT Destination FROM FLIGHT WHERE Source = "Memphis";
```

And sonofagun, the query returns `Champaign` — which you can add to the list of reachable cities (even if you have to get there in two hops). As long as you're considering multiple hops, you might as well plug in `Champaign` as a starting point:

```
SELECT Destination FROM FLIGHT WHERE Source = "Champaign";
```

Oops. This query returns a null value; Vannevar offers no outgoing flights from Champaign. (Seven queries so far. Anybody fidgeting yet?)

Of course, Vannevar doesn't offer a flight out of Daytona Beach, either, so if you go there, you're stuck there — which might not be a hardship if it's Spring Break week. (Of course, if you use up a week running individual queries to find out where to go next, you might get a worse headache than you'd get from a week of partying.) Or you might get stuck in Champaign — in which case, you might as well enroll in the University of Illinois and take a few database courses. (They might even help you figure out how to get out of Daytona or Champaign.)

Granted, this method will (eventually) answer the question, *What cities are reachable from Portland?* But running one query after another, making each one depend on the results of a previous query, is complicated, time-consuming, and (frankly) fidgety.

Saving time with a recursive query

A simpler way to get the info you need would be to craft a single recursive query that does the entire job in one operation. And (will wonders never cease?) here's the syntax for just such a query:

```
WITH RECURSIVE
    ReachableFrom (Source, Destination)
        AS (SELECT Source, Destination
              FROM FLIGHT
            UNION
            SELECT in.Source, out.Destination
              FROM ReachableFrom in, FLIGHT out
              WHERE in.Destination = out.Source
        )
    SELECT * FROM ReachableFrom
    WHERE Source = "Portland";
```

The first time through the recursion, FLIGHT has seven rows and ReachableFrom has none. The UNION takes the seven rows from FLIGHT and copies them into ReachableFrom. At this point, ReachableFrom has the data shown in Table 12-2.

Table 12-2	ReachableFrom after One Pass through Recursion
Source	*Destination*
Portland	Orange County
Portland	Charlotte
Portland	Daytona Beach
Orange County	Montgomery
Charlotte	Memphis
Memphis	Champaign
Montgomery	Memphis

The second time through the recursion, things start to get interesting. The WHERE clause (WHERE in.Destination = out.Source) means that you're looking only at rows where the Destination field of the ReachableFrom table equals the Source field of the FLIGHT table. For those rows, you're taking the Source field from ReachableFrom and the Destination field from FLIGHT, and adding those two fields to ReachableFrom as a new row. Table 12-3 shows the result of this iteration of the recursion.

Table 12-3	ReachableFrom after Two Passes through the Recursion
Source	*Destination*
Portland	Orange County
Portland	Charlotte
Portland	Daytona Beach
Orange County	Montgomery
Charlotte	Memphis
Memphis	Champaign
Montgomery	Memphis
Portland	Montgomery
Portland	Memphis
Orange County	Memphis
Charlotte	Champaign

The results are looking a lot more useful. ReachableFrom now contains all the `Destination` cities that are reachable from any `Source` city in two hops or less. The recursion will next process three-hop trips, and so on until all possible destination cities have been reached.

After the recursion is complete, the third and final `SELECT` statement (which is outside the recursion) extracts from ReachableFrom only those cities you can reach from Portland by flying Vannevar. In this example, all six other cities are reachable from Portland — in few enough hops that you won't think you're going by pogo stick.

Well, okay, if you scrutinize the code in the recursive query, it doesn't *look* any simpler than the seven individual queries that it replaces. It does, however, have two advantages:

- ✔ When you set it in motion, it completes the entire operation without any further intervention.
- ✔ It can do the job really fast.

Imagine, if you will, a real-world airline with many more cities on its route map. The more possible destinations, the bigger the advantage of using the recursive method.

What makes this query recursive? It is the fact that we are defining ReachableFrom in terms of itself. The recursive part of the definition is the second `SELECT` statement, the one just after the `UNION`. ReachableFrom is a temporary table that progressively gets filled with data as the recursion proceeds. Processing continues until all possible destinations have been added to ReachableFrom. Any duplicates are eliminated, because the `UNION` operator does not add duplicates to the result table. After the recursion completes, ReachableFrom contains all the cities that are reachable from any starting city. The third and final `SELECT` statement returns only those destination cities that you can reach from Portland. Bon voyage.

Where Else Might I Use a Recursive Query?

Any problem that you can lay out as a tree-like structure can potentially be solved using a recursive query. The classic industrial application is materials processing (the process of turning raw stuff into finished things). Suppose your company is building a new gasoline-electric hybrid car. Such a machine is built of subassemblies — engine, batteries, and so on — which in turn are constructed from smaller subassemblies (crankshaft, electrodes, and so on) — which are made of even smaller parts. Keeping track of all the parts of parts can be very difficult in a relational database that does not use recursion. Recursion allows you to start with the complete machine and ferret your way along any path to get to the smallest part. Want to find out the specs for the fastening screw that holds the clamp to the negative electrode of the auxiliary battery? Can do — in nearly no time. The `WITH RECURSIVE` structure gives SQL the capability to address such problems.

Recursion is also a natural for 'What if?' processing. In the Vannevar Airlines example, what if management decides to discontinue service from Portland to Charlotte? How will that affect the cities that are reachable from Portland? A recursive query will quickly give you the answer.

Chapter 13

Providing Database Security

A system administrator has to have various kinds of special knowledge that cover the ways a database works. That's why, in preceding chapters, I discuss the parts of SQL that create databases and manipulate data — and then (in Chapter 3) introduce SQL's facilities for protecting databases from harm or misuse. In this chapter, I go into more depth on the subject of misuse.

The person in charge of a database can determine who has access to the database — and can set the level of access that a user receives, granting or revoking access to certain aspects of the system. The system administrator can even grant — or revoke — the right to grant and revoke access privileges. If you use them correctly, the security tools that SQL provides are powerful protectors of important data. Used incorrectly, these same tools can tie up the efforts of legitimate users in a big knot of red tape when they're only trying to do their jobs.

Granted, databases often contain sensitive information that you shouldn't make available to everyone. That's why SQL provides different levels of access — from complete to none, with several levels in between. By controlling exactly which operations each authorized user can perform, the database administrator (about whom more in a moment) can make available all the data that the users need to do their jobs — but restrict access to parts of the database that not everyone should see or change.

The SQL Data Control Language

The SQL statements that you use to create databases form a group known as the *Data Definition Language (DDL)*. After you create a database, you can use another set of SQL statements — known collectively as the *Data Manipulation Language (DML)* — to add, change, and remove data from the database. SQL includes additional statements that don't fall into either of these categories. Programmers sometimes refer to these statements collectively as the *Data Control Language (DCL)*. DCL statements primarily protect the database from unauthorized access, from harmful interaction among multiple database users, and from power failures and equipment malfunctions. In this chapter, I discuss protection from unauthorized access.

User Access Levels

SQL:1999 provides controlled access to six database management functions: creating, seeing, modifying, deleting, referencing, and using. *Creating, seeing, modifying,* and *deleting* correspond to the INSERT, SELECT, UPDATE, and DELETE operations that I discuss in Chapter 6. *Referencing* — that is, using the REFERENCES keyword (which I discuss in Chapters 3 and 5) — involves applying referential integrity constraints to a table that depends on another table in the database. *Using,* which you specify with the USAGE keyword, pertains to domains, character sets, collations, and translations. (I define domains, character sets, collations, and translations in Chapter 5.)

The database administrator

In most installations large enough to have more than a few users, the supreme authority for a database is the *database administrator (DBA)*. The DBA has all rights and privileges to all aspects of the database. Being a DBA can give you a real feeling of power, but the position is also a great responsibility. With all that power at your disposal, you can easily mess up your database and destroy thousands of hours of work. DBAs must think clearly and carefully about the consequences of every action they perform.

Not only does the DBA have all rights to the database, but the DBA also controls the rights that other users can have. This way, highly trusted individuals can access more functions — and, perhaps, more tables — than can the majority of users.

The best way to become a DBA is to install the database-management system yourself. If you do, the installation manual gives you an account, or *login,* and a password. That login identifies you as a specially privileged user. Sometimes, the system calls this privileged user the DBA, sometimes the *system administrator,* and sometimes the *super user* (sorry, no cape and boots provided). In any event, as your first official act after logging in, you should change your password from the default to a secret one of your own. If you don't change the password, anyone who reads the manual can also log in with full DBA privileges. This situation may not prove very healthy for your database. After you change the password, only people who know the new password can log in as DBA.

I suggest that you share the new DBA password with only a small number of highly trusted people. After all, a falling meteor could strike you tomorrow; you could win the lottery; or you may become unavailable to the company in some other way. Your colleagues must be able to carry on in your absence. Anyone who knows the DBA login and password becomes the DBA after the person uses that information to access the system.

If you have DBA privileges, I suggest that you log in as DBA only if you need to perform a specific task that requires DBA privileges. After you finish, log out. For routine work, log in by using your own personal login ID and password. This approach may save you from making mistakes that have serious consequences for other users' tables (as well as for your own).

Database object owners

Another class of privileged user, along with the DBA, is the *database object owner.* Tables and views, for example, are database objects. Any user who creates such an object can specify its owner. A table owner enjoys every possible privilege associated with that table, including the privilege to grant access to the table to other people. Because you can base views on underlying tables, someone other than a table's owner can actually create a view based on that owner's table. In such a case, however, the view owner receives only the same privileges for the view as that user normally does for the underlying table. The bottom line, therefore, is that a user can't circumvent the protection on another user's table simply by creating a view based on that table.

It's a tough job, but . . .

You're probably wondering how you can become a DBA (database administrator) and accrue for yourself all the status and admiration that goes with the title. The obvious answer is to kiss up to the boss in the hope of landing this plum assignment. Demonstrating competence, integrity, and reliability in the performance of your everyday duties may even help. (Actually, the key requisite is that you're sucker enough to take the job. I was kidding when I said that stuff about status and admiration. Mostly, the DBA gets the blame if anything goes wrong with the database — and invariably, sooner or later, something does.) So it helps to have the fortitude of a superhero, even if you don't have the cape and boots.

The public

In network terms, "the public" consists of all users who are not specially privileged users (that is, either DBAs or object owners) and to whom a privileged user hasn't specifically granted access rights. If a privileged user grants certain access rights to PUBLIC, then everyone who can access the system gains those rights.

In most installations, a hierarchy of user privilege exists, in which the DBA stands at the highest level and the public at the lowest. Figure 13-1 illustrates the privilege hierarchy.

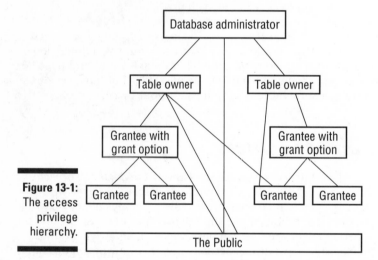

Figure 13-1:
The access
privilege
hierarchy.

Granting Privileges to Users

The DBA, by virtue of his or her position, has all privileges on all objects in the database. After all, the owner of an object has all privileges with respect to that object — and the database itself is an object. No one else has any privileges with respect to any object, unless someone who already has those privileges (and the authority to pass them on) specifically grants the privileges. You grant privileges to someone else by using the GRANT statement, which has the following syntax:

```
GRANT privilege-list
    ON object
    TO user-list
    [WITH GRANT OPTION] ;
```

In this statement, `privilege-list` is defined as follows:

```
privilege [, privilege] ...
```

or

```
ALL PRIVILEGES
```

Here `privilege` is defined as follows:

```
SELECT
  | DELETE
  | INSERT [(column-name [, column-name]...)]
  | UPDATE [(column-name [, column-name]...)]
  | REFERENCES [(column-name [, column-name]...)]
  | USAGE
```

In the original statement, `object` is defined as follows:

```
[TABLE] table-name
  | DOMAIN domain-name
  | CHARACTER SET character-set-name
  | COLLATION collation-name
  | TRANSLATION translation-name
```

And `user-list` in the statement is defined as follows:

```
login-ID [, login-ID]...
  | PUBLIC
```

The preceding syntax considers a view to be a table. The SELECT, DELETE, INSERT, UPDATE, and REFERENCES privileges apply to tables and views only. The USAGE privilege applies to domains, character sets, collations, and translations. The following sections give examples of the various ways you can use the GRANT statement and the results of those uses.

Roles

A *user name* is one type of authorization identifier but not the only one. It identifies a person (or a program) who is authorized to perform one or more functions on a database. In a large organization with many users, granting privileges to every individual employee could become tedious and time-consuming in a hurry. SQL:1999 addresses this problem by introducing the notion of roles.

A *role,* identified by a role name, is a set of zero or more privileges that can be granted to multiple people who all require the same level of access to the database. For example, all the people who perform the role SECURITY_GUARD would have the same privileges. These privileges would probably be different from those granted to the people who have the role SALES_CLERK.

Because roles are not a part of the core SQL:1999 specification, they may not be present in some implementations. Check your DBMS documentation before you try to use roles.

You can create roles using syntax similar to the following:

```
CREATE ROLE SALES_CLERK ;
```

After you create a role, you can grant it privileges in exactly the same way that you grant privileges to users, with one exception: It won't argue or complain.

Inserting data

To grant someone the privilege of adding data to a table, follow this example:

```
GRANT INSERT
    ON CUSTOMER
    TO SALES_CLERK ;
```

This privilege enables the clerk in the sales department to add new customer records to the CUSTOMER table.

Looking at data

To enable someone to view the data in a table, use the following example:

```
GRANT SELECT
    ON PRODUCT
    TO PUBLIC ;
```

This privilege enables anyone with access to the system (PUBLIC) to view the contents of the PRODUCT table.

Actually, this statement can be dangerous. Columns in the PRODUCT table may contain information that not everyone should see, such as COST_OF_GOODS. To provide access to most information while withholding access to sensitive information, define a view on the table that doesn't include the sensitive columns. Then grant SELECT privileges on the view rather than on the underlying table. The following example shows the syntax for this procedure:

```
CREATE VIEW MERCHANDISE AS
    SELECT MODEL, PRODNAME, PRODDESC, LISTPRICE
        FROM PRODUCT ;
GRANT SELECT
    ON MERCHANDISE
    TO PUBLIC ;
```

Using the MERCHANDISE view, the public doesn't get to see the PRODUCT table's COST_OF_GOODS column or any other column except the four listed in the CREATE VIEW.

Modifying table data

In any active organization, table data changes over time. You need to grant to some people the right and power to make changes and to prevent everyone else from doing so. To grant change privileges, follow this example:

```
GRANT UPDATE (BONUSPCT)
    ON BONUSRATE
    TO SALES_MGR ;
```

The sales manager can adjust the bonus rate that salespeople receive for sales (the BONUSPCT column), based on changes in market conditions. The sales manager can't, however, modify the values in the MINAMOUNT and MAX-AMOUNT columns that define the ranges for each step in the bonus schedule. To enable updates to all columns, you must either specify all column names or not specify any column names at all, as shown in the following example:

```
GRANT UPDATE
    ON BONUSRATE
    TO VP_SALES ;
```

Deleting obsolete rows from a table

Customers go out of business or stop buying for some other reason. Employees quit, retire, are laid off, or die. Products become obsolete. Life goes on, and things that you tracked in the past may no longer be of interest to you. Someone needs to remove obsolete records from your tables. On the other hand, you want to carefully control who can remove which records. Regulating such privileges is another job for the GRANT statement, as shown in the following example:

```
GRANT DELETE
    ON EMPLOYEE
    TO PERSONNEL_MGR ;
```

The personnel manager can remove records from the EMPLOYEE table. So can the DBA and the EMPLOYEE table owner (who's probably the DBA also). No one else can remove personnel records (unless another GRANT statement gives that person the power to do so).

Referencing related tables

If one table includes a second table's primary key as a foreign key, information in the second table becomes available to users of the first table. This situation potentially creates a dangerous "back door" through which unauthorized users can extract confidential information. In such a case, a user doesn't need access rights to a table to discover something about its contents. If the user has access rights to a table that references the target table, those rights are often enough to enable him to access the target table as well.

Suppose, for example, that the table LAYOFF_LIST contains the names of the employees who are to be laid off next month. Only authorized management people have SELECT access to the table. An unauthorized employee, however, deduces that the table's primary key is EMPID. The employee then creates a new table SNOOP, which has EMPID as a foreign key, enabling him to sneak a peek at LAYOFF_LIST. (I describe how to create a foreign key with a REFERENCES clause in Chapter 5. It's high on the list of techniques every system administrator should know.)

```
CREATE TABLE SNOOP
   (EMPID INTEGER REFERENCES LAYOFF_LIST) ;
```

Now all the employee needs to do is try to INSERT rows corresponding to the employee ID numbers of all employees into SNOOP. The inserts that the table accepts are those for the employees on the layoff list. All rejected inserts are for employees not on the list.

SQL:1999 prevents this kind of security breach by requiring that a privileged user explicitly grant any reference rights to other users, as shown in the following example:

```
GRANT REFERENCES (EMPID)
   ON LAYOFF_LIST
   TO PERSONNEL_CLERK ;
```

Using domains, character sets, collations, and translations

Domains, character sets, collations, and translations also have an effect on security issues. Created domains, in particular, must be watched closely to avoid their use as a way to undermine your security measures.

You can define a domain that encompasses a set of columns. In doing so, you want all these columns to have the same type and to share the same constraints. The columns you create in your CREATE DOMAIN inherit the type and constraints of the domain. You can override these characteristics for specific columns, if you want, but domains provide a convenient way to apply numerous characteristics to multiple columns with a single declaration.

Domains come in handy if you have multiple tables that all contain columns with similar characteristics. Your business database, for example, may consist of several tables, each of which contains a PRICE column that should have a type of DECIMAL(10,2) and values that are nonnegative and no greater than 10,000. Before you create the tables that hold these columns, you must create a domain that specifies the columns' characteristics, as does the following example:

```
CREATE DOMAIN PRICE_TYPE_DOMAIN  DECIMAL (10,2)
    CHECK (PRICE >= 0 AND VALUE <= 10000) ;
```

Perhaps you identify your products in multiple tables by PRODUCT_CODE, which is always of type CHAR (5), with a first character of X, C, or H and a last character of either 9 or 0. You can create a domain for these columns, too, as in the following example:

```
CREATE DOMAIN PRODUCT_CODE_DOMAIN CHAR (5)
    CHECK (SUBSTR (VALUE, 1,1) IN ('X', 'C', 'H')
    AND SUBSTR (VALUE, 5, 1) IN (9, 0) ) ;
```

With the domains in place, you can now proceed to create tables, as follows:

```
CREATE TABLE PRODUCT
    (PRODUCT_CODE PRODUCT_CODE_DOMAIN,
    PRODUCT_NAME CHAR (30),
    PRICE PRICE_TYPE_DOMAIN) ;
```

In the table definition, instead of giving the data type for PRODUCT_CODE and PRICE, specify the appropriate domain instead. This action gives those columns the correct type and also applies the constraints you specify in your CREATE DOMAIN statements.

Certain security implications go with the use of domains. What if someone else wants to use the domains you create — may such use cause problems? Yes. What if someone creates a table with a column that has a domain of PRICE_TYPE_DOMAIN? That person can assign progressively larger values to that column until it rejects a value. By doing so, the person can determine the upper bound on PRICE_TYPE that you specify in the CHECK clause of your CREATE DOMAIN statement. If you consider that upper bound private information, you don't want to enable others to use the PRICE_TYPE domain. To protect you in situations such as this example, SQL enables only those to whom the domain owner explicitly grants permission to use domains. Thus only the domain owner (as well as the DBA, of course) can grant such permission. You can grant permission by using a statement such as the one shown in the following example:

```
GRANT USAGE ON DOMAIN PRICE_TYPE TO SALES_MGR ;
```

Different security problems may arise if you DROP domains. Tables that contain columns that you define in terms of a domain cause problems if you try to DROP the domain. You may need to DROP all such tables first. Or you may find yourself unable to DROP the domain. How a domain DROP is handled may vary from one implementation to another. SQL Server may do it one way, whereas Oracle does it another. At any rate, you may want to restrict who can DROP domains. The same applies to character sets, collations, and translations.

Granting the Power to Grant Privileges

The DBA can grant any privileges to anyone. An object owner can grant any privileges on that object to anyone. Users who receive privileges this way, however, can't in turn grant those privileges to someone else. This restriction helps the DBA or table owner retain a good measure of control. Only people the DBA or object owner empowers to do so can gain access to the object in question.

From a security standpoint, putting limits on the capability to delegate access privileges makes a lot of sense. Many occasions arise, however, in which users need such delegation authority. Work can't come to a screeching halt every time someone is ill, on vacation, or out to lunch. You can trust *some* users with the power to delegate their access rights to reliable designated alternates. To pass such a right of delegation to a user, the GRANT uses the WITH GRANT OPTION clause. The following statement shows one example of how you can use this clause:

```
GRANT UPDATE (BONUSPCT)
    ON BONUSRATE
    TO SALES_MGR
    WITH GRANT OPTION ;
```

Now the sales manager can delegate the UPDATE privilege by issuing the following statement:

```
GRANT UPDATE (BONUSPCT)
    ON BONUSRATE
    TO ASST_SALES_MGR ;
```

After the execution of this statement, the assistant sales manager can make changes to the BONUSRATE table — a power she didn't have before.

A tradeoff exists between security and convenience. The owner of the BONUSRATE table relinquishes considerable control in granting the UPDATE privilege to the sales manager by using the WITH GRANT OPTION. One hopes that the sales manager takes this responsibility seriously and is careful about passing on the privilege.

Taking Privileges Away

If you have a way to give access privileges to people, you'd better have a way of taking those privileges away, too. People's job functions change, and with the change, their need for access to data changes. People may even leave the organization to join a competitor. You should probably revoke all the access privileges of such people. SQL provides for the removal of access privileges by using the REVOKE statement. This statement acts just as the GRANT statement does, except that it has the reverse effect. The syntax for this statement is as follows:

```
REVOKE [GRANT OPTION FOR] privilege-list
    ON object
    FROM user-list [RESTRICT|CASCADE] ;
```

You can use this structure to revoke specified privileges while leaving others intact. The principal difference between the REVOKE statement and the GRANT statement is the presence of the optional RESTRICT or CASCADE keyword in the REVOKE statement. If you used WITH GRANT OPTION to grant the privileges you're revoking, using CASCADE in the REVOKE statement revokes privileges for the grantee and also for anyone to whom that person granted those privileges as a result of the WITH GRANT OPTION clause. On the other hand, the REVOKE statement with the RESTRICT option works only if the grantee hasn't delegated the specified privileges. In the latter case, the REVOKE statement revokes the grantee's privileges. If the grantee passed on the specified privileges, the REVOKE statement with the RESTRICT option doesn't revoke anything but instead returns an error code.

You can use a REVOKE statement with the optional GRANT OPTION FOR clause to revoke only the grant option for specified privileges while enabling the grantee to retain those privileges for himself. If the GRANT OPTION FOR clause and the CASCADE keyword are both present, you revoke all privileges that the grantee granted, along with the grantee's right to bestow such privileges — as if you'd never granted the grant option in the first place. If the GRANT OPTION FOR clause and the RESTRICT clause are both present, one of two things happens. If the grantee didn't grant to anyone else any of the privileges you're revoking, then the REVOKE statement executes and removes the grantee's ability to grant privileges. If the grantee has already granted at least one of the privileges you're revoking, the REVOKE doesn't execute but returns an error code instead.

The fact that you can grant privileges by using WITH GRANT OPTION, combined with the fact that you can also selectively revoke privileges, makes system security much more complex than the concept appears at first glance. Multiple grantors, for example, can conceivably grant a privilege to any single user. If one of those grantors then revokes the privilege, the user still retains that privilege because of the still-existing grant from another grantor. If a privilege passes from one user to another by way of the WITH GRANT OPTION, this situation creates a *chain of dependency,* in which one user's privileges depend on those of another user. If you're a DBA or object owner, always remain aware that, after you grant a privilege by using the WITH GRANT OPTION, that privilege may show up in unexpected places. Revoking the privilege from unwanted users while letting legitimate users retain the same privilege may prove challenging. In general, the GRANT OPTION and CASCADE clauses encompass numerous subtleties. If you use these clauses, check both the SQL:1999 standard and your product documentation carefully to ensure that you understand how the clauses work.

Using GRANT and REVOKE Together Saves Time and Effort

Multiple privileges for multiple users on selected columns of a table may require a lot of typing. Consider this example: The VP of sales wants everyone in sales to see everything in the CUSTOMER table. Only sales managers, however, should update, delete, or insert rows. *Nobody* should update the CUSTID field. The sales managers' names are Tyson, Keith, and David. You can grant appropriate privileges to these managers with GRANT statements, as follows:

```
GRANT SELECT, INSERT, DELETE
    ON CUSTOMER
    TO TYSON, KEITH, DAVID ;
GRANT UPDATE
    ON CUSTOMER (COMPANY, CUSTADDRESS, CUSTCITY,
        CUSTSTATE, CUSTZIP, CUSTPHONE, MODLEVEL)
    TO TYSON, KEITH, DAVID ;
GRANT SELECT
    ON CUSTOMER
    TO JENNY, VALERIE, MELODY, NEIL, ROBERT, SAM,
        BRANDON, MICHELLE_T, ALLISON, ANDREW,
        SCOTT, MICHELLE_B, JAIME, LINLEIGH, MATT, AMANDA;
```

That should do the trick. Everyone has SELECT rights on the CUSTOMER table. The sales managers have full INSERT and DELETE rights on the table, and they may update any column but the CUSTID column. However, there's an easier way to get the same result:

```
GRANT SELECT
    ON CUSTOMER
    TO PUBLIC ;
GRANT INSERT, DELETE, UPDATE
    ON CUSTOMER
    TO TYSON, KEITH, DAVID ;
REVOKE UPDATE
    ON CUSTOMER (CUSTID)
    FROM TYSON, KEITH, DAVID ;
```

You still take three statements in this example for the same protection of the three statements in the preceding example. No one may change data in the CUSTID column; only Tyson, Keith, and David have INSERT, DELETE, and UPDATE privileges. These latter three statements, however, are significantly shorter than those in the preceding example because you don't name all the users in the sales department and all the columns in the table. (The time you spend typing names is also significantly shorter. That's the idea.)

Part IV
Controlling Operations

The 5th Wave   By Rich Tennant

It's really made the job a lot less complicated. Oh jeez—now what?

In this part . . .

After you create a database and fill it with data, you want to protect your new database from harm or misuse. In this part, I discuss in detail SQL's tools for maintaining the safety and integrity of your data. SQL's Data Control Language (DCL) enables you to protect your data from misuse by selectively granting or denying access to the data. You can protect your database from other threats — such as interference from simultaneous access by multiple users — by using SQL's transaction-processing facilities. You can use constraints to help keep users from entering bad data in the first place. Of course, even SQL can't defend you against bad application design (that's strictly a live-and-learn proposition). If you take full advantage of the tools that SQL provides, however, using SQL *can* protect your data from most problems.

Chapter 14

Protecting Data

● ●

● ●

*E*veryone has heard of Murphy's Law — usually stated, *If anything can go wrong, it will go wrong*. We joke about this pseudo-law because most of the time things go fine. At times we seem to be among the lucky few who remain untouched by one of the basic laws of the universe. Usually, when unexpected problems arise, we recognize what has happened and deal with it.

In a very complex structure, however, the potential for unanticipated problems shoots way up (a mathematician might say it "increases approximately as the square of the complexity"). Thus large software projects are almost always delivered late and are often loaded with bugs. A nontrivial, multiuser DBMS application is a large, complex structure. In the course of operation, a number of things can go wrong. Methods have been developed for minimizing the impact of these problems, but the problems can never be eliminated completely. This is good news for professional database maintenance and repair people, because automating them out of a job will probably never be possible.

Threats to Data Integrity

Cyberspace (including your network) may be a nice place to visit — but for the data living there, it's no picnic. Data can be damaged or corrupted in a variety of ways. In Chapter 5, problems resulting from bad input data, operator error, deliberate destruction, and concurrent access are discussed. Poorly formulated SQL statements and improperly designed applications can also damage your data, and figuring out how doesn't take much imagination. But two relatively obvious threats — platform instability and equipment failure — can also trash your data. Both of these hazards are detailed in this section as well as problems that can be caused by concurrent access.

Platform instability

Platform instability is a category of problem that shouldn't even exist, but alas, it does. It is most prevalent when you are running one or more new and relatively untried components in your system. Problems can lurk in a new DBMS release, a new operating system version, or new hardware. Conditions or situations that have never appeared before show up while you are running a critical job. Your system locks up and your data is damaged. Beyond directing a few choice words at your computer and the people who built it, there isn't much you can do except hope that your latest backup was a good one.

Never put important production work on a system that has *any* unproven components. Resist the temptation to put your bread-and-butter work on an untried beta release of the newest, most function-laden version of your DBMS or operating system. If you feel that you must gain some hands-on experience with something new, do so on a machine that is completely isolated from your production network.

Equipment failure

Even well-proven, highly reliable equipment fails sometimes, sending your data to the great beyond. Everything physical wears out eventually — even modern, solid-state computers. If such a failure happens while your database is open and active, you can lose data — and sometimes (even worse) not realize it. Be assured that such a failure will happen sooner or later. If Murphy's Law is in operation that day, it happens at the worst possible time.

One way to protect data against equipment failure is *redundancy.* Keep extra copies of everything. For maximum safety (provided your organization can swing it financially), have duplicate hardware configured exactly the same as your production system. Have backups of your database and applications that can be loaded and run on your backup hardware when needed. If cost constraints keep you from duplicating everything (which effectively doubles your costs), at least be sure to back up your database and applications frequently enough that an unexpected failure doesn't require you to re-enter a large amount of data.

Another way to avoid the worst consequences of equipment failure is to use transaction processing — a topic that takes center stage later in this chapter. A *transaction* is an indivisible unit of work. Either the entire transaction is executed or none of it is. If this all-or-nothing approach seems drastic, consider: The worst problems arise when a series of database operations is only partially processed.

Concurrent access

Assume that you are running on proven hardware and software, your data is good, your application is bug-free, and your equipment is inherently reliable. Data utopia, right? Not quite. Problems can still arise when multiple people try to use the same database table at the same time *(concurrent access)* and their computers argue about who gets to go first *(contention)*. Multiple-user database systems have to be able to handle the ruckus efficiently.

Transaction interaction trouble

Contention troubles can lurk even in applications that seem straightforward. Consider, for example, the following case: You are writing an order-processing application that involves four tables: ORDER_MASTER, CUSTOMER, LINE_ITEM, and INVENTORY. The following conditions apply:

- ✔ The ORDER_MASTER table has `ORDER_NUMBER` as a primary key and `CUSTOMER_NUMBER` as a foreign key that references the CUSTOMER table.

- ✔ The LINE_ITEM table has `LINE_NUMBER` as a primary key, `ITEM_NUMBER` as a foreign key that references the INVENTORY table, and `QUANTITY` as one of its columns.

- ✔ The INVENTORY table has `ITEM_NUMBER` as a primary key; it also has a field named `QUANTITY_ON_HAND`.

- ✔ All three tables have other columns, but they don't enter into this example.

Your company policy is to ship each order completely or not at all. No partial shipments or back orders are allowed. (Relax. It's a hypothetical situation.) You write the `ORDER_PROCESSING` application to process each incoming order in the ORDER_MASTER table as follows: It first determines whether shipping *all* the line items is possible. If so, it writes the order, then decrements the `QUANTITY_ON_HAND` column of the INVENTORY table as required. (This deletes the affected entries from the ORDER_MASTER and LINE_ITEM tables.) So far, so good. You set up the application to process orders in one of two ways:

> Method 1 processes the INVENTORY row that corresponds to each row in the LINE_ITEM table. If `QUANTITY_ON_HAND` is large enough, the application decrements that field. If `QUANTITY_ON_HAND` is not large enough, it rolls back the transaction to restore all inventory reductions made to other LINE_ITEMs in this order.

> Method 2 checks every INVENTORY row that corresponds to a row in the order's LINE_ITEMs. If they are *all* big enough, then it processes those items by decrementing them.

Normally Method 1 is more efficient when you succeed in processing the order; Method 2 is more efficient when you fail. Thus, if most orders can be filled most of the time, you're better off using Method 1. If most orders can't be filled most of the time, you're better off with Method 2. Suppose this hypothetical application is up and running on a multiuser system that doesn't have adequate concurrency control. Yep. Trouble is brewing, all right. It looks like this:

✔ User 1 starts using Method 1 to process an order: Ten pieces of Item 1 are in stock, and User 1's order takes them all. The order-processing function chugs along, decrementing the quantity of Item 1 to zero. Then things get (as the Chinese proverb says) *interesting*. User 2 processes a small order for one piece of Item 1 — and finds that not enough Item 1s are in stock to fill the order. User 2's order is rolled back because it can't be filled. Meanwhile, User 1 tries to order five pieces of Item 37, but only four are in stock. User 1's order is rolled back because it can't be completely filled. The INVENTORY table is now back to the state it was in before either user started operating. Neither order is filled, even though User 2's order could be.

✔ Method 2 fares no better, although for a different reason. User 1 could check all the items ordered and decide that all the items ordered *are* available. If User 2 comes in and processes an order for one of those items *before* User 1 performs the decrement operation, then User 1's transaction could fail.

Serialization eliminates harmful interactions

No conflict occurs if transactions are executed *serially* rather than concurrently. (Taking turns — what a concept.) In the first example, if User 1's unsuccessful transaction was completed before User 2's transaction started, then the ROLLBACK function would have made the item ordered by User 2 available during User 2's transaction. If the transactions had run serially in the second example, then User 2 would have had no opportunity to change the quantity of any item until User 1's transaction was complete. User 1's transaction completes successfully — and User 2 can see how much of the desired item is *really* on hand.

If transactions are executed serially, one after the other, they have no chance of interacting destructively. Execution of concurrent transactions is *serializable* if the result is the same as it would be if the transactions were executed serially.

Serializing concurrent transactions isn't a cure-all. Tradeoffs exist between performance and protection from harmful interactions. The more you isolate transactions from each other, the more time it takes to perform a function (in cyberspace as in real life, waiting in line takes time). Be aware of what the tradeoffs are so you can configure your system for adequate protection — but not more protection than you need. Controlling concurrent access too tightly can kill overall system performance.

Reducing Vulnerability to Data Corruption

You can take precautions at several levels to reduce the chances of losing data through some mishap or unanticipated interaction. You can set up your DBMS to take some of these precautions for you — like guardian angels, they protect you from harm and operate behind the scenes. You don't see them and probably don't even know they are helping you. Your database administrator (DBA) can take still other precautions at his or her discretion. You may or may not be aware of them directly. Finally, as the developer, you can take some precautions yourself as you write your code. You can avoid a great deal of grief if you get into the habit of adhering to a few simple principles automatically so they are always included in your code or in your interactions with your database:

- ✔ Use SQL transactions.
- ✔ Tailor the level of isolation to balance performance and protection.
- ✔ Know when and how to set transactions, lock database objects, and perform backups.

Details coming right up.

Using SQL transactions

The transaction is one of SQL's main tools for maintaining database integrity. An *SQL transaction* encapsulates all the SQL statements that can have an effect on the database. An SQL transaction is completed with either a COMMIT or a ROLLBACK statement. If the transaction finishes with a COMMIT, the effects of all the statements in the transaction are applied to the database in one rapid-fire sequence. If the transaction finishes with a ROLLBACK, the effects of all the statements are *rolled back* (that is, undone) and the database returns to the state it was in before the transaction began.

In this discussion, the term *application* means either an execution of a program (whether in COBOL, C, or some other programming language) or a series of actions performed at a terminal during a single logon.

An application can include a series of SQL transactions. The first SQL transaction begins when the application begins; the last SQL transaction ends when the application ends. Each COMMIT or ROLLBACK that the application performs ends one SQL transaction and begins the next. For example, an application with three SQL transactions would have the following form:

```
Start of the application
    Various SQL statements (SQL transaction-1)
COMMIT or ROLLBACK
    Various SQL statements (SQL transaction-2)
COMMIT or ROLLBACK
    Various SQL statements (SQL transaction-3)
End of the application
```

"SQL transaction" is used because the application may be using other facilities (such as for network access) that do other sorts of transactions. In the following discussion, "transaction" is used to mean "SQL transaction" specifically.

A normal SQL transaction has an access mode that is either READ-WRITE or READ-ONLY; it has an isolation level that is either SERIALIZABLE, REPEATABLE READ, READ COMMITTED, or READ UNCOMMITTED. (Find transaction characteristics in the "Isolation levels" section.) The default characteristics are READ-WRITE and SERIALIZABLE. If you want any other characteristics, you have to specify them with a SET TRANSACTION statement such as the following:

```
SET TRANSACTION READ ONLY ;
```

or

```
SET TRANSACTION READ ONLY REPEATABLE READ ;
```

or

```
SET TRANSACTION READ COMMITTED ;
```

You can have multiple SET TRANSACTION statements in an application, but you can specify only one of them in each transaction — and it must be the first SQL statement executed in the transaction. If you want to use a SET TRANSACTION statement then execute it either at the beginning of the application or after a COMMIT or ROLLBACK. You must perform a SET TRANSACTION at the beginning of every transaction for which you want nondefault properties, because each new transaction after a COMMIT or ROLLBACK is automatically given the default properties.

A SET TRANSACTION statement can also specify a DIAGNOSTICS SIZE, which determines the number of error conditions for which the implementation should be prepared to save information. (Such a numerical limit is necessary because an implementation can detect more than one error during a statement.) The SQL default for this limit is implementor-defined, and that default is almost always adequate.

The default transaction

The default SQL transaction has characteristics that are satisfactory for most users most of the time. If necessary, however, you can specify different transaction characteristics with a SET TRANSACTION statement, as described in the previous section. (SET TRANSACTION gets its own spotlight treatment later in the chapter as well.)

The default transaction makes a couple of other implicit assumptions:

- ✔ That the database will change over time.
- ✔ Always better to be safe than sorry.

It sets the mode to READ-WRITE which, as you may expect, enables you to issue statements that change the database. It also sets the isolation level to SERIALIZABLE, which is the highest level of isolation possible (thus the safest). The default diagnostics size is implementation-dependent. Have a look at your SQL documentation to see what that size is for your system.

Isolation levels

Ideally, the work that the system performs for your transaction is completely isolated from anything being done by other transactions that happens to execute concurrently with yours. On a real-world, multiuser system, however, complete isolation is not always feasible. It may exact too large a performance penalty. A tradeoff question arises: *How much isolation do you really want, and how much are you willing to pay for it in terms of performance?*

Getting mucked up by a dirty read

The weakest level of isolation is called READ UNCOMMITTED, which allows the sometimes-problematic dirty read. A *dirty read* is a situation in which a change made by one user can be read by a second user before the first user COMMITs (that is, finalizes) the change. The problem arises when the first user aborts and rolls back his transaction. The second user's subsequent operations are now based on an incorrect value. The classic example of this foul-up can appear in an inventory application: One user decrements inventory; a second user reads the new (lower) value. The first user rolls back his transaction (restoring the inventory to its initial value), but the second user, thinking inventory is low, orders more stock and possibly creates a severe overstock. And that's if you're lucky.

Don't use the READ UNCOMMITTED isolation level unless you don't care about accurate results.

You *can* use READ UNCOMMITTED if you want to generate approximate statistical data, such as:

- ✔ Maximum delay in filling orders
- ✔ Average age of salespeople who don't make quota
- ✔ Average age of new employees

In many such cases, approximate information is quite sufficient; the extra (performance) cost of the concurrency control required to give an exact result may not be worthwhile.

Getting bamboozled by a nonrepeatable read

The next highest level of isolation is READ COMMITTED: A change made by another transaction doesn't become visible to your transaction until the other user has COMMITted the other transaction. This level gives you a better result than you can get from READ UNCOMMITTED but it's still subject to a *nonrepeatable read* — a serious problem that happens like a comedy of errors. To illustrate, consider the classic inventory example. User 1 queries the database to see how many of a particular product are in stock. The number is ten. At almost the same time, User 2 starts — and then COMMITs — a transaction that records an order for ten units of that same product, decrementing the inventory, leaving none. Now User 1, having seen that ten are available, tries to order five of them. Five are no longer left, however. User 2 has, in effect, raided the pantry. User 1's initial read of the quantity available is not repeatable. The quantity has changed out from under User 1; any assumptions made on the basis of the initial read are not valid.

Risking the phantom read

An isolation level of REPEATABLE READ guarantees that the nonrepeatable-read problem doesn't happen. This isolation level, however, is still haunted by the *phantom read* — a problem that arises when the data a user is reading changes in response to another transaction (and does not show the change on-screen) *while the user is reading it.* Suppose, for example, that User 1 issues a command whose search condition (the WHERE clause or HAVING clause) selects a set of rows — and (immediately afterward) User 2 performs and commits an operation that changes the data in some of those rows. Those data items met User 1's search condition at the start of this snafu, but now they no longer do. Maybe some other rows that first did *not* meet the original search condition now *do* meet it. User 1, whose transaction is still active, has no inkling of these changes; the application behaves as if nothing has happened. The hapless User 1 issues another SQL statement with the same search conditions as the original one, expecting to retrieve the same rows. Instead (and alas) the second operation is performed on rows other than those used in the first operation. Reliable results go out the window, spirited away by the phantom read.

Getting a reliable (if slower) read

An isolation level of SERIALIZABLE is not subject to any of the problems that beset the other three levels. At this level, concurrent transactions can (in principle) be run serially — one after the other — rather than in parallel, and the results come out the same. If you're running at this isolation level, hardware or software problems can still cause your transaction to fail, but at least you don't have to worry about the validity of your results if you know that your system is functioning properly.

Of course, superior reliability may come at the price of slower performance, so we're back in Tradeoff City. Table 14-1 sums up the terms of the tradeoff, showing the four isolation levels and the problems they solve.

Table 14-1	Isolation Levels and Problems Solved
Isolation Level	*Problems Solved*
READ UNCOMMITTED	None
READ COMMITTED	Dirty read
REPEATABLE READ	Dirty read
	Nonrepeatable read
SERIALIZABLE	Dirty read
	Nonrepeatable read
	Phantom read

The implicit transaction-starting statement

Some implementations of SQL require that you signal the beginning of a transaction with an explicit statement, such as BEGIN or BEGIN TRAN. SQL:1999 does not. If you don't have an active transaction and you issue a statement that calls for one, SQL:1999 starts a default transaction for you. CREATE TABLE, SELECT, and UPDATE are examples of statements that require the context of a transaction. Issue one of these statements, and SQL starts a transaction for you.

SET TRANSACTION

On occasion, you may want to use transaction characteristics that are different from those set by default. You can specify different characteristics with a SET TRANSACTION statement before you issue your first statement that actually requires a transaction. The SET TRANSACTION statement enables you to specify mode, isolation level, and diagnostics size.

To change all three, for example, you may issue the following statement:

```
SET TRANSACTION
    READ ONLY,
    ISOLATION LEVEL READ UNCOMMITTED,
    DIAGNOSTICS SIZE 4 ;
```

With these settings, you can't issue any statements that change the database (READ ONLY), and you have set the lowest and most hazardous isolation level (READ UNCOMMITTED). The diagnostics area has a size of 4. You are making minimal demands on system resources.

In contrast, you may issue this statement:

```
SET TRANSACTION
    READ WRITE,
    ISOLATION LEVEL SERIALIZABLE,
    DIAGNOSTICS SIZE 8 ;
```

These settings enable you to change the database, give you the highest level of isolation, and give you a larger diagnostics area. This setting makes larger demands on system resources. Depending on your implementation, these settings may turn out to be the same as those used by the default transaction. Naturally, you can issue SET TRANSACTION statements with other choices for isolation level and diagnostics size.

Set your transaction isolation level as high as you need to, but no higher. Always setting your isolation level to SERIALIZABLE just to be on the safe side may seem reasonable but may not be so for all systems. Depending on your implementation and what you are doing, however, you may not need to do so, and performance can suffer significantly if you do. If you don't intend to change the database in your transaction (for example), set the mode to READ ONLY. Bottom line: Don't tie up any system resources that you don't need.

COMMIT

Although SQL:1999 doesn't have an explicit transaction-starting keyword, it has two that terminate a transaction: COMMIT and ROLLBACK. Use COMMIT when you have come to the end of the transaction and you want to make permanent the changes that you have made to the database (if any). You may include the optional keyword WORK (COMMIT WORK) if you want. If an error is encountered or the system crashes while a COMMIT is in progress, you may have to roll the transaction back and try it again.

ROLLBACK

When you come to the end of a transaction, you may decide that you don't want to make permanent the changes that have occurred during the transaction. In fact, you want to restore the database to the state it was in before the transaction began. To do this, issue a ROLLBACK statement. ROLLBACK is a failsafe mechanism. Even if the system crashes while a ROLLBACK is in progress, you can restart the ROLLBACK after the system is restored, and it restores the database to its pretransaction state.

Locking database objects

The isolation level set either by default or by a SET TRANSACTION statement tells the DBMS how zealous to be in protecting your work from interaction with the work of other users. The main protection from harmful transactions that the DBMS gives to you is its application of locks to the database objects you are using. Sometimes it locks the table row you are accessing, preventing anyone else from accessing that record while you are using it. Sometimes it locks an entire table, if you are performing an operation that could affect the whole table. Sometimes it allows reading but not writing; other times it prevents both. Each implementation handles locking in its own way. Some implementations are more bulletproof than others, but most up-to-date systems protect you from the worst problems that can arise in a concurrent-access situation.

Backing up your data

Backup is a protective action that your DBA should perform on a regular basis. All elements of your system should be backed up at intervals that depend on how frequently they are updated. If your database is updated daily, it should be backed up daily. Your applications, forms, and reports may change, too, though less frequently. Whenever you make changes to them, your DBA should back up the new versions.

Keep several generations of backups. Sometimes database damage doesn't become evident until some time has passed. To return to the last good version, you may have to go back several backup versions.

Many different ways exist to perform backups. One way is to use SQL to create backup tables and copy data into them. A second way is to use an implementation-defined mechanism that backs up the whole database or portions of it. This mechanism is generally much more convenient and efficient than using SQL. Finally, your installation may have a mechanism in place for backing up everything, including databases, programs, documents, spreadsheets, utilities, and computer games. If so, you may not have to do anything beyond assuring yourself that the backups are performed frequently enough to protect you.

You may hear database designers say they want their databases to have ACID. Well, no, they're not planning to zonk their creations with a 1960s psychedelic or dissolve the data they contain into a bubbly mess. ACID is simply an acronym for Atomicity, Consistency, Isolation, and Durability. These four characteristics are necessary to protect a database from corruption:

- **Atomicity:** Database transactions should be atomic — in the classic sense of the word: The entire transaction is treated as an indivisible unit. Either it is executed in its entirety *(committed),* or the database is restored (rolled back) to the state it would have been in if the transaction had not been executed.

- **Consistency:** Oddly enough, the meaning of *consistency* is not consistent; it varies from one application to another. When you transfer funds from one account to another in a banking application, for example, you want the total amount of money in both accounts at the end of the transaction to be the same as it was at the beginning of the transaction. In a different application, your criterion for consistency might be different.

- **Isolation:** Ideally, database transactions should be totally isolated from other transactions that execute at the same time. If the transactions are serializable, then total isolation is achieved. If the system has to process transactions at top speed, sometimes lower levels of isolation can enhance performance.

- **Durability:** After a transaction has committed or rolled back, you should be able to count on the database being in the proper state: well stocked with uncorrupted, reliable, up-to-date data. Even if your system suffers a hard crash after a commit — but before the transaction is stored to disk — a durable DBMS can guarantee that upon recovery from the crash, the database can be restored to its proper state.

Savepoints and subtransactions

Ideally, transactions should be atomic — as indivisible as the ancient Greeks thought atoms were. However, atoms are not really indivisible. Since the time of the ancient Greeks, natural philosophers and scientists thought that atoms, such as oxygen atoms or molybdenum atoms were the smallest units of matter. In the late nineteenth and early twentieth centuries it became clear that atoms were actually divisible into smaller particles (electrons, protons, and neutrons) and by the late twentieth century, it was discovered that even protons and neutrons were not "atomic," since they are built up out of quarks and gluons.

Sure enough, with the implementation of SQL:1999, database transactions are not atomic, either. A transaction is divisible into multiple *subtransactions*. Each subtransaction is terminated by a SAVEPOINT statement. The SAVE-POINT statement is used in conjunction with the ROLLBACK statement. Before the introduction of *savepoints* (the point in the program where the SAVE-POINT statement takes effect) the ROLLBACK statement could be used only to cancel an entire transaction. Now it can be used to roll back a transaction to a savepoint within the transaction. What good is this, you might ask?

Granted, the primary use of the ROLLBACK statement is to prevent data corruption if a transaction is interrupted by an error condition. And no, rolling back to a savepoint does not make sense if an error occurred while a transaction was in progress; you'd want to roll back the *entire* transaction to bring the database back to the state it was in before the transaction started. But such a situation isn't the whole story; you might have other reasons for rolling back part of a transaction.

Say you are performing a complex series of operations on your data. Partway through the process, you receive results that lead you to conclude that you're going down an unproductive path. If you had put a SAVEPOINT statement just before you started on that path, you could roll back to the savepoint and try another option. Provided the rest of your code was in good shape before you set the savepoint, this approach works better than aborting the current transaction and starting a whole new one just to try a new path.

To insert a savepoint into your SQL code, use the following syntax:

```
SAVEPOINT savepoint_name ;
```

You can cause execution to roll back to that savepoint with code such as the following:

```
ROLLBACK TO SAVEPOINT savepoint_name ;
```

The SAVEPOINT and ROLLBACK statements are not part of core SQL. If your implementation does not include them, you will not be able to use them.

Constraints within Transactions

Ensuring the validity of the data in your database means doing more than just making sure the data is of the right type. Perhaps some columns, for example, should never hold a null value — and maybe others should hold only values that fall within a certain range. Such restrictions, called *constraints,* are discussed in Chapter 5.

Constraints are relevant to transactions because they can conceivably prevent you from doing what you want. For example, suppose that you want to add data to a table that contains a column with a NOT NULL constraint. One common method of adding a record is to append a blank row to your table and then insert values into it later. The NOT NULL constraint on one column, however, causes the append operation to fail. SQL doesn't allow you to add a row that has a null value in a column with a NOT NULL constraint, even though you plan to add data to that column before your transaction ends. To address this problem, SQL:1999 enables you to designate constraints as either DEFERRABLE or NOT DEFERRABLE.

Constraints that are NOT DEFERRABLE are applied immediately. You can set DEFERRABLE constraints to be either initially DEFERRED or IMMEDIATE. If a DEFERRABLE constraint is set to IMMEDIATE, it acts like a NOT DEFERRABLE constraint — it is applied immediately. If a DEFERRABLE constraint is set to DEFERRED, it is not enforced. (No, your code doesn't have an attitude problem; it's simply following orders.)

To append blank records or perform other operations that may violate DEFERRABLE constraints, you can use a statement similar to the following:

```
SET CONSTRAINTS ALL DEFERRED ;
```

This statement puts all DEFERRABLE constraints in the DEFERRED condition. It does not affect the NOT DEFERRABLE constraints. After you have performed all operations that could violate your constraints, and the table reaches a state that doesn't violate them, you can reapply them. The statement that reapplies your constraints looks like this:

```
SET CONSTRAINTS ALL IMMEDIATE ;
```

If you made a mistake and any of your constraints are still being violated, you find out as soon as this statement takes effect.

If you do not explicitly set your DEFERRED constraints to IMMEDIATE, SQL does it for you when you attempt to COMMIT your transaction. If a violation is still present at that time, the transaction does not COMMIT; instead, SQL gives you an error message.

SQL's handling of constraints protects you from entering invalid data (or an invalid *absence* of data — just as important) while giving you the flexibility to violate constraints temporarily while a transaction is still active.

Consider a payroll example to see why being able to defer the application of constraints is important.

Assume that an EMPLOYEE table has columns EMP_NO, EMP_NAME, DEPT_NO, and SALARY. DEPT_NO is a foreign key referencing the DEPT table. Assume also that the DEPT table has columns DEPT_NO and DEPT_NAME. DEPT_NO is the primary key.

Suppose that, in addition, you want to have a table like DEPT that also contains a PAYROLL column that holds the sum of the SALARY values for employees in each department.

You can create the equivalent of this table with the following view:

```
CREATE VIEW DEPT2 AS
    SELECT D.*, SUM(E.SALARY) AS PAYROLL
        FROM DEPT D, EMPLOYEE E
        WHERE D.DEPT_NO = E.DEPT_NO
        GROUP BY D.DEPT_NO ;
```

You can also define this view equivalently as follows:

```
CREATE VIEW DEPT3 AS
    SELECT D.*,
        (SELECT SUM(E.SALARY)
            FROM EMPLOYEE E
            WHERE D.DEPT_NO = E.DEPT_NO) AS PAYROLL
        FROM DEPT D ;
```

But suppose that, for efficiency, you don't want to calculate the SUM every time you reference DEPT.PAYROLL. Instead, you want to store an actual PAYROLL column in the DEPT table. You will then update that column every time you change a SALARY.

And to make sure that the SALARY column is accurate, you can include a CONSTRAINT in the table definition:

```
CREATE TABLE DEPT
    (DEPT_NO CHAR(5),
    DEPT_NAME CHAR(20),
    PAYROLL DECIMAL(15,2),
    CHECK (PAYROLL = (SELECT SUM(SALARY)
            FROM EMPLOYEE E WHERE E.DEPTNO= DEPT.DEPT_NO)));
```

Now, suppose that you want to increase the SALARY of employee 123 by 100. You can do it with the following update:

```
UPDATE EMPLOYEE
    SET SALARY = SALARY + 100
    WHERE EMP_NO = '123' ;
```

And you must remember to do the following as well:

```
UPDATE DEPT D
   SET PAYROLL = PAYROLL + 100
   WHERE D.DEPT_NO = (SELECT E.DEPT_NO
             FROM EMPLOYEE E
             WHERE E.EMP_NO = '123') ;
```

(You use the subquery to reference the DEPT_NO of employee 123.)

But there's a problem: Constraints are checked after each statement. In principle, *all* constraints are checked. In practice, implementations check only the constraints that reference the values modified by the statement.

After the first preceding UPDATE statement, the implementation checks all constraints that reference values that the statement modifies. This includes the constraint defined in the DEPT table, because that constraint references the SALARY column of the EMPLOYEE table, and the UPDATE statement is modifying that column. After the first UPDATE statement, that constraint is violated. You assume that before you execute the UPDATE statement the database is correct, and each PAYROLL value in the DEPT table equals the sum of the SALARY values in the corresponding columns of the EMPLOYEE table. When the first UPDATE statement increases a SALARY value, this equality is no longer true. The second UPDATE statement corrects this, and again leaves the database values in a state for which the constraint is True. Between the two updates, the constraint is False.

The SET CONSTRAINTS DEFERRED statement lets you temporarily disable or "suspend" all constraints, or only specified constraints. The constraints are deferred until either you execute a SET CONSTRAINTS IMMEDIATE statement, or you execute a COMMIT or ROLLBACK statement. So you surround the previous two UPDATE statements with SET CONSTRAINTS statements. The code looks like this:

```
SET CONSTRAINTS DEFERRED ;
UPDATE EMPLOYEE
   SET SALARY = SALARY + 100
   WHERE EMP_NO = '123' ;
UPDATE DEPT D
   SET PAYROLL = PAYROLL + 100
   WHERE D.DEPT_NO = (SELECT E.DEPT_NO
             FROM EMPLOYEE E
     WHERE E.EMP_NO = '123') ;
SET CONSTRAINTS IMMEDIATE ;
```

This procedure defers all constraints. If you insert new rows into DEPT, the primary keys won't be checked; you have removed protection that you may want to keep. Specifying the constraints that you want to defer is preferable. To do this, name the constraints when you create them:

```
CREATE TABLE DEPT
    (DEPT_NO CHAR(5),
    DEPT_NAME CHAR(20),
    PAYROLL DECIMAL(15,2),
    CONSTRAINT PAY_EQ_SUMSAL
    CHECK (PAYROLL = SELECT SUM(SALARY)
    FROM EMPLOYEE E      WHERE E.DEPT_NO = DEPT.DEPT_NO)) ;
```

With constraint names in place, you can then reference your constraints individually:

```
SET CONSTRAINTS PAY_EQ_SUMSAL DEFERRED;
UPDATE EMPLOYEE
    SET SALARY = SALARY + 100
    WHERE EMP_NO = '123' ;
UPDATE DEPT D
    SET PAYROLL = PAYROLL + 100
    WHERE D.DEPT_NO = (SELECT E.DEPT_NO
                        FROM EMPLOYEE E
                        WHERE E.EMP_NO = '123') ;
SET CONSTRAINTS PAY_EQ_SUMSAL IMMEDIATE;
```

Without a constraint name in the CREATE statement, SQL generates one implicitly. That implicit name is in the schema information (catalog) tables. But specifying the names explicitly is more straightforward.

Now suppose that, in the second UPDATE statement, you mistakenly specified an increment value of 1000. This value is allowed in the UPDATE statement, because the constraint has been deferred. But when you execute SET CON-STRAINTS . . . IMMEDIATE, the specified constraints are checked. If they fail, SET CONSTRAINTS raises an exception. If, instead of a SET CONSTRAINTS . . . IMMEDIATE statement, you execute COMMIT and the constraints are found to be False, then COMMIT instead performs a ROLLBACK.

Bottom line: You can defer the constraints only *within* a transaction. When the transaction is terminated by a ROLLBACK or a COMMIT, the constraints are both enabled and checked. The SQL capability of deferring constraints is meant to be used within a transaction. If used properly, it doesn't create any data that violates a constraint available to other transactions.

Chapter 15

Using SQL within Applications

*P*revious chapters address SQL statements mostly in isolation. For example, questions are asked about data and SQL queries are developed that retrieve answers to the questions. This mode of operation, interactive SQL, is a fine way to discover what SQL can do, but it's not the way SQL is typically used.

Even though SQL syntax can be described as similar to English, it isn't an easy language to master. The overwhelming majority of computer users today are not fluent in SQL. You can reasonably assume that the overwhelming majority of computer users will never be fluent in SQL, even if this book is wildly successful. When a database question comes up, Joe User will probably not sit down at his terminal and enter an SQL SELECT statement to find the answer. Systems analysts and application developers are the people who are likely to be comfortable with SQL, and they typically do not make a career of entering ad hoc queries into databases. They develop applications that make queries. If you plan to perform the same operation repeatedly, you shouldn't have to rebuild it every time from the console. Write an application to do the job and then run it as often as you like. SQL can be a part of an application, but when it is, it works a little differently from the way it does in an interactive mode.

SQL in an Application

In Chapter 2, SQL is set forth as an incomplete programming language. To use SQL in an application, you have to combine it with a *procedural* language such as Pascal, FORTRAN, Visual Basic, C, C++, Java, or COBOL. Because of the way it is structured, SQL has some strengths and some weaknesses. Procedural languages, which are structured differently, have different strengths and weaknesses. Happily, the strengths of SQL tend to make up for the weaknesses of procedural languages, and the strengths of the procedural languages are in those areas where SQL is weak. By combining the two, you can build powerful applications with a broad range of capabilities. Recently, object-oriented rapid application development (RAD) tools such as Borland's Delphi and C++ Builder have appeared, which incorporate SQL code into applications developed by manipulating objects instead of writing procedural code.

While discussing interactive SQL in previous chapters, the asterisk is used (*) as a shorthand substitute for "all columns in the table." If the table has numerous columns, the asterisk can save a lot of typing. A danger lurks in using the asterisk this way, however, whenever you use SQL in an application program.

After your application is written, you or someone else may add new columns to a table or delete old ones. Doing so, however, changes the meaning of "all columns." Your application, when it specifies "all columns" with an asterisk, may retrieve columns other than those it thinks it's getting.

Such a change to a table won't affect existing programs until they have to be recompiled to fix a bug or make some change. Then the effect of the * wildcard expands to include all the now-current columns. This change may cause the application to fail in a way totally unrelated to the bug fix (or other change made, causing a debugging nightmare).

To be safe, specify all column names explicitly in an application, rather than using the asterisk.

SQL strengths and weaknesses

SQL is strong in data retrieval. If important information is buried somewhere in a single-table or multitable database, SQL gives you the tools you need to retrieve it. You don't need to know the order of the rows or columns in a table because SQL doesn't deal with rows or columns individually. The SQL transaction-processing facilities ensure that your database operations are unaffected by any other users who may be simultaneously accessing the same tables that you are.

A major weakness of SQL, however, is its rudimentary user interface. It has no provision for formatting screens or reports. It accepts command lines from the keyboard and sends retrieved values to the terminal, one row at a time.

Sometimes a strength in one context can be a weakness in another. One strength of SQL is that it can operate on an entire table at once.Whether the table has one row, a hundred rows, or a hundred thousand rows, a single SELECT statement can extract the data you want. SQL can't easily operate on one row of a multirow table at a time, however, and sometimes you do want to deal with each row individually. In such cases, you can use SQL's cursor facility, described in Chapter 20, or you can use a procedural host language.

Procedural language strengths and weaknesses

In contrast to SQL, procedural languages are designed for one-row-at-a-time operation, which allows the application developer precise control over the way a table is processed. This detailed control is a great strength of procedural languages. A corresponding weakness exists, however. The application developer must have detailed knowledge of the way data is stored in the database tables. The order of the database's columns and rows is significant and must be taken into account.

Because of the step-by-step nature of procedural languages, they have the flexibility to produce user-friendly screens for data entry and viewing. You can also produce printed reports of great sophistication, with any desired layout.

Problems in combining SQL with a procedural language

In view of how the strengths of SQL complement the weaknesses of procedural languages and vice versa, trying to combine them in such a way that you can benefit from their strengths and not be penalized by their weaknesses makes sense. As valuable as such a combination may be, some challenges must be overcome before it can be achieved practically.

Contrasting operating modes

A big problem in combining SQL with a procedural language is that SQL operates on tables a set at a time, whereas procedural languages work on them a row at a time. Sometimes this is not a big deal. You can separate set operations from row operations, doing each with the appropriate tool. Other times, however, you may want to search a table for records meeting certain conditions and perform different operations on the records depending on whether or not they meet the conditions. Such a process requires both the retrieval power of SQL and the branching capability of a procedural language. Embedded SQL gives you this combination of capabilities by enabling you to "embed" SQL statements at strategic locations within a program that you have written in a conventional procedural language.

Data type incompatibilities

Another hurdle to the smooth integration of SQL with any procedural language is that SQL's data types are different from those of all major procedural languages. This circumstance shouldn't be surprising, because the data types defined for any procedural language are different from the types for the other procedural languages. No standardization of data types exists across languages. In releases of SQL prior to SQL-92, data-type incompatibility was a major concern. In SQL-92, however (and also in SQL:1999), the CAST statement addresses the problem. Chapter 8 goes into detail on how you can use CAST to convert a data item from the procedural language's data type to one recognized by SQL, as long as the data item itself is compatible with the new data type.

Hooking SQL into Procedural Languages

Though many potential difficulties exist with integrating SQL into procedural languages, it can be done. In many instances, it *must* be done to produce the desired result in the allotted time — or at all. Luckily, several methods for combining SQL with procedural languages are available to you. Three of the methods — *embedded SQL, module language,* and *RAD tools* — are outlined in the following section.

Embedded SQL

The most common method of mixing SQL with procedural languages is called *embedded SQL*. The name is descriptive: SQL statements are dropped right into the middle of a procedural program, wherever they are needed. As you may expect, an SQL statement that appears suddenly in the middle of (for example) a C program can present a challenge for a compiler who isn't expecting it. For that reason, programs containing embedded SQL are usually passed through a preprocessor before being compiled or interpreted. The preprocessor is warned of the imminent appearance of SQL code by the EXEC SQL directive.

As an example of embedded SQL, look at a program written in Oracle's Pro*C version of the C language. The program, which accesses a company employee table, prompts the user for an employee name and then displays that employee's salary and commission. It then prompts the user for new salary and commission data and updates the employee table with it:

```
EXEC SQL BEGIN DECLARE SECTION;
     VARCHAR uid[20];
     VARCHAR pwd[20];
     VARCHAR ename[10];
     FLOAT salary, comm;
     SHORT salary_ind, comm_ind;
EXEC SQL END DECLARE SECTION;
main()
{
     int sret;              /* scanf return code */
     /* Log in */
     strcpy(uid.arr,"FRED");     /* copy the user name */
     uid.len=strlen(uid.arr);
     strcpy(pwd.arr,"TOWER");    /* copy the password */
     pwd.len=strlen(pwd.arr);
     EXEC SQL WHENEVER SQLERROR STOP;
     EXEC SQL WHENEVER NOT FOUND STOP;
EXEC SQL CONNECT :uid;
printf("Connected to user: percents \n",uid.arr);
     printf("Enter employee name to update:  ");
     scanf("percents",ename.arr);
     ename.len=strlen(ename.arr);
     EXEC SQL SELECT SALARY,COMM INTO :salary,:comm
               FROM EMPLOY
               WHERE ENAME=:ename;
     printf("Employee: percents salary: percent6.2f comm:
          percent6.2f \n",
          ename.arr, salary, comm);
     printf("Enter new salary:  ");
     sret=scanf("percentf",&salary);
     salary_ind = 0;
     if (sret == EOF !! sret == 0)    /* set indicator */
          salary_ind =-1;      /* Set indicator for NULL */
     printf("Enter new commission:  ");
     sret=scanf("percentf",&comm);
     comm_ind = 0;     /* set indicator */
     if (sret == EOF !! sret == 0)
          comm_ind=-1;         /* Set indicator for NULL */
```

```
        EXEC SQL UPDATE EMPLOY
                SET SALARY=:salary:salary_ind
                SET COMM=:comm:comm_ind
                WHERE ENAME=:ename;
printf("Employee percents updated. \n",ename.arr);
        EXEC SQL COMMIT WORK;
        exit(0);
}
```

You don't have to be an expert in C to understand the essence of what this program is doing and how the program does it. First, SQL declares host variables. Next, C code controls the user login procedure, and then SQL sets up error handling and connects to the database. C code then solicits an employee name from the user and places it in a variable. An SQL SELECT statement retrieves the named employee's salary and commission data and stores them in the host variables :salary and :comm. C then takes over again and displays the employee's name, salary, and commission and then solicits new values for salary and commission. It also checks to see that an entry has been made, and if one has not, it sets an indicator. Next, SQL updates the database with the new values. C then displays an "operation complete" message. SQL commits the transaction, and C finally exits the program.

You can intermix the commands of two languages like this because of the pre-processor. The preprocessor separates the SQL statements from the host language commands, placing the SQL statements in a separate external routine. Each SQL statement is replaced with a host language CALL of the corresponding external routine. The language compiler can now do its job. The way the SQL part is passed to the database is implementation-dependent. You, as the application developer, don't have to worry about any of this. The preprocessor takes care of it. You should be concerned about a few things, however, that do not appear in interactive SQL — things such as host variables and incompatible data types.

Declaring host variables

Some information must be passed between the host language program and the SQL segments. You do this with host variables. In order for SQL to recognize the host variables, you must declare them before you use them. Declarations are included in a declaration segment that precedes the program segment. The declaration segment is announced by the following directive:

```
EXEC SQL BEGIN DECLARE SECTION ;
```

The end of the declaration segment is signaled by

```
EXEC SQL END DECLARE SECTION ;
```

Every SQL statement must be preceded by an EXEC SQL directive. The end of an SQL segment may or may not be signaled by a terminator directive. In COBOL, the terminator directive is "END-EXEC"; in FORTRAN, it is the end of a line; in Ada, C, Pascal, and PL/I, it is a semicolon.

Converting data types

Depending on the compatibility of the data types supported by the host language and those supported by SQL, you may have to use CAST to convert certain types. You can use host variables that have been declared in the DECLARE SECTION. Remember to prefix host variable names with a colon (:) when you use them in SQL statements, as in the following example:

```
INSERT INTO FOODS
    (FOODNAME, CALORIES, PROTEIN, FAT, CARBOHYDRATE)
    VALUES
    (:foodname, :calories, :protein, :fat, :carbo) ;
```

Module language

Module language provides another method of using SQL with a procedural programming language. With module language, you explicitly put all the SQL statements into a separate SQL module.

An SQL module is simply a list of SQL statements. Each of the SQL statements is called an SQL *procedure* and is preceded by a specification of the name of the procedure and the number and types of the parameters.

Each SQL procedure contains one or more SQL statements. In the host program, you explicitly call an SQL procedure at whatever point in the host program you want to execute the SQL statement in that procedure. You call the SQL procedure as if it were a host language subprogram.

Thus, an SQL module and the associated host program are essentially a way of explicitly hand-coding the result of the SQL preprocessor for embedded syntax.

Embedded SQL is much more common than module language. Most vendors offer some form of module language, but few emphasize it in their documentation. Module language does have several advantages:

✔ Because the SQL is completely separated from the procedural language, you can hire the best SQL programmers available to write your SQL modules, whether they have any experience with your procedural language or not. In fact, you can even defer deciding on which procedural language to use until after your SQL modules are written and debugged.

✔ You can hire the best programmers who work in your procedural language, even if they know nothing about SQL.

✔ Most importantly, no SQL is mixed in with the procedural code, so your procedural language debugger works — which can save you considerable development time.

Once again, what can be looked at as an advantage from one perspective may be a disadvantage from another. Because the SQL modules are separated from the procedural code, following the flow of the logic isn't as easy as it is in embedded SQL when you're trying to understand how the program works.

Module declarations

The syntax for the declarations in a module is as follows:

```
MODULE [module-name]
    [NAMES ARE character-set-name]
    LANGUAGE {ADA|C|COBOL|FORTRAN|MUMPS|PASCAL|PLI|SQL}
    [SCHEMA schema-name]
    [AUTHORIZATION authorization-id]
    [temporary-table-declarations...]
    [cursor-declarations...]
    [dynamic-cursor-declarations...]
    procedures...
```

As indicated by the square brackets, the module name is optional. Naming it anyway is probably a good idea, just to help keep things from getting too confusing. The optional NAMES ARE clause specifies a character set. If you don't include a NAMES ARE clause, the default set of SQL characters for your implementation is used. The LANGUAGE clause tells the module which language it is to be called from. The compiler must know what the calling language is, because it's going to make the SQL statements appear to the calling program as if they are subprograms in that program's language.

Although the SCHEMA clause and the AUTHORIZATION clause are both optional, you must specify at least one of them. You can also specify both. The SCHEMA clause specifies the default schema, and the AUTHORIZATION clause specifies the authorization identifier. The authorization identifier establishes the privileges you have. If you don't specify an authorization ID, the DBMS uses the authorization ID associated with your session to determine the privileges your module is allowed. If you don't have the privilege to perform the operation your procedure calls for, your procedure isn't executed.

If your procedure requires temporary tables, declare them with the temporary table declaration clause. Declare cursors and dynamic cursors before any procedures that use them. Declaring a cursor after a procedure is permissible as long as that procedure doesn't use the cursor. Doing this for cursors used by later procedures may make sense. More in-depth information is provided on cursors in Chapter 20.

Module procedures

Finally, after all these declarations, the functional parts of the module are the procedures. An SQL module language procedure has a name, parameter declarations, and executable SQL statements. The procedural language program calls the procedure by its name and passes values to it through the declared parameters. Procedure syntax is as follows:

```
PROCEDURE procedure-name
    (parameter-declaration [, parameter-declaration ]... )
    SQL statement ;
    [SQL statements] ;
```

The parameter declaration should take the following form:

```
parameter-name data-type
```

or

```
SQLSTATE
```

The parameters you declare may be input parameters, output parameters, or both. SQLSTATE is a status parameter through which errors are reported. To delve deeper in to parameters, skip on over to Chapter 21.

Object-oriented RAD tools

By using state-of-the-art RAD tools, you can develop sophisticated applications without knowing how to write a single line of code in C, Pascal, COBOL, or FORTRAN. Instead, you choose objects from a library and place them in appropriate spots on the screen.

Objects of different standard types have characteristic properties, and selected events are appropriate for each object type. You can also associate a method with an object. The *method* is a procedure written in a procedural language. Building very useful applications without writing any methods is possible, however.

Although you can build complex applications without using a procedural language, sooner or later you will probably need SQL. SQL has a richness of expression that is difficult, if not impossible, to duplicate with the object paradigm. As a result, full-featured RAD tools offer you a mechanism for injecting SQL statements into your object-oriented applications. Borland C++Builder is an example of an object-oriented development environment that offers SQL capability.

Chapter 4 shows you how to create database tables with C++Builder. That operation, of course, represents only a small fraction of C++Builder's capabilities. The tool's primary purpose is the development of applications that process the data in database tables. The developer places objects on forms and then customizes the objects by giving them properties, events, and possibly methods as well. Out of sight of the developer, C++Builder converts the graphic representation of the application into a C++ program, which can then be compiled and run.

Although RAD tools such as C++Builder can deliver high-quality applications in less time, they are usually specific to one platform — or to only a few platforms. C++Builder, for instance, runs only under Microsoft Windows operating systems. Keep that in mind if you think you may want to migrate your application to a different platform.

RAD tools such as C++Builder represent the beginning of the eventual merger of relational and object-oriented database design. The structural strengths of relational design and SQL will both survive. They will be augmented by the rapid — and comparatively bug-free — development that comes from object-oriented programming.

Part V

SQL in the Real World

The 5th Wave   By Rich Tennant

"OH, SCARECROW – I DON'T THINK YOU'LL NEED YOUR LAPTOP IN THE EMERALD CITY ANYWAY."

In this part . . .

Okay, if you've been reading this book one chapter at a time, enthralled by the unfolding saga of SQL:1999, then you've looked at SQL in isolation — you may even have begun to dream that you could solve all your data-handling problems by using SQL alone. Alas, reality intrudes. (Doesn't it always?) Many things you simply can't do with SQL, at least not with SQL by itself. By combining SQL with traditional procedural languages, such as COBOL, FORTRAN, or C, you can achieve results that you could not get with SQL alone. In this part, I show you how to combine SQL with procedural languages. Then I describe how SQL databases operate over the Internet and over organizational intranets. Suddenly reality starts to look pretty good . . .

Chapter 16

ODBC and JDBC

● ●

In This Chapter

▶ Defining ODBC

▶ Describing the parts of ODBC

▶ Using ODBC in a client/server environment

▶ Using ODBC on the Internet

▶ Using ODBC on an intranet

▶ Using JDBC

● ●

*I*n the last several years, computers have become increasingly interconnected, both within and between organizations. With this connection
comes the need for sharing database information across networks. The major
obstacle to the free sharing of information across networks is the incompatibility of the operating software and applications running on different
machines. A major step toward overcoming this incompatibility has been the
creation and ongoing evolution of SQL.

Unfortunately, "standard" SQL is not all that standard. Even DBMS vendors
who claim to be SQL:1999-compatible have included extensions in their implementations that make them incompatible with the extensions in the implementations of other vendors. The vendors are loath to give up their extensions
because their customers have designed them into their applications and have
become dependent on them. User organizations, particularly large ones, need
another way to make cross-DBMS communication possible — something that
does not require vendors to "dumb down" their implementations to the lowest
common denominator. This other way is ODBC (Open Database Connectivity).

ODBC

ODBC is a standard interface between a database and an application that accesses the data in the database. Having a standard enables any application front end to access any database back end by using SQL. The only requirement is that the front end and the back end both adhere to the ODBC standard. ODBC 3.5 is the current version of the standard. An application accesses a database by using a *driver* that is specifically designed to interface with that particular database. The front end of the driver, the side that goes to the application, rigidly adheres to the ODBC standard. It looks the same to the application, regardless of what database engine is on the back end. The back end of the driver is customized to the specific database engine that it is addressing. With this architecture, applications don't have to be customized to — or even aware of — which back-end database engine controls the data they are using. The driver masks the differences between back ends.

ODBC interface

The *ODBC interface* is essentially a set of definitions that is accepted as standard. The definitions cover everything that is needed to establish communication between an application and the database that holds its data. The ODBC interface defines the following:

- **A function call library**

  The ODBC function calls provide for connecting to a back-end database engine, executing SQL statements, and passing results back to the application.

- **Standard SQL syntax**
- **Standard SQL data types**
- **Standard protocol for connecting to a database engine**
- **Standard error codes**

To perform an operation on a database, include the appropriate SQL statement as an argument of an ODBC function call. As long as you use the ODBC-specified standard SQL syntax, the operation works — regardless of what database engine is on the back end.

Components of ODBC

The ODBC interface consists of four functional components. Each component plays a role in giving ODBC the flexibility that enables it to provide transparent communication from any compatible front end to any compatible back end. The four layers of the ODBC interface are between the user and the data that the user wants, as follows:

- ✔ **Application:** The application is the part of the ODBC interface that is closest to the user. Of course, even systems that don't use ODBC include an application. Nonetheless, including the application as a part of the ODBC interface makes sense. The application must be cognizant that it is communicating with its data source through ODBC. It must connect smoothly with the ODBC driver manager, in strict accordance with the ODBC standard.

- ✔ **Driver manager:** The driver manager is a *dynamic link library* (DLL), which is generally supplied by Microsoft. It loads appropriate drivers for the system's (possibly multiple) data sources and directs function calls coming in from the application to the appropriate data sources via their drivers. The driver manager also handles some ODBC function calls directly and detects and handles some types of errors.

- ✔ **Driver:** Because data sources can be different from each other (in some cases, they can be very different indeed), you need a way to translate standard ODBC function calls into the native language of each different data source. Translation is the job of the driver DLL. Each driver DLL accepts function calls through the standard ODBC interface and then translates them into code that is understandable to its associated data source. When the data source responds with a result set, the driver reformats it in the reverse direction into a standard ODBC result set. The driver is the key element that enables any ODBC-compatible application to manipulate the structure and the contents of an ODBC-compatible data source.

- ✔ **Data source:** The data source may be one of many different things. It may be a relational DBMS (and associated database) residing on the same computer as the application. It may be such a database on a remote computer. It may be an *ISAM* (Indexed Sequential Access Method) file with no DBMS, either on the local or a remote computer. It may include a network, or it may not. The myriad of different forms that the data source can take requires that a custom driver be available for each one.

ODBC in a Client/Server Environment

In a client/server system, the interface between the client part and the server part is called the *application programmer's interface* (API). An API can be either proprietary or standard. A *proprietary* API is one in which the client part of the interface has been specifically designed to work with one particular back end on the server. The actual code that forms this interface is a driver, and in a proprietary system it is called a *native driver*. I discuss native drivers in more detail in Chapter 17. A native driver is optimized for use with a specific front-end client and its associated back-end data source. Because native drivers are optimized for both the specific front-end application and the specific DBMS back end that they are working with, the drivers tend to pass commands and information back and forth quickly, with a minimum of delay.

If your client/server system always accesses the same type of data source, and you're sure that you'll never need to access data on another type of data source, then you may want to use the native driver that is supplied with your DBMS. On the other hand, if you need to access data that is stored in a different form sometime in the future, then using an ODBC interface now may save you from a great deal of rework later.

ODBC drivers are also optimized to work with specific back-end data sources, but they all have the same front-end interface to the driver manager. Any driver that hasn't been optimized for a particular front end, therefore, is probably not as fast as a native driver that is specifically designed for that front end. A major complaint about the first generation of ODBC drivers was their poor performance compared to native drivers. Recent benchmarks, however, have shown that ODBC 3.5 drivers are quite competitive in performance to native drivers. The technology is now mature enough that it is no longer necessary to sacrifice performance to gain the advantages of standardization.

ODBC and the Internet

Database operations over the Internet are different in several important ways from database operations on a client/server system. The most visible difference from the user's point of view is the client portion of the system, which includes the user interface. In a client/server system, the user interface is part of an application that communicates with the data source on the server via ODBC-compatible SQL statements. Over the World Wide Web, though, the client portion of the system is a Web browser, which communicates with the data source on the server via *HTML* (HyperText Markup Language).

Because anyone with a Web browser can access data that is accessible on the Web, the act of putting a database on the Web is called *database publishing*. Databases that are placed on the Web are potentially accessible by many more people than can access data on a LAN server. Furthermore, on the Web, you usually don't have very strict control over who those people are. Thus, the act of putting data on the Web is more akin to publishing to the world than it is to sharing with a few coworkers. See Figure 16-1 for illustrations comparing client/server systems with Web-based systems.

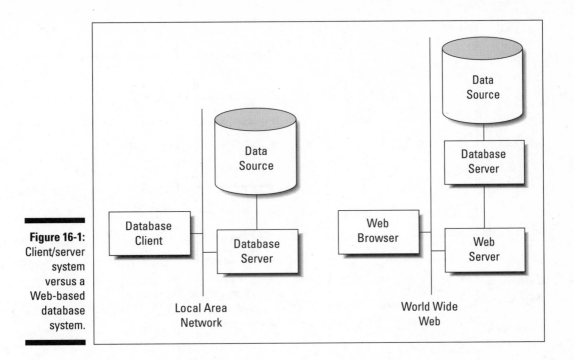

Figure 16-1:
Client/server
system
versus a
Web-based
database
system.

Server extensions

In the Web-based system, communication between the browser on the client machine and the Web server on the server machine takes place in HTML. A system component called a *server extension* translates the HTML into ODBC-compatible SQL, then the database server acts on the SQL, which in turn deals directly with the data source. In the reverse direction, the data source sends the result set that is generated by a query through the database server to the server extension, which then translates it into a form that the Web server can handle. The results are then sent over the Web to the Web browser on the client machine, where they are displayed to the user. Figure 16-2 shows the architecture of this type of system.

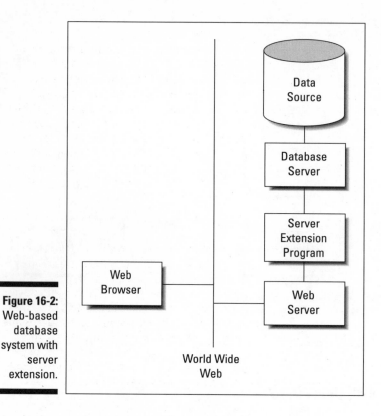

Client extensions

Web browsers were designed — and are now optimized — to be easy-to-understand and easy-to-use interfaces to Web sites of all kinds. The most popular browsers, Netscape Navigator and Microsoft Internet Explorer, were not designed or optimized to be database front ends. In order for meaningful interaction with a database to occur over the Internet, the client side of the system needs functionality that the browser does not provide. To fill this need, several types of *client extensions* have been developed. These extensions include helper applications, Navigator plug-ins, ActiveX controls, Java applets, and scripts. The extensions communicate with the server via HTML, which is the language of the Web. Any HTML code that deals with database access is translated into ODBC-compatible SQL by the server extension before being forwarded to the data source.

Helper applications

The first client extensions were called *helper applications*. A helper application is a standalone program that runs on the user's PC. It is not integrated with a Web page and it does not display in a browser window. You can use a helper application as a viewer for graphics file formats that are not supported by the browser. To use a helper application, the user must first download it from its source site and install it on his or her browser. From then on, when the user downloads a file in that format, the browser automatically prompts the viewer to display the file. One negative feature of this scheme is that the entire data file must be downloaded into a temporary file before the helper application starts. Thus, for large files, your wait can be quite long before you see any part of your downloaded file.

Netscape Navigator plug-ins

Netscape Navigator plug-ins are similar to helper applications in that they help process and display information that the browser can't handle alone. They differ in that they work only with Netscape browsers and are much more closely integrated with them. The tighter integration enables a browser that is enhanced by plug-ins to start displaying the first part of a file before the download operation is complete. The ability to display early output while later output is still being downloaded is a significant advantage. The user doesn't have to wait nearly as long before beginning work. A large and ever-growing number of Netscape plug-ins is available that enable enhancements such as sound, chats with similarly equipped users, animation, video, and interactive 3-D virtual reality. Aside from these uses, some plug-ins facilitate accessing remote databases over the Web.

ActiveX controls

Microsoft's ActiveX controls provide similar functionality to Netscape's plug-ins but they operate by an entirely different technology. ActiveX is based on Microsoft's earlier OLE technology. Netscape has committed to support ActiveX as well as other strategic Microsoft technologies in the Netscape environment. Of course, Microsoft's own Internet Explorer is also compatible with ActiveX. Between the two, Netscape and Microsoft control an overwhelming majority of the browser market.

Java applets

Java is a C++-like language that was developed by Sun Microsystems specifically for the development of Web client extensions. After a connection is made between a server and a client over the Web, the appropriate Java applet is downloaded to the client, where the applet commences to run. The applet, which is embedded in an HTML page, provides the database-specific functionality that the client needs in order to provide flexible access to server data. Figure 16-3 is a schematic representation of a Web database application with a Java applet running on the client machine.

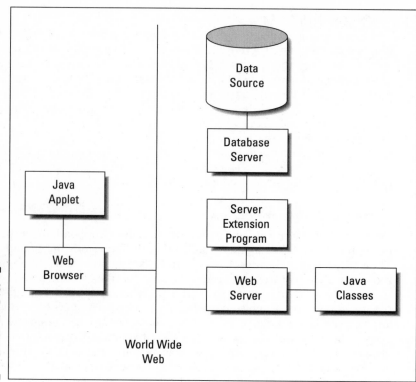

Figure 16-3:
Web
database
application
using a Java
applet.

A major advantage to using Java applets is that they are always up to date. Because the applets are downloaded from the server every time they are used (as opposed to being retained on the client), the client is always guaranteed to have the latest version whenever it runs one. If you are responsible for the server, you never have to worry about losing compatibility with some of your clients when you upgrade the server software. Just make sure that your downloadable Java applet is compatible with the new server configuration, and all your clients automatically become compatible too.

Scripts

Scripts are the most flexible tools for creating client extensions. Using a scripting language, such as Netscape's JavaScript or Microsoft's VBScript, gives you maximum control over what happens at the client end. You can put validation checks on data entry fields, thus enabling the rejection or correction of invalid entries without ever going out onto the Web. This can save you a good deal of time as well as reduce traffic on the Web, thus benefiting other users as well. As with Java applets, scripts are embedded in an HTML page and execute as the user interacts with that page.

ODBC and an Intranet

An *intranet* is a local or wide area network that operates exactly like a simpler version of the Internet. Because an intranet is entirely contained within a single organization, you don't need complex security measures such as fire-walls. (More about intranets in Chapter 18.) All the tools that are designed for application development on the World Wide Web operate equally well as development tools for intranet applications. ODBC works on an intranet in the same way that it does on the Internet. If you have multiple different data sources, clients using Web browsers and the appropriate client and server extensions can communicate with them with SQL that passes through HTML and ODBC stages. At the driver, the ODBC-compliant SQL is translated into the database's native command language and executed.

JDBC

JDBC (Java DataBase Connectivity) is very similar to ODBC but it differs in a few important respects. One such difference is hinted at by its name. JDBC is a data-base interface that looks the same to the client program — regardless of what data source is sitting on the server (back end). The difference is that JDBC expects the client application to be written in the Java language, rather than another language such as C++ or Visual Basic. A third difference is that Java and JDBC were both designed from the start to run on the World Wide Web.

Java is a full-featured programming language, and it is entirely possible to write robust applications with Java that can access databases in some kind of client-server system. When used this way, a Java application that accesses a database via JDBC is very similar to a C++ application that accesses a data-base via ODBC. The major difference between a Java application and a C++ application, however, concerns the Internet (or an intranet).

When the system that you are interested in is on the Net, however, the oper-ating conditions are quite different from the conditions in a client-server system. The client side of an application that operates over the Internet is a browser, with minimal computational capabilities. These capabilities must be augmented in order for significant database processing to be done; Java applets provide these capabilities.

An *applet* is a small application that resides on a server. When a client con-nects to that server over the Web, the applet is downloaded and starts run-ning in the client computer. Java applets are specially designed so that they run in a *sandbox*. A sandbox is a well-defined area in the client computer's memory where the downloaded applet can run. The applet is not allowed to affect anything outside the sandbox. This architecture is designed to protect the client machine from potentially hostile applets that may try to extract sensitive information or cause malicious damage.

You face a certain amount of danger when you download anything from a server that you do not know to be trustworthy. If you download a Java applet, that danger is much reduced, but not completely eliminated. Be wary about letting executable code enter your machine from a questionable server.

Like ODBC, JDBC passes SQL statements from the front-end application (applet) running on the client to the data source on the back end. It also serves to pass result sets or error messages from the data source back to the application. The value of using JDBC is that the applet writer can write to the standard JDBC interface, without needing to know or care what database is located at the back end. JDBC performs whatever conversion is necessary for accurate two-way communication to take place.

Chapter 17

SQL on the Internet

• •

• •

*T*he Internet, and particularly the portion of it known as the World Wide Web (WWW), has mushroomed in importance in the last several years. Just about every aspect of computing seems to be viewed according to how it relates to the Web, and database is no exception. The World Wide Web lives up to its name. It provides a web of connectivity that envelops the globe. With an Internet connection, anyone, anywhere, can access data residing on a Web server on the other side of town or, just as easily, on the other side of the world.

The ability to make your data available to anyone, anywhere in the world opens up a whole new kind of database usage. This new usage, *database publishing,* is more akin to book publishing or radio broadcasting than it is to the point-to-point communication characteristic of operations on a local-area network (LAN). The information that you make available on the Web can be accessed and used by thousands or even millions of people that you will never meet. The most popular sites on the Web today receive more than a million visits, or *hits,* per day. You can make a substantial impact with your Web-based database, however, even if you are nowhere near that league.

The LAN Is SQL's Ancestral Home

SQL was originally created by IBM to facilitate communication between large databases residing on mainframe computers and users on client machines that were connected to those mainframes by a local-area network (LAN). SQL gradually became a de facto standard means, and then an official ANSI and ISO standard means of communicating between users and databases.

Companies producing relational databases designed to operate across LANs embraced the SQL standard and made it the communications medium of choice on systems in which the user was located on a different machine from the database, with a LAN connecting them.

SQL, coupled with ODBC, enabled an application running on a user's machine to simultaneously access data located on two or even more server machines. This combination proved to be a great boon to organizations whose information-processing infrastructure had grown up over time without the benefit of centralized planning. Different machines, running different operating systems and different applications, can now share information. Marvelous as this kind of flexibility is, it pales in comparison with what is possible over the Internet.

How the Internet Differs From a Classic LAN

A *local-area network* (LAN) is a collection of computers that are all in physical proximity (thus, the word *local*). The computers, forming *nodes* on the network, are interconnected by wired or wireless communication links. Many local-area networks are small, having anywhere from 10 to 50 nodes. Large organizations are better served by LANs that have more than a thousand nodes. In either case, you can exercise some centralized control over the network. This control makes specifying a proprietary database interface possible, and you can expect all the users to be using access tools that are compatible with it.

The Internet, however, is an entirely different story. It has millions of nodes, and they are not in physical proximity. No one has centralized control over what goes on. In this environment, the owner of a database server can't make any assumptions about what kind of access tools the user has. The user has a Web browser, possibly supplemented with a plug-in that hosts the client end of a client/server database system. Because the most popular Web browsers run on all the popular client platforms, the client software doesn't have to be specifically tailored to run on a specific back-end database.

Note: The ordinary Web browser, such as Netscape Navigator or Microsoft Internet Explorer, comes close to being that Holy Grail of database access, the *Universal Front End*. If it existed, the Universal Front End would interface seamlessly with any database server of your choice. It would enable the user to easily create tables, manipulate data, and operate database applications regardless of what kind of server the database is on or what kind of DBMS is controlling it. A browser by itself can't do these tasks, of course. But by downloading the appropriate Netscape plug-in or ActiveX component (see Chapter 16 for more about these items) before attempting to deal with the database, the browser can come very close. When a connection is established, state-of-the-art database publishers check the client machine for the appropriate plug-in. If they find it, they download the client part of their application and proceed. If they do not find the appropriate plug-in on the client, they first download the plug-in to the client machine, then they download the client part of their application. This whole sequence can be relatively transparent to the user.

Two areas where operation on the Internet may differ significantly from operation on a LAN are

  ✔ Network protocol
  ✔ Security

If you are considering allowing remote access to your database from over the Internet, you should carefully consider the impact of these two aspects of operation.

Network protocol

In order for the nodes on a network to communicate with each other, they must all speak the same language. When a node sends a message, it must be formatted in such a way that the receiving node can understand it and then take appropriate action. The people who first hooked personal computers together to form local-area networks were not concerned with making their systems compatible with the Internet. At that time, the Internet was running only on large mainframe computers that ran the UNIX operating system and that were located at government organizations and research universities. The personal computer world seemed far removed from that of the mainframes used by "big science." Consequently, the languages, or *protocols*, that were developed for PC LANs were different from what the Internet used.

Today, many PC LANs still operate with protocols that have evolved from those early PC protocols. The IPX/SPX protocol and the NetBEUI protocol are probably the most common of these. In contrast, the Internet uses the TCP/IP — Transmission Control Protocol/Internet Protocol. Anyone who wants to engage in database operations over the Web must use TCP/IP. Generally, switching to TCP/IP doesn't require any kind of a hardware change, but it can require a software reconfiguration.

Security

Security is a much bigger issue on the Internet than it is on any organizational LAN. On a LAN, you can be reasonably sure that no one is going to purposely try to sabotage your system. On the Internet, this assumption is very foolish and dangerous. All kinds of people are out there on the Internet, and some of them may want to hurt you — just for the sheer, twisted fun of it. Competitors or even enemies may have stronger reasons to give you trouble. When you are exposing your database server to the Internet, you must take significant extra precautions, beyond the normal precautions for a LAN.

The principal defense against attacks by hackers or other malefactors on the Internet is to install a firewall between your organizational network and the Internet. A *firewall* is a software system, or combination of hardware and software, that insulates your network from the Internet. All traffic, both in and out, must pass through the firewall. The firewall authenticates the packets passing through it according to standards that you set up. It passes packets that meet your criteria and throws away those that don't. It also enables you to monitor traffic for suspicious activity and to trace attempts at breaching your security.

When you make the decision to take the big step of putting your server on the Internet, be sure to provide adequate protection for sensitive information that you don't want inquisitive outsiders to know or malicious outsiders to damage.

From Client/Server to Internet-Based Database

Most database systems found on LANs are structured according to client/server architecture. Data is stored on one or more servers whose specific task is providing access to that data. Smaller client machines are spread throughout the organization — they host the user interface of the applications that access the database. Users, interacting with the client part of the application, access the data on the server by communicating over the LAN.

Compelling reasons exist to make database data available over the Internet. A commercial enterprise may want certain parts of its operational data to be available to vendors or customers with which it works closely. An enterprise like this may also want to make detailed information about its products available to the general public, in hopes that some of them will become customers. Entities that are in the information dissemination business, such as libraries, may want to make their information available to a wider audience than those who are able to make a physical visit. For these and other reasons, many groups have decided to establish a presence on the Internet.

Beyond posting a simple Web page, many organizations are engaging in database publishing — making selected internal information available to those who access their Web site. Some such information is freely available to anyone who logs on to the Web site. Using passwords, publishers can restrict access to authorized users, enabling them to access proprietary databases on the site or databases for which a fee is being charged.

The client/server architecture provides many of the key ingredients of a successful Web database publishing installation. Clients on the Web have similar equipment and operating environments to what is typical for clients on a corporate LAN. The database server of a Web-based system is no different from the database server on a LAN. Yes, you must address protocol and security issues, but good solutions exist for both. Investigating how client/server architecture may be applied to Web database publishing makes sense.

Two-tier client/server architecture

The original implementation of client/server computing on PC LANs used a two-tier architecture. This architecture had two main elements — the database client and the database server — connected by the LAN. You can implement a two-tier client/server system in several ways. One way, the so-called *fat client* architecture, places most of the computational burden on the client machine and relatively little on the server. A second way is the *thin client* architecture (also called *fat server*) model. In this model, the server does most of the computation, and the client provides little more than the user interface. Figure 17-1 is a schematic representation of a two-tier client/server system.

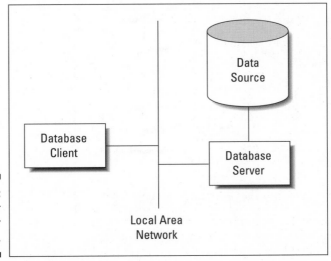

Figure 17-1:
Two-tier
client/server
system.

Regardless of how a two-tier client/server system is implemented, all the necessary functions are performed by either the database client software on the client machine or by the database server software on the server machine.

Three-tier client/server architecture

Three-tier client/server architecture is a relatively new development that is rapidly replacing the older two-tier model. It adds another functional block or level to the server side of the system. This new functional block, often called *middleware,* assumes some of the responsibilities that are normally handled by both the database client and the database server, allowing both of them to be *thinner.* Thinning the client is good, because potentially there are lots of clients, and the less capable the client machines need to be, the cheaper the overall system will be. Thinning the database server is also good because, when freed of computational tasks, the server can concentrate on moving data into and out of the database, speeding up operations. The higher level of modularization in a three-tier system also makes maintenance and troubleshooting easier. Figure 17-2 is a schematic representation of a three-tier client/server system.

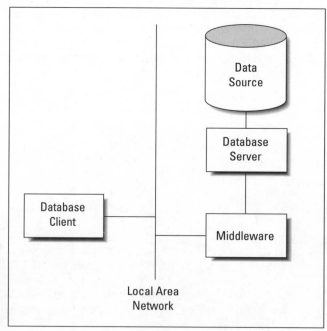

Figure 17-2:
Three-tier
client/server
system.

Two-tier Web architecture

The traditional architecture of the World Wide Web can also be viewed as a two-tier structure. A Web server hosts HTML (HyperText Markup Language) pages, which are accessible over the Internet to Web browsers running on client machines. This architecture is similar to a two-tier client/server system in that the Web browser on an Internet client performs the same function as the user interface running on a client/server database client. The Web server performs a similar job to that of the client/server database server — dispensing information. The main differences are: A Web browser is thinner than even the thinnest database client in a thin-client client/server system, and a Web server is incapable of the database manipulation required of even a thin-server implementation of a client/server system. This state of affairs is fine as long as you aren't trying to perform database operations over the Web. If all you're doing is putting HTML pages up for people to read, you don't need to do anything more. Figure 17-3 shows the structure of a two-tier Web system.

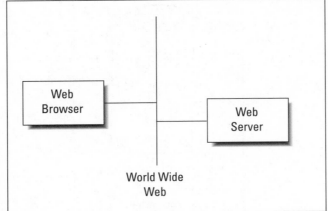

Figure 17-3:
Two-tier
Web
system.

Three-tier Web database architecture

To perform database operations over the Web effectively, you must combine elements from a two-tier client/server system with elements from a two-tier Web system to produce a composite three-tier solution. On the client side, the Web browser — perhaps enhanced by a Netscape plug-in or ActiveX component — provides the database application user interface. On the server side, the database server interfaces directly with the data source, just as it does in a classic client/server system.

The three-tier Web database architecture differs from the three-tier client/server database architecture in the *middleware*. The third tier (middleware) of a three-tier Web database system incorporates the Web server of a two-tier system and adds to it a *server extension program*. The signals and protocols handled by the Web server grew up in the Web environment and are accepted as standards in that realm. The signals and protocols that the database server is accustomed to seeing grew up in the client/server environment and are accepted as standards in that realm. The server extension program translates between these two incompatible standards. When requests are traveling from the client out on the Web to the data source behind the database server, the server extension program translates HTML to a form that the database server can understand, such as ODBC-compliant SQL. When result sets are traveling in the opposite direction, the server extension program translates them back into HTML for transmission over the Web. Figure 17-4 schematically shows the structure of a three-tier Web database system.

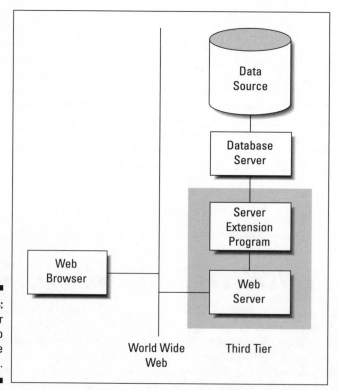

Figure 17-4:
Three-tier Web database system.

The Role of SQL

SQL was originally developed as a means for a remote client to communicate with a database. Local-area networks (or wide area networks) passed the SQL from client to server, encoding it according to a network protocol on the source end and decoding it at the destination end. A Web-based system adds an additional level of complication. The Web browser on the client end transforms a user request into packets in TCP/IP format for transmission over the Web. At the server end, the Web server passes these packets on to the server extension program, which translates them back into SQL that the database server can understand and respond to. So whether you are accessing a database over the Web or on a LAN, SQL is the means by which communication is conducted.

Where ODBC fits in

Whereas SQL is a standard language for communicating with a database, database vendors comply with that standard (commonly called SQL:1999) to a greater or lesser extent. An application using SQL for database access is by no means guaranteed to communicate successfully with a DBMS that claims to be SQL:1999 compliant. You have two ways to address this problem. One is to write native drivers for all the popular database servers. A *native driver* is specifically written to communicate with one, and only one, database server. For example, Netscape provides native drivers for Informix, Oracle, and Sybase databases as well as IBM's DB2 database. Microsoft provides native driver support for its own SQL Server database.

Native drivers are fast and efficient because they are specifically written for the database client and database server that they are connecting. The disadvantage is that a different native driver must be written for each database that you want to access — for each database client to which you want that access to be provided. The magnitude of the task of providing all those drivers for all those combinations of clients and servers motivated Microsoft to develop — and the industry to adopt — ODBC as the standard method for conveying SQL statements from clients to servers. If the SQL on the client end is always ODBC-compliant, then only one driver must be written for each type of server, and far fewer different server types exist than do clients. ODBC-compliant drivers are now available for the overwhelming majority of servers that anyone would want to connect to.

Java and SQL

Java is a language developed by Sun Microsystems specifically for use on the World Wide Web. It is similar in many respects to C++ but is simpler to learn and use. People maintaining Web sites create applications written in Java — called *applets* — that reside on their Web server. When a user connects to a database server, the server downloads an applet to the user's browser, where it serves as a client-side extension to the browser. This system enables the user to access much more of the functionality available on the server than what is possible with just a "plain vanilla" browser.

SQL is a data sub-language — it was never meant to be a complete language in itself, but was designed to be embedded in programs written in some other "host" language. Java can serve the function of being that host language just as well as can C++, Basic, or any other commonly used programming language. Sun has published a specification for JDBC (Java DataBase Connectivity) that performs the same function that ODBC performs in making a client-generated SQL statement understandable to a wide array of possible database servers. The JDBC standard provides writers of Java applets with the ground rules that they need to produce applets that will work with multiple, different database servers.

Chapter 18

Database on the Organizational Intranet

A dramatic transformation is sweeping through all types of organizations — large and small. Organizational LANs are being converted into intranets. If you work in a company, you will likely be a witness to some of the changes that are happening right under your nose! What is an intranet, and how does it compare to a LAN? How does it relate to the Internet, from which it derives its name?

LAN versus Intranet

An intranet differs from a *LAN* (local area network) in that the client-user interface is always the same — a Web browser — regardless of the hardware that the client runs on or the operating system that it uses. Platform independence is a big advantage in an organization with a heterogeneous installed base. Because you have to learn the Web browser interface only once, all applications then become easier to learn.

Physically, an intranet can be virtually identical to the LAN that it replaces. A network connects one or more servers to multiple client machines that are all located fairly close to each other. The difference is in the software — and possibly in the network protocols, as well. A database client on a LAN may run a database application, potentially requiring substantial client computing power in the process. A client on an intranet may run a browser, supplemented by a plug-in, ActiveX component, or a Java applet. In general, a much less capable (and cheaper) machine can do the job.

The database server on a LAN takes ODBC-compliant SQL (or database native commands) from the network interface as input and performs appropriate operations on the database, possibly returning a result set to the client. On an intranet, a Web server and server extension program stand between the network and the database server. As with the LAN, this combination delivers ODBC-compliant SQL or database native commands to the server. The interface that the database server sees is the same, regardless of whether it connects to a LAN or an intranet.

One possible difference between the two environments (although the database server may never know it) is the network protocol. An intranet must use TCP/IP. A LAN may use TCP/IP, but it may just as well use IPX/SPX or NetBEUI. Even if you convert an existing IPX/SPX network to an intranet, the protocol change is almost as easy as it would be if your LAN were already using TCP/IP — no big deal.

Internet-Intranet Commonality and Contrast

The organizational intranet is truly a child of the Internet. It is a "chip off the old block" — a smaller version of its parent. An intranet has clients running browsers, just like the Internet. An intranet has servers hosting Web pages and database sources, just like the Internet. And just like the Internet, a network that runs the TCP/IP protocol connects these elements. Anything that works on the Internet also works on an intranet.

Although the Internet and intranets are similar, many important differences also exist between them. The Internet is huge and essentially uncontrollable. Neither you nor anyone else can exercise any degree of authority over it. Even the world's largest intranet is small compared to the Internet, and because a single organization completely contains that intranet, it is subject to that organization's control.

Security is another big area of difference. For all practical purposes, the Internet has no security. Anybody can get an Internet account and do what he or she pleases with it. If you connect your organizational network directly to the Internet, you multiply the threats to the integrity of your data. Get expert advice and put a robust firewall in place before you make the connection. Being unprotected would make Charlie Brown's pal Linus run for his security blanket — or the nearest intranet. On an intranet, you have far fewer security concerns. You have control over physical access to all the computers on the network. You can control not only who has network access, but also what they are allowed to do.

Intranets enjoy one of the biggest advantages of the Internet, but at the same time they avoid one of the Internet's biggest disadvantages. Intranets, like the Internet, give you the advantage of a single, easy-to-learn user interface; the browser that your organization has established as a standard. After your users learn this one interface, they are a major step closer toward fluency in any network application that your organization uses. Unlike the Internet, intranets are not subject to strong attacks by outside hackers or other undesirable characters. No wonder so many organizations are converting their LANs to intranets.

A Database Is Safer and Faster on an Intranet

You have an easier time writing database applications for the intranet (assuming that they are never exposed to the Internet) than writing Internet database applications. The main reason is that you don't need to be paranoid about database security. On the Internet, you have plenty of reason to be paranoid about security.

To enable an Internet user to view a particular aspect of your database, you typically download a Web page with a data-entry form that contains invisible, embedded SQL statements. The Internet user then enters data into the form that translates "behind the scenes" into an SQL statement. It's easy for an Internet user to save an HTML page locally and make changes to it. A hostile person could change any embedded SQL statements in your form to statements that destroy data or cause some other unintended effect, and then submit the modified form. Your database may then proceed to self-destruct. Even if you plug this particular security breach, plenty of others are ready to take its place.

A hacker of only moderate skill and cleverness has numerous ways to attack you. You don't ever want to become a target of a highly skilled hackerAt any rate, you shouldn't worry about this problem if you're on an intranet, because (theoretically) everyone who has access to the system is a friend.

Speed is another advantage of intranets. The Internet is congested, and response time is often slow. This situation is bound to get worse before it gets better. Your own intranet should be faster. If it isn't, you can upgrade it until it is.

The added speed makes better use of your users' time and also gives you some added options. You can make more use of graphics and multimedia than you can on the Internet. A word of advice: Make very little use of graphics and multimedia effects in applets that you place on your Internet Web server, because the download times for these large files are excessive. On a high-bandwidth intranet, download times aren't nearly so much of an issue. You can spruce up the user interface and make your applet more appealing, without worrying overmuch about download times.

Intranet Challenges

Along with the advantages of switching your LAN to an intranet, you also face some possible disadvantages. One of these is the *HTTP* (HyperText Transfer Protocol) that forms the basis for all Web traffic. HTTP operates on a higher level than the popular LAN protocols and thus doesn't handle large amounts of data as efficiently. For applications that heavily update database files, operating over an intranet may be noticeably slower than on a LAN running on the same hardware.

Aside from speed, another HTTP characteristic is that it is stateless. SQL enables you to encapsulate a series of statements in a transaction to protect them from harmful interactions with the statements of other users. The transaction also protects the statements from system failures that occur after only some of the statements have been executed. (Take a look at Chapter 14 for more details.) Because HTTP is stateless, you have no way to specify that a transaction is operating. Thus, you can't use transactions on an intranet (or on the Internet either). You can find ways around this problem, but they add complication to application development and slow the operation of any application that uses them.

Note: To say that HTTP is *stateless* doesn't mean that HTTP is a protocol without a country. It means that mechanisms don't exist for tracking how many of a sequence of operations have actually been performed and for informing the server that a series of related operations is now complete.

Don't panic! You can use cookies as one possible solution to the lack of transactions over the Web. A *cookie* is a data file that a server sends to a client that gets stored on the client's hard drive. It can contain up to 4,000 bytes of information. Each time the client connects to that server, the cookie gets sent to the server along with the request for the server's Web page. In this way, the client and server can exchange state information, allowing a partially completed transaction to pick up where it left off. Newer development tools, through state management features, offer more advanced solutions to the lack of persistent connections across the Web.

The Intranet Back End

The intranet back end is the stuff on the server side of the Web. Back-end elements consist of the data source, the database server, and the middleware that connects them to the Web. The middleware may take several different forms but always includes a Web server, which interfaces directly with the Web. In addition to the Web server, the middleware usually also includes some sort of server extension that connects the Web server to the database server.

The middleware, whatever form it takes, transforms requests coming in from the Web to the standard form that the database server is accustomed to receiving. It doesn't matter what the database server is — Microsoft SQL Server, Borland InterBase, Informix, Oracle, Sybase SQL Server, or anything else. As far as the server can tell, it is dealing with an ordinary LAN client. It neither knows nor cares that an intranet is involved in its interactions with its clients.

Building Intranet Database Applications

Building database applications that are to run over an intranet requires skill in two different, and largely disjointed, areas. If you're an expert at producing client/server database applications, you may be unaware of the most elementary aspects of Web programming. On the other hand, if you're a whiz at Web programming, you may not be a programming pundit with client/server database applications. Practitioners with a high level of skill in both areas are rare. Because of this situation, tool vendors produce tools specifically aimed at Web database development that require less skill than those that have been traditionally available.

Traditional application-development tools

Back in my day, I used to walk 16 miles to school, through slippery mud flats in the spring and waist-deep snowdrifts in the winter . . . wait a minute. That's a different book. What I mean to say is that in the early days of Web database development, conditions were pretty primitive. The tools available for database application development were not particularly appropriate for interfacing to a Web server. For their part, Web page design tools were not designed for connecting Web pages to databases either. Web pages were created and formatted using HTML. People wrote server extension programs from scratch using PERL, C, C++, or shell scripts, according to the Common Gateway Interface (CGI) protocol. State management programming required another tool.

To do a good job, you had to understand the interfaces of the Web server and the database server on a low level, and you had to be an expert in your language of choice. Development was slow and laborious. Significant performance issues arose, particularly if you were using PERL. PERL is an interpretive language, and the interpreter is over 500K in size. Every time a Web browser made a request, this 500K file had to be loaded and a PERL script executed. This arrangement tended to make database access slow and to load down the server, slowing operation for other users, too. You can still write server extensions this way, if you want to, but now better alternatives are available.

Integrated development environments

Products in this category are a big step up from a plain-vanilla language compiler because they incorporate a visual design paradigm, automatic generation of code for standard components, an array of wizards, and other development tools.

ColdFusion

ColdFusion comes in two complementary parts. ColdFusion Server is a scalable, open platform for delivering Web applications that range from simple database-driven pages to full e-commerce solutions on intranets, extranets, and the Internet. ColdFusion Studio is an integrated development environment consisting of an array of visual tools for creating ColdFusion applications. ColdFusion Studio supports advanced project management and source control integration. ColdFusion Server supports multi-server clusters, providing scalability across a wide range of sizes.

Borland C++Builder

In a general purpose Windows 9x, Windows ME, Windows NT, or Windows 2000 visual development environment, you can use C++Builder to create stand-alone EXE and DLL files, drivers, action games — practically anything. Although it has broad general applicability, C++Builder is well endowed in the database development area. Available in Enterprise, Professional, and Standard editions, you can find a version appropriate to any size task. The Enterprise and Professional Editions include an extensive array of tools and utilities that specifically target the creation of database applications. A key feature of the C++Builder database application development support is the data-aware component. You can drop these easy-to-use and fast-executing components into your applications, speeding both development and execution.

Microsoft's Visual Studio

Visual Studio is a suite of application development tools that includes Visual Basic, Visual C++, Visual J++ or Visual FoxPro, and Visual InterDev. Visual C++ is Microsoft's visual application development environment that uses the C++ language. Like C++Builder, you can use Visual C++ to create any kind of stand-alone program. You can apply the Microsoft development environment to Web database application development as easily as you can apply it to any other kind of development. A variety of wizards greatly simplify application development. Visual C++ makes it easy to include ActiveX components in your programs, as well as elements from the Microsoft Foundation Classes library. You can use the templates included in the Active Template Library to build custom components quickly.

Visual J++ is Microsoft's visual development environment for creating applications and applets in an extended version of Java that includes ActiveX controls. Visual J++ includes all the things that you expect in a full-featured development environment, including a visual debugger, wizards for building applets and ActiveX controls, an editor, a compiler, and a class viewer to promote easy comprehension of Java objects. A database wizard makes it easy to hook Java applications to ODBC and SQL databases. Microsoft promotes Visual J++ as an improved version of Java — improved because of its ActiveX support. Visual InterDev is a full Web page-authoring environment. You can use Visual InterDev to develop applications in Visual Basic, Visual C++, Visual J++, or Visual FoxPro.

Borland JBuilder

JBuilder is a visual application development tool specifically designed to develop Java applications and applets. In structure and features, JBuilder has much in common with C++Builder, because both are descendants of the popular Borland Delphi development environment. However, although Delphi produces Pascal code and C++Builder produces C++ code, JBuilder produces Java code and runs on non-Microsoft platforms as well as the Microsoft operating systems that C++ Builder runs on. JBuilder's drag-and-drop development structure is based on Sun Microsystems's Enterprise JavaBeans standard. JBuilder supports the industry-standard Common Object Request Broker Architecture (CORBA) for creating distributed object systems. This means that a JBuilder system can run on a network consisting of different computer types running different, incompatible operating systems. Two-way tools enable you to switch back and forth seamlessly between the graphical environment and the code environment. Any applications that you develop according to the JavaBeans standard can run on any computer platform that supports Java.

SQL Builder is a graphical query editor that automatically generates SQL:1999 statements. SQL Explorer is an integrated database schema and content management utility. Rounding out JBuilder's SQL tools is SQL Monitor, which you can use to test, debug, and tune SQL queries.

JBuilder includes what Borland calls *DataExpress architecture,* which supports all JDBC-compliant data sources. In addition, JBuilder has native drivers for Oracle, Sybase, Informix, InterBase, and other desktop and client/server database-management systems.

The pure Java/extended Java battle

A battle is raging for control of the Web development tools market. Sun Microsystems originally envisioned Java as a cross-platform language that would allow Web-based applications to be completely platform-independent. The particular hardware or operating system that you developed an application on would no longer matter because it would run on any other hardware or operating system that supported a standard Web browser. This idea caught on like a brushfire on a hot summer day in Malibu. People started building Java applets for mainframes, minicomputers, PCs, and even Sun workstations. Java became an overnight success.

At first, Microsoft did not perceive the sudden emergence of the Web as a threat to its dominance of the personal-computer software marketplace, so Microsoft mounted only a modest effort in the Web area. Coming late to the realization that a platform-independent Web was indeed a serious problem for the Intel-Microsoft axis, Microsoft went on *red alert* and started developing a strategy to deflect any move toward platform independence and to promote a move back into the Microsoft Windows camp.

Microsoft decided to get back into the battle zone by extending its version of Java with the ActiveX control. You can speed development of your Java applications and applets with pre-built ActiveX controls or you can create your own custom ActiveX controls. Such applications can run within a browser on any platform, but you must develop the applications on a Microsoft Windows machine. Because the overwhelming majority of computers in the world are Intel machines running Windows, Microsoft has been able to gain substantial support for its view of the future of the Web and of Java.

Meanwhile, Sun and a host of other companies who view Microsoft as intent on taking over the world are fighting to keep Java "pure." These companies want to make sure that pure Java has no extensions that tie it to any single development platform, such as Windows. They want Java to retain the idea that brought it into existence in the first place — platform independence.

At this point, it appears that both pure and extended Java will be around for a long time. Pure Java dominates in the Linux/Unix environments, and extended Java dominates on Windows systems. No surprise there, I guess. In both cases, SQL mediates any communication between the applet (or application) and its corresponding data source on the server.

Chapter 19

Triggers

● ●

● ●

*I*n pistols, rifles, shotguns, and bazookas, a trigger is a small, seemingly insignificant piece of metal — that when moved ever so slightly — causes a powerful explosion that propels a projectile toward a target at near the speed of sound. The trigger is a very small cause that can have a very large effect.

What Do Triggers Have to Do with Databases?

Databases — specifically, active databases — can also have triggers. The analogy to firearms is apt, because in the database context a seemingly small trigger can cause a very large effect on a database — hopefully not a destructive effect!

A *trigger* is a procedure that the DBMS automatically invokes in response to a pre-specified change in the database. This procedure can cause additional changes, perhaps major ones, to be made to the database.

Three things are relevant to a trigger:

✔ **Event:** A change to the database that activates the trigger.

✔ **Condition:** A query or test that is run when the trigger is activated.

✔ **Action:** A procedure that is executed when the trigger is activated and its condition is true.

The event can be any change to the database, large or small. The condition can be any query or test that evaluates to either a true or false result. The action can be a procedure that contains any number of SQL statements, some of which may have a major effect on the database.

A trigger may initiate an action that changes the database in such a way as to activate another trigger. A whole cascade of events might be initiated by a single trigger, which in turn, sets off a string of other triggers.

When May You Want to Use a Trigger?

Most likely, you may want to use a trigger just before or just after an INSERT, UPDATE, or DELETE statement. These are statements that change the contents of a database table. Before an INSERT, UPDATE, or DELETE statement, you may want to capture the old state of the table before it is changed and archive it. After an INSERT, UPDATE or DELETE operation, you may want to write the operation that you just performed to a log file. Later, if you want to roll back the operation, you have the information that enables you to do so. Triggers are such flexible tools, you will probably think of many other uses for them.

Triggers are often used as alternatives to constraints. For example, you may have a constraint on an order entry application that aborts the transaction if the value of a credit order exceeds the customer's credit limit. This makes sense, but this may not be the best way to handle the situation in all cases. What if the order exceeds the customer's limit by only a small amount — say, 5 percent? What if, in addition, the customer has had a good payment history for over a year? In a case like this, you may want to allow the transaction, and add the customer to a table of people to be considered for a credit increase. A trigger that fires before this order is inserted into the ORDERS table gives you the flexibility to make a series of checks and perform a sequence of actions instead of merely aborting the transaction.

Creating a Trigger

You create a trigger with a CREATE TRIGGER statement. Consider the case mentioned in the section "When May You Want to Use a Trigger": Assume ORDER_TOTAL is the total amount being charged, and CREDIT_LIMIT is the credit limit for the customer making the purchase:

```
CREATE TRIGGER CREDIT_CHECK
    BEFORE INSERT ON ORDERS
    FOR EACH ROW
    WHEN (((ORDER_TOTAL - CREDIT_LIMIT) > 0.05 * CREDIT_LIMIT)
        OR CREDIT_STATUS = Bad) ;
    BEGIN ATOMIC
        SELECT ORDER_TOTAL / 0 from ORDER ;
    END ;
```

We want to allow the insertion of an order that is less than 5 percent over the credit limit of a customer in good standing. The trigger specified in the previous example checks for the opposite condition. If the order is more than 5 percent over the credit limit or if the customer has a bad credit status, then the trigger action is performed. In this case, the trigger action is a SELECT that incorporates a divide by zero. This causes the trigger to fail which in turn causes the INSERT statement (that it is triggered by) to also fail. This has the effect of accepting the orders of good customers who are just slightly over their credit limit, but rejecting orders that are more than 5 percent over the purchaser's credit limit — or orders made by customers with a bad credit rating.

In this case, the BEGIN ATOMIC ... END structure was not really necessary, because only one SQL statement was in the action part of the trigger. When the action part contains more than one SQL statement, the BEGIN ATOMIC ... END structure assures that either all or none of the action statements will be executed.

The trigger in this example is defined so that it occurs *before* the event that "pulls" the trigger. You can also create a trigger that fires *after* the triggering event.

Firing a Trigger

In the previous example, the condition specified by the WHEN clause in the CREDIT_CHECK trigger executes any time the ORDERS table calls for an INSERT. If it evaluates to a TRUE value, the trigger fires, a divide by zero executes, and the error condition that is produced prevents the addition of a credit order to the ORDERS table. If the WHEN clause evaluates to a FALSE, the trigger doesn't fire and the INSERT into the ORDERS table takes place.

In general, if a trigger's WHEN condition evaluates to TRUE when the event that invokes the trigger (an INSERT, UPDATE, or DELETE) occurs, the trigger fires and its action takes place.

The SQL-92 specification did not provide for triggers, but many DBMS vendors included them anyway because they are so useful. As a result, when SQL:1999 finally specified a standard syntax for triggers, much code had already been written using other syntaxes. Depending on which DBMS you use, the syntax for triggers may vary from what was shown in the code example in the section "Creating a Trigger." As time goes on, vendors typically phase in the standard syntax, while retaining their pre-existing proprietary syntax, so that their customers do not have to modify applications that are already running fine.

Part VI
Advanced Topics

The 5th Wave   By Rich Tennant

And finally, do you feel your client/server environment keeps you well connected to your department?

In this part . . .

You can approach SQL on many levels. In earlier parts, I cover the major topics that you are likely to encounter in most applications. This part deals with subjects that are significantly more complex. SQL deals with data a set at a time. Cursors come into play only if you want to violate that paradigm and grapple with the data a row at a time. Error handling is important to every application, whether simple or sophisticated — but you can approach it either simplistically or on a much deeper level. (Hint: The more depth you give to your error handling, the better off your users are if problems arise.) Dynamic SQL can be deep indeed, not to mention confusing. With it you can write SQL statements without having to know what data you are manipulating or what actions you are performing on it (ideal if you're working on a secret weapon and don't want yourself to know). In this part, I give you a view of the depths as well as of the shallows. The Persistent Stored Modules update adds procedural extensions to SQL that give SQL some hefty new powers without making the programmer revert to a host language for procedural operations.

The SQL:1999 international standard added object-oriented enhancements to SQL — and they can be a bear to master. Folks who are schooled in traditional procedural programming have to wrestle their assumptions into a whole different shape to handle object-oriented programming. Once you make that mental shift, however, you can make your code perform in ways that were not possible when everyone was playing by the old rules.

Chapter 20

Cursors

A major incompatibility between SQL and the most popular application development languages is that SQL operates on the data of an entire set of table rows at a time, whereas the procedural languages operate on only a single row at a time. A *cursor* enables SQL to retrieve (or update, or delete) a single row at a time so that you can use SQL in combination with an application written in any of the popular languages.

A cursor is like a pointer that locates a specific table row. When a cursor is active, you can SELECT, UPDATE, or DELETE the row at which the cursor is pointing.

Cursors are valuable if you want to retrieve selected rows from a table, check their contents, and perform different operations based on those contents. SQL can't perform this sequence of operations by itself. SQL can retrieve the rows, but procedural languages are better at making decisions based on field contents. Cursors enable SQL to retrieve rows from a table one at a time and then feed the result to procedural code for processing. By placing the SQL code in a loop, you can process the entire table row by row.

In embedded SQL, the most common flow of execution looks like this:

```
EXEC SQL DECLARE CURSOR statement
EXEC SQL OPEN statement
Test for end of table
Procedural code
```

```
Start loop
    Procedural code
    EXEC SQL FETCH
    Procedural code
    Test for end of table
End loop
EXEC SQL CLOSE statement
Procedural code
```

The SQL statements in this listing are DECLARE, OPEN, FETCH, and CLOSE. Each of these statements is discussed in detail in this chapter.

If you can perform the operation that you want with normal SQL (set-at-a-time) statements, then do so. Declare a cursor, retrieve table rows one at a time, and use your system's host language only when normal SQL can't do what you want.

Declaring a Cursor

To use a cursor, you first must declare its existence to the DBMS, and you do this with a DECLARE CURSOR statement. The DECLARE CURSOR statement doesn't actually cause anything to happen; it just announces the name of the cursor to the DBMS and specifies what query the cursor is going to operate on. An SQL:1999 DECLARE CURSOR statement has the following syntax:

```
DECLARE cursor-name [INSENSITIVE][SCROLL] CURSOR FOR
    query expression
    [ORDER BY order-by expression]
    [FOR updatability expression] ;
```

Note: The cursor name uniquely identifies a cursor, so it must be unlike that of any other cursor name in the current module or compilation unit.

To make your application more readable, give the cursor a meaningful name. Relate it to the data that the query expression requests or to the operation that your procedural code performs on the data.

The query expression

The *query expression* can be any legal SELECT statement. The rows that the SELECT statement retrieves are the ones that the cursor steps through one at a time. These rows are the scope of the cursor.

The query is not actually performed when the DECLARE CURSOR statement is read. You can't retrieve data until you execute the OPEN statement. The row-by-row examination of the data starts after you enter the loop that encloses the FETCH statement.

The ORDER BY clause

You may want to process your retrieved data in a particular order, depending on what your procedural code is going to do with the data. You can sort the retrieved rows before processing them by using the optional ORDER BY clause. The clause has the following syntax:

```
ORDER BY sort-specification [ , sort-specification ]...
```

You can have multiple sort specifications. Each has the following syntax:

```
( column-name ) [ COLLATE BY collation-name ] [ ASC | DESC ]
```

You sort by column name, and to do so, the column must be in the select list of the query expression. Columns that are in the table but not in the query select list do not work as sort specifications. For example: You want to perform an operation that is not supported by SQL on selected rows of the CUSTOMER table. You can use a DECLARE CURSOR statement like this:

```
DECLARE cust1 CURSOR FOR
    SELECT CUST_ID, F_NAME, L_NAME, CITY, STATE, PHONE
        FROM CUSTOMER
    ORDER BY STATE, L_NAME, F_NAME ;
```

In this example, the SELECT statement retrieves rows sorted first by state, then by last name, and then finally by first name. The statement retrieves all customers in Alaska (AK) before it retrieves the first customer from Alabama (AL). The statement then sorts customer records from Alaska by the customer's last name (*Aaron* before *Abbott*). Where the last name is the same, sorting then goes by first name (*George Aaron* before *Henry Aaron*).

Have you ever made 40 copies of a 20-page document on a photocopy machine without a collator? What a drag! You must make 20 stacks on tables and desks, then walk by the stacks 40 times, placing a sheet on each stack. This process is called *collation*. A similar process plays a role in SQL.

A collation is a set of rules that determines how strings in a character set compare. A character set has a default collation sequence that defines the order in which elements are sorted. But, you can apply a collation sequence other than the default to a column. To do so, use the optional `COLLATE BY` clause. Your implementation probably supports several common collations. Pick one, then make the collation *ascending* or *descending* by appending an `ASC` or `DESC` keyword to the clause.

In a `DECLARE CURSOR` statement, you can specify a calculated column that doesn't exist in the underlying table. In this case, the calculated column doesn't have a name that you can use in the `ORDER BY` clause. You can give it a name in the `DECLARE CURSOR` query expression, which enables you to identify the column later. Consider the following example:

```
DECLARE revenue CURSOR FOR
    SELECT model, units, price,
           units * price AS extprice
      FROM TRANSDETAIL
    ORDER BY model, extprice DESC ;
```

In this example, no `COLLATE BY` clause is in the `ORDER BY` clause, so the default collation sequence was used. Notice that the fourth column in the select list comes from a calculation on the data in the second and third columns. The fourth column is an extended price named `extprice`. In the `ORDER BY` clause, I first sort by model name, then by `extprice`. The sort on `extprice` is descending, as specified by the DESC keyword; transactions with the highest dollar value are processed first.

The default sort order in an ORDER BY clause is ascending. If a sort specification list includes a DESC sort and the next sort should be in descending order also, you must explicitly specify DESC for the next sort. For example:

```
ORDER BY A, B DESC, C, D, E, F
```

is equivalent to

```
ORDER BY A ASC, B DESC, C ASC, D ASC, E ASC, F ASC
```

The updatability clause

Sometimes, you may want to update or delete table rows that you access with a cursor. At other times, you may want to guarantee that such updates or deletions can't be made. SQL:1999 gives you control over this issue with the updatability clause of the `DECLARE CURSOR` statement. If you want to prevent updates and deletions within the scope of the cursor, use the clause:

```
FOR READ ONLY
```

For updates of specified columns only — leaving all others protected — use:

```
FOR UPDATE OF column-name [ , column-name ]...
```

Of course, any columns listed must appear in the DECLARE CURSOR's query expression. If you don't include an updatability clause, the default assumption is that all columns listed in the query expression are updatable. In that case, an UPDATE statement can update all the columns in the row to which the cursor is pointing, and a DELETE statement can delete that row.

Sensitivity

The query expression in the DECLARE CURSOR statement determines the rows that fall within the scope of a cursor. Consider this possible problem: What if a statement in your program, located between the OPEN and the CLOSE statements, changes the contents of some of those rows so that they no longer satisfy the query? What if such a statement deletes some of those rows entirely? Does the cursor continue to process all the rows that originally qualified, or does it recognize the new situation and ignore rows that no longer qualify or that have been deleted?

Changing the data in columns that are part of a DECLARE CURSOR query expression after some — but not all — of the query's rows have been processed results in a big mess. Your results are likely to be inconsistent and misleading. To avoid this problem, make your cursor insensitive to any changes that statements within its scope may make. Add the INSENSITIVE keyword to your DECLARE CURSOR statement. As long as your cursor is open, it is insensitive to table changes that otherwise affect rows qualified to be included in the cursor's scope. A cursor can't be both insensitive and updatable. An insensitive cursor must be read-only.

Think of it this way: A normal SQL statement, such as UPDATE, INSERT, or DELETE, operates on a set of rows in a database table (perhaps the entire table). While such a statement is active, SQL's transaction mechanism protects it from interference by other statements acting concurrently on the same data. If you use a cursor, however, your "window of vulnerability" to harmful interaction is wide open. When you open a cursor, you are at risk until you close it again. If you open one cursor, start processing through a table, then open a second cursor while the first is still active, the actions you take with the second cursor can affect what the statement controlled by the first cursor sees. For example, suppose that you write these queries:

```
DECLARE C1 CURSOR FOR SELECT * FROM EMPLOYEE
   ORDER BY SALARY ;
DECLARE C2 CURSOR FOR SELECT * FROM EMPLOYEE
   FOR UPDATE OF SALARY ;
```

Now, suppose you open both cursors and fetch a few rows with C1 and then update a salary with C2 to increase its value. This change can cause a row that you have fetched with C1 to appear again on a later fetch of C1.

The peculiar interactions that are possible with multiple open cursors, or opened cursors and set operations, are the sort of concurrency problems that transaction isolation avoids. If you operate this way, you are asking for trouble. So remember: Don't operate with multiple open cursors.

Scrollability

Scrollability is a capability that cursors didn't have prior to SQL-92. In implementations adhering to SQL-86 or SQL-89, the only allowed movement of the cursor was sequential, starting at the first row retrieved by the query expression and ending with the last row. SQL-92's SCROLL keyword in the DECLARE CURSOR statement gives you the capability to access rows in any order that you want. SQL:1999 retains this capability. The syntax of the FETCH statement controls the movement of the cursor. I describe the FETCH statement later in this chapter.

Opening a Cursor

Although the DECLARE CURSOR statement specifies which rows to include in the cursor, it doesn't actually cause anything to happen, because DECLARE is a declaration and not an executable statement. The OPEN statement actually brings the cursor into existence. It has the following form:

```
OPEN cursor-name ;
```

To open the cursor that I use in the discussion of the ORDER BY clause (earlier in this chapter) use the following:

```
DECLARE revenue CURSOR FOR
    SELECT model, units, price,
           units * price AS extprice
       FROM TRANSDETAIL
    ORDER BY model, extprice DESC ;
OPEN revenue ;
```

You can't fetch rows from a cursor until you open the cursor. When you open a cursor, the values of variables referenced in the DECLARE CURSOR statement become fixed, as do all current date-time functions. Consider the following example:

The fix is in (for date-times)

A similar "fixing" of date-time values exists in set operations. Consider:

```
UPDATE ORDERS SET RECHECK_DATE
    = CURRENT_DATE WHERE....;
```

Now suppose that you have a bunch of orders. You begin executing this statement at a minute before midnight. At midnight, the statement is still running, and it doesn't finish executing until five minutes after midnight. It doesn't matter. If a statement has any reference to CURRENT_DATE (or TIME or TIMESTAMP), the value is fixed when the statement begins, so all of the ORDERS rows in the statement get the same RECHECK_DATE. Similarly, if a statement references TIMESTAMP, the whole statement uses only one timestamp value, no matter how long the statement runs.

Here's an interesting example of an implication of this rule:

```
UPDATE EMPLOYEE SET KEY=
    CURRENT_TIMESTAMP;
```

You may expect that statement to set a unique value in the key column of each EMPLOYEE. You'd be disappointed: It sets the same value in every row.

So when the OPEN statement fixes date-time values for all statements referencing the cursor, it treats all of these statements like an extended statement.

```
DECLARE CURSOR C1 FOR SELECT * FROM ORDERS
    WHERE ORDERS.CUSTOMER = :NAME
        AND DUE_DATE < CURRENT_DATE ;
NAME := 'Acme Co';    //A host language statement
OPEN C1;
NAME := 'Omega Inc.';  //Another host statement
...
UPDATE ORDERS SET DUE_DATE = CURRENT_DATE;
```

The OPEN statement fixes the value of all variables referenced in the declare cursor and also fixes a value for all current date-time functions. Thus the second assignment to the name variable (NAME := 'Omega Inc.') has no effect on the rows that the cursor fetches. (That value of NAME is used the next time you open C1.) And even if the OPEN statement is executed a minute before midnight and the UPDATE statement is executed a minute after midnight, the value of CURRENT_DATE in the UPDATE statement is the value of that function at the time the OPEN statement executed. This is true even if DECLARE CURSOR doesn't reference the date-time function.

Fetching Data from a Single Row

Whereas the DECLARE CURSOR statement specifies the name of the cursor and its scope and the OPEN statement collects the table rows selected by the DECLARE CURSOR query expression, the FETCH statement actually retrieves the data. The cursor may point to one of the rows in the scope of the cursor, or to the location immediately before the first row in the scope, or to the location immediately after the last row in the scope, or to the empty space between two rows. You can specify where the cursor points with the orientation clause in the FETCH statement.

Syntax

The syntax for the FETCH command is:

```
FETCH [[orientation] FROM] cursor-name
    INTO target-specification [, target-specification ]... ;
```

Six orientation options are available:

- NEXT
- PRIOR
- FIRST
- LAST
- ABSOLUTE
- RELATIVE

The default option is NEXT, which was the only orientation available in versions of SQL prior to SQL-92. It moves the cursor from wherever it is to the next row in the set specified by the query expression. If the cursor is located before the first record, it moves to the first record. If it points to record n, it moves to record n+1. If the cursor points to the last record in the set, it moves beyond that record and notification of a no data condition is returned in the SQLSTATE system variable. (Chapter 21 details SQLSTATE and the rest of SQL's error-handling facilities.)

The target specifications are either host variables or parameters, respectively, depending on whether embedded SQL or module language is using the cursor. The number and types of the target specifications must match the number and types of the columns specified by the query expression in the DECLARE CURSOR. So in the case of embedded SQL, when you fetch a list of five values from a row of a table, five host variables must be there to receive those values, and they must be the right types.

Orientation of a scrollable cursor

Because the SQL:1999 cursor is scrollable, you have other choices besides NEXT. If you specify PRIOR, the pointer moves to the row immediately preceding its current location. If you specify FIRST, it points to the first record in the set, and if you specify LAST, it points to the last record.

An integer value specification must accompany ABSOLUTE and RELATIVE. For example, FETCH ABSOLUTE 7 moves the cursor to the seventh row from the beginning of the set. FETCH RELATIVE 7 moves the cursor seven rows beyond its current position. FETCH RELATIVE 0 doesn't move the cursor.

FETCH RELATIVE 1 has the same effect as FETCH NEXT. FETCH RELATIVE -1 has the same effect as FETCH PRIOR. FETCH ABSOLUTE 1 gives you the first record in the set, FETCH ABSOLUTE 2 gives you the second record in the set, and so on. Similarly, FETCH ABSOLUTE -1 gives you the last record in the set, FETCH ABSOLUTE -2 gives you the next-to-last record, and so on. Specifying FETCH ABSOLUTE 0 returns the *no data* exception condition code, as does FETCH ABSOLUTE 17 if only 16 rows are in the set.

Positioned DELETE and UPDATE statements

You can perform delete and update operations on the row that the cursor is currently pointing to. The syntax of the DELETE statement is as follows:

```
DELETE FROM table-name WHERE CURRENT OF cursor-name ;
```

If the cursor doesn't point to a row, the statement returns an error condition. No deletion occurs.

The syntax of the UPDATE statement is as follows:

```
UPDATE table-name
   SET column-name = value [,column-name = value]...
   WHERE CURRENT OF cursor-name ;
```

The value you place into each specified column must be a value expression or the keyword DEFAULT. If an attempted positioned update operation returns any error, the update isn't performed.

Closing a Cursor

After you finish with a cursor, make a habit of closing it immediately. Leaving a cursor open as your application goes on to other issues may not cause any harm, but then again it may. Also, open cursors use system resources.

If you close a cursor that was insensitive to changes made while it was open, reopen it; the reopened cursor now reflects any such changes.

Chapter 21

Persistent Stored Modules

• •

In This Chapter

▶ Tooling up compound statements with atomicity, cursors, variables, and conditions

▶ Regulating the flow of control statements

▶ Doing loops that do loops that do loops

▶ Retrieving and using stored procedures and stored functions

▶ Assigning privileges with practical panache

▶ Creating and using stored modules

• •

S ome of the leading practitioners of database technology have been working on the standards process for years. Even right after a standard has been issued and accepted by the worldwide database community, progress toward the next standard does not slow down. Such was the case for SQL-92. A seven-year gap separated the issuance of SQL-92 and the release of the first component of SQL:1999. The intervening years were not without activity, however. During this interval, ANSI and ISO issued an addendum to SQL-92, called SQL-92/PSM (Persistent Stored Modules). The release of this addendum formed the basis for a part of SQL:1999 with the same name. The SQL/PSM part of SQL:1999 defines a number of new statements that give SQL flow of control structures comparable to the flow of control structures available in full-featured programming languages. The new features added to SQL by SQL/PSM allow you to do many things entirely within SQL. Earlier versions of SQL would have required repeated swapping between SQL and its procedural host language.

Compound Statements

Throughout this book, SQL is set forth as a non-procedural language, that deals with data a set at a time rather than a record at a time. With the addition of the new facilities covered in this chapter, however, this statement is not as true as it used to be. SQL is becoming more procedural, although it still deals with data a set at a time. Because archaic SQL (that defined by SQL-92) does not follow the procedural model — where one instruction follows another in a sequence to produce a desired result — early SQL statements were standalone entities, perhaps embedded in a C++ or Visual Basic program. With these early versions of SQL, users typically did not pose a query or perform some other operation by executing a series of SQL statements. If users did execute such a series of statements, they suffered a performance penalty. Every SQL statement that is executed requires a message to be sent from the client where the user is located, to the server where the database is located, and then a response in the reverse direction. This network traffic slows operations as the network becomes congested.

SQL:1999 now allows compound statements, made up of individual SQL statements, that execute as a unit. This capability eases network congestion because all of the individual SQL statements in the compound statement are sent to the server as a unit, executed as a unit, and a single response is sent back to the client.

All the statements included in a compound statement are enclosed between a BEGIN keyword at the beginning of the statement and an END keyword at the end of the statement. For example, to insert data into multiple related tables, you use syntax similar to the following:

```
void main {
    EXEC SQL
BEGIN
  INSERT INTO students (StudentID, Fname, Lname)
     VALUES (:sid, :sfname, :slname) ;
  INSERT INTO roster (ClassID, Class, StudentID)
     VALUES (:cid, :cname, :sid) ;
  INSERT INTO receivable (StudentID, Class, Fee)
     VALUES (:sid, :cname, :cfee)
        END ;
/* Check SQLSTATE for errors */
}
```

This little fragment from a C program includes an embedded compound SQL statement. The comment about SQLSTATE deals with error handling. If, for some reason, the compound statement does not execute successfully, an error code is placed in the status parameter SQLSTATE. Of course, placing a comment after the END keyword doesn't correct the error. The comment is placed there simply to remind us that in a real program, error-handling code belongs in that spot. Error handling is described in detail in Chapter 22.

Atomicity

Compound statements introduce a possibility for error that does not exist for simple SQL statements. A simple SQL statement either completes successfully or it doesn't. If it doesn't complete successfully, the database is unchanged, but this is not necessarily the case for a compound statement. Consider the example in the previous section.

1999 STANDARD SQL

What's in a name?

As a name for a feature of SQL, *persistent stored modules* is pretty descriptive — so descriptive, in fact, that you may already have reasoned out what it probably means. You already know what a *module* is; if not, sneak a peek at Chapter 15. (Not to worry. All quizzes in this book are open-book.) Logic may then lead you to expect that a *stored* module must be one that's kept somewhere till it's needed — and that a *persistent* stored module must be one that sticks around for an extended time. And that's gotta be what this chapter is about — right?

Well, you're close, but logic has led you a little astray. Granted, you can find *some* handy facts about such modules in this chapter — but the part of SQL:1999 known as Persistent Stored Modules (PSM) is mostly concerned with other SQL features. In SQL:1999, the bulk of PSM defines important functions that should have made it into SQL-92, but didn't. These functions dramatically increase the power and utility of SQL — and hey, they had to put 'em *somewhere.* And some of them do have *stored* in their names (in particular, stored functions and stored procedures). So much for pure logic. What's important is that it's good new stuff and it works.

What if the Insert to the Students table and the Insert to the Roster table both took place, but because of interference from another user, the Insert to the Receivable table failed? A student would be registered for a class but would not be billed. This kind of error can be hard on a university's finances. The concept that is missing in this scenario is *atomicity.* An atomic statement is indivisible — it either executes completely or not at all. Simple SQL statements are atomic by nature, but compound SQL statements are not. However, you can make a compound SQL statement atomic by specifying it as such. In the following example, the compound SQL statement is safe by introducing atomicity:

```
void main {
     EXEC SQL
BEGIN ATOMIC
  INSERT INTO students (StudentID, Fname, Lname)
     VALUES (:sid, :sfname, :slname) ;
  INSERT INTO roster (ClassID, Class, StudentID)
     VALUES (:cid, :cname, :sid) ;
  INSERT INTO receivable (StudentID, Class, Fee)
     VALUES (:sid, :cname, :cfee)
          END ;
/* Check SQLSTATE for errors */
  }
```

By adding the keyword ATOMIC after the keyword BEGIN, you can assure that either the entire statement executes, or — if an error occurs — the entire statement rolls back, leaving the database in the state it was in before the statement began executing.

Variables

One feature that full computer languages such as C or Basic offer that SQL didn't offer until SQL/PSM is *variables*. Variables are symbols that can take on a value of any given data type. Within a compound statement, you can declare a variable and assign it a value. The variable can then be used within the compound statement. Then, after you exit a compound statement, all the variables declared within it are destroyed. Thus, variables in SQL are local to the compound statement within which they are declared. Here is an example:

```
BEGIN
    DECLARE prezpay NUMERIC ;
    SELECT salary
    INTO prezpay
    FROM EMPLOYEE
    WHERE jobtitle = 'president' ;
END;
```

Cursors

You can declare a cursor within a compound statement. As I mentioned in Chapter 20, you use cursors to process a table's data one row at a time. Within a compound statement, you can declare a cursor, use it, and then forget it because the cursor is destroyed when you exit the compound statement. Here's an example of this usage:

```
BEGIN
    DECLARE ipocandidate CHARACTER(30) ;
    DECLARE cursor1 CURSOR FOR
  SELECT company
  FROM biotech ;
    OPEN CURSOR1 ;
    FETCH cursor1 INTO ipocandidate ;
    CLOSE cursor1 ;
END;
```

Conditions

When people say that a person has a "condition," they usually mean that something is wrong with that person — he or she is sick or injured. People usually don't bother to mention that a person is in good condition; rather, we talk about people who are in serious condition, or even worse, in critical condition. This idea is very similar to the way programmers talk about the condition of an SQL statement. The execution of an SQL statement leads to a successful result, a questionable result, or an outright erroneous result. Each of these possible results corresponds to a condition.

Every time an SQL statement executes, the database server places a value into the status parameter SQLSTATE. SQLSTATE is a five-character field. The value that is placed into SQLSTATE indicates whether the preceding SQL statement executed successfully. If it did not execute successfully, the value of SQLSTATE provides some information about the error.

The first two of the five characters of SQLSTATE (the class value) give you the major news as to whether the preceding SQL statement executed successfully, returned a result that may or may not have been successful, or produced an error. Table 21-1 shows the four possible results.

Table 21-1	SQLSTATE Class Values
Class	*Description*
'00'	Successful completion
'01'	Warning
'02'	Not Found
other	Exception

A class value of '00' indicates that the preceding SQL statement executed successfully. This is a very happy and welcome result — most of the time.

A class value of '01' indicates a warning. This means that something unusual happened during the execution of the SQL statement. This occurrence may or may not be an error — the DBMS cannot tell. The warning is a "heads-up" to the developer, suggesting that perhaps he or she should check the preceding SQL statement carefully to assure that it is operating correctly.

A class value of '02' indicates that no data was returned as a result of the execution of the preceding SQL statement. This may or may not be good news, depending on what the developer was trying to do with the statement. For example, sometimes an empty result table is exactly what the developer wanted the SQL statement to return.

Any class code other than '00', '01', or '02' indicates an error condition. An indication of the nature of the error appears in the three characters that hold the subclass value. The two characters of the class code, plus the three characters of the subclass code together comprise the five characters of SQLSTATE.

Handling conditions

You can have your program look at SQLSTATE after the execution of every SQL statement. Now what do you do with the knowledge that you gain? If you find a class code of '00', you probably don't want to do anything at all — you want execution to proceed as you originally planned. If you find a class code of '01' or '02', however, you may or may not want to take special action. If you expected the "Warning" or "Not found" indication, then you probably want to let execution proceed normally. If you didn't expect either of these class codes, then you probably want to have execution branch to a procedure that is specifically designed to handle the unexpected, but not totally unanticipated warning or 'not found' result. If you received any other class code, then something is definitely wrong, and you should branch to an exception-handling procedure. The specific procedure that you choose to branch to depends on the contents of the three sub-class characters, as well as the two class characters of SQLSTATE. If multiple different exceptions are possible, there should be an exception-handling procedure for each one because different exceptions often require different responses. Some errors may be correctable, or you may find a work-around. Other errors may be fatal, calling for termination of the application.

Handler declarations

You can put a condition handler within a compound statement. To create a condition handler, you must first declare the condition that it will handle. The condition declared can be some sort of exception, or it can just be something that is true. Table 21-2 lists the possible conditions and includes a brief description of what causes each type of condition.

Table 21-2	Conditions That May Be Specified in a Condition Handler
Condition	*Description*
SQLSTATE VALUE 'xxyyy'	Specific SQLSTATE value
condition name	declared condition
SQLEXCEPTION	SQLSTATE class other than '00', '01', or '02'
SQLWARNING	SQLSTATE class '01'
NOT FOUND	SQLSTATE class '02'

The following is an example of a condition declaration:

```
BEGIN
    DECLARE constraint_violation CONDITION
    FOR SQLSTATE VALUE '23000' ;
END ;
```

This example is not realistic because typically, the SQL statement that may cause the condition to occur — as well as the handler that would be invoked if the condition did occur — would also be enclosed within the BEGIN ... END structure.

Handler actions and handler effects

If a condition occurs that invokes a handler, the action specified by the handler executes. This action is an SQL statement, which can be a compound statement. If the handler action completes successfully, then the handler effect executes. The following is a list of the three possible handler effects:

- ✔ CONTINUE. Continue execution immediately after the statement that caused the handler to be invoked.

- ✔ EXIT. Continue execution after the compound statement that contains the handler.

- ✔ UNDO. Undo the work of the previous statements in the compound statement, and continue execution after the statement that contains the handler.

If the handler was able to correct whatever problem invoked the handler, then the CONTINUE effect may be appropriate. The EXIT effect may be appropriate if the handler didn't fix the problem, but the changes made to the compound statement do not need to be undone. The UNDO effect is appropriate if you want to return the database to the state it was in before the compound statement started execution. Consider the following example:

```
    BEGIN ATOMIC
    DECLARE constraint_violation CONDITION
FOR SQLSTATE VALUE '23000' ;
    DECLARE UNDO HANDLER
        FOR constraint_violation
RESIGNAL ;
    INSERT INTO students (StudentID, Fname, Lname)
        VALUES (:sid, :sfname, :slname) ;
    INSERT INTO roster (ClassID, Class, StudentID)
        VALUES (:cid, :cname, :sid) ;
    END ;
```

If either of the INSERT statements causes a constraint violation, such as adding a record with a primary key that duplicates a primary key already in the table, then SQLSTATE assumes a value of 23000, thus setting the constraint_violation condition to a true value. This action causes the handler to UNDO any changes that have been made to any tables by either INSERT command. The RESIGNAL statement transfers control back to the procedure that called the currently executing procedure.

If both INSERT statements execute successfully, then execution continues with the statement following the END keyword.

Remember that the ATOMIC keyword is mandatory whenever a handler's effect is UNDO. This is not the case for handlers whose effect is either CONTINUE or EXIT.

Conditions that aren't handled

In the preceding example, consider this possibility: What if an exception occurred that returned an SQLSTATE value other than '23000'? Something is definitely wrong, but the exception handler that you coded can't handle it. What happens now? Because the current procedure doesn't know what to do, a RESIGNAL occurs. This bumps the problem up to the next higher level of control. If the problem does not get handled there, then it continues to be elevated to higher levels until either it is handled or it causes an error condition in the main application. The idea that I want to emphasize here is that if you write an SQL statement that may possibly cause exceptions, then you should write exception handlers for all such possible exceptions. If you don't, you will have more difficulty isolating the source of the problem when it inevitably occurs.

Assignment

With SQL/PSM, SQL finally gains a function that even the most lowly procedural languages have had since their inception: the ability to assign a value to a variable. Essentially, an assignment statement takes the following form:

```
SET target = source ;
```

In this usage, target is a variable name and source is an expression. Several examples might be:

```
SET vfname = 'Brandon' ;
```

```
SET varea = 3.1416 * :radius * :radius ;
```

```
SET vhiggsmass = NULL ;
```

Flow of Control Statements

Since its original formulation in the SQL-86 standard, one of the main drawbacks that has prevented people from using SQL in a procedural manner has been its lack of flow of control statements. Until now, you couldn't branch out of a strict sequential order of execution without reverting to a host language like C or Basic. SQL/PSM introduces the traditional flow of control structures that other languages provide, thus allowing SQL programs to perform needed functions without switching back and forth between languages.

IF . . . THEN . . . ELSE . . . END IF

The most basic flow of control statement is the `IF...THEN...ELSE...END IF` statement. `IF` a condition is true, then execute the statements following the `THEN` keyword. Otherwise execute the statements following the `ELSE` keyword. For example:

```
IF
    vfname = 'Brandon'
THEN
    UPDATE students
        SET Fname = 'Brandon'
    WHERE StudentID = 314159 ;
ELSE
    DELETE FROM students
    WHERE StudentID = 314159 ;
END IF
```

In this example, if the variable `vfname` contains the value 'Brandon', then the record for student `314159` is updated with 'Brandon' in the Fname field. If the variable `vfname` contains any value other than 'Brandon', then the record for student 314159 is deleted from the `students` table.

The `IF...THEN...ELSE...END IF` statement is great if you want to take one of two actions, based on the value of a condition. Often, however, you want to make a selection from more than two choices. At such times, you should probably use a `CASE` statement.

CASE . . . END CASE

`CASE` statements come in two different forms: the simple `CASE` statement and the searched `CASE` statement. Both kinds allow you to take different execution paths, based on the values of conditions.

Simple CASE statement

A simple `CASE` statement evaluates a single condition. Based on the value of that condition, execution may take one of any number of branches. For example:

```
CASE vmajor
    WHEN 'Computer Science'
    THEN INSERT INTO geeks (StudentID, Fname, Lname)
            VALUES (:sid, :sfname, :slname) ;
    WHEN 'Sports Medicine'
    THEN INSERT INTO jocks (StudentID, Fname, Lname)
            VALUES (:sid, :sfname, :slname) ;
    ELSE INSERT INTO undeclared (StudentID, Fname, Lname)
            VALUES (:sid, :sfname, :slname) ;
END CASE
```

The ELSE clause handles everything that doesn't fall into the explicitly named categories in the THEN clauses.

The ELSE clause is optional. However, if it is not included, and the CASE statement's condition is not handled by any of the THEN clauses, SQL returns an exception.

Searched CASE statement

A searched CASE statement is similar to a simple CASE statement, but it evaluates multiple conditions rather than just one. For example:

```
CASE
    WHEN vmajor
        IN ('Computer Science', 'Electrical Engineering')
        THEN INSERT INTO geeks (StudentID, Fname, Lname)
            VALUES (:sid, :sfname, :slname) ;
    WHEN vclub
        IN ('Amateur Radio', 'Rocket', 'Computer')
        THEN INSERT INTO geeks (StudentID, Fname, Lname)
            VALUES (:sid, :sfname, :slname) ;
    ELSE
        INSERT INTO poets (StudentID, Fname, Lname)
            VALUES (:sid, :sfname, :slname) ;
END CASE
```

You avoid an exception by putting all students who are not geeks into the poets table. Because not all nongeeks are poets, this may not be strictly accurate in all cases. If it isn't, you can always add a few more WHEN clauses.

LOOP . . . ENDLOOP

The LOOP statement allows you to execute a sequence of SQL statements multiple times. After the last SQL statement enclosed within the LOOP . . . ENDLOOP statement executes, control loops back to the first such statement and makes another pass through the enclosed statements. The syntax is as follows:

```
SET vcount = 0 ;
LOOP
    SET vcount = vcount + 1 ;
    INSERT INTO asteroid (AsteroidID)
        VALUES (vcount) ;
END LOOP
```

This code fragment pre-loads your asteroid table with unique identifiers. You can fill in other details about the asteroids as you find them, based on what you see through your telescope when you discover them.

Notice the one little problem with the code fragment in the preceding example: It is an infinite loop. No provision is made for leaving the loop, so it will continue inserting rows into the asteroid table until the DBMS fills all available storage with asteroid table records. If you are lucky, the DBMS will raise an exception at that time. If you are unlucky, you will merely crash the system.

For the LOOP statement to be useful, you need a way to exit loops before you raise an exception. That way is the LEAVE statement.

LEAVE

The LEAVE statement works just like you might expect it to work. When execution encounters a LEAVE statement embedded within a labeled statement, it proceeds to the next statement beyond the labeled statement. For example:

```
AsteroidPreload:
SET vcount = 0 ;
LOOP
   SET vcount = vcount + 1 ;
   IF vcount > 1000
      THEN
         LEAVE AsteroidPreload ;
   END IF ;
   INSERT INTO asteroid (AsteroidID)
      VALUES (vcount) ;
END LOOP AsteroidPreload
```

The above code inserts 1000 sequentially numbered records into the asteroids table, then passes out of the loop.

WHILE . . . DO . . . END WHILE

The WHILE statement provides another method of executing a series of SQL statements multiple times. While a designated condition is true, the WHILE loop continues to execute. When the condition becomes false, looping stops. For example:

```
AsteroidPreload2:
SET vcount = 0 ;
WHILE
   vcount < 1000 DO
      SET vcount = vcount + 1 ;
      INSERT INTO asteroid (AsteroidID)
         VALUES (vcount) ;
END WHILE AsteroidPreload2
```

This code does exactly the same thing that was done in the previous section by AsteroidPreload. This is just another example of the often-cited fact that with SQL, you usually have multiple ways to accomplish any given task. Use whichever method you feel most comfortable with, assuming your implementation allows both.

REPEAT . . . UNTIL . . . END REPEAT

The REPEAT loop is very much like the WHILE loop, except that the condition is checked after the embedded statements execute rather than before. Example:

```
AsteroidPreload3:
SET vcount = 0 ;
REPEAT
    SET vcount = vcount + 1 ;
    INSERT INTO asteroid (AsteroidID)
        VALUES (vcount) ;
    UNTIL X = 1000
END REPEAT AsteroidPreload3
```

Although I perform the same operation three different ways in the preceding example (with LOOP, WHILE, and REPEAT) you will encounter some instances where one of these structures is clearly better than the other two. It is good to have all three methods in your "bag of tricks" so that when a situation like this arises, you can decide which one is the best tool available for the situation.

FOR . . . DO . . . END FOR

The SQL FOR loop declares and opens a cursor, fetches the rows of the cursor, and executes the body of the FOR statement once for each row, and then closes the cursor. This loop makes processing possible entirely within SQL, rather than switching out to a host language. If your implementation supports SQL FOR loops, you can use them as a simple alternative to the cursor processing described in Chapter 20. Here's an example:

```
FOR vcount AS Curs1 CURSOR FOR
    SELECT AsteroidID FROM asteroid
DO
    UPDATE asteroid SET Description = 'stony iron'
        WHERE CURRENT OF Curs1 ;
END FOR
```

In this example, you update every row in the asteroid table by putting 'stony iron' into the Description field. This is a really fast way to identify the compositions of asteroids, but the table may suffer some in the accuracy department. Perhaps you'd be better off checking the spectral signatures of the asteroids and then entering their types individually.

ITERATE

The ITERATE statement provides a way to change the flow of execution within an iterated SQL statement. The iterated SQL statements are LOOP,

WHILE, REPEAT, and FOR. If the iteration condition of the iterated SQL statement is true or not specified, then the next iteration of the loop commences immediately after the ITERATE statement executes. If the iteration condition of the iterated SQL statement is false or unknown, then iteration ceases after the ITERATE statement executes. For example:

```
AsteroidPreload4:
SET vcount = 0 ;
WHILE
    vcount < 1000 DO
        SET vcount = vcount + 1 ;
        INSERT INTO asteroid (AsteroidID)
          VALUES (vcount) ;
        ITERATE AsteroidPreload4 ;
        SET vpreload = 'DONE' ;
END WHILE AsteroidPreload4
```

Execution loops back to the top of the WHILE statement immediately after the ITERATE statement each time through the loop until vcount equals 999. On that iteration, vcount increments to 1000, the INSERT performs, the ITERATE statement ceases iteration, vpreload is set to 'DONE', and execution proceeds to the next statement after the loop.

Stored Procedures

Stored procedures reside in the database on the server, rather than executing on the client — where all procedures were located before SQL/PSM. After you have defined a stored procedure, you can invoke it with a CALL statement. Keeping the procedure located on the server rather than the client reduces network traffic, thus speeding performance. The only traffic that needs to pass from the client to the server is the CALL statement. You can create this procedure in the following manner:

```
EXEC SQL
    CREATE PROCEDURE MatchScore
        ( IN white CHAR (20),
          IN black CHAR (20),
          IN result CHAR (3),
          OUT winner CHAR (5) )
    BEGIN ATOMIC
        CASE result
            WHEN '1-0' THEN
                SET winner = 'white' ;
            WHEN '0-1' THEN
                SET winner = 'black' ;
            ELSE
                SET winner = 'draw' ;
        END CASE
    END ;
```

After you have created a stored procedure like the one in this example, you can invoke it with a CALL statement similar to the following statement:

```
CALL MatchScore ('Kasparov', 'Karpov', '1-0', winner) ;
```

The first three arguments are input parameters that are fed to the MatchScore procedure. The fourth argument is the output parameter that the MatchScore uses to return its result to the calling routine. In this case it returns 'white'.

Stored Functions

A stored function is similar in many ways to a stored procedure. Collectively, the two are referred to as stored routines. They are different in several ways, including the way in which they are invoked. A stored procedure is invoked with a CALL statement, and a stored function is invoked with a function call, which can replace an argument of an SQL statement. The following is an example of a function definition, followed by an example of a call to that function:

```
CREATE FUNCTION PurchaseHistory (CustID)
    RETURNS CHAR VARYING (200)

    BEGIN
        DECLARE purch CHAR VARYING (200)
            DEFAULT '' ;
        FOR x AS SELECT *
                FROM transactions t
                WHERE t.customerID = CustID
        DO
            IF a <> ''
                THEN SET purch = purch || ', ' ;
            END IF ;
            SET purch = purch || t.description ;
        END FOR
        RETURN purch ;
    END ;
```

This function definition creates a comma-delimited list of purchases made by a customer that has a specified customer number, taken from the TRANSACTIONS table. The following UPDATE statement contains a function call to PurchaseHistory that inserts the latest purchase history for customer number 314259 into her record in the customer table:

```
SET customerID = 314259 ;
UPDATE customer
    SET history = PurchaseHistory (customerID)
    WHERE customerID = 314259 ;
```

Privileges

The various privileges that you can grant to users are discussed in Chapter 13. The database owner can grant to other users:

- The right to DELETE rows from a table
- The right to INSERT rows into a table
- The right to UPDATE rows in a table
- The right to create a table that REFERENCES another table
- The right of USAGE on a domain

SQL/PSM adds one more privilege that can be granted to a user — the EXECUTE privilege. Here are two examples:

```
GRANT EXECUTE on MatchScore to TournamentDirector ;
```

```
GRANT EXECUTE on PurchaseHistory to SalesManager ;
```

These statements allow the tournament director of the chess match to execute the MatchScore procedure, and the sales manager of the company to execute the PurchaseHistory function. People lacking the EXECUTE privilege for a routine aren't able to use it.

Stored Modules

A stored module can contain multiple routines (procedures and/or functions) that can be invoked by SQL. Anyone who has the EXECUTE privilege for a module has access to all the routines in the module. Privileges on routines within a module can't be granted individually. The following is an example of a stored module:

```
CREATE MODULE mod1
    PROCEDURE MatchScore
        ( IN white CHAR (20),
          IN black CHAR (20),
          IN result CHAR (3),
          OUT winner CHAR (5) )
    BEGIN ATOMIC
        CASE result
            WHEN '1-0' THEN
                SET winner = 'white' ;
            WHEN '0-1' THEN
                SET winner = 'black' ;
```

```
        ELSE
            SET winner = 'draw' ;
    END CASE
  END ;
```

```
  FUNCTION PurchaseHistory (CustID)
  RETURNS CHAR VARYING (200)
  BEGIN
     DECLARE purch CHAR VARYING (200)
        DEFAULT '' ;
     FOR x AS SELECT *
             FROM transactions t
             WHERE t.customerID = CustID
     DO
        IF a <> ''
           THEN SET purch = purch || ', ' ;
        END IF ;
        SET purch = purch || t.description ;
     END FOR
     RETURN purch ;
  END ;
END MODULE ;
```

The two routines in this module don't have much in common, but then —
they don't have to. You can gather related routines into a single module, or if
you'd rather, you can stick all the routines you are likely to use into a single
module, regardless of whether they have anything in common.

Chapter 22

Error-Handling

. . . .

. . . .

*W*ouldn't it be great if every application you wrote worked perfectly every time? Yeah, and it would also be really cool to win $57 million in the Oregon state lottery. Unfortunately, both possibilities are equally likely to happen. Error conditions of one sort or another are inevitable, so it's helpful to know what causes them. SQL:1999's mechanism for returning error information to you is the *status parameter* (or *host variable*) SQLSTATE. Based on the contents of SQLSTATE, you can take different actions to remedy the error condition.

For example, the WHENEVER directive enables you to take a predetermined action whenever a specified condition (if SQLSTATE has a non-zero value, for example) is met. You can also find detailed status information about the SQL statement that you just executed in the diagnostics area. In this chapter, I explain these helpful error-handling facilities and how to use them.

SQLSTATE

SQLSTATE specifies a large number of anomalous conditions. SQLSTATE is a five-character string in which only the uppercase letters A through Z and the numerals 0 through 9 are valid characters. The five-character string is divided into two groups: a two-character class code and a three-character subclass code. Figure 22-1 illustrates the SQLSTATE layout.

The SQL:1999 standard defines any class code that starts with the letters *A* through *H* or the numerals 0 through 4; therefore, these class codes mean the same thing in any implementation. Class codes that start with the letters *I* through *Z* or the numerals 5 through 9 are left open for implementors (the people who build database management systems) to define because the SQL specification can't anticipate every condition that may come up in every implementation. Clearly, however, implementors should use these non-standard class codes as little as possible to avoid migration problems from one DBMS to another. Ideally, implementors should use the standard codes most of the time and the nonstandard codes only under the most unusual circumstances.

Figure 22-1:
SQLSTATE
status
parameter
layout.

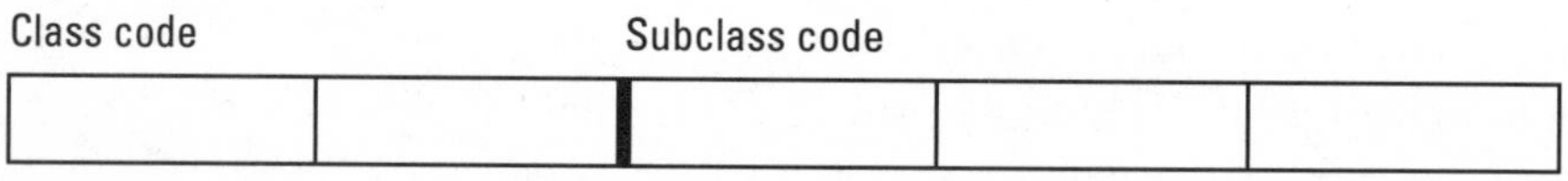

Class code   Subclass code

In SQLSTATE, a class code of 00 indicates successful completion. Class code 01 means that the statement executed successfully but produced a warning. Class code 02 indicates a no-data condition. Any SQLSTATE class code other than 00, 01, or 02 indicates that the statement did not execute successfully.

Because SQLSTATE updates after every SQL operation, you can check it after every statement executes. If SQLSTATE contains 00000 (successful completion), then you can proceed with the next operation. If it contains anything else, you may want to branch out of the main line of your code to handle the situation. The specific class code and subclass code that an SQLSTATE contains determines which of several possible actions you should take.

To use SQLSTATE in a module language program (described in Chapter 15), include a reference to it in your procedure definitions, as the following example shows:

```
PROCEDURE NUTRIENT
    (SQLSTATE, :foodname CHAR (20), :calories SMALLINT,
        :protein DECIMAL (5,1), :fat DECIMAL (5,1),
        :carbo DECIMAL (5,1))
INSERT INTO FOODS
    (FOODNAME, CALORIES, PROTEIN, FAT, CARBOHYDRATE)
    VALUES
    (:foodname, :calories, :protein, :fat, :carbo) ;
```

At the appropriate spot in your procedural language program, you can make values available for the parameters (perhaps by soliciting them from the user) and then call up the procedure. The syntax of this operation varies from one language to another, but it looks something like this:

```
foodname = "Okra, boiled" ;
calories = 29 ;
protein = 2.0 ;
fat = 0.3 ;
carbo = 6.0 ;
NUTRIENT(state, foodname, calories, protein, fat, carbo);
```

The state of SQLSTATE is returned in the variable state. Your program can examine this variable and then take the appropriate action based on the variable's contents.

WHENEVER Directive

What's the point of knowing that an SQL operation didn't execute success-fully if you can't do anything about it? If an error occurs, you don't want your application to continue executing as if everything is fine. You need to be able to acknowledge the error and do something to correct it. If you can't correct the error, at the very least you want to inform the user of the problem and bring the application to a graceful termination. The WHENEVER directive is the SQL mechanism for dealing with execution exceptions.

The WHENEVER directive is actually a declaration and is therefore located in your application's SQL declaration section, before the executable SQL code. The syntax is as follows:

```
WHENEVER condition action ;
```

The condition may be either SQLERROR or NOT FOUND. The action may be either CONTINUE or GOTO *address*. SQLERROR is True if SQLSTATE has a class code other than 00, 01, or 02. NOT FOUND is True if SQLSTATE is 02000.

If the action is CONTINUE, nothing special happens and the execution continues normally. If the action is GOTO *address* (or GO TO *address*), execution branches to the designated address in the program. At the branch address, you can put a conditional statement that examines SQLSTATE and takes different actions based on what it finds. Here are some examples of this scenario:

```
WHENEVER SQLERROR GO TO error_trap ;
```

or

```
WHENEVER NOT FOUND CONTINUE ;
```

The GO TO option is simply a macro: The *implementation* (that is, the embed-ded language precompiler) inserts the following test after every EXEC SQL statement:

```
IF SQLSTATE <> '00000'
   AND SQLSTATE <> '00001'
   AND SQLSTATE <> '00002'
THEN GOTO error_trap;
```

The CONTINUE option is essentially a NO-OP that says, "ignore this."

Diagnostics Area

Although SQLSTATE can give you some information about why a particular statement failed, this information is still pretty brief. So SQL:1999 provides for the capture and retention of additional status information in a diagnostics area. The additional status information can be particularly helpful in cases in which the execution of a single SQL statement generates multiple warning followed by an error. SQLSTATE only reports the occurrence of one error, but the diagnostics area has the capacity to report on multiple (hopefully all) errors.

The diagnostics area is a DBMS-managed data structure that has two components:

  ✔ **Header.** The header contains general information about the last SQL statement that was executed.

  ✔ **Detail area.** The detail area contains information about each code (error, warning, or success) that the statement generated.

The diagnostics header area

In Chapter 14, the SET TRANSACTION statement is examined. In this statement, you can specify DIAGNOSTICS SIZE. The SIZE that you specify is the number of detail areas allocated for status information. If you don't include a DIAGNOSTICS SIZE clause in your SET TRANSACTION statement, then your DBMS assigns its default number of detail areas, whatever that happens to be.

The header area contains five items, listed in Table 22-1.

Table 22-1	The Diagnostics Header Area
Fields	*Data Type*
NUMBER	INTEGER
ROW_COUNT	INTEGER

Item	Data Type
COMMAND_FUNCTION	VARCHAR (>=128)
COMMAND_FUNCTION_CODE	INTEGER
MORE	INTEGER
TRANSACTIONS_COMMITTED	INTEGER
TRANSACTIONS_ROLLED_BACK	INTEGER
TRANSACTION_ACTIVE	INTEGER

The NUMBER field is the number of detail areas that have been filled with diagnostic information about the current exception. The ROW_COUNT field holds the number of rows affected if the previous SQL statement was an INSERT, UPDATE, or DELETE.

The COMMAND_FUNCTION field describes the dynamic SQL statement that was just executed (if in fact the last SQL statement to be executed was a dynamic SQL statement). The COMMAND_FUNCTION_CODE field gives the code number for the dynamic SQL statement that was just executed (if the last SQL statement executed was a dynamic SQL statement). Every dynamic function has an associated numeric code.

The MORE field may be either a '1' or an '0.' '1' indicates that there are more status records than the detail area can hold. 'N' indicates that all the status records generated are present in the detail area. Depending on your implementation, you may be able to expand the number of records you can handle using the SET TRANSACTION statement.

The TRANSACTIONS_COMMITTED field holds the number of transactions that have been committed. The TRANSACTIONS_ROLLED_BACK field holds the number of transactions that have been rolled back. The TRANSACTION_ACTIVE field holds a '1' if a transaction is currently active and a '0' otherwise. A transaction is deemed to be active if a cursor is open or if the DBMS is waiting for a deferred parameter.

The diagnostics detail area

The detail areas contain data on each individual error, warning, or success condition. Each detail area contains 29 items, as Table 22-2 shows.

Table 22-2	The Diagnostics Detail Area
Item	*Data Type*
CONDITION_NUMBER	INTEGER
RETURNED_SQLSTATE	CHAR (6)
MESSAGE_TEXT	VARCHAR (>=128)
MESSAGE_LENGTH	INTEGER
MESSAGE_OCTET_LENGTH	INTEGER
CLASS_ORIGIN	VARCHAR (>=128)
CONNECTION_NAME	VARCHAR (>=128)
SERVER_NAME	VARCHAR (>=128)
CONSTRAINT_CATALOG	VARCHAR (>=128)
CONSTRAINT_SCHEMA	VARCHAR (>=128)
CONSTRAINT_NAME	VARCHAR (>=128)
CATALOG_NAME	VARCHAR (>=128)
SCHEMA_NAME	VARCHAR (>=128)
TABLE_NAME	VARCHAR (>=128)
COLUMN_NAME	VARCHAR (>=128)
CURSOR_NAME	VARCHAR (>=128)
CONDITION_IDENTIFIER	VARCHAR (>=128)
PARAMETER_NAME	VARCHAR (>=128)
ROUTINE_CATALOG	VARCHAR (>=128)
ROUTINE_SCHEMA	VARCHAR (>=128)
ROUTINE_NAME	VARCHAR (>=128)
SPECIFIC_NAME	VARCHAR (>=128)
TRIGGER_CATALOG	VARCHAR (>=128)
TRIGGER_SCHEMA	VARCHAR (>=128)
TRIGGER_NAME	VARCHAR (>=128)

CONDITION_NUMBER holds the sequence number of the detail area. If a statement generates five status items that fill up five detail areas, the CONDITION_ NUMBER for the fifth detail area is five. To retrieve a specific detail area for examination, use a GET DIAGNOSTICS statement (I describe this statement later in this chapter in the "Interpreting the information returned by SQL-STATE" section) with the desired CONDITION_NUMBER. RETURNED_SQLSTATE holds the SQLSTATE value that caused this detail area to be filled.

CLASS_ORIGIN tells you the source of the class code value returned in SQLSTATE. If the SQL standard defines the value, the CLASS_ORIGIN is 'ISO 9075'. If your DBMS implementation defines the value, CLASS_ORIGIN holds a string identifying the source of your DBMS. SUBCLASS_ORIGIN tells you the source of the subclass code value returned in SQLSTATE.

CLASS_ORIGIN is important. If you get an SQLSTATE of '22012', for example, the values indicate that it is in the range of standard SQLSTATEs, so you know that it means the same thing in all SQL implementations. However, if the SQLSTATE is '22500', the first two characters are in the standard range and indicate a data exception, but the last three characters are in the implementation-defined range. And if SQLSTATE is '900001', it's completely in the implementation-defined range. SQLSTATE values in the implementation-defined range can mean different things in different implementations, even though the code itself may be the same.

So how do you find out the detailed meaning of '22500' or the meaning of '900001'? You must look in the implementor's documentation. Which implementor? If you're using CONNECT, you may be connecting to various products. To determine which one produced the error condition, look at CLASS_ORIGIN and SUBCLASS_ORIGIN: They have values that identify each implementation. You can test the CLASS_ORIGIN and SUBCLASS_ORIGIN to see whether they identify implementors for which you have the SQLSTATE listings. The actual values placed in CLASS_ORIGIN and SUBCLASS_ORIGIN are implementor-defined, but they also are expected to be self-explanatory company names.

If the error reported is a constraint violation, the CONSTRAINT_CATALOG, CONSTRAINT_SCHEMA, and CONSTRAINT_NAME identify the constraint being violated.

Constraint violation example

The constraint violation information is probably the most important information that GET DIAGNOSTICS provides. Consider the following EMPLOYEE table:

```
CREATE TABLE EMPLOYEE
(ID CHAR(5) CONSTRAINT EMP_PK PRIMARY KEY,
SALARY DEC(8,2) CONSTRAINT EMP_SAL CHECK SALARY > 0,
DEPT CHAR(5) CONSTRAINT EMP_DEPT
REFERENCES DEPARTMENT) ;
```

And this DEPARTMENT table:

```
CREATE TABLE DEPARTMENT
   (DEPTNO CHAR(5),
    BUDGET DEC(12,2) CONSTRAINT DEPT_BUDGET
    CHECK(BUDGET >= SELECT SUM(SALARY) FROM EMPLOYEE
        WHERE EMPLOYEE.DEPT=DEPARTMENT.DEPTNO),
    ...);
```

Now consider an INSERT as follows:

```
INSERT INTO EMPLOYEE VALUES(:ID_VAR, :SAL_VAR, :DEPT_VAR);
```

Now suppose that you get an SQLSTATE of '23000'. You look it up in your SQL documentation, and it says "integrity constraint violation." Now what? That SQLSTATE value means that one of the following situations is true:

- ✔ The value in ID_VAR is a duplicate of an existing ID value: You have violated the PRIMARY KEY constraint.

- ✔ The value in SAL_VAR is negative: You have violated the CHECK constraint on SALARY.

- ✔ The value in DEPT_VAR isn't a valid key value for any existing row of DEPARTMENT: You have violated the REFERENCES constraint on DEPT.

- ✔ The value in SAL_VAR is large enough that the sum of the employees' salaries in this department exceeds the BUDGET: You have violated the CHECK constraint in the BUDGET column of DEPARTMENT. (Recall that if you change the database, all constraints that may be affected are checked, not just those defined in the immediate table.)

Under normal circumstances, you would need to do a great deal of testing to figure out what is wrong with that INSERT. But you can find out what you need to know by using GET DIAGNOSTICS as follows:

```
DECLARE CONST_NAME_VAR CHAR(18) ;
GET DIAGNOSTICS EXCEPTION 1
    CONST_NAME_VAR = CONSTRAINT_NAME ;
```

Assuming that SQLSTATE is '23000', this GET DIAGNOSTICS sets CONST_NAME_VAR to either 'EMP_PK', 'EMP_SAL', 'EMP_DEPT', or 'DEPT_BUDGET'. Notice that, in practice, you also want to obtain the CONSTRAINT_SCHEMA and CONSTRAINT_CATALOG, to uniquely identify the constraint given by CONSTRAINT_NAME.

Adding constraints to an existing table

This use of GET DIAGNOSTICS — determining which of several constraints has been violated — is particularly important in the case where ALTER TABLE is used to add constraints that didn't exist when you wrote the program:

```
ALTER TABLE EMPLOYEE
   ADD CONSTRAINT SAL_LIMIT CHECK(SALARY < 200000) ;
```

Now if you insert data into EMPLOYEE or update the SALARY column of an EMPLOYEE, you get an SQLSTATE of '23000' if SALARY exceeds 200000. You can program your INSERT statement so that, if you get an SQLSTATE of '23000', and you don't recognize the particular constraint name that GET DIAGNOSTICS returns, you can display a helpful message, such as Invalid INSERT: Violated constraint SAL_LIMIT.

Interpreting the information returned by SQLSTATE

CONNECTION_NAME and ENVIRONMENT_NAME identify the connection and environment to which you are connected at the time the SQL statement is executed.

If the report deals with a table operation, CATALOG_NAME, SCHEMA_NAME, and TABLE_NAME, identify the table. COLUMN_NAME identifies the column within the table that caused the report to be made. If the situation involves a cursor, CURSOR_NAME gives its name.

Sometimes a DBMS produces a string of natural language text to explain a condition. The MESSAGE_TEXT item is for this kind of information. The contents of this item depend on the implementation; SQL:1999 doesn't explicitly define them. If you do have something in MESSAGE_TEXT, its length in characters is recorded in MESSAGE_LENGTH and its length in octets is recorded in MESSAGE_OCTET_LENGTH. If the message is in normal ASCII characters, MESSAGE_LENGTH equals MESSAGE_OCTET_LENGTH. If, on the other hand, the message is in Kanji or some other language whose characters require more than an octet to express, MESSAGE_LENGTH differs from MESSAGE_OCTET_LENGTH.

To retrieve diagnostic information from a diagnostics area header, use the following:

```
GET DIAGNOSTICS status₁ = item₁ [, status₂ = item₂]... ;
```

$Status_n$ is a host variable or parameter; $item_n$ can be any of the keywords NUMBER, MORE, COMMAND_FUNCTION, DYNAMIC_FUNCTION, or ROW_COUNT.

To retrieve diagnostic information from a diagnostics detail area the syntax is as follows:

```
GET DIAGNOSTICS EXCEPTION condition-number
   status₁ = item₁ [, status₂ = item₂]... ;
```

Again $status_n$ is a host variable or parameter, and $item_n$ is any of the 17 keywords for the detail items listed in Table 22-2. The condition number is (surprise!) the detail area's `CONDITION_NUMBER` item.

Handling Exceptions

When `SQLSTATE` indicates an exception condition by holding a value other than 00000, 00001, or 00002, you may want to handle the situation by returning control to the parent procedure that called the sub-procedure that raised the exception. Alternatively, you may want to use a `WHENEVER` directive to branch to an exception-handling routine or perform some other action. A third alternative is to handle the exception on the spot with a *compound* SQL statement. A compound SQL statement consists of one or more simple SQL statements, sandwiched between `BEGIN` and `END` keywords.

The following is an example of a compound statement exception handler:

```
BEGIN
    DECLARE ValueOutOfRange EXCEPTION FOR SQLSTATE '73003' ;
    INSERT INTO FOODS
        (CALORIES)
        VALUES
        (:cal) ;
    SIGNAL ValueOutOfRange ;
    // (Comment) 'Process the new value.'
    EXCEPTION
        WHEN ValueOutOfRange THEN
            // (Comment) 'Handling the calorie range error' ;
        WHEN OTHERS THEN
            RESIGNAL ;
END
```

With one or more `DECLARE` statements, you can give names to specific `SQLSTATE` values that you suspect may arise. The `INSERT` statement is the one that might cause an exception to occur. If the value of :cal exceeds the maximum value for a `SMALLINT` data item, `SQLSTATE` is set to "73003". The `SIGNAL` statement signals an exception condition. It clears the diagnostics area. It sets the `RETURNED_SQLSTATE` field of the diagnostics area to the `SQLSTATE` for the named exception. If no exception has occurred, the series of statements represented by the `MESSAGE` 'Process a new calorie value' statement is executed. However, if an exception has occurred, that series of statements is skipped and the `EXCEPTION` statement is executed.

If the exception was a `ValueOutOfRange` exception, then the series of statements represented by the `MESSAGE` 'Handling the calorie range error' statement is executed. If it was any other exception, the `RESIGNAL` statement is executed. `RESIGNAL` merely passes control of execution to the calling parent procedure. That procedure may have additional error-handling code to deal with exceptions other than the expected value out of range error.

Chapter 23

Dynamic SQL

• •

• •

*I*n previous chapters, I mention three different types of SQL: *interactive SQL,* *embedded SQL,* and *module language*. Embedded SQL and module language can collectively be called *static SQL,* because after the code is compiled, it doesn't change. *Dynamic SQL* is a fourth, although not frequently used, way to run SQL. It's used mainly by SQL experts performing system programming, and although dynamic SQL is rarely needed in SQL applications, you need to be able to recognize it when you see it. This chapter enables you to do just that, with a brief introduction to dynamic SQL. You can think of dynamic SQL as a hybrid that possesses some of the attributes of interactive SQL and some of the attributes of either embedded SQL or module language.

Interactive SQL, as the name implies, is a real-time conversation with the database. The user and the programmer are the same person, and no distinction exists between using and programming. Embedded SQL and module language are used in a very different way. The program is written, compiled, and debugged by the programmer long before the intended user first sets eyes on it. All decisions as to what the application can do have already been made. As a result, the user doesn't need to have nearly the level of skill and understanding of SQL that the programmer requires.

Both modes of operation have advantages and disadvantages. Interactive SQL is good because you may not know what some of the subsequent SQL statements should be until you have actually started an interactive session. Since, in interactive mode, you are getting immediate feedback after each SQL statement, you can alter your next statement, based on the results of your last statement. Embedded SQL and module language don't allow such 'mid-course corrections' because they must be cast in concrete (compiled) before they can start running. On the other hand, interactive SQL is bad because it requires the user to be as knowledgeable as a programmer and because every statement in a session must be entered by hand, even when it's the fiftieth repetition of a statement that has been entered before. Aside from all this tedious keyboarding, performance drops to a mere fraction of what it is for an equivalent compiled application.

Dynamic SQL provides a way of building a compiled application even when you don't know everything you need to know at compile time. You can supply the unknown values, known as *dynamic parameters* or *parameter markers,* at run time. Dynamic parameters are denoted by question marks (?) in a dynamic SQL statement. The following example shows one way in which they are used:

```
UPDATE NATIONAL_LEAGUER
    SET COMPLETE_GAMES = ? WHERE LAST_NAME = ? ;
```

This example contains two dynamic parameters, neither of which you know until run time.

Using dynamic SQL when more than just a couple of values may be unknown until run time can be challenging. In fact, the entire SQL statement may be unknown at run time. Despite these obstacles, however, you can write your application in such a way that the user enters all the data needed to construct the statement. You can output messages on the screen that tell the user which parameters to enter, based on the intermediate results that have been displayed thus far.

Another potential problem is the user's ability to smoothly coordinate the dynamic SQL with the procedural code that surrounds it — because the user can enter a previously unknown statement with an unknown number of parameters. To address this issue, you can set up SQL item descriptor areas that document the characteristics of the material entered at run time. The procedural code can then interrogate the descriptor areas to determine how to deal with that material.

If you know the number of dynamic parameters to expect, you can represent them with host variables or static parameters in your dynamic SQL statement. If you don't know the number of dynamic parameters, you have to extract that information from the descriptor areas, described later in this chapter.

Prepared and Unprepared Dynamic SQL

Dynamic SQL has two modes of execution. One is more similar to the static modes (embedded and module language), and the other is more similar to the interactive mode. The first mode uses the PREPARE/EXECUTE statement pair. The second mode uses the EXECUTE IMMEDIATE statement.

Be prepared (or how the Boy Scout motto applies to SQL)

When you use the PREPARE/EXECUTE statement pair, you break your dynamic SQL activity into two parts:

✔ Preparation

✔ Execution

The preparation activity is analogous to the compilation of static SQL. The PREPARE statement analyzes the dynamic SQL statement for proper syntax and then determines the types of any dynamic parameters. The PREPARE statement also gives the dynamic SQL statement a name and sets it up to optimize its execution.

You realize the main advantage of breaking a dynamic SQL activity into two parts when you must execute the activity repeatedly. You can do the preparation part once, repeating only the execution part. This division slashes overhead, enabling faster completion of the entire job. Another advantage is the ability to use dynamic parameters.

Just do it (the Nike approach)

EXECUTE IMMEDIATE is handy when you're going to execute an SQL statement only once (and therefore, you don't care about separating out the preparation part), or when your statement doesn't include any dynamic parameters. If your statement does include dynamic parameters, you can't use EXECUTE IMMEDIATE.

Consider this pseudo-code example that doesn't involve dynamic parameters and doesn't produce any output:

```
DECLARE STMNT_VAR CHAR (200);
BEGIN
   DO WHILE condition = true
      DISPLAY ('Enter an SQL statement') ;
      READ (:STMNT_VAR) ;
      EXEC SQL EXECUTE IMMEDIATE STMNT_VAR ;
      ...
   END DO ;
END ;
```

This program DISPLAYs the prompt, 'Enter an SQL statement', READs whatever the user enters, and then EXECUTEs the entry as an SQL statement. The user can enter any SQL statement that doesn't include host variables or dynamic parameters and that doesn't produce an output. Here are two examples:

```
UPDATE EMPLOYEE SET SALARY=SALARY+100 WHERE AGE>50 ;
```

or

```
INSERT INTO DEPT VALUES('Sales', 1200, 1450) ;
```

If the user enters anything other than a valid SQL statement, he or she gets an error message, just like in static SQL.

The PREPARE statement

The format of the PREPARE statement is:

```
PREPARE statement-name
FROM statement-variable ;
```

One example of its use may be:

```
PREPARE game_update
    FROM 'UPDATE NATIONAL_LEAGUER
    SET COMPLETE_GAMES = ?
    WHERE LAST_NAME = ?' ;
```

This statement prepares an update of the NATIONAL_LEAGUER table, using dynamic parameters whose values are determined at run time.

Describing a Dynamic SQL Statement

Because important details of a dynamic SQL statement may not become known until run time, they can't be coded into your application. This information must be captured and stored somewhere so that it is available when you need it.

An SQL *item descriptor area* is an area used by a DBMS to store information about the dynamic parameters in your dynamic SQL statements.

The DESCRIBE statement causes a dynamic parameter to be represented in the item descriptor area. When the user enters a value for a dynamic parameter, SQL analyzes the value and puts the result of its analysis in the item descriptor area. Table 23-1 illustrates the information stored about a dynamic parameter.

Table 23-1	Dynamic Parameter Information Stored in SQL Item Descriptor Area	
Field Name	*Field Data Type*	*Comment*
TYPE	Exact numeric, scale 0	Code for the data type
LENGTH	Exact numeric, scale 0	Length in characters or bits for string types
OCTET_LENGTH	Exact numeric, scale 0	Length in octets for strings
RETURNED_ LENGTH	Exact numeric, scale 0	Length in characters or bits returned from DBMS for strings
RETURNED_ OCTET_LENGTH	Exact numeric, scale 0	Length in octets returned from DBMS for strings
PRECISION	Exact numeric, scale 0	Precision for numeric types
SCALE	Exact numeric, scale 0	Scale for exact numeric types
DATETIME_ INTERVAL_CODE	Exact numeric, scale 0	Code for datetime/interval subtype
DATETIME_ INTERVAL_ PRECISION	Exact numeric, scale 0	Precision of interval's leading field
NULLABLE	Exact numeric, scale 0	Is column nullable?
NAME	Character string, length <= 128	Name of associated database column
UNNAMED	Exact numeric, scale 0	Is name real, or supplied by DBMS?
COLLATION_ CATALOG	Character string, length <= 128	Catalog name for column's collation
COLLATION_ SCHEMA	Character string, length <= 128	Schema name for column's collation
COLLATION_NAME	Character string, length <= 128	Collation name for column's collation
CHARACTER_ SET_CATALOG	Character string, length <= 128	Catalog name for column's character set
CHARACTER_ SET_SCHEMA	Character string, length <= 128	Schema name for column's character set

(continued)

Table 23-1 *(continued)*

Field Name	Field Data Type	Comment
CHARACTER_ SET_NAME	Character string, length <= 128	Collation name for column's character set
DATA	Specified by code in TYPE field	The actual data itself
INDICATOR	Exact numeric, scale 0	Value for indicator parameter

Some fields in the descriptor area contain codes rather than actual data. One of these is the TYPE field, which holds a code representing the data type of the column or parameter being described. Table 23-2 displays the codes and the data types that they represent.

Table 23-2 **TYPE Codes**

Code	Data Type
Negative	Implementor-defined data types
1	CHARACTER
2	NUMERIC
3	DECIMAL
4	INTEGER
5	SMALLINT
6	FLOAT
7	REAL
8	DOUBLE PRECISION
9	DATE, TIME, or TIMESTAMP
10	INTERVAL
11	Reserved for future use
12	CHARACTER VARYING
13	ENUMERATED
14	BIT
15	BIT VARYING
17	Abstract data types

Code	Data Type
30	BLOB
31	BLOB LOCATOR
40	CLOB
41	CLOB LOCATOR

DATETIME_INTERVAL_CODE is another field in the descriptor area that contains a code. This code distinguishes between the various DATETIME types. Table 23-3 gives the five possibilities for non-INTERVAL types.

(Type code = 9.)

Table 23-3	DATETIME Codes for DATE, TIME, or TIMESTAMP Data
Code	**Data Type**
1	DATE
2	TIME
3	TIMESTAMP
4	TIME WITH TIME ZONE
5	TIMESTAMP WITH TIME ZONE

Table 23-4 displays the codes in DATETIME_INTERVAL_CODE that apply to INTERVAL type data.

(Type code = 10.)

Table 23-4	DATETIME Codes for INTERVAL Data
Code	**Data Type**
1	YEAR
2	MONTH
3	DAY
4	HOUR

(continued)

Table 23-4 *(continued)*

Code	Data Type
5	MINUTE
6	SECOND
7	YEAR TO MONTH
8	DAY TO HOUR
9	DAY TO MINUTE
10	DAY TO SECOND
11	HOUR TO MINUTE
12	HOUR TO SECOND
13	MINUTE TO SECOND

The ALLOCATE DESCRIPTOR statement

If you want to pass data from your procedural code to your dynamic SQL code via a dynamic parameter, you can use a DESCRIBE INPUT statement to place information about that parameter into the descriptor area. Conversely, if you want to pass data from a database column to your procedural code via a dynamic parameter, you can use a DESCRIBE OUTPUT statement to place information about the parameter into the descriptor area.

Before you can put data into a descriptor, you must allocate space for it in the descriptor area. Do this with an ALLOCATE DESCRIPTOR statement, which has the following syntax:

```
ALLOCATE DESCRIPTOR descriptor-name
   [WITH MAX occurrences] ;
```

After you establish a descriptor name, you can refer to it in the DESCRIBE, SET DESCRIPTOR, GET DESCRIPTOR, and DEALLOCATE DESCRIPTOR statements that follow. The optional WITH MAX *occurrences* clause (a positive integer) tells how many items to make space for. If you don't specify a WITH MAX *occurrences* clause, your implementation gives you its default maximum number of occurrences.

The DESCRIBE statement

The DESCRIBE statement places information into the descriptor table, based on the data entered by the user. Look at the example in the following paragraphs to see dynamic SQL in action. Getting everything properly declared, allocated, and described is a lengthy process. In fact, when you see how lengthy the process is, you may be discouraged from ever using dynamic SQL — unless you have absolutely no other way to accomplish your objectives.

Suppose that you want to update the values of a column in selected rows of a table. At compile time, you don't know the name of the table, the primary keys of the rows, or the values to be placed in the column. This looks like a job for dynamic SQL.

The first thing that you need to do is define the variables to hold the quantities that you are interested in. You need a variable for the name of the table, another for the name of its primary key column, and a third variable for the name of the column to update. Call these variables table_name, col_name_1, and col_name_2. That takes care of the names of the data items. The SQL statement that you want to construct is of the following form:

```
UPDATE table_name
    SET col_name_2 = V2
    WHERE col_name_1 = V1 ;
```

The name of the column that serves as the primary key of the table is captured into the col_name_1 variable, and the name of the column to be updated is captured into the col_name_2 variable.

In the following example, I use generic pseudo-code with embedded SQL statements to show what must be done:

```
DECLARE table_name CHAR (18) ;
DECLARE col_name_1 CHAR (18) ;
DECLARE col_name_2 CHAR (18) ;
```

You also need to declare variables to hold the data itself and information about its type. To keep the example from getting too tedious (it's tedious enough as it is!), make the simplifying assumption that the data is of either CHARACTER or INTEGER type:

```
DECLARE CHAR_V1 CHAR (100) ;
DECLARE INT_V1 INTEGER ;
DECLARE CHAR_V2 CHAR (100) ;
DECLARE INT_V2 INTEGER ;
DECLARE TYPE_VAR1 INTEGER ;
DECLARE TYPE_VAR2 INTEGER ;
DECLARE UPDATE_STMNT CHAR (100) ;
```

Next, you need to solicit the names of the table and the two columns of interest from the user:

```
DISPLAY ('Enter the table name, the key column name, '
    || 'and the data column name') ;
READ (table_name, col_name_1, col_name_2) ;
```

Now, with the variable data in hand, you can construct the UPDATE statement:

```
UPDATE_STMNT := 'UPDATE ' || table_name
               || ' SET ' || col_name_2 || '= ?'
               || 'WHERE ' || col_name_1 || '= ?' ;
```

This statement produces a dynamic SQL statement that looks like this:

```
UPDATE table_name SET col_name_2 =? WHERE col_name_1 =?;
```

Now, at last, you get to some SQL, which prepares your dynamic UPDATE statement for execution:

```
EXEC SQL PREPARE S FROM UPDATE_STMT ;
```

Before executing the UPDATE, you have to determine the data types of the values being entered:

```
EXEC SQL ALLOCATE DESCRIPTOR 'D' ;
EXEC SQL DESCRIBE INPUT INTO SQL DESCRIPTOR 'D' ;
EXEC SQL GET DESCRIPTOR 'D' VALUE 1 TYPE_VAR1 = TYPE ;
EXEC SQL GET DESCRIPTOR 'D' VALUE 2 TYPE_VAR2 = TYPE ;
IF (TYPE_VAR1 <> 1 AND TYPEVAR1 <> 4)
    OR (TYPE_VAR2 <> 1 AND TYPE_VAR2 <> 4)
   THEN DISPLAY ('This program only handles '
       || 'character and integer data. ') ;
END IF ;
```

Recall from Table 23-2 that 1 is the TYPE code for CHARACTER data and that 4 is the TYPE code for INTEGER data. At last, you're ready to have the user start entering data and to perform the updates:

```
DO WHILE condition = true
   DISPLAY ('Enter values for '
         || col_name_1 || ' AND ' || col_name_2) ;
   IF TYPE_VAR1 = 1 AND TYPE_VAR2 = 1
      THEN READ (CHAR_V1, CHAR_V2) ;
         EXEC SQL EXECUTE S USING (CHAR_V1, CHAR_V2) ;
   END IF ;
   IF TYPE_VAR1 = 1 AND TYPE_VAR2 = 4
      THEN READ (CHAR_V1, INT_V2) ;
         EXEC SQL EXECUTE S USING (CHAR_V1, INT_V2) ;
   END IF ;
   IF TYPE_VAR1 = 4 AND TYPE_VAR2 = 1
```

```
      THEN READ (INT_V1, CHAR_V2) ;
          EXEC SQL EXECUTE S USING (INT_V1, CHAR_V2) ;
   END IF ;
   IF TYPE_VAR1 = 4 AND TYPE_VAR2 = 4
      THEN READ (INT_V1, INT_V2) ;
          EXEC SQL EXECUTE S USING (INT_V1, INT_V2) ;
   END IF ;
   ...
END DO WHILE ;
```

In this skeleton of a program, you have no error-checking, loop termination condition, or any other items that you would normally have in a real program. This program contains only enough to show a broad outline of what is involved in using dynamic SQL in an application.

It's fair to say that, conceptually, dynamic SQL is simple. But it's not easy to use in practice. Every line of code in the preceding examples is simple, performing rudimentary actions. But programs like these aren't easy to write, because rudimentary actions abound. If you include error-checking, null-checking, and a full range of data types — as of course you should — the application becomes even more difficult to write, although perhaps no more complex.

The DESCRIBE statement loads the allocated descriptor areas with information about the dynamic parameters. Assuming that the primary key is of the CHARACTER type and the data to be updated is of INTEGER type, Table 23-5 shows the contents of the first descriptor area, and Table 23-6 shows the contents of the second descriptor area.

Table 23-5	Descriptor Area 1
Field Name	*Field Contents*
TYPE	1
LENGTH	100
OCTET_LENGTH	100 (assuming ASCII characters)
RETURNED_LENGTH	100
RETURNED_OCTET_LENGTH	100
PRECISION	n/a
SCALE	n/a
DATETIME_INTERVAL_CODE	n/a
DATETIME_INTERVAL_PRECISION	n/a

(continued)

Table 23-5 *(continued)*

Field Name	Field Contents
NULLABLE	1
NAME	EMPLOYEE_ID
UNNAMED	0
COLLATION_CATALOG	Implementation dependent
COLLATION_SCHEMA	Implementation dependent
COLLATION_NAME	Implementation dependent
CHARACTER_SET_CATALOG	Implementation dependent
CHARACTER_SET_SCHEMA	Implementation dependent
CHARACTER_SET_NAME	Implementation dependent
DATA	Set when data is retrieved
INDICATOR	Set when data is retrieved

Table 23-6 **Descriptor Area 2**

Field Name	Field Contents
TYPE	4
LENGTH	n/a
OCTET_LENGTH	n/a
RETURNED_LENGTH	n/a
RETURNED_OCTET_LENGTH	n/a
PRECISION	9
SCALE	0
DATETIME_INTERVAL_CODE	n/a
DATETIME_INTERVAL_PRECISION	n/a
NULLABLE	1
NAME	SALARY
UNNAMED	0
COLLATION_CATALOG	Implementation dependent

Field Name	Field Contents
COLLATION_SCHEMA	Implementation dependent
COLLATION_NAME	Implementation dependent
CHARACTER_SET_CATALOG	Implementation dependent
CHARACTER_SET_SCHEMA	Implementation dependent
CHARACTER_SET_NAME	Implementation dependent
DATA	Set when data is retrieved
INDICATOR	Set when data is retrieved

The GET DESCRIPTOR statement

After you've described a dynamic parameter, information about it is stored in a descriptor area. Your application can now access the information and take appropriate action. The GET DESCRIPTOR statement is the tool you use to do this.

You can use the GET DESCRIPTOR statement two ways: First, to give you a count of how many parameters are described in the selected area, and second, to find out the nature of those parameters. You may need the count if you don't know the number of dynamic parameters that are contained in the SQL statement, which is entered or constructed at run time. After you know the count, hopefully you can deduce what each of the dynamic variables is.

To get a count of the number of dynamic parameters in an area, issue a statement in this form:

```
GET DESCRIPTOR  descriptor-name
   number-of-parameters = COUNT ;
```

Follow up with statements that return information about the parameter of interest within the descriptor area. For example, if you want information about the first parameter stored in the descriptor area named 'D', you can issue the following statement:

```
GET DESCRIPTOR 'D' VALUE 1
    :type = TYPE,
    :length = LENGTH,
    :name = NAME,
    :nullable = NULLABLE,
    :data = DATA,
    :indicator = INDICATOR ;
```

In the previous example, you were only interested in retrieving the data types of the values to be entered, so you used these statements:

```
GET DESCRIPTOR 'D' VALUE 1 TYPE_VAR1 = TYPE ;
```

and

```
GET DESCRIPTOR 'D' VALUE 2 TYPE_VAR2 = TYPE ;
```

You can select whatever information you want from the descriptor table, retrieve it, and then cause your program to take one action or another, based on what you retrieve.

The SET DESCRIPTOR statement

After a descriptor area has been described, it begins to fill up with information based on the data coming to it at run time. However, you (the programmer/developer) can also set values for fields of selected items in an area. The SET DESCRIPTOR statement, with syntax very similar to that of the GET DESCRIPTOR statement, does this — as illustrated in this example:

```
SET DESCRIPTOR  descriptor-name
    COUNT = number-of-parameters ;
```

This statement sets the total number of items that you plan to use in a descriptor area. Of course, COUNT can't be greater than the maximum number of occurrences set in the preceding ALLOCATE DESCRIPTOR statement. If it is, an error is returned.

To specify values for an item in the descriptor area, use this syntax:

```
SET DESCRIPTOR descriptor-name
    VALUE item-number
    item-field-name = value [,item-field-name = value]... ;
```

Here's an example:

```
SET DESCRIPTOR 'D'
    VALUE 1
    TYPE = :type,
    LENGTH = :length,
    NAME = :name,
    NULLABLE = :nullable,
    DATA = :data,
    INDICATOR = :indicator ;
```

You can set whatever fields you want to whatever values you want, as long as those values are valid for the field that you are trying to place them in.

The EXECUTE statement

After a dynamic SQL statement is prepared and its descriptor area is allocated and described, you can (at last!) execute it. The EXECUTE statement specifies the name of the statement being executed, the identity of input parameters (if any), and the identity of results (if any). The syntax is:

```
EXECUTE statement-name
    USING input-parameter-list
    INTO result-list ;
```

The DEALLOCATE PREPARE and the DEALLOCATE DESCRIPTOR statements

After you're finished with a dynamic SQL statement that you've prepared — and you're sure that you won't need it again — you can free up the resources that it has been using with a DEALLOCATE PREPARE statement. Similarly, when you're finished with a descriptor area, DEALLOCATE DESCRIPTOR releases whatever system resources it was using.

If resources are tight, pay attention to your usage of descriptors and prepared dynamic SQL statements. Deallocate them as soon as they have served their purposes.

If you're only going to execute a dynamic SQL statement one time, and it has no dynamic parameters, then you gain no benefit by preparing it in advance. The processor is going to have to perform all the same actions anyway; so it may as well do them all at once. Not only that, but as you may have gathered from the previous discussion, using the PREPARE/EXECUTE approach can get pretty involved. If the statement that you want to execute contains no host variables or dynamic parameters and returns no output, then it's much easier using EXECUTE IMMEDIATE.

Cursors and Dynamic SQL

The dynamic SQL I have discussed so far deals with non-SELECT statements and SELECT statements that are guaranteed to return no more than one row. To handle SELECT statements that return more than one row, you must invoke cursors, because your application's host language probably can't handle data a set at a time.

The dynamic cursor is very similar to the static cursor described in Chapter 20. It is also set up by a DECLARE CURSOR statement, but with a slight difference in syntax:

```
DECLARE cursor-name [INSENSITIVE][SCROLL] CURSOR
   FOR statement-name ;
```

In static SQL, the FOR clause holds a query expression. In dynamic SQL, you probably don't know what the query is at compile time. Instead, the FOR clause argument is a statement name that is equated to a character string at run time. This character string is the query expression.

The dynamic OPEN CURSOR statement is similar to the analogous static statement, but with one additional restriction: If one or more dynamic parameters appear in the cursor declaration, they must be listed in a USING clause. If no dynamic parameters are involved, the USING clause is not needed:

```
OPEN cursor-name [USING dynamic-parameter-list] ;
```

The dynamic FETCH has the form:

```
FETCH [[orientation] FROM] cursor-name
   USING dynamic-parameter-list ;
```

Here the USING clause is mandatory. The FETCH must return at least one value, and the USING clause tells the DBMS where to put it.

After you're done using a dynamic cursor, close it with:

```
CLOSE cursor-name ;
```

The dynamic OPEN, FETCH, and CLOSE statements are static statements, even though they operate on dynamic cursors. Thus, you don't need to PREPARE them. The only fact about the operation that you need to know at compile time is whether you want the cursor to be insensitive or scrollable. All other aspects of the operation are determined at run time.

Dynamic positioned statements

In Chapter 20, I cover the static positioned DELETE and UPDATE statements. These statements enable you to delete or update selected rows in a table, which are accessed by a cursor. You can perform positioned deletes and updates with a dynamic cursor, too. The syntax is identical to the static DELETE and UPDATE statements:

```
DELETE FROM table-name WHERE CURRENT OF cursor-name ;
UPDATE table-name
   SET column-name = value [,column-name = value]...
   WHERE CURRENT OF cursor-name ;
```

One problem with this UPDATE statement is that in a dynamic situation, you may not know the column names at compile time. In that case, you have to prepare the dynamic positioned update statement. When the update has been prepared, the table-name becomes optional in the UPDATE statement, because it has already been specified in the PREPARE statement. The syntax becomes:

```
UPDATE [table-name]
   SET column-name = value [,column-name = value]...
   WHERE CURRENT OF cursor-name ;
```

To keep DELETE syntax consistent with UPDATE syntax, table-name is also optional in the dynamic positioned DELETE statement:

```
DELETE [FROM table-name] WHERE CURRENT OF cursor-name ;
```

A final word of advice on dynamic SQL

Dynamic SQL isn't commonly used because it's intended for writing utility programs that provide generalized access to data. Most SQL applications are intended to do specific things to specific tables, and thus they can be written in static SQL. Many SQL sites have no programs that use dynamic SQL, and the rest have only a few such programs.

When you need to write a program using dynamic SQL, find some other program using dynamic SQL that has a function similar to the one that you want to perform. Copy that other program and modify it as needed. You should be able to find such a program, because relatively few varieties of dynamic SQL programs are available. You may find what you need in the programmer's manual for the DBMS that you're using.

Chapter 24

Major New Features Added to SQL by the SQL:1999 Specification

• •

In This Chapter

▶ How the object-oriented paradigm applies to database management

▶ Marrying object-oriented programming to relational database management

▶ New data types require extensions to SQL

▶ How SQL:1999 sanctions the use of unnormalized data

▶ Defining your own data types

▶ How SQL:1999 changes the way you work with relational databases

▶ Miscellaneous new stuff in SQL :1999

• •

SQL is the standard language that is used worldwide for dealing with relational databases. Of all the models in use for structuring databases, the relational model is the most widespread. When you need to deal with data in the form of text strings or numbers, databases that are structured according to the relational model are unparalleled in power and ease of use. As a result, the relational model has been the dominant database model for the past 20 years. However, the relational model doesn't handle certain types of data very well.

In recent years, nontextual and nonnumeric data have risen in importance. Remote sensing and other scientific applications have given image data a place of importance. Speech processing and multimedia presentations have brought sound data into prominence. If you want to do more with an image than just look at it, or do more with a sound file than just listen to it, you need some way of structuring the data and allowing selective retrievals. In other words, you need a database. Unfortunately, the relational database model cannot accommodate these new data types. You need something with more representational power. In this chapter some of the new features of SQL:1999 expand the number of types of data that you can handle with a database, and other new features add expanded functionality.

Object-Oriented Database Management Systems

Object-Oriented Programming (OOP) was invented to extend the abilities of traditional programming languages to handle more general situations. OOP languages like Smalltalk and C++ allow programmers to define new data types. OOP languages have other features that add a lot of flexibility and power to programming. They also add a lot of complexity, and as a result, are harder to learn. Object-Oriented Database Management Systems (OODBMS) are OOP languages that have been extended to include database management functionality. Because the heritage of the OODBMS is in the language arena rather than the database arena, commercial OODBMS products typically are not based on SQL. Furthermore, OODBMS have not achieved widespread acceptance in the marketplace. Consequently, I don't discuss OODBMS further in this book.

Object-Relational Database Management Systems

Object-Relational Database Management Systems (ORDBMS) were developed for many of the same reasons that motivated the developers of the OODBMS. However, the ORDBMS model was developed from the point of view of relational database management rather than programming. Consequently, rather than discarding SQL, products that follow the ORDBMS model seek to extend it. By extending SQL, ORDBMS can handle nontraditional data types, but in the process, they break some of the cardinal rules of the relational model. As a result, the object-relational model is harder to understand than the relational model. The benefit for anyone experienced in relational database systems is that you don't have to use any of the extensions that you don't understand. The core relational part of object-relational databases continues to work the old fashioned way.

Object-Relational Database Management Systems use many of the fundamental concepts of OOP, such as encapsulation and inheritance. OOP is a major topic — worthy of a book all by itself. Many books have been written on this topic, such as *C++ For Dummies,* written by Stephen Randy Davis and published by IDG Books Worldwide, Inc.

Dealing with Non-textual, Non-numerical Data

If you are dealing with data that is neither text nor numbers, then what kind of data is it? The data may be image data, and if it is, it may be in any of a large number of formats, such as jpeg, gif, tiff, pict, bmp, pdf, and so on. It may be sound data, and if it is, it also may be in any of a large number of formats, including wav and mp3. Or it may be a movie in any of several formats. Or it may be a virtual reality environment, a three-dimensional topographic map from a remote sensing satellite, or any number of things that are not easily reducible to text and numbers. In recent years, these complex data types have increased in importance, and figuring out how to deal with them in a structured way has become a priority. The extensions to the relational model that are included in SQL:1999 address the need for handling these complex data types in useful ways.

In order to deal with complex data, the SQL:1999 specification has relaxed some of the most fundamental restrictions that have been a part of the relational model since its inception. For example, the relational model was designed to work with relations that are defined to have certain characteristics, and these characteristics define *first normal form* (1NF). Dr. Codd and other computer scientists devised the normal forms, described in detail in Chapter 5, to help prevent the introduction of anomalies into databases. These normal forms have been the cornerstone of relational database theory ever since their creation. A database incorporating a new data type that conforms to SQL:1999, however, may not even be in 1NF!

Does SQL:1999 Really Dump Normalization?

Normalization has been one of the cardinal principles of relational database design since the introduction of the relational model. To even suggest that it may be not only possible, but also desirable, to deal with non-normalized tables seems not just strange, but downright heretical. We need to examine what normalization does for us in the first place, and what it costs us. For textual and numerical data, the tradeoff leans toward normalization. The newer complex data types sometimes violate the most fundamental principles of normalization. For these data types the cost of normalization is unacceptably high. Normalization would not allow these types to be used at all.

What is normalization?

Normalization is a procedure that takes a conceptually complex table and breaks it down into multiple tables that are simpler. The value of normalization is that it reduces the chance of modification anomalies being introduced into a database when data is added to, changed in, or deleted from one of its tables. This is a major advantage for anyone who cares about the accuracy and reliability of their data. You pay a price for this advantage, however. When data is distributed across multiple tables, the retrieval process becomes complicated. Usually, the retrieval process takes data from more than one table. This means that a JOIN operation must put the disjoint tables back together again before the needed information can be extracted and displayed. Another disadvantage is that data types that allow more than one value in a table cell are not allowed. This type of organizational structure may be desirable in many applications. SQL:1999 addresses this need by extending the standard data types defined by SQL-92 to include new predefined types (see Chapter 2 for more info), array types, and user-defined abstract data types (ADTs).

Array types

The inclusion of array types in SQL:1999 is a clear violation of one of the defining characteristics of first normal form (1NF), namely "Each cell of a table must have only a single value." Data of an array type can have multiple values in a single cell. For example, in a fully SQL:1999-compliant DBMS, you may declare an array attribute as part of a table definition:

```
CREATE TABLE CLIENT (
    CLIENT_ID   INTEGER                    NOT NULL,
    PHONE    CHARACTER (13) ARRAY[3] ) ;
```

The PHONE attribute can accommodate as many as three different telephone numbers.

Array types are not a part of core SQL and thus may not be available in commercial implementations for some time. Make sure the implementation that you are working with supports array types before you build a design based on them.

User-defined Abstract Data Types

Databases are being used today in every field imaginable — and a few that are not imaginable. They are being applied to many different kinds of data, including a large number of kinds that do not easily translate to the SQL-92 standard types. SQL:1999 breaks this logjam by allowing users to define their own data types.

User-defined abstract data types are not a part of core SQL and thus may not be available in commercial implementations for some time. Make sure the implementation that you are working with supports ADTs before you build a design based on them.

Borrowing much of its structure from object-oriented programming, an abstract data type includes both attributes and methods, which are revealed to the outside world only through the type's interface. *Encapsulation* is the process by which the internal structure of these attributes and methods are hidden. Furthermore, an abstract data type (serving as a *supertype*) can have subtypes that inherit attributes and methods from the supertype, and in addition, the subtypes can have attributes and methods of their own. This ability, borrowed from object-oriented programming, is called *inheritance*.

Creating a new type

SQL:1999 supports more than one kind of ADT; it supports both *structured types* and *distinct types*. Of the two varieties, distinct types are simpler and easier to understand. You create a distinct type out of an already existing type. For example, suppose you are working on a financial application for a trading company that does business in both the USA and Europe. Sometimes payments are made in dollars and sometimes in euros. You want to make sure that the two kinds of payments are not mixed up — you want to keep dollar amounts distinct from euro amounts. You can create distinct types for dollars and euros, based on the DECIMAL type, as shown in the following example:

```
CREATE TYPE dollar AS DECIMAL(10,2) FINAL ;
CREATE TYPE euro AS DECIMAL(10,2) FINAL ;
```

The FINAL keyword means that these types may not serve as supertypes of other types — they may not have any subtypes. Because the types are distinct, it isn't possible to add a dollar amount to a euro amount, even though both distinct types are derived from the same DECIMAL type. If you want to convert a payment of the dollar type to a payment of the euro type (or vice versa), you can do so with a CAST operation.

Structured types are the most object-oriented feature of SQL:1999. They are analogous to classes in object-oriented programming. The following list further defines structured types:

  ✔ A structured type may be defined to have one or more attributes, each of which can be of any SQL type, including structured types. You can nest structured types to any desired level of nesting.

  ✔ Structured types can have behaviors, which are specified by the type's methods, functions, and procedures.

✔ Structured type attributes are encapsulated. Their values can only be accessed through system-generated observer and mutator functions, which allow those values to be read and written.

✔ Comparisons of the values of the attributes of a structured type can be done only with user-defined functions.

✔ Structured types may have subtypes.

You can create a type to keep track of people, as shown in the following example:

```
CREATE TYPE person_type
AS ( NAME            CHAR(30),
     ADDRESS         CHAR(30),
     CITY            CHAR(20),
     STATE_OR_PROV   CHAR(20),
     COUNTRY         CHAR(20) )
NOT FINAL
REF ( NAME ) ;
```

This new type has multiple attributes, but no methods. NOT FINAL means that subtypes of this type may be created. The REF clause indicates that the person_type can be referenced by the NAME attribute.

Creating subtypes

SQL:1999 not only permits you to create new data types, it also allows the creation of subtypes that inherit all the attributes and methods of their 'parent' supertype. (A subtype may have only one parent.) In addition to the attributes and methods that a subtype inherits from its parent, you can define additional attributes and methods that distinguish it from its parent and from any siblings that might also exist. For example, suppose you want to create a subtype of person_type for employees of a company. The subtype may look something like this:

```
CREATE TYPE employ_type
     UNDER person_type
AS ( EMPLOY_ID       INTEGER,
     EXEMPT          BOOLEAN,
     WAGE            REAL )
INSTANTIABLE
NOT FINAL
REF ( EMPLOY_ID )
INSTANCE METHOD
     ChangePay
          ( AMOUNT          REAL )
          RETURNS REAL ;
```

This subtype starts with the characteristics of the `person_type` and adds characteristics that apply specifically to employees. `employ_type` includes a method that allows the pay of an employee to be changed. Because this type is `NOT FINAL`, subtypes of `employ_type` can be created, such as `developer_type` or `qa_tester_type`.

What's a method?

A *method* is very much like a SQL-invoked function, but with some important differences:

✔ Methods are tightly bound to a single user-defined type (UDT), but functions are not. In the preceding example, the `ChangePay` method is bound to the `employ_type` UDT.

✔ The UDT to which a method is bound is the data type of a distinguished argument of the method. This argument is the first argument and is undeclared. Functions have no such argument.

✔ Functions are specified at compile time, but selection of which method to execute can be deferred until execute time.

✔ Methods must be stored in the same schema as the definition of their tightly-bound structured type. Functions are not limited in this way.

Methods may be written in SQL:1999 or in any of several other host languages. Methods expand the concept of a data type by allowing the type to actually *do* something rather than just *be* something.

How Do These New Features of SQL Affect Me?

The new features specified in SQL:1999 can either have a great effect or no effect at all on the way you develop databases and database applications. If the DBMS that you are using implements only core SQL:1999, the most dramatic new features aren't available. On the other hand, if your DBMS includes these new features and you are trying to deal with object data, the new object-relational features of SQL:1999 can make life a lot easier for you.

If you are experienced in creating relational databases, you will have to make a major paradigm shift in your mind in order to successfully use the new object-oriented features of SQL:1999. Don't try to do too much too soon. Add the new features one-by-one to your repertoire of tools as the need for them arises. You have a lot to learn, and even more important, you have a lot to unlearn before you can effectively use the new features of SQL.

More New Features of SQL:1999

The SQL:1999 specification heaps major new features on SQL, and for the sake of sanity, this book sticks to the most significant features. But what the heck, here's a sampling of some other nifty new features. . . .

Dot notation

User-defined types contain attributes and methods in a way that is very similar to the way tables contain columns. And the *dot notation* way of referring to these attributes and methods is similar to the way programmers refer to columns of tables. For example:

```
WHERE person_type.NAME = 'Smith'
```

compares the NAME attribute of the UDT person_type to 'Smith'. Notice the similarity between this representation and a similar WHERE clause dealing with the PERSON table and the lname column:

```
WHERE PERSON.lname = 'Smith'
```

Functional notation

Functional notation is just a different way of representing the same element that dot notation represents. It looks like this:

```
WHERE NAME(person_type) = 'Smith'
```

Depending on the situation and your personal preferences, you may decide to use either functional notation or dot notation, but keep in mind the one important difference between the two notations: Only dot notation works for method invocations. Functional notation doesn't work for that purpose.

Objects

You may have noticed that user-defined types seem awfully similar to objects. After all, they have type hierarchies, inheritance, and encapsulation in common. However, user-defined types lack a sense of identity that can be referenced. By adding that sense of identity, SQL can be truly said to support objects. In SQL:1999, this sense of identity comes from allowing database designers to specify typed tables.

Typed tables

Typed tables are tables whose column definitions are derived from the attributes of a structured type. For example:

```
CREATE TABLE PEOPLE OF person_type ;
```

Tables of this sort have one column for each attribute in the underlying structured type. The functions, methods, and procedures defined to operate on instances of this type also operate on rows of the table. This means that the rows of the table are instances of the type. Each row is given a unique identity that acts as an object identifier.

REF types

SQL:1999 provides the REF type, whose values are the unique identifiers for typed tables. A given REF type is always associated with a specific structured type. You can define a table that contains a column, whose values refer to rows in a typed table. Suppose this type of table has a column named 'surgeons' that references appropriate rows in the typed table physician_type. The specification of that column in the CREATE TABLE statement is:

```
surgeons    REF(physician_type) ,
```

REF types can also be used to follow a reference and retrieve a value from the referenced structured type. For example:

```
SELECT PARTNERS.surgeons -> lname ;
```

The surgeons column of the partners table references the typed table physician_type. The SELECT statement retrieves the lname column from the referenced table.s

Part VII
The Part of Tens

The 5th Wave   By Rich Tennant

It started as a little experiment in data compression, and...well...just close the door and call the zoo!

In this part . . .

If you've read this far, congratulations! You may now consider yourself an SQL weenie (spicy mustard optional). To raise your status that final degree from weenie to wizard, you must master two sets of ten rules. But don't make the mistake of just reading the section headings. Taking some of these headings at face value could have dire consequences. All the tips in this part are short and to the point, so reading them all (in their entirety, if you please) shouldn't be too much trouble. Put them into practice and you can be a true SQL wizard.

Chapter 25

Ten Common Mistakes

*I*f you're reading this book, then you must be interested in building relational database systems. Let's face it — nobody studies SQL for the fun of it. You use SQL to build database applications, but before you can build one, you need a database for it to work on. Unfortunately, many projects go awry before the first line of the application is coded. And if you don't get the database definition right, your application is doomed — no matter how well you write it. Here are ten common database creation mistakes that you should be on the lookout for.

Assuming That Your Clients Know What They Need

Generally, clients call you in to design a database system when they have a problem and their current methods are not working. Clients often believe that they have identified the problem and its solution. They figure that all they need to do is tell *you* what to do.

Giving clients exactly what they ask for is usually a sure-fire prescription for disaster. Most users (and their managers) don't possess the knowledge or skills necessary to accurately identify the problem, so they have no chance of determining the best solution.

Your job is to tactfully convince your client that you are the expert in systems analysis and design and that you must do a proper analysis to uncover the real cause of the problem. Usually the real cause of the problem is hidden behind the more obvious symptoms.

Ignoring Project Scope

Your client tells you what he or she expects from the new application at the beginning of the development project. Unfortunately, the client almost always forgets to tell you something — usually several things. Throughout the job, these new requirements crop up and are tacked onto the project. And if you're being paid on a project basis rather than on an hourly basis, this kind of growth in scope can change what was once a profitable project into a loser. Make sure that everything you're obligated to deliver is specified in writing before you start the project. Any new requirements that emerge during a project justify additional time and budget.

Considering Only Technical Factors

Application developers often consider potential projects in terms of their technical feasibility and then they base their estimates of effort and time on that determination. However, issues of cost maximums, resource availability, schedule requirements, and organization politics can have a major effect on the project. In fact, these issues may turn a project that is technically feasible into a nightmare. Make sure that you understand all relevant factors before you start any development project. You may decide that it makes no sense to proceed, and you're much better off coming to that conclusion at the beginning of the project than after you have expended considerable effort.

Not Asking for Client Feedback

Your first inclination might be to listen to the managers who hire you. The users themselves don't have any clout. On the other hand, there may be good reason to ignore the managers, too. They usually don't have a clue about what the users really need. Wait a minute! Don't automatically assume that you know more than your client groups about what they need. Data-entry clerks don't typically have much organizational clout, and many managers have only a dim understanding of some aspects of their areas of responsibility. But isolating yourself from either of these groups is almost certain to result in a system that solves a problem that nobody has. An application that works perfectly, but solves the wrong problem, is of no value to anybody.

Always Using Your Favorite Development Environment

You've probably spent months or even years becoming proficient in the use of a particular DBMS or application development environment. But your favorite environment — no matter what it is — has strengths and weaknesses. Occasionally, you come across a development task that makes heavy demands in an area where your preferred development environment is weak. So rather than kludge together something that isn't really the best solution, bite the bullet. You have two options: Either climb the learning curve of a more appropriate tool and then use it, or candidly tell your clients that their job would best be done with a tool that you're not an expert at using. Then suggest that they hire someone who can be productive with that tool right away. Professional conduct of this sort raises your clients' respect for you. (Unfortunately, if you work for a company instead of for yourself, that conduct may also get you laid off or fired.)

Using Your Favorite System Architecture Exclusively

Nobody can be an expert at everything. Database management systems that work in a teleprocessing environment are different from systems that work in client/server, resource sharing, or distributed database environments. The one or two systems that you are expert in may not be the best for the job at hand. Choose the best architecture anyway, even if it means passing on the job. Not getting the job is better than getting it and producing a system that doesn't serve the client's needs.

Designing Database Tables in Isolation

Incorrect identification of data objects and their relationships to each other leads to database tables that have a tendency to introduce errors into the data, which can destroy the validity of any results. To design a sound database, you must consider the overall organization of the data objects and carefully determine how they relate to each other. Usually, no one *right* design exists. You must determine what is appropriate, considering the present and projected future needs of your client.

Neglecting Design Reviews

Nobody's perfect. Even the best designer and developer can miss important points that are evident to someone looking at the situation from a different perspective. Actually, if you must present your work before a formal design review, it makes you more disciplined in your work — probably helping you avoid numerous problems that you may otherwise have experienced. Have a competent professional review your proposed design before you start development.

Skipping Beta Testing

Any database application complex enough to be truly useful is also complex enough to contain bugs. Even if you test it in every way you can think of, the application is sure to contain failure modes that you didn't uncover. Beta testing means giving the application to people who don't understand it as well as you do. They're likely to have all kinds of problems that you never encountered because you know too much about the application. You need to fix anything that others find before the product goes officially into use.

Not Documenting

If you think your application is so perfect that it never needs to be looked at, even once more — think again. The only thing you can be absolutely sure of in this world is change. Count on it. Six months from now, you aren't going to remember why you designed things the way you did, unless you carefully document what you did and why you did it that way. If, heaven forbid, you transfer to a different department or win the lottery and retire, your replacement has almost no chance of modifying your work to meet new requirements if you didn't document your design. Without documentation, your replacement may need to scrap the whole thing and start from scratch. Don't just document your work adequately — over-document your work. Put in more detail than you think is reasonable. If you come back to this project after six or eight months away from it, you'll be glad you documented.

Chapter 26

Ten Retrieval Tips

A database can be a virtual treasure trove of information, but like the treasure of the Caribbean pirates of long ago, the stuff that you really want is probably buried and hidden from view. The `SQL SELECT` statement is your tool to dig up this hidden information. Even if you have a clear idea of what you want to retrieve, translating that idea into SQL can be a real challenge. If your formulation is just a little off, you may end up with the wrong results — but results that are so close to what you expect that they mislead you. To reduce your chances of being misled, use the following ten principles.

Verify the Database Structure

If you retrieve data from a database and your results don't seem reasonable, check the database design. Many poorly-designed databases are in use, and if you're working with one, fix the design before you try any other remedy. Remember — good design is a prerequisite of data integrity.

Try Queries on a Test Database

Create a test database that has exactly the same structure as your production database, but with only a few representative rows in the tables. Choose the data so that you know in advance what the result of your query should be. Run the query on the test data and see whether the result matches your expectations. If it doesn't, you may need to reformulate your query. If the query is properly formulated, you may need to restructure your database.

Build several sets of test data and be sure to include odd cases, such as empty tables and extreme values at the very limit of allowable ranges. Try to think of extremely unlikely scenarios, and check for proper behavior when they occur. In the course of checking for unlikely cases, you may gain insight into problems that are more likely to happen.

Double-Check Queries with JOINs

JOINs are notorious for being counterintuitive. If your query contains one, make sure that it's doing what you expect before you add WHERE clauses or other complicating factors.

Triple-Check Queries with Subselects

Because subselects can entangle data taken from one table with data taken from another, they are frequently misapplied. You must make sure the data that the inner SELECT retrieves is the data that the outer SELECT needs to produce the desired end result. If you have two or more levels of subselects, you need to be even more careful.

Summarize Data with GROUP BY

Say that you have a table (NATIONAL) giving the name (PLAYER), team (TEAM), and number of home runs hit (HOMERS) by every baseball player in the National League. You can retrieve the team homer total for all teams with a query like this:

```
SELECT TEAM, SUM (HOMERS)
    FROM NATIONAL
    GROUP BY TEAM ;
```

This query lists each team, followed by the total number of home runs hit by all the players on that team.

Watch GROUP BY Clause Restrictions

Suppose that you want a list of power hitters in the National League. Consider the following query:

```
SELECT PLAYER, TEAM, HOMERS
    FROM NATIONAL
    WHERE HOMERS >= 20
    GROUP BY TEAM ;
```

In most implementations, this query returns an error. Generally, only columns used for grouping or columns used in a set function may appear in the select list. The following formulation works:

```
SELECT PLAYER, TEAM, HOMERS
    FROM NATIONAL
    WHERE HOMERS >= 20
    GROUP BY TEAM, PLAYER, HOMERS ;
```

Because all the columns you want to display appear in the GROUP BY clause, the query succeeds and delivers the results you want. This formulation has the effect of sorting the resulting list first by TEAM, then by PLAYER, and finally by HOMERS.

Use Parentheses with AND, OR, and NOT

Sometimes when you mix AND and OR, SQL doesn't process the expression in the order that you expect. Use parentheses in complex expressions to make sure that the result you get is the one that you intend to get. The few extra keystrokes are a small price to pay for better results. Parentheses also help to assure that the NOT keyword is applied to the term or expression that you want it to apply to.

Control Retrieval Privileges

Many people don't use the security features available on their DBMS. They just don't want to bother with them, and they consider misuse and misappropriation of data to be something that only happens to other people. Don't wait to get burned. Establish and maintain security for all databases that have any value.

Back Up Your Databases Regularly

Data is hard to retrieve after a power surge, fire, earthquake, or mortar attack destroys your hard drive. Make frequent backups and remove the backup media to a safe place. What constitutes a safe place depends on how critical your data is. It might be a fireproof safe in the same room as your computer. It might be in another building. It might be in a concrete bunker under a mountain that has been hardened to withstand a nuclear attack. Decide on what level of safety is appropriate for your data.

Handle Error Conditions Gracefully

Whether you're making ad hoc queries from the console or embedding queries in an application, occasionally SQL returns an error message rather than the desired results. At the console, you can decide what to do next based on the message returned and then take appropriate action. In an application, the situation is different. The application user probably doesn't know what action is appropriate. Put extensive error handling into your applications to cover every conceivable error that may occur. Creating error-handling code takes a great deal of effort, but it's better than having the user stare quizzically at a frozen screen.

Part VIII
Appendixes

The 5th Wave   By Rich Tennant

THE GENIE in the MACHINE

"YES, I'M NORMALLY LARGER AND MORE AWE-INSPIRING,
BUT THIS IS ONLY A 4MB SYSTEM!"

In this part . . .

For completeness, and as a potentially valuable reference, this part contains an appendix that lists SQL:1999's reserved words. These words are reserved for specific purposes in SQL; you may not use them for any other purpose in your applications. Part VIII also contains a glossary of important terms.

Appendix A

SQL:1999 Reserved Words

ABSOLUTE	CATALOG	DEALLOCATE	EXEC
ACTION	CHAR	DEC	EXECUTE
ADD	CHARACTER	DECIMAL	EXTERNAL
ADMIN	CHECK	DECLARE	FALSE
AFTER	CLASS	DEFAULT	FETCH
AGGREGATE	CLOB	DEFERRABLE	FIRST
ALIAS	CLOSE	DEFERRED	FLOAT
ALL	COLLATE	DELETE	FOR
ALLOCATE	COLLATION	DEPTH	FOREIGN
ALTER	COLUMN	DEREF	FOUND
AND	COMMIT	DESC	FREE
ANY	COMPLETION	DESCRIBE	FROM
ARE	CONNECT	DESCRIPTOR	FULL
ARRAY	CONNECTION	DESTROY	FUNCTION
AS	CONSTRAINT	DESTRUCTOR	GENERAL
ASC	CONSTRAINTS	DETERMINISTIC	GET
ASSERTION	CONSTRUCTOR	DIAGNOSTICS	GLOBAL
ASSERTIONS	CONTINUE	DICTIONARY	GO
AT	CORRESPONDING	DISCONNECT	GOTO
AUTHORIZATION	CREATE	DISTINCT	GRANT
BEFORE	CROSS	DOMAIN	GROUP
BEGIN	CUBE	DOUBLE	GROUPING
BINARY	CURRENT	DROP	HAVING
BIT	CURRENT_DATE	DYNAMIC	HOST
BLOB	CURRENT_PATH	EACH	HOUR
BOOLEAN	CURRENT_ROLE	ELSE	IDENTITY
BOTH	CURRENT_TIME	EMBEDDED	IGNORE
BREADTH	CURRENT_TIMESTAMP	END	IMMEDIATE
BY	CURRENT_USER	END-EXEC	IN
CALL	CURSOR	EQUALS	INDICATOR
CASCADE	CYCLE	ESCAPE	INITIALIZE
CASCADED	DATA	EVERY	INITIALLY
CASE	DATE	EXCEPT	INNER
CAST	DAY	EXCEPTION	INOUT

INPUT	NO	REF	TABLE
INSERT	NONE	REFERENCES	TEMPORARY
INT	NOT	REFERENCING	TERMINATE
INTEGER	NULL	RELATIVE	THAN
INTERSECT	NUMERIC	RESTRICT	THEN
INTERVAL	OBJECT	RESULT	TIME
INTO	OF	RETURN	TIMESTAMP
IS	OFF	RETURNS	TIMEZONE_HOUR
ISOLATION	OLD	REVOKE	TIMEZONE_MINUTE
ITERATE	ON	RIGHT	TO
JOIN	ONLY	ROLE	TRAILING
KEY	OPEN	ROLLBACK	TRANSACTION
LANGUAGE	OPERATION	ROLLUP	TRANSLATION
LARGE	OPTION	ROUTINE	TREAT
LAST	OR	ROW	TRIGGER
LATERAL	ORDER	ROWS	TRUE
LEADING	ORDINALITY	SAVEPOINT	UNDER
LEFT	OUT	SCHEMA	UNION
LESS	OUTER	SCROLL	UNIQUE
LEVEL	OUTPUT	SCOPE	UNKNOWN
LIKE	PAD	SEARCH	UNNEST
LIMIT	PARAMETER	SECOND	UPDATE
LOCAL	PARAMETERS	SECTION	USAGE
LOCALTIME	PARTIAL	SELECT	USER
LOCALTIMESTAMP	PATH	SEQUENCE	USING
LOCATOR	POSTFIX	SESSION	VALUE
MAP	PRECISION	SESSION_USER	VALUES
MATCH	PREFIX	SET	VARCHAR
MINUTE	PREORDER	SETS	VARIABLE
MODIFIERS	PREPARE	SIZE	VARYING
MODIFY	PRESERVE	SMALLINT	VIEW
MODULE	PRIMARY	SOME	WHEN
MONTH	PRIOR	SPACE	WHENEVER
NAMES	PRIVILEGES	SPECIFIC	WHERE
NATIONAL	PROCEDURE	SPECIFICTYPE	WITH
NATURAL	PUBLIC	SQL	WITHOUT
NCHAR	READ	SQLEXCEPTION	WORK
NCLOB	READS	SQLSTATE	WRITE
NEW	REAP	SQLWARNING	YEAR
NEXT	RECURSIVE	START	ZONE

Glossary

ActiveX control: A reusable software component that can be added to an application, reducing development time in the process. ActiveX is a Microsoft technology; ActiveX components can be used only by developers who work on Windows development systems.

aggregate function: A function that produces a single result based on the contents of an entire set of table rows. Also called a *set function*.

alias: A short substitute or "nickname" for a table name.

applet: A small application, written in the *Java* language, stored on a Web server that is downloaded to and executed on a Web client that connects to the server.

Application Programmer's Interface (API): A standard means of communicating between an application and a database or other system resource.

assertion: A constraint that is specified by a CREATE ASSERTION statement (rather than by a clause of a CREATE TABLE statement). Assertions commonly apply to more than one table.

atomic: Incapable of being subdivided.

attribute: A component of a structured type or of a relation.

back end: That part of a DBMS that interacts directly with the database.

catalog: A named collection of *schemas*.

client: An individual user workstation that represents the *front end* of a DBMS — the part that displays information on a screen and responds to user input.

client/server system: A multiuser system in which a central processor (the server) is connected to multiple intelligent user workstations (the clients).

cluster: A named collection of *catalogs*.

CODASYL DBTG database model: The network database model. *Note:* This use of the term "network" refers to the structuring of the data ("network" as opposed to "hierarchy"), rather than to network communications.

collating sequence: The ordering of characters in a character set. All collating sequences for character sets that have the Latin characters (a, b, c) define the obvious ordering (a, b, c, . . .). They differ, however, in the ordering of special characters (+, -, <, ?, and so on) and in the relative ordering of the digits and the letters.

column: A component of a table that holds a single attribute of the table.

composite key: A key made up of two or more table columns.

conceptual view: The *schema* of a database.

concurrent access: Two or more users operating on the same rows in a database table at the same time.

constraint: A restriction you specify on the data in a database.

constraint, deferred: A constraint that is not applied until you change its status to *immediate* or until you COMMIT the encapsulating transaction.

cursor: An SQL feature that specifies a set of rows, an ordering of those rows, and a current row within that ordering.

Data Control Language (DCL): That part of SQL that protects the database from harm.

Data Definition Language (DDL): That part of SQL used to define, modify, and eradicate database structures.

Data Manipulation Language (DML): That part of SQL that operates on database data.

data redundancy: Having the same data stored in more than one place in a database.

data source: A source of data used by a database application. It may be a DBMS or a data file.

data sublanguage: A subset of a complete computer language that deals specifically with data handling. SQL is a data sublanguage.

data type: A set of representable values.

database: A self-describing collection of integrated records.

database, organizational: A database containing information used by an entire organization.

database, personal: A database designed for use by one person on a single computer.

database, workgroup: A database designed to be used by a department or workgroup within an organization.

Database Administrator (DBA): The person ultimately responsible for the functionality, integrity, and safety of a database.

database engine: That part of a DBMS that directly interacts with the database (serving as part of the *back end*).

database publishing: The act of making the contents of a database available on the Internet or over an intranet.

database server: The server component of a *client/server* system.

DBMS: A database management system.

deletion anomaly: An inconsistency in a multitable database that occurs when a row is deleted from one of its tables.

descriptor: An area in memory used to pass information between an application's procedural code and its dynamic SQL code.

diagnostics area: A data structure, managed by the DBMS, that contains detailed information about the last SQL statement executed and any errors that occurred during its execution.

distributed data processing: A system in which multiple servers handle data processing.

domain: The set of all values that a database item can assume.

domain integrity: A property of a database table column where all data items in that column fall within the domain of the column.

driver: That part of a database management system that interfaces directly with a database. Drivers are part of the *back end*.

driver manager: A component of an *ODBC*-compliant database interface. On Windows machines, the driver manager is a dynamic link library (DLL) that coordinates the linking of data sources with appropriate drivers.

entity integrity: A property of a database table that is entirely consistent with the real-world object that it models.

file server: The server component of a resource-sharing system. It does not contain any database management software.

firewall: A piece of software (or a combination of hardware and software) that isolates an *intranet* from the Internet, allowing only trusted traffic to travel between them.

flat file: A collection of data records having minimal structure.

foreign key: A column or combination of columns in a database table that references the primary key of another table in the database.

front end: That part of a DBMS (such as the client in a *client/server* system) that interacts directly with the user.

functional dependency: A relationship between or among attributes of a relation.

hierarchical database model: A tree-structured model of data.

host variable: A variable passed between an application written in a procedural host language and embedded SQL.

HTML (HyperText Markup Language): A standard formatting language for Web documents.

implementation: A particular relational DBMS running on a specific hardware platform.

index: A table of pointers used to locate rows rapidly in a data table.

information schema: The system tables, which hold the database's *metadata*.

insertion anomaly: An inconsistency introduced into a multitable database when a new row is inserted into one of its tables.

Internet: The worldwide network of computers.

intranet: A network that uses World Wide Web hardware and software, but restricts access to users within a single organization.

IPX/SPX: A local-area network protocol.

Java: A platform-independent compiled language designed specifically for Web application development.

JavaScript: A script language that gives some measure of programmability to HTML-based Web pages.

JDBC (Java DataBase Connectivity): A standard interface between a Java *applet* or application and a database. The JDBC standard is modeled after the ODBC standard.

join: A relational operator that combines data from multiple tables into a single result table.

logical connectives: Used to connect or change the truth value of predicates to produce more complex predicates.

metadata: Data about the structure of the data in a database.

modification anomaly: A problem introduced into a database when a modification (insertion, deletion, or update) is made to one of the tables in the database.

module language: A form of SQL in which SQL statements are placed in modules, which are called by an application program written in a host language.

mutator function: A function associated with a user-defined type, having two parameters whose definition is implied by the definition of some attribute of the type. The first parameter (the result) is of the same type as the *UDT*. The second parameter has the same type as the defining attribute.

nested query: A statement that contains one or more subqueries.

NetBEUI: A local-area network protocol.

Netscape plug-in: A software component downloaded from a Web server to a Web client, where it is integrated with the client's browser, providing additional functions.

network database model: A way of organizing a database to get minimum redundancy of data items by allowing any data item (node) to be directly connected to any other.

normalization: A technique that reduces or eliminates the possibility that a database is subject to modification anomalies.

object: Any uniquely identifiable thing.

ODBC (Object DataBase Connectivity): A standard interface between a database and an application that is trying to access the data in that database. ODBC is defined by an international (ISO) and a national (ANSI) standard.

Oracle: A relational database management system marketed by Oracle Corporation.

parameter: A variable within an application written in SQL module language.

precision: The maximum number of digits allowed in a numeric data item.

predicate: A statement that may be either logically true or logically false.

primary key: A column or combination of columns in a database table that uniquely identifies each row in the table.

procedural language: A computer language that solves a problem by executing a procedure in the form of a sequence of steps.

query: A question you ask about the data in a database.

rapid application development (RAD) tool: A proprietary graphically oriented alternative to SQL. A number of such tools are on the market.

record: A representation of some physical or conceptual object.

reference type: A data type whose values are all potential references to sites of one specified data type.

referential integrity: A state in which all the tables in a database are consistent with each other.

relation: A two-dimensional array of rows and columns, containing single-valued entries and no duplicate rows.

reserved words: Words that have a special significance in SQL and cannot be used as variable names or in any other way that differs from their intended use.

row: A sequence of `(field name, value)` pairs.

row value expression: A list of value expressions enclosed in parentheses and separated by commas.

scale: The number of digits in the fractional part of a numeric data item.

schema: The structure of an entire database. The information that describes the schema is the database's *metadata*.

schema owner: The person who was designated as the owner when the schema was created.

SEQUEL: A data sublanguage created by IBM that was a precursor of SQL.

set function: A function that produces a single result based on the contents of an entire set of table rows. Also called an *aggregate function*.

SQL: An industry standard data sublanguage, specifically designed to create, manipulate, and control relational databases. SQL:1999 is the latest version of the standard.

SQL, dynamic: A means of building compiled applications that does not require all data items to be identifiable at compile time.

SQL, embedded: An application structure in which SQL statements are embedded within programs written in a host language.

SQL, interactive: A real-time conversation with a database.

SQL/DS: A relational database management system marketed by IBM Corporation.

subquery: A query within a query.

subtype: A data type is a subtype of a second data type if every value of the first type is also a value of the second type.

supertype: A data type is a supertype of a second data type if every value of the second type is also a value of the first type.

table: A relation.

TCP/IP (Transmission Control Protocol/Internet Protocol): The network protocol used by the Internet and by intranets.

teleprocessing system: A powerful central processor connected to multiple dumb terminals.

transaction: A sequence of SQL statements whose effect is not accessible to other transactions until all the statements are executed.

transitive dependency: One attribute of a relation depends on a second attribute, which in turn depends on a third attribute.

translation table: Tool for converting character strings from one character set to another.

trigger: A small piece of code that tells a DBMS what other actions to perform after certain SQL statements have been executed.

update anomaly: A problem introduced into a database when a table row is updated.

user-defined type: A type whose characteristics are defined by a type descriptor specified by the user.

value expression: An expression that combines two or more values.

value expression, conditional: A value expression that assigns different values to arguments, based on whether a condition is logically true.

value expression, datetime: A value expression that deals with `DATE`, `TIME`, `TIMESTAMP`, or `INTERVAL` data.

value expression, numeric: A value expression that combines numeric values using the addition, subtraction, multiplication, or division operators.

value expression, string: A value expression that combines character strings with the concatenation operator.

value function: A function that performs an operation on a single character string, number, or date/time.

view: A database component that behaves exactly like a table but has no independent existence of its own.

virtual table: A view.

World Wide Web: An aspect of the Internet that has a graphical user interface. The Web is accessed by applications called *Web browsers,* and information is provided to the Web by installations called *Web servers.*

Index

Notes

Notes

Notes